PAPERS FROM THE 3rd ICHL

AMSTERDAM STUDIES IN THE THEORY AND
HISTORY OF LINGUISTIC SCIENCE

General Editor
E.F. KONRAD KOERNER
(University of Ottawa)

Series IV - CURRENT ISSUES IN LINGUISTIC THEORY

Volume 13

J. Peter Maher, Allan R. Bomhard & E.F.K. Koerner (eds.)

Papers from the
3rd International Conference
on Historical Linguistics

PAPERS

from the

3rd INTERNATIONAL CONFERENCE

on

HISTORICAL LINGUISTICS

edited by

J. Peter Maher, Allan R. Bomhard
and E.F. Konrad Koerner

AMSTERDAM / JOHN BENJAMINS B.V.

1982

© Copyright 1982 – John Benjamins B.V.
ISSN 0304 0763 / ISBN 90 272 3505 8

PREFACE

The Third International Conference on Historical Linguistics (3rd ICHL) met from 22nd to 26th August 1977 at the University of Hamburg. In attendance were over ninety scholars from Asia, Africa, the Americas, Australia, and Europe.

3rd ICHL took place at a time of great turmoil in the political life of the German Federal Republic and of German universities in particular, though our conference itself came during a blessed lull. Just weeks before, the International Conference on the Future of the University had sent its German Universities Commission to investigate, and ultimately to confirm, the reports of chaos. Few 3rd ICHL parti-- cipants, except for those familiar with Hamburg, sensed the relevance of this and the symbolism of academic solidarity for a victim of the new totalitarians in German life in my inviting to speak on "Drei literaturwissenschaftliche Auffassungen der Wirklichkeit" my colleague in the Seminar für Englische Sprache und Kultur, Professor Dr. Johannes Kleinstück, a scholar himself of no mean linguistic accomplishments. Earlier in the Summer Term he had been "host" in his commandeered office to a delegation of fifteen "Reformers" wearing stocking masks. Apart from this gesture of fraternal support for a persecuted colleague, Professor Kleinstück's paper, as linguists informed in the philosophy of science appreciated at the time, represents an issue of paramount importance to historical linguistics.

As for the papers read by the regular participants in 3rd ICHL, the widely hoped for debate on recent controversial issues, such as the theoretical status of "Analogy", failed to materialize through the absence of principals in the debate. Indeed, partisans of both sides of this controversy were jointly diappointed. My repeated dispatch of registered invitations was to no avail.

The present volume could not accommodate all the papers read at 3rd ICHL, and various factors, apart from editorial selection, affecc the mix. The long delay in publication stemming from my problems of relocating home and career discouraged several colleagues, who have since published their work elsewhere. Others, for a variety of reasons, withheld theirs. Yet others who were not present at sessions of 3rd ICHL at which publication was discussed unfortunately were unaware that proceedings would be published. Still others, and we all know the agony, did not succeed in writing the definitive draft. We wish one day to see all this remedied.

At midweek 3rd ICHL participants and their guests treated them-selves to an epicurean buffet feast in the Provence Restaurant high above the night life of Sankt Pauli, overlooking the harbor lights of the Elbe. Our wandering scholars next day tasted the sights and sounds, the seafood and good beer of the world of the Hansa, under the bluest skies and balmiest breezes that ever blew over the waves of the Elbe. Unser Dank gilt dem Mäzen, der Firma Pätz + Co., Hamburg.

3rd ICHL participants have on the whole been immensely considerate to the harried director, who accepted the kind offer of technical assis-tance from E.F.Konrad Koerner (Ottawa) and Allan R. Bomhard (Boston), without whom no proceedings ever would have appeared. The publishers, John and Claire Benjamins have exceeded the very patience of Job in this case. At Hamburg, colleagues who helped find solutions for 3rd ICHL are Dr. Rudolf Beier, Professor Dr. Margarethe Schwerdtfeger, Pro-fessor Dr. Rudolf Haas, and, above all, Dr. Hans-Jürgen Höhling, with-out whom there would have been no Third International Conference on Historical Linguistics.

Generous funding for 3rd ICHL came from the Free and Hanseatic City of Hamburg, through its Second Mayor and Kultursenator Biallas, together with the Deutsche Forschungsgemeinschaft, Bonn-Bad Godesberg.

Chicago, March 1982

                                           J. Peter Maher

PROGRAM OF

III.≡3.ICHL

Third International Conference on Historical Linguistics

22–26 August 1977
Hamburg

Monday, 22 August.

09:15   OPENING OF 3.ICHL: J. Peter Maher (Universität Hamburg)*

Historiography: scholars and schools in historical linguistics.

Chair: Raimo Anttila (University of California at Los Angeles)

[* As it is now impossible to reconstruct the program changes that occurred during the conference, the program presented here is the one drawn up before and distributed at the beginning of the meeting.]

09:30   John Hewson (Memorial University of Newfoundland):

Determinism in Linguistics: Neogrammarian and Trans-
formationalist

10:00   W. Keith Percival (University of Kansas):

The Neogrammarian View of Synchronic Variability

10:30   Boyd H. Davis (University of North Carolina at Charlotte):

Archibald Henry Sayce (1845-1933)

11:00   BREAK

11:30   Michael Studemund (Universität Hamburg):

The History of Yudezmo Lexicography

12:00   Bengt Löfstet (UCLA):

Die vulgärlateinische Sprachforschung in diesem Jahr-
hundert: Rückschau und Ausblick

12:30   E.F.Konrad Koerner (University of Ottawa):

The Sources, Development and Meaning of the Term
"Indo-European"

13:00   LUNCH

HISTORY AS AUTONOMOUS THEORY: PANCHRONY, SYNCHRONY,
DIACHRONY.

Chair: Saul Levin (SUNY Binghamton)

14:30   Göran Hammarström (Monash University):

Diachrony in Synchrony

15:00   William M. Christie, Jr. (University of Arizona):

Synchronic, Diachronic, and Panchronic Linguistics

15:30   Eugenio Coseriu (Universität Tübingen):

Sprachzustand und Sprachenwicklung

16:30   BREAK

17:00   Hans-Heinrich Lieb (Freie Universität Berlin):

Language Systems and the Problem of Abstraction

17:30   Pieter Muysken (Instituut voor Algemene Taalweten-
schap, Amsterdam):

The Independence of Synchronic Analyses from Diachronic
Considerations: Changes in Grammatical Categories

18:00   Thomas L. Markey (University of Michigan):

   An Historical Necessity: Non-paradogmatic Paradigms

18:30   Closing Announcements

•   •   •

Tuesday, 23 August.

   LINGUISTIC MICROTHEORY; PRINCIPLES OF LANGUAGE CHANGE
   ONTOGENY - FREQUENCY - DIALECT - STYLE - SOUND CHANGE
   - ANALOGY.

Chair: Elizabeth Closs Traugott (Stanford University)

09:00   Fred C. C. Peng (International Christian University,
   Tokyo):

   Sound Change and Language Change

09:30   Janine K. Reklaitis (University of Illinois at Chicago Circle):

   Empirical Evidence from Lithuanian for some Principles
   of Language Change

10:00   Irmengard Rauch (University of Illinois):

   Historical Analogy and the Peircean Categories

10:30   Lynn A. Ness and Caroline Duncan-Rose (California
   S C, Dominguez Hills):

   A Syntactic Correlate of Style-switching in the Canterbury Tales

11:00   BREAK

11:20   Marinel Gerritsen (Institute of Dialectology, Royal
   Academy of Arts and Sciences, Amsterdam):

   The Interplay between Diachronic Linguistics and Dialectology: Some Refinements of Trudgill's Formulae
   for Dialect Influence

11:50   Brian Newton (Simon Fraser University):

   Verbal Aspect and Modality in Hellenistic and Modern
   Greek

12:20   Rocky V. Miranda (University of Minnesota):

   Frequency of Grammatical Categories and the Direction
   of Leveling

12:50   Tore Janson (University of Stockholm):

   The Loss of Distinctive Vowel Quantity in Late Latin:
   The Experimental Reconstruction of Structural Reinter
   pretation

13:15   LUNCH

MICROTHEORY CONTINUED: CLASSIC PRINCIPLES; THE COM-
PARATIVE METHOD: WITHIN AND ACROSS FAMILIES

Chair: Fred C. C. Peng (International Christian University,
Tokyo)

14:30   Herbert Penzl (University of California, Berkeley):

Gottscheds Sprachkunst (1748) und die deutsche Hoch-
lautung

15:00   Consuelo J. Paz (University of the Philippines):

The Comparative Method Applied to the Languages of the
Philippines

15:30   Edgar C. Polomé (University of Texas):

Italic-Germanic Isoglosses

16:00   Otto Sadovszky (California State University, Fuller-
ton/Los Angeles):

The Uralo-Penutian Case System

16:30   BREAK

16:45   H. Christoph Wolfart (University of Manitoba):

The Word-and-Paradigm Model and Linguistic Change:
The Ojibwa Verb System

17:15   Gerald Cohen (University of Missouri/Rolla):

Etymology of Greek πατασσ- "strike" and Related Words

17:45   Manfred Betz (Universität Mainz):

Galloromanisch *drut*:   russisch *drug*;   deutsch *traut*

18:15   Hans-Jürgen Höhling (Oxford University):

The Efficacy of History in Language Pedagogy

18:45   Closing Announcements

20:00   Buffet Supper: Restaurant Provence / Hafenblick
Restaurant, Millerntorplatz 1, 2000 Hamburg 4

●   ●   ●

Wednesday, 24 August.

Barkassenfahrt auf der Elbe / Boat ride on the Elbe (cour-
tesy of Paetz + Co., through the good offices of Prof. Rudolf Haas).

Embarcation at 10:00

Bei dem Neuen Kraan 2 (between the Katharinenkirche
and Überseebrücke).

<u>Afternoon Free</u>

IMPORTANT NOTICE:

The session on Macro-theoretical approaches to historical linguistics had to be shifted from its intended spot because of
the boat ride. This was determined by the hour of the tides on
this day. Consequently, the following papers will be presented
on Friday morning before the session on Typology and Diachrony
which, therefore, will begin an hour later. The paper by B.
Newton would also more properly have fit in here.

09:00 Joan B. Hooper (SUNY Buffalo):

On Rule-death and Restructuring

09:30 Peter Cole (University of Illinois at Champaign-
Urbana):

The Subject Hierarchy and Syntactic Change

● ● ●

<u>Thursday, 25 August.</u>

MICROTHEORETICAL LINGUISTICS CONTINUED: PARTICULAR
PROBLEMS, METHODS, GENERAL PRINCIPLES, AND DYNAMICS

Chair: Niels Danielson (University of Odense)

09:00 Karl Odwarka (University of Northern Iowa):

Evidence of Auslautsverhärtung in Old Saxon

09:30 Leena Löfstedt (University of Helsinki):

The Place of -*(e)sse* in French Derivational Morphology

10:00 Frances McSparran (University of Michigan):

A Case of Grammaticalization: The Modern English
Modals

10:30 Yoshihiko Ikegami (University of Tokyo):

English *make* and *do*: Typology and Evolution of Causative Verbs

11:00 BREAK

11:20 Yakov Malkiel (University of California at Berkeley):

Between Polygenesis and Monogenesis

12:20 Elizabeth Closs Traugott (Stanford University):

From Space to Time to Logical Relation; Evidence for a
Dynamic Theory of Language

12:50 Esa Itkonen (University of Helsinki):

Short-term and Long-term Teleology in Linguistic Change

13:20   LUNCH

MICROTHEORY CONTINUED: PSYCHOLOGICAL AND SOCIAL
DYNAMICS

Chair: H.-J. Niederehe (Universität Trier)

14:30   Henning Andersen (University of Copenhagen):

Wave-theory as Adaptive-evolutive Change

15:00   Ernst Pulgram (University of Michigan):

Redundancy in the Dynamics of Change

15:30   Saul Levin (State University of New York at Binghamton):

Latin *homo* : *humus* and the Semitic Counterparts: The
Oldest Culturally Significant Etymology?

16:00   Stephan Langhoff (Universität Hamburg):

The Semantic Investiture of Underspecified Units in
Syntax

16:30   BREAK

17:00   Johannes Kleinstück (Universität Hamburg):

Drei literaturwissenschaftliche Auffassungen von Wirklichkeit

17:30   Uhlan V. Slagle (Arlington, VA) and Raimo Anttila
(Los Angeles):

On the Dynamics of Mind and Meaning

18:15   Closing Announcements

• • •

Friday, 26 August.

TYPOLOGY AND DIACHRONY   [N.B.:   See **IMPORTANT NOTICE**
under Wednesday, above.]

Chair: Yoshihiko Ikegami (University of Tokyo)

10:00   Paul J. Hopper (State University of New York at Binghamton):

Diachronic and Typological Implications of Foregrounding

10:30   Martin Harris (University of Salford):

Alternatives to the Morphological Passive in Romance

11:00   BREAK

11:20   Marianne Mithun (State University of New York at
        Albany):

        Comparative Syntax: Priorities and Pitfalls

11:50   Lyle Campbell (State University of New York at Albany):

        Universals of Ergative Languages in the Light of Proto-
        Mayan Syntax

12:20   Frans Plank (Technische Universität Berlin):

        Can Case-marking and Serialization Theories that Rely
        on the Principle of Ambiguity Avoidance Explain Syn-
        tactic and Morphological Change in Anglo-Saxon?

12:50   LUNCH

        TONOGENESIS: DEVELOPMENT AND LOSS OF TONE SYSTEMS

Chair: Henning Andersen (University of Copenhagen)

14:00   Jean-Marie Hombert (UCLA) and John J. Ohala (UC
        Berkeley):

        Historical Development of Tone Patterns

14:45   Edward T. Purcell and Philip Regier (University of
        Southern California):

        The Phonetic Origins of Balto-Slavic Tone

15:15   Alice Wyland Grundt (California State University at
        Fresno):

        Tonal Accents in Basque and Greek

15:45   Kristian Ringgaard (University of Aarhus):

        On the Problem of Merger

16:15   BREAK

16:30   Ilse Lehiste (Ohio State University) and Pavle Ivić
        (Novi Sad):

        The Phonetic Nature of the Neo-Štokavian Accent Shift
        in Serbo-Croatian

17:00   Jadranka Gvozdanović (University of Amsterdam):

        Development of Tones in Languages with Distinctive
        Tonal Accents

17:30   Kay Williamson (University of Ibadan):

        From Tone to Pitch-accent: The Case of Ijo

18:00   Vit Bubenik (Memorial University of Newfoundland):

        Historical Development of the Ancient Greek Accent Sys-
        tem

●   ●   ●

TABLE OF CONTENTS

SYNCHRONIC, DIACHRONIC, AND PANCHRONIC LINGUISTICS

WILLIAM M. CHRISTIE, JR.
University of Arizona

The distinction between synchrony and diachrony is one of the sacred dogmas of our discipline. Antedating both de Saussure and Baudoin,
with whom it is often first associated, it has been observed more or
less scrupulously by most of their successors. Recently, however,
there have been some hints that the two aspects of language study are
not being kept apart as rigorously as they once were. The most explicit and far reaching proposal along these lines has been Lightner's
suggestion (1975:630) that synchrony reflects diachrony and should be
described accordingly. The consequences of Lightner's proposal, by
now familiar to many who have read and clucked over his article, are
interesting in their immoderation. He suggests, for example, that in
the synchronic grammar of an ideal native speaker/hearer such forms as
*generate, genius, halogen, photogenic, gonorrhea, pregnant, cognate,
natal, nation, noel, renaissance, kin,* and *kindergarten* (and there are
many more) are all to be regarded as morphologically related. Note
that this is in a synchronic grammar.

To the average linguist such a proposal as this is preposterous.
It is simply too extreme. Few take Lightner seriously, according him
nothing more than an incredulous shake of the head. But I would like
to suggest that we ought to take Lightner very seriously indeed. To
see why let us look at the principles that led him to his conclusions.
They are, I believe, two in number. The first, though never stated
explicitly, can be inferred from his remark following his list of *gen-

forms: "The important point of this example is that if the words listed above are NOT all synchronically derived from the same root, one
will miss semantic and phonological generalizations right and left"
(1975:618). In other words, the objective of his undertaking is to
capture all the significant generalizations he can about the language.
The relationships, phonological and semantic, among *kin*, *noel*, *cognate*,
halogen, and *generate* are in some way significant, so they are to be
captured. The principle of capturing all relevant generalizations is,
of course, not new in phonology, or even in linguistics in general.
The problem is with deciding which generalizations are significant and
which are not. Chomsky and Halle (*SPE*) do try to limit the range of
generalizations described when they say that the formal devices of a
grammar must "permit us to formulate general statements about the language which are true and significant, and must provide a basis for distinguishing these from other generalizations which are false, or which
are true but not significant" (1968:330). This latter restriction is
the important one for our purposes, for despite their best efforts to
assert that the notion of "linguistically significant generalization"
has "real empirical content", Chomsky and Halle never come anywhere
near giving us empirical criteria by which to decide whether any given
generalization is significant. Lacking such criteria, of course, we
have no way whatever to rule Lightner's generalizations linguistically
non-significant.

Lightner's second principle, expressed toward the end of his article, is that one should "assume that the synchronic analysis mirrors
the diachronic analysis, and write up the grammar on the basis of this
assumption" (1975:630). Now this proposal may seem radical, as I mentioned above, but in fact it is not in essence so extreme as it first
appears. Note that the synchronic description is written up following
a synchronic analysis that mirrors a diachronic analysis. But this
does not mean that the synchronic description will be the same as a
diachronic description. If it were, Lightner would have said to write
a diachronic description and let that be the synchronic description.

He did not. A synchronic description still has to observe all the necessary conventions of grammars. It will thus reflect, but not be identical to, a diachronic analysis. Understood thus, Lightner's principle
may differ in degree of application, but in its essentials it in no way
conflicts with the position taken on this issue by Chomsky and Halle.
Although Chomsky and Halle observe that it "does not happen to be the
case" that "a grammar of a language contains nothing but rules that at
one time or another were introduced into the language by the 'operation'
of a 'sound law'" (1968:251), their reason for their denial is that numerous rules were not so introduced. In other words, they are merely
denying that all rules were introduced in this way. They are not at
all denying that many were. Thus although Lightner may well disagree
with Chomsky and Halle on the proportion of historically introduced
rules, a difference of degree, there is no disagreement that there are
many, no difference of principle.

The conclusion to be drawn from the foregoing considerations is
that the principles that lead Lightner to his conclusions are not in
conflict with the principles that underlie *SPE*. He has just carried
them to their logical conclusions. It is for this reason that Lightner's work must be taken seriously, very seriously indeed, for there is
no principled way to prevent the methods and conclusions found in such
conventional works as *SPE* from being extended to the very extremes that
Lightner reaches. For all his apparent absurdity, Lightner is directly
following the principles of standard generative phonology.

Now we come to the real problem in dealing with Lightner. Our in-
tuitions tell us that something is very wrong here, but defining it is
more difficult. The heart of the matter, to turn to the expressed topic
of this paper, is that descriptions such as Lightner's have no "home"
in linguistic science. They are not synchronic (despite Lightner's futile protestations about the "perfect knowledge" of his ideal speaker/
hearer), for the relationships he suggests are neither consciously nor
unconsciously productive in the language today. Neither, however, are
they diachronic, for he thoroughly confounds certain diachronic proces-

ses while totally ignoring others. He has attempted a force-fit of
selected diachronic phenomena into a rule framework that does violence
to them. The whole undertaking is thus left in a never-never land suspended between synchrony and diachrony. The metaphor of never-never
land is appropriate, for to practitioners of this kind of linguistics
time no longer exists. It seems to me that the only way to escape
the pitfalls of such unwarranted extensions of grammar is to review
and renew our definitions of our subfields and the distinctions among
them, and to adhere strictly to the definitions and distinctions we
have established.

Let us, then, offer a preliminary definition of synchronic linguistics as the study of an état de langue in which all generalizations and relationships must be verifiable by reference to the observed behavior of native speakers. We can next tentatively define
diachronic linguistics as the study of the transitions within a
speech community from one état de langue to another. These definitions may seem rather conventional and obvious, and in a sense they
are. But let us adhere strictly to them and see what results we obtain. If synchronic description is always to be tested against the
observed behavior of native speakers, it follows that derivationally
related forms must show a replicable morphologic generalization. By
this I mean that the relationship obtaining between two forms must
be generally usable by native speakers. If it is not, it will fail
the empirical test. Now we do not require that native speakers be observed replicating the relationship. Many chance factors may prevent
such observation. But we should require that native speakers at least
recognize the generalization when it is used. A brief example will
both illustrate my intent and show the somewhat surprising results of
strict adherence to this requirement.

Most grammars of English would show the three forms *horror*, *horrid*, and *horrible* to be morphologically related. If such is the case,
the relationship among them should be replicable and recognizable by
native speakers. Therefore to *terror* it should be possible to form

and recognize a word *terrid*. But no native speaker I have asked has
ever associated *terrid* with *terror*. Asked the meaning of *terrid*,
native speakers produce associations with *torrid* or with *terrestrial*,
but not with *terror*. Likewise *candible* yields no associations with
candor or *candid*, only with *cannibal*. We must thus conclude that the
relationships among *horror*, *horrid*, and *horrible* are not replicable
and recognizable. It is therefore necessary in a strictly synchronic
grammar of English to list these as three separate and grammatically
unrelated lexical items. That semantic and phonic associations of
some kind exist need not be denied. What I deny is that these associations are grammatical. Now it is worth noting that if we continue
to apply principles such as these to further relationships in the language, the end result is likely to be a striking increase in the size
of the lexicon, and a striking decrease in its complexity, and in the
complexity of the grammar as a whole, changes which strike at the very
heart of many of our most cherished preconceptions of our great ability
as linguists to undo the intricate Gordian knots of linguistic structure. It may well be that the knots are not really so complex after
all. While I do not intend to pursue further this matter of simplification of grammars, I would note that Bolinger (1978), starting from
a somewhat different perspective and working in syntax rather than
phonology, has reached essentially the same conclusion.

Now it may appear, especially to us at this conference, that our
beloved and venerable historical linguistics will not hold any such
surprises for us when we hold strictly to our definitions. But let us
continue our discussion of our friend *horror*. It might seem inevitable
that if the relationships posited above are not appropriately to be
expressed in a synchronic grammar, a diachronic statement will be their
proper home. After all, synchrony and diachrony together have custom-
arily been held to exhaust the range of linguistics. But consider
what such an assignment must imply. If there is some relationship
among *horror*, *horrid*, and *horrible*, and if that relationship is not
now synchronically productive, and if an explanation of the phenomenon

is to be found in a diachronic description, then, according to our definition, we must find the explanation in the transition within the
English speech community from one état de langue to the present one.
Now we certainly cannot concern ourselves with an earlier état in
which there was no synchronic relationship among the three forms. For
our purposes there would be no change from that état to the present,
hence no explanation. Rather we must start with an earlier état in
which these three forms were synchronically related, and from which
we have changed. The earlier état plus the intervening changes would
serve to explain the present lack of a synchronic relationship but the
existence of some kind of relationship observable to the grammarian.
Such is the task and service of diachrony. At this point, however, we
run into a minor difficulty. To the best of my knowledge there never
was in English an état de langue in which these three words were synchronically related. The earliest of them to appear (*OED*) is *horrible*,
a direct borrowing from Norman French *orrible*, first making its appearance as *orryble* around 1303. The form *horror*, does not show up until
nearly three quarters of a century later, first appearing around 1375.
Note that one might expect a primary form like *horror* to show up earlier. Or, if we treat *horror* as derived from the verb *horre*, we would
certainly expect *horre* to show up before its derivatives, not over a
century after the first. The verb *horre* holds a very tenuous existence,
mainly in the sense of "bristle", from about 1430 to perhaps 1530, after
which it is heard from no more. As for *horrid*, it first appears as a
very obvious Latinism in the sense of "bristling" in Spenser's *Faerie
Queene* (1590). As an approximate synonym for *horrible* it pops up a
decade later in *Twelfth Night*. But with the Spenserian predecessor
and with the Latin having both meanings available, there is no reason
whatever to believe that a synchronic relationship ever existed between
horrid and either of the other forms in English.

    We are now left in something of a quandary. Synchrony and dia-
chrony exhaust the field, some relationship exists, yet that relationship is assignable neither to synchrony nor diachrony. The problem,

I believe, lies in our definition of our whole discipline. Our definitions, including the ones offered here, have treated linguistics as a
branch of psychology. So considered, the field is, indeed, exhausted
by synchrony and diachrony. But suppose that instead of considering
ourselves historical linguists we consider ourselves linguistic historians. The difference is not trivial. If we are first of all linguists, looking at the present state of the system, and then giving
consideration to the systems that have preceded it, we will certainly
be concerning ourselves with a branch of psychology, perhaps several
branches. In our study of diachrony, for example, we will in effect
be doing historical social psychology. But suppose we are first of
all historians, examining as a historian would the present system as
a product of its history. No historian would limit the history of
a community to phenomena strictly within that community. Outside
phenomena that may have even an indirect effect must be considered.
The approach of the historian I would denominate panchrony, which for
us will be pure linguistic description, not a sub-branch of some other
discipline, but drawing freely on any other discipline that might contribute something of value.

   A word of definition is appropriate here. In defining panchrony
I am not referring to that study of the same name that was discussed
by de Saussure and Hjelmslev.[1] Both of them refer by this term to the
study of what we would today refer to as synchronic universals, those
principles that will be always and everywhere valid in human language
studied synchronically. Such a study would certainly be a part of the
panchronic approach as I would define it, but it would not constitute
the whole of the approach. The panchronic linguist will range as widely as the historian, drawing on any piece of information that might
illuminate the nature of his subject matter. Panchrony, thus defined,
will resemble very closely an inversion of our old friend, nineteenth
century philology. Just as the philologist used language as a tool for
the study of various cultures and all aspects of their histories, so
now the panchronic linguist must use history in all its aspects as a

tool for the study of language. But panchrony is not merely an inversion of philology, for it will also accept any contribution forthcoming from psychology, including pure synchronic linguistics, as well as from ancillary disciplines such as mathematical linguistics. It will use these contributions, but it will not be allowed to become limited by them. And now we return to Lightner.

Synchronic description, as a branch of psychology, will most certainly have to supply itself with precise formalisms for the expression of its generalizations. These formalisms have been essential in recent linguistic work. Many generalizations could not easily have been seen without them, and the generalizations will not be integrated with generalizations from other branches of psychology without the eventual development of shared formalisms. Diachrony, too, will require formalisms of description, and it may well be that these will have to be as strictly applied as in synchrony. But it is most important to note that, although some of the generalizations found in a synchronic description will have their roots in diachronic description, there is no necessity whatever for the diachronic formalism to follow the synchronic in form. Nor, incidentally, is there any need at all for a synchronic formalism to adopt the form of a diachronic one. They are separate and must be kept so to avoid the dangers of confounding them that have been preached at us from the time of de Saussure on. This, to return to the beginning of this essay, was one of Lightner's greatest faults. By forcing diachronic phenomena into a synchronic formalism he will do great violence to the diachronic description. But even greater is the violence done to a panchronic description. Many of Lightner's phenomena need, according to our definitions, panchronic treatment. But I would submit that panchronic statements need not be constrained by any formalism at all, any more than any other history needs to follow particular formulaic patterns. It must, to be sure, respect the formalisms of the disciplines from which it draws data, but that is all. It would be the most serious kind of error to try to force these highly varied panchronic data into a particular formal strightjacket, and that

is exactly what Lightner does. It would, for example, do violence to
the examples we have been treating, to the problem posed concerning
horror, *horrid*, and *horrible*. The solution, of course, is panchronic.
There did exist among these a relationship in Latin, which relationship may or may not still have existed in Norman French. Whether it
did is a question for Romance diachrony. Either way, they were borrowed as individual items into English, and no systematic relationship
was established here. The perceived relationship is merely a reflection of the original Latin situation. But how could one possible capture all these disparate facts within a single formalism, be that formalism diachronic or, even worse, synchronic?

The panchronic approach I have just defined is not, of course,
new. Much of the work of Anttila and Maher, to name just two, is done
in just these terms. I believe, however, that it is useful to make
the definitions explicit and to fit a strictly defined panchrony into
a whole system of strictly defined linguistic disciplines. One can
justify such a treatment in two ways, by showing the benefits of ad-
hering to the defined system, and by showing the consequences of fail-
ing to adhere to it. Anttila, Maher, and others have done the former.
Here I have made a brief attempt at the latter.

We may, then, here at the end ask ourselves what we are doing.
Is this undertaking of ours at a conference on historical linguistics
to be concerned with diachrony or synchrony? Really it matters little.
Both have their contributions to make. Each is a valid line of inquiry.
The important thing is to be absolutely clear about what we have chosen,
for confusion on either side can lead to unnecessary violence to the
data we seek to elucidate.

NOTE:

1) The term "panchronique" was, I believe, first used by de Saussure (*Cours*: 134-35). His discussion is very brief, but Hjelmslev
(1928:101-07) adopts much the same position and gives a much fuller
exposition. Hjelmslev's discussion is also useful for his treatment of
distinctions quite similar to some made in the present essay.

REFERENCES:

Bolinger, Dwight. 1976. "Meaning and Memory", *Forum Linguisticum*
    1.1-14.
Chomsky, Noam and Halle, Morris. 1968. *The Sound Pattern of English.*
    New York.
Hjelmslev, Louis. 1928. *Principes de grammaire générale.* København.
Lightner, Theodore. 1975. "The Role of Derivational Morphology in
    Generative Grammar", *Language* 51.617-38.
de Saussure, Ferdinand. 1916. *Cours de linguistique générale.* Paris.

THE INTERPLAY BETWEEN
DIACHRONIC LINGUISTICS AND DIALECTOLOGY:
SOME REFINEMENTS OF TRUDGILLS FORMULA

MARINEL GERRITSEN and FRANK JANSEN
Royal Netherlands Academy   *Moller Institute,*
of Arts and Sciences   *Tilburg*

0.   ABSTRACT

The purpose of this paper is twofold: in the first place it will
be demonstrated how a formula evaluating the influence of one dialect
on another, as suggested by Trudgill (1974), can be used for diachronic
linguistic ends. In the second place, we will propose two refinements
of Trudgill's formula.

First, some examples of the use of dialect borrowing as an explanation in diachronic linguistics are given. In the second section Chen's
vehement criticism of explanations which rely on dialect borrowing will
be discussed and it will be shown how it should be possible to give
more content to the label "dialect borrowing". The third section is
devoted to Trudgill's investigation and to the formula for explaining
the influence one dialect has on another, which was the result of his
examination.

In the fourth section the result of a survey similar to Trudgill's
carried out in the dialect area around Amsterdam, are given and the
allied refinements of Trudgill's formula are proposed.

The fifth and last section deals with possibilities for further
research and the uses of diachronic linguistics of formulas such as the
one proposed here.

1.   DIALECT BORROWING AS A MEANS OF LANGUAGE CHANGE

Since the invention of exceptionless sound changes, scholars have
been needing an explanation of the persistent exceptions.*

The most successful and according to Bloomfield (1933:479) the only
explanation of exceptions to sound changes is dialect borrowing: the
spread of a form from one dialect to other dialects. General remarks

on dialect borrowing appear already in Paul (1880:399), but the romanist Schuchardt (see Vennemann and Wilbur [1972]) was the major propa-
gandist for the use of dialect borrowing as an explanation for linguistic change. The notion of dialect borrowing as an explanatory tool for
the spread of dialect phenomena was developed only in the first decen-
nia of the twentieth century, essentially in the work of German and
Dutch dialectologists.

Frings (1926) could only account for the spread of a number of
words in Rhineland (Germany) by assuming influence from Cologne.

In Debus (1962) we can find far more examples of the spread of
certain dialect phenomena around German cities, examples which can only
be explained satisfactorily with the aid of dialect borrowing.

Kloeke (1927), a Dutch dialectologist, also made a strong case for
dialect borrowing as the most important factor in language change. He
tried to demonstrate that the Dutch dialect areas as defined by currently important isoglosses (for example, the palatalization and diphthongization of West Germanic $\hat{u}$) are the result of borrowing from a
southern dialect in the 16th and 17th century (see Bloomfield 1933:
328). As far as we know, the most basic claim, viz. that dialect borrowing must play some role in a theory of language change, has not been
refuted, despite much criticism of details.

2.   CRITICISM OF DIALECT BORROWING AS AN EXPLANATION OF LANGUAGE
      CHANGE

The use of dialect borrowing for explanatory ends has been criticized by Chen (1973:462ff.). His closing argument against the use of
dialect borrowing as an explanatory tool is the most important one:

> Lastly, there is one more reason why 'dialect mixture' has been
> used as a favourite cover-symbol for exceptions to sound laws,
> namely it is in most cases almost impossible to rule out the
> possibility of dialect borrowing. Spatially speaking, geographical
> distance cannot serve to factor out interdialectal loans; we have
> known cases of saltatory sound changes and lexical interference

especially between distant urban centers. Temporally, the absence
of evidence of cross-linguistic or cross-dialectal interference
at any point in time cannot be adduced as proof that such interference could not have taken place before or after that point in
time.

The arguments against dialect borrowing presented by Chen are
methodological in character: dialect borrowing is less successful as
a scientific means of explanation because it cannot be refuted. Nevertheless, a theory of language change must contain a theory of dialect
borrowing, for it can be proved from some well-attested changes that
dialect borrowing does indeed exist.

To set some bounds to the term dialect borrowing will not be a
very easy task. Several difficulties are mentioned in Chen (1973),
such as the alleged influence of town A on another town B, with a
great distance between A and B, while no influence can be attested in
the regions between A and B. We know of course of these cases, but
don't think that it is useful to try to explain everything at once.
The preferable strategy seems to be, as in other sciences, one of beginning with a very simple case: for example, the influence of the
dialect of a big town on the dialects of its surroundings during a
limited period. The reasons for doing so are the following:

1. In detailed investigations, for example Debus (1962), it has
    been proved that certain large towns have influenced the dia-
    lects of their surroundings.

2. In most cases there is no mutual influence between the town
    and its surroundings; it is "one-way traffic" influence.

3. By choosing the right location for the survey, it is possible
    to limit the number of surrounding dialects.

We cannot but hope that the results of studying more or less simple
cases will make it possible to explore later the complex and intricate
ones.

3.   TRUDGILL'S FORMULA

The first step towards a better definition of the label "dialect borrowing" has been taken in Peter Trudgill (1974). This article shows, on the basis of dialect investigations in Norway and East England, how recent developments in theoretical geography can be applied to linguistic geography and how this can lead to more adequate explanations for the geographical spread of certain linguistic facts. Since our explanation relies in large part on Trudgill's, it is necessary to discuss his article in more detail.

Trudgill carried out his Norwegian research in Brunlanes, a small rural peninsula on the south coast of Norway; he explored the influence of the rather big town Larvik on the other towns of this peninsula. For his investigation, Trudgill used a technique of division of the dialect area which for some time has been successfully employed by geographers to describe and explain, for example, technical innovations. He divided the landscape under investigation into areas of uniform size and shape, forming in this case a hexagon grid.

Subsequently, he selected at random one named locality in each cell and recorded casual speech (as defined in Labov [1966]) of members of the population of different ages in each locality.

In examining the influence of Larvik on the other cities of the peninsula, he looked for only one linguistic phenomenon, the realization of the /æ/, which was originally realized as [ɛ] on the whole peninsula, but as [a] in Larvik.

The different variants of the phoneme /æ/ were set on a value scale in the manner of Labov (1966), the individual scores for its pronunciation were calculated for each informant, and then the average scores for each cell were worked out for three different age groups: 24 years old and younger; between 25 and 69; older than 69.

On the base of these data three different maps for the three age groups could be constructed with isoglosses indicating greater or less influence from Larvik.

Next Trudgill tried to explain why the influence from Larvik was as it was for the three different age groups, making use of a formula, the gravity model, often used by geographers to investigate the interaction between two centers.

The gravity model has the following form:

$$1. \quad M_{AB} = \frac{P_A \cdot P_B}{(d_{A-B})^2}$$

where M_{AB} is the interaction between A and B, P is the population in thousands, and d_{A-B} is the distance between A and B.

Since Trudgill was not interested in interaction, but merely in the influence of one center on another, and since he assumed that interaction consisted of influence in each direction proportional to population size, he amended this formula to yield 2:

$$2. \quad I_{AB} = \frac{P_A \cdot P_B}{(d_{A-B})^2} \cdot \frac{P_A}{P_A + P_B}$$

where I_{AB} is the influence of town A on town or village B, P is the population in thousands, and d_{A-B} is the distance between A and B.

Furthermore, he added to the formula a factor s, expressing prior existing linguistic similarity. This final version of the formula as suggested in Trudgill's article is as given in 3:

$$3. \quad I_{AB} = s \cdot \frac{P_A \cdot P_B}{(d_{A-B})^2} \cdot \frac{P_A}{P_A + P_B}$$

where I_{AB} is the influence of town A on town or village B, P is the population in thousands, d_{A-B} is the distance between A and B, and s is a factor expressing prior existing linguistic similarity between the dialects of A and B.

However, since the dialects of the Norwegian peninsula were very similar to each other, Trudgill did not need to take into account the possible values of s in the Norwegian survey, and he used the formula without any factor s.

He gives some suggestions, based on his intuition, for the possible values of s. For example, s is 4 for the towns and villages near town A, 3 for the region around town A, etc.

He suggests further that the factor s is still a rather vague one which needs to be defined more precisely.

To explain the map of the influence that Larvik had on the towns and villages of the peninsula on the basis of the data obtained from persons older than 70, Trudgill used the formula taking into consideration the distances by sea between Larvik and the other towns and villages.

At the time that these people learned to speak, around 1900, roads had not yet been constructed on this peninsula and therefore travel by sea between Larvik and the cities on the coast was far more important than overland travel was. On the other hand, in order to explain the map of the influence that Larvik had on the peninsula on the basis of the data obtained from people younger than 24, he used the distances by land, because by the time that this generation learned their language, road traffic was far more important than sea traffic.

The linguistic map of the Larvik [a·] spoken by people older than 69 now indicates exactly those towns with a Larvik [a·] that have been predicted by the formula calculated for sea distances.

The linguistic map of Larvik [a·] spoken by people younger than 24 indicates precisely those towns and villages with a Larvik [a·] which have been forecasted by the formula calculated for distances by road.

In this Norwegian instance the formula exactly corresponded with the facts. This is the case not only for this example, but also for word initial *h*-deletion, a change in progress in East England, which is explained in Trudgill's article by the same formula. Thus it ap-

peared from his investigation that with the aid of a rather simple formula employing easily obtainable main factors such as distance and population size, dialect influence can be explained. On the other hand,
such a formula can also be used to determine whether or not it is plausible to consider a language change to be the result of dialect influence.

Trudgill himself explicitly points out that this formula has to be
considered as a starting point and that some other things should eventually be incorporated:

- the extent to which a factor has prestige or covered prestige;

- in which particular social group the innovation has arisen;

- refinement of the factor s. (Some linguistic systems will
  offer more resistance to an innovation than others.)

In the present article we will restrict ourselves to redefining Trudgill's formula only with respect to factor s.

4. TESTING TRUDGILL'S FORMULA: THE INFLUENCE OF THE DIALECT OF
    AMSTERDAM ON THE DIALECTS OF THE NEIGHBORHOOD

4.0. A formula can be tested by confronting the data which are
found in the real world with the data expected on the grounds of that
formula. In this section the data found in our investigation will be
compared with the expectations yielded through Trudgill's formula.

However, before discussing our investigation, it is necessary to
pay attention to the most important difference between our investigation and Trudgill's.

4.1. We try to become aware of language change by collecting data
from different points of time (real time), while Trudgill tried to do
so by collecting data from people of different age groups (apparent
time). Studying language change in real time is rather traditional;

one studies the differences between the speech of, e.g., forty-year-old
people in a certain society and the speech of people of the same age
60 years ago. On the other hand, study of language change by employing
apparent time has been initiated and stimulated by sociolinguists (Labov 1966, Trudgill 1974). The principle of apparent time is based on
the idea that the speech of a person of 80 can be considered as a reflection of the speech of the younger generation 60 years ago, and that
the speech of a person of 60 can be considered as a reflection of the
speech of the younger generation 40 years ago, etc. In studying language change in apparent time, one studies at a certain moment the differences between the speech of people of different ages. The use of apparent time is based on the hypothesis that changes in the speech of
adults are of minor importance. Both types of diachronic investigation
have their pro's and con's. *Apparent time* investigations share the following *advantages*:

A.   It is possible to get a corpus of data which is in principle
     unlimited: every classification according to the age of the
     informants can be made (within the limits of the human race:
     ±55 years). It is therefore possible to enlarge the data
     whenever one notices that one lacks the information to sol-
     ving a particular problem.

B.   Collecting, transcribing and processing the data can be done
     in a uniform way.

C.   It is possible to elicit different styles of speaking.

Apparent time investigations have the following *disadvantages*:

A.   It has to be emphasized that up until now the equation of ap-
     parent and real time was a working hypothesis and that results
     of very recent research have cast some doubt upon its correct-
     ness (Fred Peng, paper presented at the III ICHL).

B.   Investigations of changes over a period which surpasses 55
     years is impossible, just as is the study of changes taking
     place more than 55 years ago, during a relative short period
     of time.

Real time investigations share the following *advantages*:

A. Depending on quality and quantity of the material, in prin-
    ciple any period whatsoever can be studied.

B. There is no need for the doubtful equation mentioned above
    as a disadvantage of apparent time investigations.

Real time investigations have the following *disadvantages*:

A. The data are limited: the selection of the periods under in-
    vestigation is dependent on the presence or absence of mate-
    rial from the dialects.

B. The recordings can be unequal in quality, the gravest problem
    being that one can never be sure about their quality. Ob-
    served differences between two recordings can be attributed
    to differences in collecting, transcribing and processing the
    data.

Despite the disadvantages of the real time method, we had to use
it because of the rather long period we wished to explore (about 90
years).

4.2. Method: Collecting the data.

For our investigation of the influence of the Amsterdam dialect on
neighboring dialects, we collected data from the province of North Holland, the area surrounding the city of Amsterdam. This province is a
peninsula, for the most part surrounded by the North Sea, the Wadden
Sea and the (former) Zuider Sea. In past centuries North Holland was
scattered with lakes and seas, most of which have now been reclaimed,
the famous polders.

In our investigation the area was covered with a hexagon grid (see
map 1), with the cross section of a hexagon being approximately 5 kilo-
meters (3 miles). Subsequently we tried to find a town or village in
each grid for which data for three different points of time was available, namely from the following sources:[1]

1. The last quarter of the 19th century: the questionnaires of the Aardrijkskundig Genootschap (the Dutch Geographic Society) which sent out two questionnaires, a rather short one in 1879 and a very large one in 1895.

2. About 1950: the recorded sentences of the Reeks Nederlandse Dialektatlassen (RNDA, Dutch Dialect Atlas Series) of North Holland (Daan 1969) and partly of South Holland (Van Ooyen 1968).

3. About 1970: recordings of casual speech (along the lines of Labov 1966) of dialect speakers, made by us and other members of the staff of the Institute for Dialectology in Amsterdam.

Although we studied several phonological variables, in this article we shall only report on the reflexes of WGm. $\hat{\imath}$ and WGm. ai, which are both realized as [ε$_{\iota}$] in current Standard Dutch.

The method used to determine the Amsterdam variants per grid was the same for each of the three points in time. First, all words containing the phonemes under consideration were counted per point in time; the totals are presented in Table I:

Table I

		WGm. $\hat{\imath}$	WGm. ai
Aardrijkskundig genootschap	1879	19	14
	1895	14	11
RNDA	1950	20	15
Recordings	1970	±100	±25

The data from the 1879 survey can be considered as a supplement to those from the 1895 questionnaire, for there were not many differences between them. Besides, the first one was filled up for less towns and villages than the second one.

Next, the Amsterdam variants (see Table II) were counted and their frequency in each grid was computed per point of time with the aid of the "formula" expressed in (4).

Table II

	A	B
Standard Dutch	Amsterdam Variants	Dialect Variants
ɛļ WGm. $\hat{\imath}$	ɛ_T· æ· a·	æļ ɛ_Tļ aļ ɔļ ι
ɛļ WGm. ai	ɛ_T· æ· a·	æļ ɛ_Tļ aļ ɔļ

4. $\dfrac{\text{Number of Amsterdam variants in dialect D in point of time P}}{\text{Number of Amsterdam variants + number of all other variants in dialect D in point of time P}}$ = Percentage of Amsterdam variants in dialect D in point of time P

One must realize that in using such a method mistakes and errors can easily creep in, and that the precise percentages suggest more exactness than is justified. That is why we took increases in the number of the Amsterdam variants into account only if the growth of the percentage of Amsterdam variants between two points of time exceeded 20%. We are inclined to believe that an increase of 20% cannot be due to coincidence.

In Map 1 each increase of the Amsterdam variants greater than 20% has been depicted. Map 2 contains the indexes for Amsterdam influence, computed per period with the help of Trudgill's formula as given in (2), without any factor s.[2] For towns and villages situated between Amsterdam and another big town, two values have been calculated: one for the influence from Amsterdam and another for the influence from the other town, for example, Utrecht. After that, the value of the other town's influence was subtracted from the value of Amsterdam's influence. The resulting values have been circled.

4.3. The refinement of s.

A comparison of Map 1 and Map 2 reveals that there are a number of grids in which there are both a high index for influence in a certain period and a rise of Amsterdam variants, in the same period. These cases indicate that the formula works. However, there are also grids in which Trudgill's formula apparently does not work:

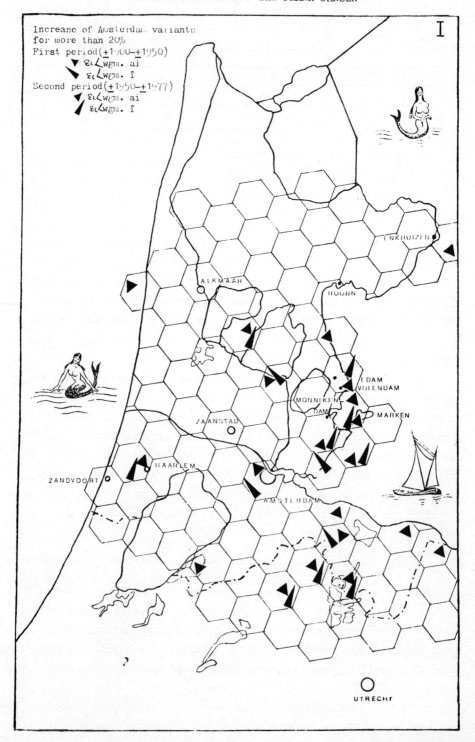

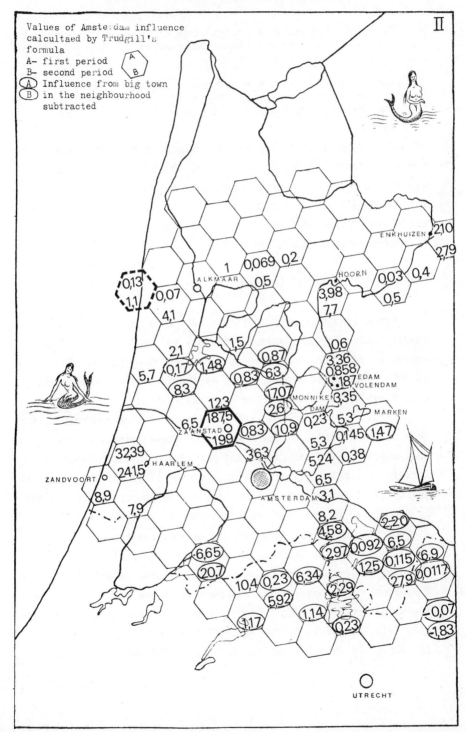

Values of Amsterdam influence
calcultaed by Trudgill's
formula
A- first period
B- second period
Ⓐ Influence from big town
Ⓑ in the neighbourhood
subtracted

A.   There are instances of a high index of influence according to
      Trudgill's formula and yet no increase of the Amsterdam vari-
      ants.

B.   There are also instances of a low index of influence accord-
      ing to Trudgill's formula co-occurring with an increase of
      the Amsterdam variants.

In our opinion, most incongruencies between attested influence and
the indexes according to the formula can be resolved by refining the
factor s in two respects. These refinements of the factor s will be
discussed in detail in subsections 4.3.1. and 4.3.2., which deal with
the restraining effect of "unnatural changes" and the restraining effect of "unfavorable system", respectively.

         4.3.1. Unnatural Changes.

      For a long time past linguists have noted that some sound
changes occur frequently in the history of the languages of the
world, while other sound changes occur seldom or never. This idea
is being elaborated upon nowadays as the "search for substantive
universals of sound change" or "natural changes".
      Labov, Yaeger, and Steiner (1972) report some tendences which
they call principles of sound changes. These principles are based
upon ongoing sound changes recently observed in sociolinguistic
surveys by comparing the spectrograms made of vowels in the casual
speech of different generations in the same speech community, and
by comparison of the vowel spectrograms of the casual speech of
dialect informants speaking closely related dialects.
      The tendencies found again and again were confirmed by the
philological evidence of sound changes in former stages in diverse
languages. The observations of Labov which are relevant for our
investigation are the following: in chain shifts, lax vowels usually fall, particularly the lax nuclei of upgliding diphthongs
(p. 106). If this lax nucleus arrives at the lowest position of

the vowel triangle, in the neighborhood of the [a·], the glide
of the diphthong is deleted and the former dissimilated diphthong
is converted into a new long and low monophthong (p. 225).   In
Fig. 1 this typical development is depicted in the vowel triangle:
a tensed long high vowel [i·] diphthongizes to [ɪ̯ʟ], then the nucleus lowers to [ɛʟ] and further to [æʟ] and [aʟ].   Finally the
glide [ʟ] is deleted and there is a new long and low monophthong
[a·].

Figure 1

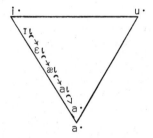

→   =   lowering of the lax vocal nucleus of the diphthong.

>   =   monophthongization of the most dissimilated diphthong.

(Based on Labov, Yaeger, and Steiner 1972.)

A slight digression about the status of "principles" of sound
changes such as these, seems called for here.   Every claim about
something universal is somewhat presumptuous, for strictly speaking it can never be based on sufficient data.   Therefore, one must
in general be very cautious with universals.

However, we think that the ample documentation by Labov et al.
can be backed up by material about changes in still other languages
and dialects.   See, for example, Andersen (1972:42), Schmitt (1931:
100), Stampe (1972), and Miller (1973).

Therefore we believe the principles we shall use here are established enough to build upon.

We call a change which is just in line with the Labovian principles of sound changes a "natural change" and those which are not
in line with those principles "unnatural changes".

With the aid of the distinction between natural and unnatural
changes it is possible to differentiate between a rise of Amsterdam variants due to natural change (a "natural rise" of Amsterdam
variants) and a rise of Amsterdam variants due to unnatural change
(an "unnatural rise" of Amsterdam variants).[3] This distinction is
important for two reasons:

A. The rise of Amsterdam variants due to a natural change is a
    less certain case of Amsterdam influence than is the rise of
    Amsterdam variants due to an unnatural change.[4] If, for ex-
    ample, there is a rise of Amsterdam variants brought about by
    a natural change, and a very low index of influence according
    to Trudgill's formula, this can be explained in either of two
    ways:

    1. there is no influence at all in that dialect: the rise
        of the Amsterdam variant is a spontaneous development;

    2. the formula doesn't work.

    The consequences of the formula are much more severe in the
    case of a low index and an unnatural change, when one is
    forced to assume that the formula does not work. Conversely,
    when there is a high index and a rise of Amsterdam variants
    brought about by a natural change, one *can* assume Amsterdam
    influence, although a spontaneous development is also pos-
    sible. In the same circumstances with an unnatural change,
    the Amsterdam influence is certain. With the aid of the dis-
    tinction between natural and unnatural changes, it is possible
    to discard some counterexamples, and, on the other hand, to
    establish firm and falsifiable cases of influence.

B. Since there are two types of rising of Amsterdam variants --
    natural changes, which can be considered as the stimulation
    or backing up of a natural development by Amsterdan influence,
    and unnatural changes, in which the Amsterdam variants had to
    substitute for one or more dialect variants -- it is not un-
    reasonable to postulate that there will be a difference in

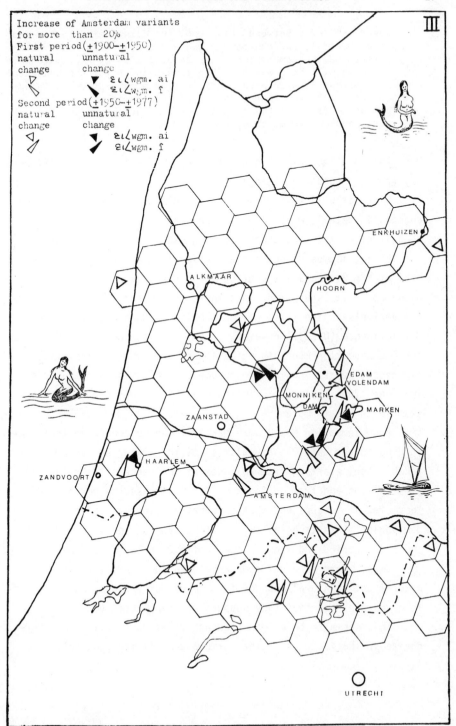

Increase of Amsterdam variants
for more than 20%
First period(±1900-±1950)
natural   unnatural
change   change
              ▼   εɪ ⟨ wgm. ai
                   εɪ ⟨ wgm. ī
Second period(±1950-±1977)
natural   unnatural
change   change
              ▼   εɪ ⟨ wgm. ai
                   εɪ ⟨ wgm. ī

ENKHUIZEN

ALKMAAR

HOORN

EDAM
VOLENDAM

MONNIKEN
DAM

MARKEN

ZAANSTAD

HAARLEM

ZANDVOORT

AMSTERDAM

UTRECHT

speed and force between these two, the first being faster and more powerful. We can assume that if there is an observable difference the lowest index for natural rise of the Amsterdam variants will be lower than the lowest index for the unnatural rise of the Amsterdam variants. If this assumption is in accordance with the facts, it can be considered an important argument in favor of the reality of the distinction between natural and unnatural changes.

In Map 3 the natural changes have been depicted in a different way from the unnatural changes.

Since it will obviously be impossible to discuss all of the changes in detail, we shall only consider those cases which can shed light on the more theoretical considerations mentioned above.

First, let us direct our attention to the thickly hatched grid of Map 2, the village of Egmond. From comparison of Map 2 with Map 3, it is apparent that there is a natural rise of Amsterdam variants in the first period combined with a very low index for influence (0.13). However, since this is a question of a natural change, the monophthongization of a maximally dissimilated diphthong, we are inclined to assume a development not caused by influence from Amsterdam. That's why this is not a true counterexample to the formula.

From comparing Map 2 with Map 3 it can be concluded that, according to our data, a natural rise of the Amsterdam variants has taken place, starting from an index of influence of 4.58 for the first period and from an index of 1.4 in the second period. Furthermore, it is apparent that an unnatural increase of the Amsterdam variants has taken place, starting from an index of 6.3 on in the first period and from an index of 5.3 in the second period.[5]

Thus, there is a difference between the minimal values for natural and unnatural changes in both of our periods and these differences are such that they support our hypothesis (cf. B).

This seems to be evidence enough to warrant trying to incorporate in the factor s of the formula the ability that influence due to natural change is taking place in an easier way than does influence due to unnatural change.

In order to do so, one first has to take one type of change, either natural or unnatural, as the basic one. Our choice was the less marked change, the natural one.

As has already been mentioned, the lowest index for a natural change was 4.5, and for an unnatural change 6.3, in the first period. In other words, the restraining power of the factor for accounting for unnatural change in this period is so strong that the index for Amsterdam influence has to be $\frac{6.3}{4.6}$ = 1.36 times as great as the Amsterdam influence index in the case of a natural change. There is yet another way to say the same thing: the index for influence is restrained by the factor $\frac{4.6}{6.3}$ = 0.73 when the influence is due to an unnatural change.

For the second period the procedure is the same: the restraining power of the factor accounting for unnatural change has to be $\frac{5.3}{1.5}$ = 3.5 times as great as the Amsterdam influence in the case of an unnatural change. In other words: the index for influence is restrained by the factor $\frac{1.5}{5.3}$ = 0.28 when the influence is due to an unnatural change.

On the basis of the data from two different periods we have been able to define two values for the restraining power of an unnatural change: 0.73 and 0.28. Both values are less than 1; thus in this investigation the restraining effect of an unnatural change has been demonstrated.

It is not plausible on *a priori* grounds that the value for the restraining effect of an unnatural change can ever be fixed at one and the same "universal height". Up until now we have found that in our survey the restraining factor of an unnatural change lies between 0.28 and 0.73.

Further determination of the value for the restraining effect of an unnatural change will have to be done in other investigations.

4.3.2. Unfavorable system.

In the tradition of structuralist phonology there has been a
lively debate about the probability of the assumption that certain
properties of a vowel system stimulate or restrain a sound change.
Goossens (1969:62ff.) refutes the premise that the properties of a
vowel system can have a stimulating effect on a sound change, as
has been assumed in Moulton (1962). Goossens demonstrates that,
using the same data as those presented by Moulton, his isoglosses
can be explained by assuming the contrary, namely the restraining
effect of an unfavorable system on a sound change. It is this
theory of a "negative teleology", in the words of Goossens, which
is adopted here.

In short, the argument is as follows: a sound change, for
example [aɪ] becomes [a·], caused by phonetic or extralinguistic
factors, can spread throughout a speech community until it reaches
the boundaries of a dialect in which there is already another [a·].
The spread will stop there because the collapsing of the other
[a·] and the [a·] from [aɪ] would cause too much ambiguity.

Proponents of this theory (Weijnen 1969:96) have stipulated
-- on theoretical grounds -- one important proviso: the two phonemes must have a high frequency in the dialect under investigation.

The theory that an unfavorable vowel system can have a restraining effect on a sound change corresponds with the data found
in our investigation.

The Amsterdam variants for Standard Dutch [εɪ] (see Table II)
occupy a position in the vowel triangle as indicated in Fig. 2.

From comparison of Fig. 2 with Fig. 3 it is apparent that the
position occupied by the Amsterdam variants for Standard Dutch [εɪ]
in the phonological space is the same as the position occupied by
the palatal and neutral [a·] for Standard Dutch [a·].

Figure 2

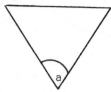

Figure 3

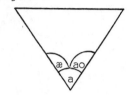

Position of Amsterdam
[a·], [æ·] for standard
[ɛ̯] in a phonological
space.

Positions of velar, neutral
and palatal [a·] in a phonological space.

According to the theory that an unfavorable system indeed has a
restraining effect on a sound change we can expect that the Amsterdam variants for Standard Dutch [ɛ̯] could not spread into dialects
with a palatal or neutral [a·], since both [ɛ̯]'s and the [a·] occur very frequently in current spoken Dutch and collapsing the two
would lead to much ambiguity.[6]

The dialects of the province of North Holland can be divided
into two groups, one with a neutral or palatal [a·] for Standard
Dutch [a·] from WGm. *a* and *ã*, the other with a velar [a·] for Standard Dutch [a·].

In Map 4 the different realizations for Standard Dutch [a·]
depicted for the first two points in time of our investigation.
The data are obtained from the same sources as those used for Maps
1 and 3. Comparing Map 4 with Map 3, one can conclude that in our
area the presence of a palatal and/or neutral [a·] indeed had a
restraining effect on the Amsterdam variants for standard [ɛ̯].

The restraining effect of an unfavorable system is powerful
enough to warrant trying to determine its force more precisely in
factor s of the formula. This can be done in the following way:
one should look first for the highest index of influence in a
place where nevertheless no Amsterdam influence has been found,
due to the unfavorable system. This would be *Zaanstad*, a large

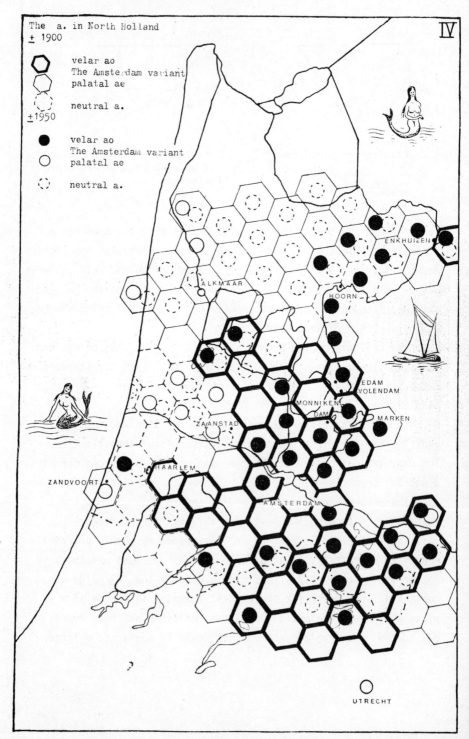

town in the neighborhood of Amsterdam with an index of 199, a
palatal [a·] and no Amsterdam influence. Secondly, one should
find out what index this 199 should be lowered to, in order to
prevent or obstruct Amsterdam influence. In our survey this
would be 1.5, the minimal value of influence due to natural
changes.

Thus it appears from the data of our investigation that the
value of s for the restraining effect of an unfavorable system
is $\frac{1.5}{199}$ = 0.00736 or less.

It seems doubtful to us whether it will be possible to determine a fixed value for the restraining effect of an unfavorable system. Only the results of other investigations will be
able to shed some light on "universality" of the value we have
determined in our survey for the restraining effect of an unfavorable system.

Up until now, the only evidence adduced for the theory of
the restraining effect of an unfavorable system, has been based
upon the interpretation of dialect isoglosses, drawn on the basis
of data for only one point in time (Moulton 1962). As a result
of our investigation we see that the influence a large town has
on its surroundings during a certain period could only be accounted for by adducing the restraining effect of an unfavorable system. The fact that the theory of an unfavorable system is also
needed in order to explain the growth of Amsterdam influence for
a certain period, can be regarded as stronger evidence in support
of this theory. Besides, the incorporation in our formula of a
factor for the restraining effect of an unfavorable system has
the advantage that Trudgill's proposal to incorporate a factor
of "prior existing dialect similarity" can be avoided when using
the formula for explanations of sound changes. This is very at-
tractive, because Trudgill's integers for the factor "prior existing dialect similarity" were rated intuitively and were not based
on any theoretical insight. Besides, they were in principle based

on all the features that two dialects have in common, which makes
it rather difficult to weigh this factor. The factor for the restraining effect of an unfavorable system, as proposed in this
paper, is more precise because it is based upon only those differences between dialects which are relevant for the sound changes
under consideration.

5.   FINAL REMARKS

In this last section a few short remarks are in order.

In the first place, one should not take this paper as a report
accounting for every decision we made and all the peculiarities we
met while working on the project. In particular, we have omitted discussion of a few exceptions to the refined formula. These exceptions
are of course very interesting, but we think that their explanation
has little, if any, bearing on the problems focussed upon here.

Secondly, our refined formula should be tested in its turn. This
could be done by investigating other Amsterdam dialect variants in the
same area, or, even more interesting, by investigating dialect influence in other areas. The purpose of these urgent follow-up investigations would not be to find a universal constant proportion among the
geographic factors in the formula. Because of the area dependency of
these factors in the formula, it will never be possible, in our opinion,
to find a fixed index above which dialect influence takes place and under which it doesn't. We think that testing the reality of the linguistic factors in the formula would be more successful.

From Labov's uniformitarian principle it follows that the linguistic factors in the formula probably will not be contingent or entirely
language-particular.

We posit that the forces operating to produce linguistic change
today are of the same kind and order of magnitude as those which
operated in the past five or ten thousand years. (Labov 1972:275.)

We hope that other investigations will yield the result that the linguistic factors in the formula are language-independent qua direction and (perhaps) force.

This brings us to our final remarks: the benefits of the use of a formula. These are twofold:

1. Regarding dialectology: a formula can give explanations for isoglosses (see Trudgill 1974) and with the aid of a formula the use of dialect borrowing as an explanatory tool can be kept within bounds, for it is now possible to demonstrate when consideration of a language change as being a result of dialect borrowing is highly improbable.

2. Regarding diachronic linguistics: whenever the reality of a restraining or stimulating linguistic factor is demonstrated and incorporated in the formula, we can take it as independent evidence for the reality of the analogue idea in diachronic linguistics. Of course, the procedure can also work the other way round: whenever the incorporation of an alleged stimulating or restraining factor in the formula gives highly inconsistent results, the reality of the analogue in diachronic linguistics has to be questioned.

NOTES:

*We are very grateful to several participants of the conference for their encouragements and criticisms on this paper. Furthermore we thank the Institute of Dialectology which gave us all the practical facilities for doing this investigation. We are in particular very grateful to Joke Wildeman and Henk Eerevelt who helped collect the data and calculate the formula, to Jan Wiegmans, who designed the maps and those lovely mermaids, and to Rob Rentenaar, who helped find the data for calculating the formula.

1) It will be clear that for some hexagons we were not able to collect sufficient data, since part of the area under investigation consists of polders with some farms but almost no villages.

2) Since travel by water in the first period was as important as traffic by road, the formula had to be modified according to our data for towns and villages which had a good connection with Amsterdam by water as follows:

$$I_{amst.-B} = \frac{P\ amst}{P\ amst + P\ B} \cdot \tfrac{1}{2} \cdot \left(\frac{P\ amst + P\ B}{(d\ amst - B)^2 \atop by\ road} + \frac{P\ amst + P\ B}{d\ Amst - B \atop by\ water} \bigvee \frac{}{d\ amst - B \atop by\ water} \right)$$

By using dAmst-B $\sqrt{\text{dAmst-B}}$ instead of (d Amst-B)[2] we have incorporated
the fact that in the first period villages and towns with both road and
water connections had more contact with Amsterdam than places with only
road connections had.

3) The standards which are applied for establishing the existence
of an unnatural change are: (A) the occurrence of 20% or more Amster-
dam variants ($[\varepsilon \cdot]$ or $[a \cdot]$) at a point in time, while there are no Amsterdam variants at a previous point in time, nor diphthongs ($[\varepsilon \iota]$ or
$[a \iota]$) which could develop into them by a natural change.   (B) the rise
of 20% or more Amsterdam variants, while there is at the previous point
in time a minimal percentage of diphthongs apt to change naturally into
them, compared with the percentage of Amsterdam variants in the latter
point of time.

This way of defining an unnatural rise of Amsterdam variants is
rather doubtful for the first period because of the long space of time
covered (50 years). In theory, it would have been possible to mistakenly conclude that a change was unnatural while it actually was
natural. We tried to exclude misinterpretation by looking for indications in several dialect surveys (especially Heeroma 1935) of intermediate stages in the development of the sounds.

4) In the first case, using Andersen's (1973) terminology it can
also be an example of evolutive change; in the latter case, it can only
be an example of adaptive change.

5) It is evident from the maps that natural changes of all the
phenomena under consideration do not take place in every grid with an
index of influence higher than 4.5 for the first period and 1.5 for the
second period. Also, unnatural changes of all the relevant phonemes
do not take place in every grid with a value higher than 6.3 for the
first period and 5.3 for the second period.

This is partly due to the fact that in some grids the same variants
as the Amsterdam variants were present from the first point of time on
(Hoorn, Marken), partly due to a factor which will be explained in
4.3.2.

6) According to the frequency list of words in spoken Dutch (Uit
den Boogaart 1975), which is based on 121.569 tokens, the frequency of
$[\varepsilon \iota]$ from WGm. $\hat{\imath}$ is 2854, of $[\varepsilon \iota]$ from WGm. ai 738, and that of $[a \cdot]$
from WGm. a and WGm. $\hat{a}$ 5866.

REFERENCES:

Andersen, H. 1972. "Diphthongization", *Language* 48.11–50.
––––––––. 1973. "Abductive and Deductive Change", *Language* 49.765–93.
Bloomfield, L. 1933. *Language*.
Boogaart, P. C. Uit den. 1975. *Woordfrequenties*.
Chen, M. 1972. "The Time Dimension: Contribution Toward a Theory of
    Sound Change", *Foundations of Language* 8.457–98.
Daan, J. 1969. *Dialektatlas van Noord-Holland*.

Debus, F. 1962. "Mundart und Hochsprache", *Zeitschrift für Mundartforschung* 29.1-43.

Frings, Th. 1926. "Sprache und Geschichte am Rhein", *Sprache und Geschichte II.* Reprinted 1956. Halle.

Goossens, J. 1969. *Strukturelle Sprachgeographie.*

Heeroma, K. H. 1935. *Hollandse Dialectstudies.* Groningen.

Kloeke, G. G. 1927. *De Hollandsche expansie in de 16e en 17e eeuw en haar weerspiegeling in de hedendaagse dialecten.* 's-Gravenhage.

Labov, W. 1966. *The Social Stratification of English in New York City.* Washington: Center for Applied Linguistics.

-------. 1972. *Sociolinguistic Patterns.* Philadelphia.

Labov, W., M. Yaeger and R. Steiner. 1972. *A Quantitative Study of Sound Change in Progress.* Report on National Science Foundation, Contract NSF-GS-3287, University of Pennsylvania. Printed and distributed by the U.S. Regional Survey, 204 N. 35th Street, Philadelphia, PA 19104.

Miller, P. D. 1973. "Bleaching and Coloring", *Papers 9th Regional Meeting Chicago Linguistic Society.* Pp. 386-97.

Moulton, W. G. 1962. "Vokalspaltung durch innere Kasualität: die Ostschweizerische Vokalspaltung", *Zeitschrift für Mundartforschung* 29.227-51.

Ooyen, L. van. 1968. *Dialectatlas van Zuid-Holland en Utrecht.* RNDA nr. 11.

Paul, H. 1880. *Prinzipien der Sprachgeschichte.* Halle.

Peng, F. C. C. 1977. *Sound Change and Language Change.* Paper presented at the IIIrd ICHL.

Schmitt, A. 1931. *Akzent und Diftongierung.* Heidelberg.

Schuchardt, H. 1885. *Ueber die Lautgesetze: gegen die Junggrammatiker.* Vennemann & Wilbur (eds.), 1972.

Stampe, D. 1972. "On the Natural History of Diphthongs", in *Papers 8th Regional Meeting of the Chicago Linguistic Society.* Pp. 443-54.

Trudgill, P. 1974. *The Social Differentiation of English in Norwich.* Cambridge.

-------. 1974. "Linguistic Change and Diffusion; Description and Explanation in Sociolinguistic Dialect Geography", *Language in Society* 3.215-47.

Vennemann, Th. & T. H. Wilbur. 1972. *Schuchardt, the Neogrammarians and the Transformational Theory of Phonological Change.* Linguistische Forschungen 26. Frankfurt.

Weijnen, A. 1969. "Lautgeschichte und Wortfrequenz", in *Actes du Xe Congrès International des Linguistes.* Bucharest. Pp. 453-62. Also in A. Weijnen, 1975, *General and Comparative Dialectology.* Pp. 95-105.

Paper completed October, 1977.

DEVELOPMENT OF TONES IN LANGUAGES
WITH DISTINCTIVE TONAL ACCENTS

JADRANKA GVOZDANOVIĆ
Universiteit van Amsterdam

1.1. Phonology was defined by Trubetzkoy (1958:29) as a study of the distinctive, the culminative, and the delimitative functions of speech sounds. The distinctive function refers to features which are capable of distinguishing between words. The culminative function refers to word accent. The delimitative function refers to boundary signals, or junctures, at the level of morphemes, words, or larger units.

Trubetzkoy (1958:241-61) describes the delimitative signals as being either phonological (referring to positional presence vs. absence of phonological oppositions) or non-phonological (in cases of complementarily distributed phonemes or variants). In addition to these segmental delimitative signals, Trubetzkoy (1958:245) points to the so-called fixed accent as a case of non-phonological delimitative signal at the level of words.

1.2. In an article on the issue whether accent is a phonological feature, Ebeling (1968:135) coined the term "configurational" as a designation of features that are relevant but not inherent in a phonological unit:

> Among the multifarious attributes of linguistic units a sharp distinction must be made between those which characterize a unit, within the larger whole to which it belongs, in comparison with the other constituents of the same whole, and those

which are established on the basis of comparison with another
element not necessarily belonging to the same utterance. I
propose to speak of configurational and inherent features,
respectively. For configurational features the compared object is *in praesentia*, for inherent features *in absentia*.

Ebeling (1968:136) states, furthermore, that "the relationship between
configurational and inherent features is such that a configurational
feature of a lower-level unit constitutes an inherent feature of the
unit of the next higher level". The accent is according to him an inherent feature of that word.

It is possible to conclude that, in languages in which word boundaries are consistently indicated by means of a delimitative signal,
this delimitative feature can be analyzed as configurational in the
same way as word accent can. Indeed, cases of a consistently present
delimitative signal are found in languages with fixed accent (such as
Czech, Polish, Hungarian, etc.), i.e., where the delimitative signal
is a suprasegmental feature. Suprasegmental features are configurational in the sense of inherent at the level of suprasegmental words.
I shall henceforth call them "prosodic words". This term equals the
term "prosodeme" as used by Hattori (1961:5ff.), referring to a word
with adjoining clitics.[1]

2.1. Concerning vowel quantity and accent assignment, Trubetzkoy (1958:
169-94) distinguishes between syllable-counting and mora-counting languages. In mora-counting languages, a long syllable nucleus (i.e.,
vowel) is evaluated as a sequence of two morae. He mentions as one
of the possible criteria for distinguishing between syllable-counting
and mora-counting that in mora-counting systems, either the first or
the second mora of a long syllable nucleus can be accented. The high
pitch of the accented mora yields phonetic contour tones in long syllable nuclei.[2] In Trubetzkoy's opinion (1958:188), it is impossible
for a mora-counting system to have contour tones in syllable nuclei
consisting of a single mora. Trubetzkoy has thus stated that a long

vowel can be analyzed as a vowel sequence (and what sorts of indication we can have concerning this analysis), but did not state when such
an analysis is impossible. In my opinion, this question goes back to
the general question of whether a sound can be analyzed as a sequence
of units or as a single unit. It was answered by Ebeling (1960:67,
etc.) in this sense that whenever there is no opposition between a
given sound and the corresponding sequence of sounds (the distinctiveness of which has been established independently) within a morpheme,
one should accept the analysis as a sequence. Consequences of this
analysis show up in the prosody, too.

2.2. Trubetzkoy (1958:190-94) mentions Standard Serbo-Croatian as an
example of a language with distinctive contour tones in both short and
long syllable nuclei. It has distinctive short and long falling accent in the initial position, and short and long rising accent in any
non-initial position. According to Trubetzkoy (1958:194), it is not
a mora-counting language. He analyzes the rising tone as an occurrence of free accent, and the falling tone as a positional variant of
tonelessness fulfilling the delimitative function. Trubetzkoy further
states that Standard Serbo-Croatian is the only language known to him
in which free accent (which is implemented as rising) is jointly relevant with a non-culminative distinction correlation (the latter term
is meant to cover the falling accent), cf. Trubetzkoy (1958:194):
"Übrigens sind uns andere Beispiele des Nebeneinanderbestehens der
freien Betonung mit einer nichtgipfelbildenden Differenzierungskorre-
lation unbekannt!".

3.1. Ivić and Lehiste's valuable phonetic investigations of Standard
Serbo-Croatian tonal accents (cf., e.g., Lehiste and Ivić 1963) have
shown that the main distinctive characteristic of the rising tonal accents is the high pitch of the first postaccentual syllable nucleus.
The final syllable of a word can never have a rising tone.

3.2. Browne and McCawley (1965) have argued that the Standard Serbo-
Croatian system can be described by marking the aforementioned high
pitch as the accent, cf. Browne and McCawley 1965:151:

> A new treatment is proposed which markes only the syllable after
> a rising (since risings never occur on the last syllable of a
> word); certain words with falling accent are marked on the first
> syllable and others, although phonetically identical, are left
> unmarked. When this is done, a rule which puts an accent on the
> first syllable of an unmarked phonological word will suffice to
> characterize the behavior of combinations of words with procli-
> tics; moreover, many accentual alternations will be describable
> very simply, namely by rules which either delete the accent mark
> from an ending or shift the accent one syllable to the left.

Browne and McCawley thus make a distinction between *br'at-a* "brother"
(gen. sg.) and *med-a* "honey" (gen. sg.), although both have a phonetically identical short falling tone. They give as their reason the
fact that in combination with a proclitic, e.g., *od* "of", we get
od-br'at-a, with a short rising tone on the first syllable, but *od-
med-a*, with an initial short falling tone. However, prosodic words
such as *od-med-a* are perceived by native speakers as having an accent
and being able to bear the prominence in a phrase, whereas clitics
such as *ga* "him" (gen-acc. sg.), *mu* "him" (dat. sg.) are not by themselves accentable and must follow the first accentable word in a phrase.
In my opinion, Browne and McCawley have failed to recognize the necessity of marking prosodic word boundaries in order to make their rules
yield the correct result. I propose that *od-med-a* as well as *med*
should be marked as *#od-med-a#* and *#med#*, as opposed to *#od*, with an
initial boundary, and *ga(#)*, with a final boundary which is obligatory
unless it is followed by another clitic. There are, consequently,
monosyllabic words which lack the status of prosodic words.

3.3. It is here that not only the problem of descriptional adequacy
vs. simplicity enters into the picture, but also the problem of whether
an analysis can be considered adequate if it does not have a direct cor-

relate in linguistic behavior. In my opinion, the Standard Serbo-Croatian tonal accents should not be analyzed as a realization of a different accent placement, because, e.g., in the short rising vs. short
falling opposition, the same syllable has both acoustic and perceptual
characteristics of accentedness (i.e., acoustically it has a relatively
non-falling and high pitch accompanied by longer duration; perception
tests [cf. Lehiste and Ivić 1963:135] have shown that the accented syllable nuclei are not mutually distinguisted).

   The Standard Serbo-Croatian rising vs. falling tones cannot be
analyzed as combinations of high and low tone levels. Whereas the
first postaccentual syllable nucleus could possibly be analyzed as
high (in the case of the rising accents) vs. low (in the case of the
falling accents), the accented syllable nucleus is not perceptually
distinguished as high vs. low (cf. also Lehiste and Ivić 1963:135).

   Each analysis of the Standard Serbo-Croatian tones necessitates
the indication of prosodic word boundaries. We have seen already
that the final syllable of each word in Standard Serbo-Croatian has
[-rising] pitch and is unaccented. This [-rising] word-final pitch
is a consistently occurring delimitative signal in Standard Serbo-
Croatian. In order to account for it, it would suffice to mark one
syllable nucleus in a prosodic word as [-rising]. A word structure
condition would then state that all of the syllables, if any, preceding
the [-rising] one have a [+rising] pitch, and all of the syllables
following it, if any, a [-rising] pitch.[3] The last rising pitch in
a prosodic word equals the [+rising] tone, and is accented. In the
absence of these, the first [-rising] pitch, which equals the [-ris-
ing] or falling tone, is perceived as accented.

   Note that the prosodic structure of a Standard Serbo-Croatian
word has been correctly described by Jakobson (1931). According to
the criteria of description adequacy that I adhere to, I cannot agree
with Jakobson's later reformulation (1949), in which he states that
the Standard Serbo-Croatian tones can be analyzed as [±high].

3.4. I cannot agree with Browne and McCawley's notation either, because in their interpretation the Standard Serbo-Croatian system looks
like the Old Serbo-Croatian one. The contemporary system emerged from
the old one after an "accent retraction" presumably between the 13th
and the 15th centuries. This "accent retraction" was a reinterpretation of distinctive accent placement in terms of distinctive tone. It
yielded the long and short rising tones, as opposed to the falling ones
in the initial position. The rising tone is characterized by a high
pitch in the next following syllable. Furthermore, the word-final delimitative signal was introduced, implemented as the [-rising] pitch.
In the contemporary system, accent is predictable on the basis of tone
and the delimitative feature -- the last rising syllable in a prosodic
word has the prominence characteristic of accentedness. In the absence
of these, the word-initial falling syllable is perceived as the accent.

     The aforementioned predictability of accent on the basis of a sin-
gle change in the tonal pattern in a word is compatible with the findings of perception tests of accentedness (e.g., with nonsense syllables,
done by Morton and Jassem [1965]), according to which a change in the
fundamental frequency pattern is normally perceived as accented.

     I have tried to show here that Standard Serbo-Croatian has distinc-
tive rising vs. falling tones which can neither be described as directly
predictable from accent, nor as combinations of tone levels. I conclude
that Standard Serbo-Croatian is a syllable-counting language in which
accent is predictable on the basis of the [±rising] tone and the delimitative signal, which is a configurational feature.

4.1. Mora-counting systems with distinctive accent placement are found,
for example, in many Čakavian and Old Štokavian local dialects of Serbo-
Croatian, many Slovenian local dialects with distinctive tonal accents,
and in Standard Japanese. An extensive analysis of Japanese has been
made, e.g., by McCawley (cf. 1968:182):

     A language with a "pitch accent" system like Japanese and a lan-
     guage with a "stress accent" system like Russian have the formal

similarity that the accentual information which must be recorded
in dictionary entries is at most the *location* of some accentual
phenomenon.

In most of the Japanese dialects which correspond to the standard
system, the morae following the accented one are characterized by a
fall in pitch.[4] For the Japanese dialects of such places as Kyōto and
Hyōgo, however, McCawley proposes a treatment according to which words
(in casu: nouns) can be treated as having from 0 to 2 underlying accents: an accent before the word or not, and an accent on one of the
syllables of the word or not (1970:527). For example:

'usagi'	"rabbit"	LLH
katati	"form"	HHH
to'bira	"door"	HLL
kata'na	"sword"	HHL
'tanu'ki	"badger"	LHL.[5]

In Kyōto and Hyōgo, the underlying form of a noun must indicate not
only where (if anywhere) the noun contributes a drop in pitch, but
also whether it starts on a high or low pitch (in McCawley's description, an initial low pitch can be treated as preceded by an underlying
accent). According to McCawley (1968:192), the Tōkyō type of accent,
which corresponds with the standard one, developed from a system of
the Kyōto type by a shift of accent one syllable to the right. Whereas the standard system has distinctive accent placement, the systems
of Kyōto and Hyōgo can be analyzed as having distinctive low vs. high
tone (cf. 4.2.).

4.2. I would like to draw attention to the existence of some similarity between the Japanese Kyōto and Hyōgo systems and the South Slavic
system of Standard Slovenian as spoken in Ljubljana. According to
Toporišič (1967, etc.), the Standard Slovenian tonal accents can be

analyzed as low vs. high tone. Whereas Slovenian presumably was originally a mora-counting language with distinctive accent placement,
the contemporary Standard Slovenian of Ljubljana has a distinctive
[±low] tone, which emerged after the abandonment of the mora-counting
principle. When it occurred in the accented syllable, the mora bearing the accent was high; otherwise it was low. In syllables which
originally contained two morae, the pitch of the first mora was preserved. This was phonologized. The following Slovenian examples resemble the aforementioned Kyōto ones:

L
junāka   "hero" (gen. sg.)
H
prismode "loony" (nom. sg.)
H
prēčnica "transversal" (nom. sg.)
H
pomlādi "spring" (gen. sg., etc.)
L
dētelja "clover" (nom. sg.).[6]

I propose to analyze the Kyōto system, just like the Standard Slovenian
one, as having a distinctive [±low] tone (in addition to a configurational feature, i.e., the accent and/or prosodic word boundaries), rather than having from 0 to 2 underlying accents. The two systems differ in that long vowels are analyzed as single units in Slovenian, but
not in Kyōto, and there is also a distinction between the final high
tone and the absence of tone in Slovenian, but not in Kyōto (as with
phonetic tone in Tōkyō). The distinction between /prismode/ (cf.
above) and the enclitic /je/ "he/she/it is", which are both pronounced
with a short final accent when occurring in isolation (cf. also Toporišič 1968:141), shows up when they form a single prosodic word, i.e.,
/prismode je/. It is pronounced with the accent on the high tone, as
the accent is predictable from tone, and in its absence from the final
prosodic word boundary.

5.1. We have seen already that the distinction between syllable-counting and mora-counting was not clearly defined in the Prague school approach, as it was not related to the problems of segmentation in general. This was a source of later misunderstanding. For example, Leben (1973) correctly pointed to the functioning of contour tones as sequences of levels in some languages with tone spreading and copying, but did not see a possibility to relate this to the segmental analysis of the vowels (and sonorants) characterized by tone as sequences, and thus erroneously assumed that contour tones must be indivisible units in a system with segmental specification of tone. This led him to suprasegmental analysis of such tone features. However, if the distinction between syllable-counting and mora-counting is viewed as a matter of segmentation which applies to long vowels and yields vowel sequences unless there is opposition with the corresponding vowel sequences within a morpheme, then there are languages with short and long vowels functioning as syllable nuclei, and languages with single vowels and vowel sequences (possibly also sequences of vowels and sonorants) functioning as syllable nuclei. An example of a system of the former type can be found in Standard Serbo-Croatian, where there is an opposition between a long vowel and the corresponding sequence of short vowels, as can be illustrated by the following examples:

> /nîn-Skī/ "pertaining to the town of Nin",
> /nín-a/   "Nin" (gen. sg.), vs.
> /niìnSki/ "Nijinsky" (proper name).[6]

An example of a system of the latter type can be found in the Posavian dialect of Serbo-Croatian, where, e.g., in proper names any expected sequence of identical vowels is pronounced as a single long vowel (cf. also Ivšić 1913), as there is no opposition between the former and the latter, and there is a pronunciation rule by which a sequence of identical segments within a morpheme is pronounced as a single long segment.

Languages with phonologically long and short vowels can have no tone (e.g., a variant of Standard Slovenian, where there is only the

accent as a suprasegmental feature), level tones (e.g., Standard Slovenian as described by Toporišič, *op. cit.*) and/or contour tones (the
latter are found in Standard Serbo-Croatian). Languages with single
vowels vs. vowel sequences can have no tone (e.g., Lapp), phonetic
tones due to accent assignment (as in the Čakavian dialect of Serbo-
Croatian, or in the Tōkyō dialect of Japanese), or phonological tones
which are inherent vowel features (e.g., in some languages discussed
by Leben and in some areas of Posavian). If in the course of language
change long vowels change from sequences to single segments or vice
versa, this has prosodic consequences.

I have tried to show that there is a clear distinction between
inherent tone, which is a segmental distinctive feature, and suprasegmental tonal features, which are relevant at the level of prosodic
words. Various cases of tone spreading and copying can be analyzed
as the latter. A consequence of this approach is that both segmental
and suprasegmental features can occur within the same language.

NOTES:

1) The term "word accent" is comparable to Hattori's (1961) term
"the kernel of a prosodeme".
2) In the terminology used in this paper, "pitch" equals "phonetic
tone".
3) A [+rising] pitch is defined as directly followed by a high
pitch within the same prosodic word.
4) A somewhat different example is found in, e.g., the Čakavian
dialect of Serbo-Croatian, where the accent on the second mora of a
long syllable nucleus yields a phonetic rising pitch, and on the first
mora, a phonetic falling pitch.
5) Cf. McCawley (1970:527): "'tanu'ki 'badger' & o'yazi 'old man'
∿ 'tanukio'yazi 'cunning old man' (note the loss of internal accent but
retention of initial low pitch in 'tanu'ki)."
6) The following abbreviations have been used: L = low tone; H =
high tone; nom. = nominative case; gen. = genitive case; and sg. = singular. (ˆ) denotes the falling tone on a long vowel, (´) the rising
tone on a long vowel, and (`) the rising tone on a short vowel; (¯) de-
notes vowel length without tone, and (-) a morpheme boundary. Capitals
denote that the feature [±voiced] of a consonant is neutralized due to
the presence of a consonant directly following it.

REFERENCES:

Browne, E. Wayles and McCawley, James D. 1965. "Srpskohrvatski ak-
cenat", *Zbornik za filologiju i lingvistiku* 8.147-51.
Ebeling, Carl L. 1960. *Linguistic Units*. The Hague.
Ebeling, Carl L. 1969. "On Accent in Dutch and the Phoneme /ə/",
Lingua 21.135-43.
Gvozdanović, Jadranka. 1976. "Tonal Accents in Scandinavian and Sla-
vic Languages", *Phonologica 1976* (Dressler, W. U. and Pfeiffer,
O. E., eds.), Innsbrucker Beiträge zur Sprachwissenschaft 1977,
pp. 195-200.
Hattori, Shiro. 1961. "Prosodeme, Syllable Structure and Laryngeal
Phonemes", *Studies in Descriptive and Applied Linguistics*. In-
ternational Christian University: Tōkyō. *Bulletin of the Summer
Institute in Linguistics* I.1-27.
Ivšić, Stjepan. 1913. "Današńi posavski govor", *Rad Jugoslavenske Aka-
demije Znanosti i Umjetnosti* 196.124-254, 197.9-138.
Jakobson, Roman. 1931. "Die Betonung und ihre Rolle in der Wort- und
Syntagmaphonologie", *Travaux du Cercle Linguistique de Prague*
5.164-82.
Jakobson, Roman. 1949. "On the Identification of Phonemic Entities",
Travaux du Cercle Linguistique de Copenhague 5.205-13.
Leben, William R. 1973. "The Role of Tone in Segmental Phonology",
Consonant Types and Tone (Hyman, L. M., ed.). *Southern Califor-
nia Occasional Papers in Linguistics* 1.115-50.
Lehiste, Ilse and Ivić, Pavle. 1963. *Accent in Serbo-Croatian*. *Mich-
igan Slavic Materials* 4.
Lehiste, Ilse and Ivić, Pavle. 1977. "The Phonetic Nature of the Neo-
Štokavian Accent Shift in Serbo-Croatian", *Proceedings of the
Third International Conference on Historical Linguistics*, i.e.,
a paper read at the present conference.
McCawley, James D. 1968. *The Phonological Component of a Grammar of
Japanese*. Mouton: The Hague.
McCawley, James D. 1970. "Some Tonal Systems that Come Close to Being
Pitch-accent Systems but Don't Quite Make It", *Papers from the
Sixth Regional Meeting, Chicago Linguistic Society*. Pp. 526-32.
Morton, John and Jassem, Wiktor. 1965. "Acoustic Correlates of Stress",
Language and Speech 8.159-81.
Toporišič, Jože. 1967. "Pojmovanje tonemičnosti slovenskega jezika",
Slavistična revija 15(1-2).64-109.
Toporišič, Jože. 1968. *Slovenski knjižni jezik 1*. Založba Obzorja:
Maribor.
Trubetzkoy, Nikolai S. 1958. *Grundzüge der Phonologie*. 2nd ed. Van-
denhoeck & Ruprecht: Göttingen.

DIACHRONY IN SYNCHRONY

GÖRAN HAMMARSTRÖM
Monash University

0. SYNCHRONY AND DIACHRONY DEFINED

In *synchrony* a language is described as it is used and known, at some point in time, by the speakers in its quality of means of communication. That a speaker knows his language means two quite different things: (a) that he can use it and (b) that he can talk about it. The second possibility, (b), does not refer to communication by language, but to what has been termed by Ungeheuer as extra-communicative dealing with language.

Thus, in synchrony, neither "older" and "younger" forms (see below) nor change can be considered, as they are not part of that knowledge which is used in communication. In a crucial observation Saussure (1949:117) states:

> La première chose qui frappe quand on étudie les faits de langue,
> c'est que pour le sujet parlant leur succession dans le temps
> est inexistante: il est devant un état.

It does, however, happen that a speaker uses older forms of his language. If he knows that the hearer knows Old English, he may well say something in Old English. He may also insert a word or a sentence from a foreign language. Such forms should, however, be considered as quotations which must be eliminated by the linguist so that they are not included in the synchronic description of a language (see Hammarström 1966:61).

It should be noted that many speakers, but not all, have ideas
about "old" and "young" forms in a language, i.e., they believe, often
correctly, that some form was more common earlier in the language or
existed before some other form. Therefore, it is "older". It is, however, important to realize that this is extra-communicative dealing
with language, i.e., reflecting on and talking about language. The
speaker is then not only the speaker, but also amateur linguist.

In *diachrony* changes in a language over a period of time are
studied. Although a speaker may make some good guesses about diachrony these are obviously of little value for a linguist who has,
in most cases, quite superior facilities and stricter requirements
for diachronic studies.

The minimal diachronic study considers language facts from two
different states of a language. This is actually the only way of
beginning a diachronic study. In a more complete study one attempts
to fill the time gap between the two states so that one obtains approximately continuous developments of the language units under study.

Below I shall deal with the problem of diachrony in synchrony,
or, more precisely, with evidence of facts from older states of a language being made part of a synchronic description or with the idea
that synchrony should somehow contain language change. I shall not
deal with the possibility that the synchronic state of a language at
a later point in time may contain clues as to earlier changes.[1]

1.   EARLIEST EVIDENCE

Before the beginnings of modern historical linguistics, because
of limited knowledge and limited interest, authors dealing with language were not so often tempted to use historical knowledge incorrectly.
However, Isidore de Seville (d. 636) is an early example of an author
who mixed diachrony into synchrony, as he believed that the origin of
words "is often necessary for interpretation, since when we see where

a name comes from, we more quickly understand its meaning" (see Din-
neen 1967:148).

All those who have believed that the etymon of a word elucidates
its meaning have not seen clearly that over a period of time a meaning
either (a) remains (roughly) the same, (b) changes somewhat, or (c)
changes completely. One cannot establish if (a), (b), or (c) is applicable before one has determined exactly the meaning at some particular point in time. After this has been done, earlier meanings obviously do not contribute to elucidating anything for the later state.[2]

2. 19TH CENTURY HISTORICAL LINGUISTICS

Although historical linguistics in the modern sense of the word
had its beginnings in the 18th century, its major achievements belong
rather to the 19th century. Predecessors to the neogrammarians and
after them the neogrammarians dominated many language departments in
Europe and they still had some strongholds in the 1950's and 1960's.
Despite their great merits these scholars did not generally recognize
the importance of coherent synchronic description. For them the main
problems were "historical", i.e., they concerned change, "evolution",
"development".

Paul rejected the idea that there could exist a "scientific"
study of language which would not be "historical" and v. Wartburg defended the "Ineinandergreifen der beiden von Saussure so säuberlich
geschiedenen Aspekte" (see Hammarström 1966:60).

A typical account of the historical phonetics of a language is
the well known manual for French by Bourciez. In such an account the
phonemes which are at the base of each section (the phonemes of Late
Latin in the case of Bourciez) are "developed" one after the other.
One usually obtains as result (a) (roughly) a modern phoneme (a modern
French phoneme in the case of Bourciez) at the end of a section, (b)
the examples of a modern phoneme spread over two or more sections in
case the phoneme has more than one source, and (c) two modern phonemes

in case they stem from the same old phoneme (see Hammarström 1966:66-70).

The nearest Bourciez comes to a synchronic description is when he
provides the Latin vowels and consonants which are the starting point
for the later developments. The book provides no answer to questions
about the vowel and consonant inventory and system at any later point
in time. It has no clear answer to questions such as: What were the
consonants in the 12th century or what were the vowels of French when
the book was written? The unclear and missing synchrony renders the
diachrony imperfect, as diachrony needs to be based on clear synchronic
descriptions. The neogrammarians being too atomistic fail to see certain relations which are seen with clarity by Jakobson, Martinet, Lausberg, Lüdtke, and others who base their diachronic conclusions on two
or more clearly defined synchronic states (see Hammarström 1966:79-82).

After the rise of structuralism, heated arguments arose between
structuralists and the last generation of neogrammarians as these pro-
grammatically underestimated the importance of synchrony. It is of
some interest for the history of linguistics that neogrammarians accused
the structuralists of being capable of no more than "mere description",
whereas the neogrammarians themselves could "explain". The diachronic
structuralists, particularly Martinet, also claimed that they could find
"explanations". (I have maintained myself that the so-called explanations of both neogrammarians and diachronic structuralists are far from
being complete causal explanations, see Hammarström 1966:75-86 and 1965.)
Another erroneous claim to "explanatory adequacy" has been common among
T.G. linguists. Chomsky seems to echo the neogrammarians (although his
explanations are of a different kind) when he quotes "philosophical grammar" with sympathy. This grammar "should not be merely a record of the
data of usage, but, rather, should offer an explanation for such data",
see Allen and van Buren 1971:1.

I have a clear memory of how I spent, between 1945 and 1965, a
great deal of time in endless arguments with neogrammarians about the
importance of synchrony. The discussions were mostly oral, but some
were published in learned journals or even in the daily press (see Ham-

marström 1959b, 1960a, b, c and, for instance, Dagens Nyheter, 4 August, 1959).

3. PHILOLOGISTS

The linguistic orientation of philologists is usually the same as that of neogrammarians, and many neogrammarians would have called themselves philologists. However, the main interest of a philologist is typically to interpret and comment on old texts because of interest in the literary qualities of the text. In this sense a neogrammarian is not a philologist, as he typically sees old texts, which sometimes do not even possess any literary qualities, as material for linguistic research. When philologists attempted to describe language details occurring in their texts, particularly phonetic details, they often squeezed them into the framework of some older stage (cf. Hammarström 1959b:9 and 17).

Their lack of a clear understanding of basic synchronic principles could have led to innumerable mistakes which were, however, mostly avoided by their intuitive knowledge of synchronies.

4. TRADITIONAL DIALECTOLOGISTS

I call by this name those dialectologists who were more or less influenced by neogrammarian thinking. Some worked within the tradition of dialect geography, which among other things involved the establishment of linguistic atlases, whereas others rather favored dialect monographs. Usually they were in search of "pure", "uncorrupted" dialects (which do not exist) and in the comparatively "pure" dialects (excluding the cities) which they found, they picked out the "old" forms and discarded the others. This orientation is incompatible with coherent synchrony (see Hammarström 1961:14-15).

When the traditional dialectologist described the sounds of his dialect, he often favored a "historical" description of the neogram-

marian kind. Some older state of the language provided him with a
basic classification despite the fact that this probably did not fit
the sounds he wished to describe. Rules changed the older forms into
the actual forms.

5. TRADITIONAL GRAMMARIANS

With all their merits, both the more research minded grammarians
and the authors of school grammars were often insufficiently synchronic.
Some formulations were certainly influenced by knowledge of older
states of the same language, but this does not seem to be the main weakness. The common confusions were rather conditioned by ideas of universal logic or, at least, by ideas of some old prestige language, such as
Latin, being so superior that its grammatical framework could and
should (partly) be used for any other language. Some modern European
languages were considered to have the same six cases as Latin although
in reality they had a much lower number. This is an example of inac-
curate synchrony which should not be considered to be conditioned primarily by diachronic interference.

6. STRUCTURALISTS

Almost every detail in the structuralist framework is contrary to
the mistaken use of diachronic knowledge in synchronic descriptions.
However, some structuralists have argued that synchrony cannot be independent of diachrony. Quoting R. Jakobson, Vachek (1967:81) argues
against pure synchrony on the ground that "some archaic elements as
well as some neologisms" [...] "have to be evaluated as synchronic
facts". However, it should be clear that such elements are to be considered as stylistic variants within the synchronic description. As a
matter of fact their particular function can only be correctly defined
if considerations of time and change are excluded (see Hammarström
1966:61).

7.   T.G. LINGUISTS

If the structuralists had almost freed linguistics from undue influences of diachrony on synchrony, Chomsky and his followers have
again made the situation worse. Many T.G. linguists have not only been
impressed by universal logic and "cross-linguistic evidence", but have
also worked knowledge of earlier states and diachrony into their description of the actual state of a language. Although one thing is as
bad as the other, we shall concentrate on the diachronic interference.
This interference is clear in "generative phonology". *The Sound Pattern of English* by Chomsky and Halle provides ample exemplification of
"underlying forms" which appear to have been influenced by knowledge
of the history of English. However, some of these forms seem more
directly to have been influenced by English orthography as argued by
myself in *The Problem of Nonsense Linguistics* (p. 106-08), where I provide some examples of particularly counter-intuitive underlying forms.
Schane provides for the modern French *travail*, *feuille*, and *framboise*
the underlying +rAvAli, fɔlia, and frAmbeza (1968:60-63). It is safe
to say that nobody who does not know the history of French could have
dreamt up these forms. Nor could one believe that such forms exist in
the mind of the speakers. (I say this independently of the fact that
it is difficult to know to what extent and in which sense particular
T.G. linguists make claims about the mind or believe that they are men-
talists.)

In a recent critical stocktaking of T.G. theory, Langacker (1976)
shows impressive clarity of perception and elegance of expression. However, it is somewhat unfortunate that in his concluding paragraph (p.
23) he expresses an opinion about a future "synthesis" which contains
two quite unacceptable points:

> The Saussurian dichotomies of competence and performance and of
> synchronic and diachronic analysis may not disappear entirely,
> but the new synthesis will not rigidly impose them on language
> and will avoid such spurious issues, so bothersome in terms of

current theories, as whether an analysis can be justified synchronically or has only historical validity, or whether certain linguistic facts should be ignored by the grammar and relegated to
the domain of performance.

In another context the same author also includes diachrony in an
unacceptable way (1973:326):

Recent syntactic investigation has failed, in my judgment, to
take sufficient cognizance of diachronic and cross-linguistic
evidence, which I feel will prove crucial in the evaluation of
competing theories of syntactic and semantic structure.

Linell (1974:127) quotes Kiparsky as believing that "evidence
from language history is the most reliable type of external evidence".
Linell contrasts this with a quotation by King who says:

To admit historical evidence into the evaluation of synchronic
grammars would be to claim that the linguistic competence of
one's forebearers should play a role in evaluating accounts of
one's own competence, and there is no reason in fact or theory
to entertain such a curious claim.

Although what King says does not exactly refute Kiparsky's view, I
agree with Linell that Kiparsky's contention is dubious.

The failure of T.G. linguistics (failure as a theory, but not as
an orientation which has given new life to linguistics by raising problems and by stimulating interest) is conditioned in a fundamental way
by lack of interest in the real competence of the speakers and in their
performance, i.e., by lack of interest in language as a means of communication. Instead, as noted recently by R. A. Hall Jr. (1976:338), the
T.G. linguists are "robbing the discipline [sc. linguistics] of its independence and making it anew into a handmaiden of logic and philosophy".

In a recent paper, Becker (1975) argues in favor of "generative
dialectology". He does not want to establish underlying forms which
are the same for all dialects (1975:339), but he does argue that historical insights should be reflected in the rules (1975:300). He quotes

(1975:278) and agrees with Karg, who said in 1930:

> Sprache nicht als Zustand, sondern als Bewegung, das ist die
> grosse Entdeckung, die wir der Sprachgeographie verdanken.

This is a rather meaningless quotation unless one points out that the
"Sprache" under discussion is not, as a reader may be led to believe,
language in general, but only an aspect of language. There is no
"movement" (Bewegung) in synchrony and synchrony does imply a "state"
(Zustand).

8. SOCIOLINGUISTS

The interest of sociolinguists in language communication and in
anything related to this kind of communication makes them rather im-
mune against the temptation of irrelevant diachronic considerations.

9. VARIATIONISTS

If variationists are considered to be a subgroup of the sociolinguists, then the sweeping statement contained in the preceding paragraph is not true. However, variationists are here considered as a
group apart.

Variationists have had considerable influence on linguistic thinking in the 1970's. Despite the importance of their studies of variants
and varieties, their variable or dynamic rules, particularly as defined
by Bailey, are capable of mixing diachrony into the description in such
a way that pure synchrony is destroyed. As not only facts concerning
diachronic change, but also considerations of dialect geography are
made part of the rules, it is clear that these rules are not those
known and used by the speakers.

Bailey (1973:14-15) quotes seven crucial passages in which Saussure requires that synchrony and diachrony be distinguished, but he
does not include the one about the speaker who "is in front of a state"

(see above, p. 51) which I believe is the most crucial of them all.[3]
Bailey disagrees with Saussure as he believes that the "dichotomy between diachronic and synchronic approaches" [...] "is a misguided one"
(1973:12). According to Bailey (1973:14):

> The attempt artificially to freeze language data and ignore the
> on-going nature of linguistic change has forced linguists into
> straitjacketed descriptions which exclude a vast amount of lin-
> guistic knowledge or language user competence, including the ele-
> mental facts of a grandchild's communicating with his grandparent.
> Erecting walls between descriptive, historical, and dialectolo-
> gical pursuits has proved a cure worse than the disease.

This kind of thinking is fundamental to Bailey's orientation. It is,
however, quite confused. There is no diachrony to account for in the
speech act in which a grandfather and his grandchild take part. They
are just using two varieties which coexist in the moment of the speech
act (see Hammarström 1966:61). How variants function in the speech act
can only be described in a synchronic way. Concerning Bailey's wish to
demolish some walls, I feel that his ideas are here so simplified as to
be meaningless. In the synchronic description a wall should keep out
history and, to a considerable extent, dialectological facts of the
usual kind. In the moment of communication, the speaker's eventual
knowledge of older stages obtained through extra-communicative considerations are not used and no speaker knows everything about all other
dialects (and sociolects) and some may even know practically nothing
but their own dialect (and sociolect). However, it is certainly true
that particularly in his capacity as hearer of other language varieties
(rather than speaker), a language user may have a rather wide competence to be described within synchrony. The diachrony deals with changes
of a language and these changes concern synchronically defined facts.
From this viewpoint there should be no wall, i.e., there must be synchrony within diachrony (and everybody would know it). It is also
clear that in the tradition of Gilliéron and other well-known early dialect geographers, evidence from dialects can provide informed guesses

on language developments in cases where direct diachronic evidence is
weak or missing. This does not mean that observed dialectal forms
are, as such, made part of diachrony, but rather that one assumes that
similar forms have existed. As for "dialectal pursuits", one can obviously describe dialectal facts within the description of a language
in a synchronic way which excludes diachrony. And the diachrony of
dialectal facts is also obviously legitimate. If Bailey does not accept the idea of pure static synchrony and if he does not see the necessity of certain basic distinctions, his results will never be more
than mediocre and somewhat confused compared with research in which the
relations between idiolects, sociolects, dialects, synchrony, and diachrony have been correctly recognized.

Not unexpectedly, Bailey quotes with sympathy Schuchardt and the
neogrammarians (1973:15-16) who also had an orientation in which incomplete understanding of diachrony prevented a correct understanding
of synchrony.

When Bailey compares his "dynamic" model to the older "static"
model which he thinks he can supersede, he describes the latter in the
following terms (1973:34):

> Variation other than morphophonemic variation is to be relegated
> to the category of performance and excluded from the work of the
> descriptionist.

This may be a partly correct description of what is contained in a
rough description of la langue, for instance in a "structural sketch",
or in Chomsky's idealized speaker-hearer, or in a school grammar, or
in what I call b-α-linguistics (see Hammarström 1973:28 and 1976:112-
13). This kind of simplification seems to be legitimate, as long as
one does not say that the rest is "just performance" which does not
require detailed study and description.

I feel that Bailey and others are wrong when they argue that static models should be replaced. On the contrary, it seems to me that they
are indispensable for synchronic description. On the other hand, a

static model for diachrony implies obviously an inconceivable contradiction as diachrony deals with change.

10. PRESCRIPTIVISTS

Prescriptivists, whether laymen or linguists, make not only the
mistake of referring to "logic" but also that of referring to older
stages of the language or perhaps even to an ancient foreign language
with high prestige when they recommend certain and condemn other forms.

The letters to the editor of daily newspapers from upset readers
who condemn "sloppy" recent language forms are frequent in many languages.

When a number of years ago a well-known Swedish neogrammarian answered a letter to his language column in a daily newspaper, he recommended the form *psykiater* rather than *psykiatriker*. He argued that the
former was correct, because it was the ancient Greek form. He thus
overlooked the fact that forms either change or do not change in diachronic perspective and that, therefore, quoting an ancient form which
has either changed or not cannot decide the problem. The diachrony
slipped into a discussion that meaningfully can be only synchronic.

11. SUMMARY AND CONCLUSION

Of the ten orientations reviewed, nine must be censured for not
keeping diachrony out of synchrony: early authors, 19th century historical linguistics, philologists, traditional dialectologists, traditional grammarians, structuralists (to some extent), T.G. linguists,
variationists, and prescriptivists. Sociolinguists (excluding variationists) can, however, hardly be faulted.

The mixing of diachrony into synchrony has serious consequences:
Impure synchrony is defective as such and its defects affect in their
turn diachrony, as diachrony is based on synchrony.

The general lack of interest in correctly describing all details of synchrony is no doubt connected with ideas of being "scientific" and of the linguist being the objective "outside" observer as in natural sciences (see my paper "Is Linguistics a Natural Science?" forthcoming in *Lingua*). It is also connected with historicism and with universalism and influences from logic. Such approaches are contrary to a truly mentalistic interest in what exactly happens in communication and what exactly is the speaker's reality.

NOTES:

1) To the extent this is a real possibility it would not be useful in the case of languages with well-documented history. However, as Sigurd points out, "for language without any history such indications might prove to be of some value" (cf. Koerner 1971:27).

2) In a similar way one must reject the idea expressed by more recent authors concerning "cross-linguistic" evidence according to which findings in other languages can support a solution suggested for some particular language (see, for instance, above p. 58).

3) However, Bailey does not seem to be completely unaware of this viewpoint of Saussure's as (without providing a page reference) he states that it is Saussure's "contention that the synchronic viewpoint is the only reality for the community of speakers" (1973:17).

REFERENCES:

Allen, J. P. B. and van Buren, P., eds. 1971. Chomsky: *Selected Readings*. London.
Bailey, C.-J. 1973. *Variation and Linguistic Theory*. Arlington (Virginia).
Becker, D. 1975. "Versuch einer generativen Dialektologie", *Orbis* XXIV/2.276-342.
Bourciez, E. 1958. *Précis historique de phonétique française*. 9th ed. Paris.
Dineen, F. P. 1967. *An Introduction to General Linguistics*. New York.
Hall, R. A., Jr. 1976. "Linguistics and Language Teaching at Cornell", *The Modern Language Journal* 60/7.335-39.
Hammarström, G. 1959a. "Språkvetenskapens förnyelse", *Dagens Nyheter* 4.8.
Hammarström, G. 1959b. "Graphème, son et phonème dans la description des vieux textes", *Studia Neophilologica* 31.5-18.
Hammarström, G. 1960a. "A propos de l'à-propos de Mlle Arthur", *Studia Neophilologica* 32.327-30.

Hammarström, G.　1960b.　"A propos de la critique de M. C. Witting", *Studia Neophilologica* 32.331-32.
Hammarström, G.　1960c.　"Philologie et linguistique. A propos d'un compte rendu de M. Félix Lecoy", *Romania* 82 (1961), pp. 129-333.
Hammarström, G.　1961.　"Inquéritos linguísticos II", *Revista de Portugal, Série A, Língua Portuguesa* 26.9-32.
Hammarström, G.　1965.　"Können Lautveränderungen erklärt werden?", *Proceedings of the 5th International Congress of Phonetic Sciences.* Basel. Pp. 336-39.
Hammarström, G.　1966.　*Linguistische Einheiten im Rahmen der modernen Sprachwissenschaft.* Berlin.
Hammarström, G.　1971.　*The Problem of Nonsense Linguistics* (= *Acta Societatis Linguisticae Upsaliensis, Nova series 2:4*).
Hammarström, G.　1973.　*Towards More Exhaustive Descriptions of Languages* (= *Umeå University, Department of Phonetics, Publication 6*). Also in *International Journal of the Sociology of Language* 9 (1976), pp. 23-41 and *Linguistics* 177 (1976), pp. 23-41.
Hammarström, G.　1976.　*Linguistic Units and Items.* Berlin.
Koerner, E. F. K.　1971.　"A Note on Transformational-Generative Grammar and the Saussurean Dichotomy of Synchrony versus Diachrony", *Linguistische Berichte* 13.25-32.
Langacker, R. W.　1973.　Review of J. M. Anderson, *The Grammar of Case: Towards a Localistic Theory, Journal of Linguistics* 9/2.319-31.
Langacker, R. W.　1976.　"Modern Syntactic Theory: Overview and Preview", *Publications of the University of Rhodesia in Linguistics* 2, pp. 1-23.
Linell, P.　1974.　*Problems of Psychological Reality in Generative Phonology. A Critical Assessment* (= *Reports from Uppsala University Department of Linguistics 4*).
Saussure, F. de.　1949.　*Cours de linguistique générale.* 4th ed. (1st ed. 1916).
Schane, S. A.　1968.　*French Phonology and Morphology.* Cambridge (Massachusetts).
Ungeheuer, G.　1970.　"Kommunikative und extrakommunikative Betrachtungsweisen in der Phonetik", *Proceedings of the 6th International Congress of Phonetic Sciences.* Prague-München. Pp. 73-86.
Vachek, J.　1967.　"The Non-static Aspect of the Synchronically Studied Phonological System", J. Hamm, ed., *Phonologie der Gegenwart.* Wien. Pp. 79-85.

DETERMINISM IN LINGUISTICS:
NEOGRAMMARIAN AND TRANSFORMATIONALIST

JOHN HEWSON
Memorial University of Newfoundland

Determinism may be defined as the name that we give to the speculation that all things are completely determined by previously existing
causes. Since the early seventeenth century, men have been much influenced by the mechanical functioning of the universe, and the immutabil-
ity of the laws of classical physics. There have, consequently, been
persistent attempts, beginning with Galileo and Descartes, to reduce
all phenomena to purely mechanical principles.

Cartesian Rationalism, to be properly appreciated, must be put in
the perspective of its own time and place. It came as a reaction to an
intellectual tradition that was based on authority rather than on empirical fact, and was not the achievement of one man: Descartes was preceded by Copernicus and Galileo and followed by Newton and Leibniz.
But like all revolutions the Cartesian Revolution had its adherents
that went too far: the work of the Eighteenth Century Encyclopaedists,
of the Nineteenth Century Darwinians, of the Twentieth Century Positiv-
ists is just as reprehensible for its narrow mindedness as was the auth-
oritarian tradition that preceded Descartes: these represent the swing
of the pendulum to the other extreme.

Darwin's *Origin of Species*, which appeared in 1859, not only
brought about general acceptance of the Theory of Evolution, which had
been in the air for a century and a half, but also gave rise to a mechanistic, deterministic explanation for Evolution: the Theory of Natu-

ral Selection. Darwin himself, of course, was not a Darwinian (which
is the name we give to those who believe in a totally deterministic
view of evolution); indeed the fifth chapter of his book deals with
causes of evolution modification other than Natural Selection and Darwin mentions love and nurture as being just as essential to survival
as strength of fang and efficiency of claw; it is therefore an irony
of fate that it was the explanation of the mechanism of Natural Selection or Adaptation that was seized upon by the followers of the demi-
religion of Determinism, and thus became associated in the popular mind
with the whole Theory of Evolution -- a contamination of two quite different theories that still goes on to this day. A mature scientific
view would not equate Natural Selection with evolution, but would instead see Natural Selection as a mechanism exploited by the general
drift of Evolution.

In the last third of the nineteenth century, with the deterministic view of Evolution very much a current of scientific fashion, it was
to be expected that some of those whose major scientific concern was
the evolution of language and languages should begin to rethink and to
reformulate the fundamentals of their discipline in deterministic terms.
And this, of course, is one of the major facets of the Neogrammarian
revolution: sound change becomes the operation of blind mechanistic
laws: *Lautgesetze wirken ausnahmlos*. Discoveries such as Verner's Law,
which showed that what were thought to be irregularities were merely
the product of another quite regular evolution, helped to establish and
popularize the view.

Linguistic change, however, comprehends not only blind mutation,
but also the intelligent or volitional adaptation and exploitation of
evolutive forms as has frequently been shown. The recent work of Labov,
for example, presents clear-cut instances of societal preferences inter-
fering with normal evolutive sound change. Morphological and syntactic
elements are also liable to exploitation. The so-called progressive
form of the modern English verb, for example, is found from the earliest
texts of English onwards; but the progressive, as a systemic element of

the English verbal system is not to be found until after Shakespeare.
We may date its systemic adaptation and exploitation from the middle
of the seventeenth century. As a mutation it exists for at least a
thousand years before its systemic exploitation.

The recognition of the role of intelligence -- which is not to be
understood simply in the naive sense of conscious intelligence -- in
linguistic evolution, is necessarily to introduce a teleological element into our theoretical considerations of linguistic change. This
tends to cause the same kind of scandal among linguists as may be seen
among physicians confronted by certain of the elements of psychosomatic
medicine. Consequently, it is necessary to keep one's sense of perspective, and to avoid commitment either to a naive teleological view or
to a naive deterministic view. In all evolution there are, unquestionably, mechanistic mutations. And likewise there are also instances of
the intelligent exploitation of mutations, as in the planned development of different strains of plants and in the breeding of animal
stocks.

Just as the teleological element is not to be ignored in diachronic studies, in like fashion the role of the speaker cannot be abstracted from synchronic studies. The speaker is a creative, imaginative
element in the construction of discourse, and speakers constantly exploit the resources that their language affords them. Discourse is
consequently creative and personal, so much so that the law allows me
to copyright, as my own personal possession, the printed discourse that
I have composed. The law, on the other hand, does not, and obviously
cannot, permit me to copyright the English language, which is the total
system of linguistic mechanisms that I exploit in the creation of discourse.

It is therefore essential to distinguish the total system of linguistic mechanisms (Saussurean *langue*) from the discourse that is created from those mechanisms, by the imaginative, intelligent intervention of the speaker (discourse is Saussurean *parole*). Consequently,
when we find Bloomfield defining a language as "The totality of utter-

ances that can be made in a speech community" (1926:154), this definition is unsatisfactory from at least two aspects: (1) no child learning his language ever learns the totality of utterances that can be
made in his community, and (2) the totality of utterances is discourse,
the product created by the intelligent activity of each and every speaker, not the linguistic means of production that is utilized in that community.

Utterances, of course, that vibrate on the air waves, are empirical in that they are the directly observable product of the acitivity
of language. But it is an empiricist or positivist bias that causes
Bloomfield to define the language of a community in this way; obviously
he is seeking to define it in empirical terms, in terms of the directly
observable, a quite unnecessary restriction since there are many theoretical substructures in the physical sciences that are not directly
observable. Scientific method is necessarily rooted in the empirical,
but in its procedure goes far beyond it. Bloomfield's definition,
therefore, amounts to an outstanding example of the intrusion of metaphysical speculation into scientific procedure: namely, the quite un-
proven speculation that the only scientific reality is the directly observable (what should be called the empiricist or positivist fallacy).

The Transformationalists, although they attack Bloomfieldian positivism and anti-mentalism as inadequate, nevertheless accept his inadequate definition of a community language without question. Chomsky defines a natural language as a set of sentences, finite or infinite, and
an adequate grammar as a set of rules that generates all those sentences, and only those sentences. Such a grammar is thereby considered
to be a description of a speaker's knowledge of his language, that is,
if we take Chomsky's definition seriously, his knowledge of his set of
sentences.

Now if all the sentences that I write or speak in so-called "performance" are not original, but are merely picked out from the pre-de-
termined set of sentences that is my language, then I have no creative
imagination of my own, and the activity of language is reduced to an

absurd determinism. And since in this model it is not the speaker but
the grammar which generates the sentences and that by purely mechanical
rules, it can be seen that, from this aspect at least, a theory which
claims to be mentalistic is in fact every bit as mechanistic as Bloomfield's anti-mentalism. It is remarkable in fact that the deterministic Rules of the Transformationalists parallel the deterministic Laws
of the Neogrammarians: in Hallean accentology, for example, the eight
derivational rules that produce Lithuanian surface forms contain, in
ordered positions 3, 4, and 5 respectively, Osthoff's Law, Saussure's
Law, and Leskien's Law as Synchronic Phonological Rules.

   Neither Behaviorism nor TG, consequently, has offered any solution
to the fundamental problem of distinguishing between linguistic mechanisms on the one hand and the imaginative exploitation of those mechanisms on the other. In fact, the anti-mentalism of the Behaviorists and
the determinism of the Transformationalists deal with this fundamental
problem by ignoring it.

   What is required, then, for further progress in the discipline of
linguistics, is the transcendance of an outmoded positivistic or deterministic view of science, and the adoption of a hermeneutic view which
is capable of accommodating both facets of the phenomenon of language
within a single holistic view. The hermeneutic viewpoint does not
force a choice between mechanism and mentalism, between the functioning
system and the imaginative mind, between that which is determined and
that which is free, but is able to accommodate both within a single comprehensive description, and without recourse to a naive dualism that
would see the temporal mind and the spatial body as two totally different and unconnected entities.

   As an analogical illustration, consider the behavior of a swimmer
in a swimming pool. His swimming activity is determined by the dimen-
sions of the pool. He is not free to swim in the spectator's gallery
nor in the parking lot outside. Yet within the bounds of the pool his
freedom is infinite in quantifiable terms. To define his possible behavior, two approaches are possible: (1) one may seek to determine and

enumerate the many billions of possible patterns he might follow, and
to do this by purely mechanical, formal means, thereby delimiting or
determining every possible particularity, or (2) one may simply define
the three dimensional parameters of the pool and then state that the
swimmer is free to move within those parameters. The former solution
entrammels that which is free in that which is truly determined; only
the latter solution succeeds in capturing the true determinism and the
real generalities of the situation. And the second solution recognizes
that the swimmer is not a robot, not an automaton, following pre-deter-
mined patterns.

For a linguistic example, let me return to the contrast of simple
and progressive in the English verb, a contrast of perfective/imperfec-
tive. The imperfective form of this pair, i.e., the progressive, has
an infinite range of stylistic usage that exploits the fact that the
progressive has an open perspective towards the future, whereas the
simple has a closed perspective:

(1) He drinks a lot

suggests the invevitability of the fact whereas

(2) He's drinking a lot

leaves open the hope that the situation is temporary and may change.
When one examines a pair such as

(3) I tell you it's true.
(4) I'm telling you it's true.

the exploitation of the progressive is different: the open perspective
of the progressive is used to suggest a failure to communicate, a failure to "get through", that the communication is recognized as incomplete.
But with the same verb in a different situation, the pair

(5) Yes, George told me

(6) Yes, George was telling me

may be used to suggest to the listener whether the speaker wants to
hear any more or not: (5) suggests that the subject is closed; (6)
suggests that it is open and the speaker wishes to hear more.

Now the range of this stylistic usage is infinite, being open to
the free situational exploitation of the speaker. And the only way
to formalize it is to entrammel every possible situation in the world
in one's grammar. The alternative is to give an accurate picture of
the underlying meaningful contrast of simple and progressive in English,
and then to show, in as large a sample as one wishes, how this contrast
is exploited stylistically in experimental situations, thereby recogniz-
ing what is determined, and what is free.

The one stage positivist or determinist model, therefore, in which
the surface features are generated directly from an underlying base,
needs to be discarded in favor of a two stage hermeneutic model in
which the speaker, in occupying an intermediary role between the underlying and the surface levels, is seen on the one hand as using the underlying mechanisms to represent his cognitive experience, and, on the
other hand exploiting the expressive potentialities of those mechanisms
in conative and creative linguistic activity. The speaker is bound in
the first case, being forced to utilize the representational mechanisms
of the language he is speaking; in the second case he is free, being
able to play with and exploit those mechanisms in whatever way he will,
to suggest whatever personal nuance he wishes to insert into his own
self-expression.

Likewise, in diachronic studies, it is clear that there is evolution which appears to be the result of accidental factors, and evolution
that appears motivated. The neutralization of final unstressed vowels
in Late Latin caused the future of the type *dicet* "he will say" and the
corresponding present *dicit* "he says" to fall together as identical in-
distinguishable forms, and with intervocalic voiced plosives becoming

fricatives, the future of the type *amābit* "he will love" likewise fell
together with its corresponding perfect *amāvit* "he has loved". Here is
a clear-cut example of phonetic attrition destroying a necessary morphological distinction. As a result the original morphology of the
future, its distinctiveness eroded by phonetic attrition, was remade
by using *habēre* "to have" as an auxiliary, so that Classical Latin
amābit and *dicet* were replaced by the fifth century *amāre habet* and
dicere habet. Three centuries later these periphrastic forms had
evolved to become single words, the reflexes of which are to be found
in the futures of the Western Romance languages and Italian.

What is remarkable here is the contrast with the Germanic languages, all of which have utilized a periphrastic future for the last
thousand years without such periphrastic forms evolving into single
words. And Rumanian, which it must be remembered has long been isolated in an area of Germanic and Slavic influence, is the only Romance
language that has maintained a periphrastic future. In this respect
one cannot fail to note that neither Slavic nor Germanic had a present/
future contrast as part of the basic system of verbal tense, as was
the case with Classical Latin, which had a future tense as part of the
basic system of the verb. What we see in Germanic and Slavic is the
representation of the future through the secondary category of aspect,
not through the primary category of tense. And what we see in Western
Romance is the re-creation of a morphology of future tense to accommodate a structural (i.e., notional) contrast that was still there in the
verbal system after the destruction of the original morphology. Such
recreation of a morphology has a motivation that is teleological, that
is, goal-oriented: the goal is achieved when the auxiliary *habēre* becomes an inflection. In the Germanic languages, where this goal is
absent, the auxiliary remains an auxiliary.

In adopting hermeneutic models in both diachronic and synchronic
studies, therefore, we should try to distinguish between the elements
that are purely mechanical and those that are not. In diachronic studies we should try to distinguish between mechanical changes and commun-

ity exploitation of those changes. And in synchronic studies we should try to distinguish between underlying structural mechanisms and the speaker's exploitation of those mechanisms.

We must, of course, be cautious in assigning reasons either teleological or deterministic for linguistic evolution. And likewise there are all kinds of constraints that need to be made operative in synchronic work so that naive determinism and naive mentalism may both be avoided. As the etymologists found out long ago, the path of the linguistic researcher is strewn with the most deadly pitfalls for the unwary.

REFERENCES:

Bloomfield, Leonard. 1926. "A Set of Postulates for the Science of
    Language", *Language* 2.153-64.

HISTORICAL DEVELOPMENT OF TONE PATTERNS

JEAN-MARIE HOMBERT and JOHN J. OHALA
University of California,   *University of California,*
Santa Barbara   *Berkeley*

INTRODUCTION

The Phonetics Laboratory at UCLA and the Phonology Laboratory at Berkeley have been engaged in studies of various aspects of tonal development ("tonogenesis") for the past 5 or 6 years. This paper constitutes a progress report on some of this research.

We should first explain our approach to tonogenesis -- or any other sound change which is found in many languages. Our primary interest is not tonogenesis in any particular language but tonogenesis as a universal or potentially universal process. Thus we are interested in every case of tonogenesis. Observing similar patterns of tonal development in many languages quite distant from each other chronologically, geographically, and genetically, we of necessity look to the universal physical properties of the human speech production and speech perception system to explain the origin and directionality of these sound patterns. We will not attempt to further justify the utility of this approach except to point out that it has had considerable success in historical phonology for a century or so; see, e.g., Passy (1890), Rousselot (1891), Lindblom (1975), Lehiste and Ivić (1963, 1977), Janson (1977).

One of the consequences of this approach -- quite surprising to some -- is that we feel justified in studying the physical causes of tonal development by examining modern languages that need not be tonal, e.g., English, French, Russian, or Japanese. As will be demonstrated, it is not at all difficult to find what we metaphorically call the *seeds* of many sound changes, including tonogenesis, in the speech of present-day speakers. Although the factors causing tonogenesis, that is, the seeds of tonogenesis, may have germinated and blossomed several centuries ago in Middle Chinese, Early Vietnamese, Punjabi, etc., nevertheless these same seeds may be found dormant in the speech of today's speakers speaking today's languages.

A graphical representation may be helpful in conveying an idea of how physical constraints of the speech mechanism can influence the form of speech via sound change in a purely mechanistic, non-teleological, way. We can liken speech communication to a transmission line with relay stations or "repeaters", as in Figure 1:

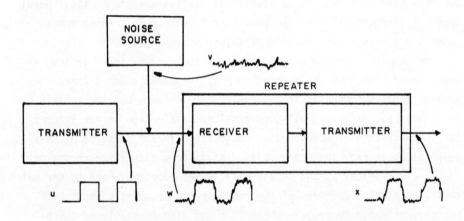

Transmission line with repeater, used as an analogue of the speech communication process.

A transmitter sends out a signal, u, to which noise, v, is added, yielding the distorted signal, w = u + v, which is picked up by the receiver, part of the repeater unit. It is the distorted signal, w, which is retransmitted as the signal, x, sent to the next repeater.

In the case of human speech, important sources of distortion are

the constraints of the transmitting and receiving systems, that is,
the vocal tract and the auditory system. This is represented in Figure 2:

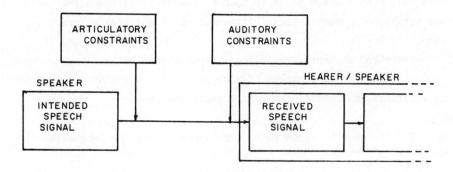

*Schematic representation of how articulatory and auditory con-
straints can introduce distortions in the speech signal.*

The speaker, although intending to produce a certain pronunciation,
may, due to vocal tract constraints, actually produce something slightly different, that is, a speech signal with unintended additional features of pronunciation.

Auditory constraints can affect pronunciation somewhat differently. Parts of the speech signal which are auditorily ambiguous, that
is, those which, as far as the listener is able to tell, may have been
produced by any of two or more distinct articulations, may be articu-
latorily re-interpreted by the listener when he repeats the signal
(Sweet 1891:238, Jonasson 1971).

There are these two ways, then, that the speech signal, by the
time it is received by the listener, may contain elements not put there
by the speaker. The listener does not have independent access to the
mind of the speaker and so cannot differentiate between parts of the
signal which were intended from those unintended. When he repeats the
words he hears, he may pronounce intentionally those features which
were unintended by the speaker he first heard the words from. We would
maintain that through such mechanisms "mini-sound changes" occur all

the time -- potentially, at least, every time someone speaks and someone else listens. Naturally, most of these changes -- misunderstandings, we might call them -- are corrected sooner or later. It is the
ones that aren't which go on to become regular "maxi-sound changes"
via normal non-phonetic social transmission of patterns of pronunciation.

There are at least the following four steps that must be taken to
show that a particular aspect of tonogenesis (or any other sound change)
is a natural, potentially universal sound change:

1.   It must be shown to be wide-spread among the languages of
     the world.

2.   It must be possible to find its "seeds", i.e., manifesta-
     tions of systematic variations in pronunciation of the
     same type and same directionality, in the articulatory or
     perceptual behavior of any speaker whose speech offers
     the proper phonetic conditions.

3.   It must be shown that these variations are unintended by-
     products of other intended elements of pronunciation.

4.   It must be shown that listeners can detect these variations.

Our claims, then, can be falsified at any one of these steps. We are
constantly in search of counterevidence ourselves but we ask the help
of all interested phonologists in this task.

TONAL DEVELOPMENT DUE TO CONSONANTAL INFLUENCE

The first pattern we will discuss is one which was first noticed by
Maspero (1912) and Karlgren (1926) and extensively documented by Haudricourt during the past 30 years (Haudricourt 1954, 1961, 1971), namely,
that represented schematically in (1):

$$(1) \quad pV \;\rightarrow\; p\acute{V}$$
$$bV \;\rightarrow\; p\grave{V}$$

Sequences of voiced obstruent + vowel give rise to low tone on the
vowel; voiceless obstruent + vowel give rise to high tone, usually
with concomitant neutralization (to voiceless) of the voicing contrast in the obstruents. This process has been extensively documented in Sino-Tibetan, many languages of Southeast Asia, and some languages of Africa (Hombert 1975a).

As for the seeds of this change, we're sure most readers are
familiar with the extensive phonetic literature showing small but
very consistent differences in pitch on the vowels following voiced
and voiceless consonants in English, Russian, Swedish, Japanese, etc.
(Ohala 1973, Hombert 1975a, Jeel 1975).

One question that came to mind in examining this pattern was whether in addition to voicing, degree of aspiration also contributed to
these pitch variations. We measured pitch after voiced and voiceless
stops in the speech of speakers of French and English since the stops
in these languages have different phonetic properties: English voiceless stops are far more aspirated than those in French (although our
study showed French /p t k/ are by no means completely unaspirated,
as the usual textbook descriptions would imply). The English voiced
stops, often phonetically voiceless in word-initial position, were
uttered in a context that would tend to guarantee their being voiced.
The resulting data, shown in figure 3,

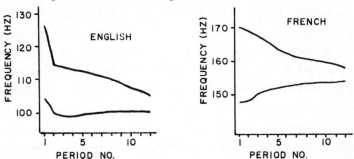

*Average fundamental frequency measurements in Hertz (vertical
axis) of vowels following /p t k/ (upper curve) and /b d g/
(lower curve) as a function of glottal period starting from
vowel onset (horizontal axis) for one male speaker of English
(left graph) and one male speaker of French (right graph).*

suggest that degree of aspiration does not significantly affect pitch; the relevant feature is presence or absence of voicing, as was stated in the traditional works on tonogenesis. (For further details of this study see Hombert and Ladefoged 1977 and Hombert 1978.)

Before discussing the physical causes of this effect we should mention another pattern, namely, that the voicing of a non-glottal obstruent can induce a distinctive tone on the vowel following, not on the vowel preceding. Most of the cases discussed in the literature are in accord with this. Moreover, virtually all instrumental phonetic studies of consonantal effects on vowels have failed to find any influence of the voicing of non-glottal consonants on the pitch of vowels preceding them (Hanson 1975, Jeel 1975).

Regarding the physical causes of these pitch perturbations, our investigations are still incomplete although we feel we have made some progress on the problem. Previously it was thought that aerodynamic differences created by the voiced/voiceless distinction would account for the pitch differences. We can say with some confidence that aerodynamic factors -- as we currently understand them -- cannot account for these pitch variations. This judgment is based on an examination of previously obtained aerodynamic data and on our own computer simulation of aerodynamic events in speech (Ohala 1976 and 1978). If it is not aerodynamic factors which perturb pitch, logically it has to be due to variations in the state of the vocal cords (their tension and/or mass) since that is the only other factor affecting the rate of vibration of the vocal cords. The question is, *how* is the vocal cords' state affected in this case? The best hypothesis we have so far is that variations in larynx height are responsible. The larynx is slightly higher for voiceless obstruents than for voiced obstruents (Jespersen 1889, Ewan and Krones 1974). Other studies have shown that larynx height varies with pitch (Ohala 1972). If this variation reflects causal factors our case is complete. Unfortunately we have not yet been able to forge this final link in our argument. We believe the larynx is lowered during voiced obstruents in order to enlarge the

oral cavity so that oral air pressure may be maintained at a level lower than subglottal air pressure; this is necessary if voicing is to
continue during the obstruent closure. Of course, the larynx lowering
should be greatest at the end of the obstruent closure and current evidence shows that it is (Ewan 1976a). This helps to explain why obstruents may affect only the pitch of the following, not the preceding vowel.

Although non-glottal consonants only affect following vowels, there
is evidence that glottal consonants [? h] may induce tone on preceding
vowels and, presumably, following vowels as well. We have phonetic data
from Arabic, a language that has word-final [?] and [h], that [?] ele-
vates the pitch on the preceding vowels and [h] lowers the pitch on preceding vowels (Hombert 1976c). This pattern parallels the influence of
these two consonants on the development of tone in Vietnamese and other
languages.

To round out this case we had to determine whether such small con-
sonantally-induced pitch changes were audible or not. In a number of
psychophysical tests involving American English listeners -- probably
the least skilled listeners where pitch variations are concerned -- we
found these small pitch perturbations were detectable (Hombert 1975a).

TONAL DEVELOPMENT AND VOWELS

One point that disturbed us as a potential disconfirmation of our
claims regarding consonantal involvement in the development of tones is
that vowel quality is also known to affect vowel pitch by about the same
magnitude as the obstruents -- higher pitch on high vowels, lower pitch
on low vowels -- but there seems to be no consistent pattern of vowel
quality leading to tonal development. There are two possible explanations for this, neither of which is sufficiently tested yet although
work is underway on them (Hombert 1976d, Hombert and Greenberg 1976).

First we note that consonants usually produce a small pitch contour on adjacent vowels, whereas the effect of vowel quality on pitch

is a steady-state higher or lower pitch. Naturally, a rapid change in
pitch is more noticeable than a steady-state difference in pitch. The
second observation we can make is that the effect of consonants on the
pitch of the vowel is in some sense separable from -- in fact it occurs
after -- the consonantal segment that produces the effect. This is not
the case with vowel quality: necessarily the vowel quality and the
changed pitch level caused by the vowel quality occur simultaneously.
Perhaps, for a sound change to occur, the phonetic perturbation must
be perceptually separable from the perturbing environment in order that
the listener have an opportunity to mistakenly regard the perturbation
as an independent and therefore intended part of the speech signal.

Additional work by our laboratories on the phonetics and phonology
of tone are listed in the references.

ACKNOWLEDGEMENTS

This work was supported by grants from the National Science Foundation, the University of California, Berkeley, Committee on Research,
and the Computer Centers and Berkeley and UCLA.

REFERENCES:

Ewan, W. G. 1976a. *Laryngeal Behavior in Speech*. Doc. diss., Univer-
     sity of California, Berkeley.
Ewan, W. G. 1976b. "Larynx Movement and Tonogenesis", *Report of the
     Phonology Laboratory* (Berkeley) 1.29-38.
Ewan, W. G. and Krones, R. 1974. "Measuring Larynx Movement Using the
     Thyroumbrometer", *Journal of Phonetics* 2.327-35.
Gandour, J. 1974. "Consonant Types and Tone in Siamese", *Journal of
     Phonetics* 2.337-50.
Hanson, R. J. 1975. "Fundamental Frequency Dynamics in VCV Sequences".
     Paper presented at the 8th International Congress of Phonetic Sci-
     ences, Leeds, August, 1975.
Haudricourt, A. G. 1954. "De l'origine des tons en vietnamien", *Jour-
     nal Asiatique* 242.69-82.
Haudricourt, A. G. 1961. "Bipartition et tripartition des systèmes de
     tons dans quelques langages d'extrême orient", *Bull. Soc. Ling. de
     Paris* 56.163-80.

Haudricourt, A. G. 1972. "Tones in Punjabi", *Pakha Sanjam* 5.xxi–xxii.
Hombert, J.-M. 1974. "Universals of Downdrift: Their Phonetic Basis and Significance for a Theory of Tone", *Studies in African Ling.*, *Suppl.* 5.169–83.
Hombert, J.-M. 1975a. *Towards a Theory of Tonogenesis: An Empirical, Physiologically and Perceptually-based Account of the Development of Tonal Contrasts in Language.* Ph.D. diss., University of California, Berkeley.
Hombert, J.-M. 1975b. "Perception of Contour Tones: An Experimental Investigation", *Proc. Annual Meeting Berkeley Linguistics Society* 1.221–32.
Hombert, J.-M. 1976a. "Phonetic Explanation of the Development of Tones from Prevocalic Consonants", *Working Papers in Phonetics* (UCLA) 33.23–39.
Hombert, J.-M. 1976b. "Consonant Types, Vowel Height, and Tone in Yoruba", *Working Papers in Phonetics* (UCLA) 33.40–54.
Hombert, J.-M. 1976c. "Phonetic Motivations for the Development of Tones from Postvocalic [h] and [?]: Evidence from Contour Tone Perception", *Report of the Phonology Laboratory* (Berkeley) 1.39–47.
Hombert, J.-M. 1976d. "Development of Tones from Vowel Height?", *Journal of Phonetics* 5.9–16.
Hombert, J.-M. 1976e. "Perception of Tones of Bisyllabic Nouns in Yoruba", *Studies in African Linguistics, Suppl.* 6.109–21.
Hombert, J.-M. 1977. "Tone Space and Universals of Tone Systems", *Journal of the Acoustic Society of America* 61.S89.
Hombert, J.-M. 1978. "Consonant Types, Vowel Quality, and Tone", in V. Fromkin, ed., *Tone: A Linguistic Survey.* Pp. 77–111. New York: Academic Press.
Hombert, J.-M. and Greenberg, S. 1976. "Contextual Factors Influencing Tone Discrimination", *Working Papers in Phonetics* (UCLA) 33. 81–89.
Hombert, J.-M. and Ladefoged, P. 1977. "The Effect of Aspiration on the Fundamental Frequency of the Following Vowel", *Working Papers in Phonetics* (UCLA) 36.33–40.
Hombert, J.-M., Ohala, J. J., and Ewan, W. E. 1976. "Tonogenesis: Theories and Queries", *Report of the Phonology Laboratory* (Berkeley) 1.48–77.
Janson, T. 1977. "The Loss of Distinctive Vowel Quantity in Late Latin: The Experimental Reconstruction of Structural Reinterpretation". Paper presented at the 3rd International Conference on Historical Linguistics, Hamburg.
Jeel, V. 1975. "An Investigation of the Fundamental Frequency of Vowels after Various Danish Consonants, in Particular Stop Consonants", *Annual Report of the Institute of Phonetics, University of Copenhagen* 9.191–211.
Jespersen, O. 1889. *The Articulations of Speech Sounds Represented by Means of Analphabetic Symbols.* Marburg in Hessen: N. G. Elwert.
Jonasson, J. 1971. "Perceptual Similarity and Articulatory Reinterpretation as a Source of Phonological Innovation", *Quarterly Prog-*

ress and Status Reports, Speech Transmission Lab., Royal Inst. of Technology, Stockholm. STL-QPSR 1/1971.30-41.

Lehiste, I. and Ivić, P. 1963. *Accent in Serbocroatian* (= *Michigan Slavic Materials No. 4*).

Lehiste, I. and Ivić, P. 1977. "The Phonetic Nature of the Neo-Što-kavian Accent in Serbo-Croatian". Paper presented at the 3rd International Conference on Historical Linguistics, Hamburg.

Lindblom, B. 1975. "Experiments in Sound Structure". Plenary address, 8th International Congress of Phonetic Sciences, Leeds.

Ohala, J. J. 1972. "How is Pitch Lowered?", *Journal of the Acoustic Society of America* 52.124.

Ohala, J. J. 1973. "The Physiology of Tone", in L. Hyman, ed., *Consonant Types and Tone* (= *Southern California Occasional Papers in Linguistics* 1.1-14).

Ohala, J. J. 1974. "Experimental Historical Phonology", in J. M. Anderson and C. Jones, eds., *Historical Linguistics II. Theory and Description in Phonology* (= *Proceedings of the 1st International Conference on Historical Linguistics, Edinburgh*). Pp. 353-89. Amsterdam: North Holland.

Ohala, J. J. 1975. "A Mathematical Model of Speech Aerodynamics", in G. Fant, ed., *Speech Communication* (= *Proceedings of the Speech Communication Seminar, Stockholm, 1-3 August 1975. Vol. 2: Speech Production and Synthesis by Rule*). Pp. 65-72. Stockholm: Almqvist and Wiksell.

Ohala, J. J. 1976. "A Model of Speech Aerodynamics", *Report of the Phonology Laboratory (Berkeley)* 1.93-107.

Ohala, J. J. 1978. "The Production of Tone", in V. Fromkin, ed., *Tone: A Linguistic Survey*. Pp. 5-39. New York: Academic Press.

Ohala, J. J. and Eukel, B. W. 1976. "Explaining the Intrinsic Pitch of Vowels", *Journal of the Acoustic Society of America* 60.S44.

Ohala, J. J. and Ewan, W. G. 1973. "Speed of Pitch Change", *Journal of the Acoustic Society of America* 53.345.

Passy, P. 1890. *Etudes sur les changements phonétiques*. Paris: Librairie Firmin-Didot.

Rousselot, L'abbe. 1891. *La modification phonétique de langage*. Paris: H. Welter.

Sweet, H. 1891. *A New English Grammar*. Oxford: Clarendon Press.

SHORT-TERM AND LONG-TERM TELEOLOGY
IN LINGUISTIC CHANGE

ESA ITKONEN
University of Helsinki

1. PRELIMINARY REMARKS

Recently there has been a renewed interest in the concept of analogy, to be employed in the explanation of sporadic linguistic changes.[1]
The analogical explanations, in turn, raise the larger issue of teleological explanation. This paper is meant to offer an analysis of teleology in diachronic linguistics. I will have to postulate two distinct
types of teleology, viz., short-term, expounded by Coseriu (1974[1958])
and the authors mentioned in the footnote 1, and long-term, expounded
by Sapir (1921, chaps. 7-8) and, more recently, by Lass (1974).

2. A JUSTIFICATION OF TELEOLOGY

What is the purpose of explanation in science? At the most abstract level, we might say that it is to bring order into chaos, that
is, into what at first *looked* like chaos, or to show that apparently
disconnected facts or entities in reality belong together. This kind
of explanation or, better, *systematization* is to be found in empirical
sciences as well as in nonempirical sciences like philosophy and logic
(cf. Itkonen 1978a, chaps. 9-11).

The basic types of empirical explanation are the causal one and
the teleological one.[2] I shall ignore here the difficult question

whether there can be genuinely simultaneous causation. At least the
diachronic variants of causal and teleological explanation can be illustrated, very roughly, by the following diagram (where x, y, and z
are entities in need of explanation):

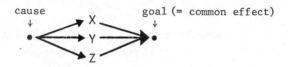

That is, x, y, and z are explained causally by relating them to
their common cause, whereas they are explained teleologically by relating them to their goal, or common effect. Notice that this diagram
does not imply that the goal literally brings about its causes. The
goal is used here merely as a *basis of systematization*.

If we accept the definition of explanation according to which explanation equals systematization, then causal and teleological explanations should be accorded an equal status. However, it is generally
felt that causal explanations are more "explanatory", and indeed several attempts have been made, in different disciplines, to *reduce* teleological explanations to causal ones (cf., e.g., Nagel 1961:401-28 and
520-35).[3] However, most often the reduction of teleological to causal
cannot be carried out in practice. And what is more, in such cases we
have no way of deciding whether we are confronted with a merely practical impossibility, or also with a logical impossibility.

This last point needs to be further clarified. To me it seems
reasonable to assume that every event or action that can be explained
teleologically can also be explained causally, in other words, that
human actions too have what might be called their "causal substrata".
However, there is nothing to guarantee that the two types of explanation are equally general or -- as the causalist would like to think --
that the causal explanation is the more general one. For instance, a
certain goal may be used to unify and explain someone's actions, but
there is no guarantee that the chemical processes that have been going

on in him exhibit the same kind of explanatory uniformity. And if they
do not, we are *missing a generalization* if we use the causal, i.e.,
chemical, level as the basis of explanation. If this argument is valid,
then there is not much point in reinterpreting teleological (or purpo-
sive) explanations of human actions as causal dispositional explanations, as Hempel (1965:472-77 and 486-87) and others have done. If the
new, causal explanation is situated at the level of actions and purposes,
then it says *precisely* the same thing as the old, teleological explanation, with the additional complication that we are committed to postulating unknown dispositional regularities;[4] and if the new explanation
is situated at some "lower", e.g., chemical, level, then it is quite
possibly false. In any case, all such lower-level explanations are un-
available today and in the foreseeable future.

   One common criticism against teleology is that also physical,
clearly causal processes can be reformulated teleologically: "A stone
rolls down the mountain *in order to* hit the valley floor". This criticism is untenable for the following reason. In the case of physical
behavior we can calculate and predict exactly the way in which the
"goal" is achieved. By contrast, the behavior that -- we feel -- is
genuinely teleological is characterized by its *plasticity* or *openness*:
Insofar as we are able to make predictions at all, we can predict *that*
the goal will be achieved -- unless, of course, some unexpected interference comes up -- but normally we are not able to predict *how*, precisely, the goal will be achieved. This is intimately connected with
the fact that the goals of (genuinely) teleological processes are necessarily much more abstract than the "goals" of causal processes. To
claim that there *must* be a causal explanation of at least equal generality "behind" the teleological one is to commit precisely that kind of
fallacy which I have already disposed of in what precedes.

   So I conclude that there are both practical and theoretical reasons for employing teleological explanations in diachronic linguistics.
The same kind of rationale, viz., equating explanation with systematization, that I have offered here is relied upon also in the general sys-

tems theory. There, explanation is felt to be achieved once it has
been shown that different types of systems exhibit the same basic characteristics:

> Of the many philosophically and scientifically acceptable state-
> ments concerning the empirical world statements from the field
> of general systems theory appear repeatedly in a wide variety of
> cases. Their relevance for the presupposition of general *order-*
> *ability* (if not necessarily *order*) in nature expresses itself in
> the isomorphism of the laws and principles formulated in regard
> to systems of different kinds. Such isomorphism (or parallelism)
> of the applicable constructs suggests a fundamental unity of
> the observables... (Laszlo 1972:18)

> ...the models give so many perspectives of what may be the common
> underlying core of events. General systems theory's task is to
> uncover that core (op. cit., p. 19).

The question of the ontological or causal basis is not even raised,
perhaps because it is thought unanswerable.

To offer a final analogy, the teleological explanation as here defined is virtually identical with what Diesing (1972) calls "pattern
explanation": A social phenomenon is explained or made understandable
by showing how it relates to other similar phenomena and, together with
them, forms a somehow meaningful and coherent whole. Here, too, the
ontological and causal aspects are left aside.

3. TERMINOLOGICAL CLARIFICATIONS

Woodfield (1976) distinguishes between "teleological" and "functional" explanations in the following way:

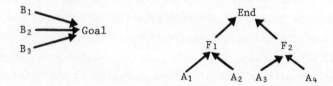

$B_1...B_3$ are (series of) *possible* actions which an animal possesses in its behavioral repertoire, and which lead to a goal (e.g., getting food). To explain, e.g., B_2 by the goal is to give a "teleological" explanation. On the other hand, $A_1...A_4$ are *actual* activities of different parts of an organism; they combine to form functions (e.g., blood circulation) which contribute to the end (i.e., survival). To explain, e.g., A_2 by F_1 (and F_1 by the end) is to give a "functional" explanation.

In linguistics we often encounter cases which have characteristics both of teleological and of functional explanations in Woodfield's sense. For instance, in a Kisseberth-type "conspiracy" several *actual* processes contribute to bring about or to maintain a preferred state (e.g., syllabic structure); on the other hand, they are all of course just one part of a large repertoire of *possible* linguistic processes. Consequently I see no cogent reason for distinguishing, in linguistics, between teleological and functional.

Coseriu (1974[1958], chap. 6) uses the term "finalistic" in a sense which is very nearly identical with the individual-psychological interpretation of my "short-term teleology" (cf. Sect. 6), whereas his term "teleological" is approximately equivalent to my "long-term teleology". It may be added that Coseriu considers the latter notion as unacceptable.

4.   THE GOAL OF SHORT-TERM TELEOLOGICAL CHANGE

What is the goal of linguistic change? Before answering this question, three comments have to be made. First, in this section my discussion will be confined to short-term change. Second, I shall be concerned mainly with morphological change. Third, all teleological behavior strives after *several* goals at the same time, and it may happen that one tries to achieve a primary goal by means of achieving subgoals which *de facto* conflict with each other; this point is well known to action theorists.

We may now repeat our question by asking: What is the primary goal

of short-term morphological change? Not surprisingly, this turns out
to be the age-old principle which Anttila (1972:107) calls the principle of "one meaning - one form", and which was formulated by Paul
(1975[1920]:227) as follows:

> Jede Sprache ist unaufhörlich damit beschäftigt, alle unnützen
> Ungleichmässigkeiten zu beseitigen, für das funktionell Gleiche
> auch den gleichen lautlichen Ausdruck zu schaffen.[5]

In what follows, the principle of "one meaning - one form" will
be called the "principle of isomorphism". There are obviously different ways in which this principle may be violated and, hence, restored.
When these cases of principle-violation are combined with von Wright's
(1968) notions of "productive" and "preventive" action, we get all
those cases which have been examined under the label of morphological
change or morphological resistance to sound change. For instance,
producing a situation where there are no longer one meaning (or function) and two forms is identical with Kiparsky's (1972) "paradigm levelling". Preventing a situation where there would be two meanings and
one form, or one meaning and no form, is in turn identical with Kiparsky's (1972) "distinctiveness condition". When von Wright's (1968)
notion of forbearance as a kind of "omissive" action is combined with
productive and preventive actions, we are able to subsume under the
general concept of teleology even the violations of the principle of
isomorphism, which then give rise to its restorations (cf. Sect. 5).

5.   SUBDIVISIONS WITHIN THE OVER-ALL LINGUISTIC SYSTEM

The reason why I have been speaking mainly of morphology is that
I, for one, cannot make (teleological) sense of linguistic change, un-
less I consider phonology, morphology, and syntax as separate even if
interacting systems each of which has its own characteristic teleology.
A somewhat similar view has been developed in considerable detail by
Dressler (1977) in his multisystematic or, as he calls it, "polycentris-

tic" conception of language. From the standpoint of morphology, phonology constitutes one of its *environments*, in the terminology of the
general systems theory. To a system its environment represents a potentially disrupting, purely causal force even if this environment,
viewed on its own terms, may possess, and in the case of phonology
does possess, a teleology of its own. It was noted above that morphological change characteristically consists in *restoring* the principle
of isomorphism. This implies that the preceding *violation* of this
principle could not have been the result of a morphological change,
but only of a sound change. The individual speaker has to balance
the conflicting teleological subsystems against each other. In the
case of sound changes leading to violations of the principle of isomorphism he *forbears* to *prevent* such changes because he (temporarily)
considers that the gain of phonological teleology is not (yet) offset
by the loss of morphological teleology.[6] For the same reason, once
the principle has been violated, he may *forbear* to *produce* a change
restoring it. If, on the other hand, the possible gains of phonological teleology are felt to be less important than the corresponding
losses of morphological teleology, then we have the cases of morphological change or morphological resistance to sound change discussed in
Sect. 4.

Furthermore, there are conflicting tendencies not only *between*
different linguistic subsystems, but also *within* one and the same sub-
system. In the latter case the tendencies are characterized by the
fact that, although conflicting, they nevertheless try to achieve the
same subsystem-internal goal. An attempted increase of isomorphism
may actually lead to its decrease: Levelling, e.g., one verb-paradigm
may make it an exception in the total class of verb-paradigms.

Different linguistic subsystems obviously constitute an overarch-
ing system, i.e., the language as a whole. I shall not discuss here
the goal of this superordinate system. I merely note that Grice's
(1975) "conversational maxims", which define some rather self-evident
requirements of clear and understandable discourse, are relevant here.

Grice says, in essence, that language is used for communication, and
that factors detrimental to effective communication tend to be avoided
or eliminated. Such maxims are in an obvious way related to our principle of isomorphism.

6. TELEOLOGICAL EXPLANATION OF SHORT-TERM CHANGE

The phenomena here discussed can be explained at two levels, viz.,
social and individual. At the social level the explanation consists
in adopting the viewpoint of the general systems theory. Morphology
is considered as a self-maintaining system whose preferred state is
represented by the principle of isomorphism. The morphological system tends to anticipate divergences from its preferred state and to
eliminate them either *ante* or *post factum*. The phonological system
guarantees, on the other hand, that such divergences continuously come
up or threaten to come up. This is a perfectly respectable type of
explanation.
     At the individual level, the change (or resistance to change) and
its spread are both explained by a modified version of von Wright's
(1971 and 1976) "practical inference (or syllogism)". The basic structure of practical inference is as follows:

> A intends to achieve B.
> A believes that he cannot achieve B, unless he does C.
> ———————————————————————————————————
> Therefore he sets himself to do C.

Here A's action C is explained by his goal B. -- The term "intention" plays an ambiguous role in most discussions of the practical inference. On the one hand, it means the mental process, or *plan*, temporally preceding the doing of C; the plan to achieve B generates the
plan to do C (in order to achieve B). On the other hand, it means the
intentional element which, once C has been done, constitutes it as an
action and distinguishes it from mere (physical) events. Von Wright

does not make this distinction explicitly, but he seems to be saying that he uses "intention" only in the latter sense (cf. von Wright 1976: 394 and 402). It follows, then, that his version of practical inference cannot properly be said to explain why C occurred. This has prompted some critics, e.g., Mackie (1974:292-93), to dismiss the whole concept of practical inference as empty and useless. I cannot accept this conclusion. The von Wright-type practical inference constitutes a valid model for *identifying* an action C, and the identification of actions is a necessary precondition for the explanation of their occurrence. So much is true, however, that in addition to intentions in von Wright's sense, or "intentions-in-the-actions", as Stoutland (1976) calls them, explaining why an action occurred requires taking plans and decisions into account.

The plan to do C (in order to achieve B) does not of course entail the occurrence of C. So it might be asked what is left of von Wright's (1971) original rationale for setting up the model of practical inference, once his "intention-in-the-actions" have been replaced by "plans". The answer is that the modified version too contains no reference to general regularities and remains, therefore, clearly different from models of natural-science explanation (cf. Sect. 7).

The actions explained by (the modified version of) the practical inference are: producing x, preventing x, or forbearing to do either. The application of these notions to diachronic linguistics was discussed in Sect. 4-5, and will become clearer in Sect. 9.

7.   THE INDIVIDUAL-PSYCHOLOGICAL VERSION OF THE TELEOLOGICAL EXPLANA-
     TION OF SHORT-TERM CHANGE EQUALS RATIONAL EXPLANATION

It is no accident that we can describe and explain the same facts either in social or in individual terms, as we did in Sect. 6. In fact, in economics it has been known for a long time, and has in particular been emphasized by Friedman (1953, chap. 1), that social selection produces essentially the same results as individual rationality. For instance, only those firms are likely to survive and prosper which are, accidentally or not, managed in a way that *de facto* coincides with the principles of economic rationality.

This last point is of paramount importance: At the individual level we indeed have to do here with a type of *rational explanation*. To this claim there is one immediate objection: Rationality is normally connected with conscious deliberation and decision-making; but surely such characteristics are absent from linguistic change. Now, I could answer simply by pointing out, first, that the means-end conceptualization provided by the practical inference clearly applies to instances of linguistic change, and, second, that the practical inference is the prototype of rational explanation. However, I can offer a slightly more detailed argument. In a series of experimental investigations on decision-making Davidson, Suppes, and Siegel (1957) noticed that test persons acted in accordance with the subjective possibilities and utilities determined by the probability theory, although they could not have consciously calculated them; nor were they just mechanically applying something that they had previously consciously learned. As the result, Davidson and the others had no other choice than to come up with the notion of *unconscious rationality*. And this, I think, is precisely what we have in those cases of linguistic change that I have been discussing.

However, if we accept this thesis, some rather important consequences follow. Rational behavior is unpredictable in more than one sense, and irreducibly so. First, the environments of rational behavior are typically of a social character. Social, including linguistic, variables cannot be ordered on a quantitative scale like physical variables, and therefore they cannot be used as a systematic and exact basis for prediction. Second, even in one and the same environment and under one and the same concept of rationality several actions may be equally rational, so reliable prediction is impossible. Third, there are actually several concepts of rationality, e.g., the minimax and the maximin strategies of the game theory, and there seems to be no

"super-rationality" which could be used to predict the choice of one
or another concept of (sub-)rationality. Fourth, in the social or human sphere the concept of environment is not constant. Environment is
what people *interpret* to be environment; and this process of interpretation too is unpredictable.

In fact, it would be a logical contradiction to claim that rational behavior is entirely predictable. The *only* reason why we do not
call stones rational is that their behavior is entirely predictable on
the basis of the laws of mechanics. Rational behavior is predictable
only on the rather abstract level of goals. If we know people's goals,
we know *that* they will try to achieve them -- assuming that they are
going to act rationally -- but we do not know *how*, precisely, they will
try to do so. The concepts of teleology and rationality coincide in the
openness of the behavior subsumable under them.

The preceding paragraph can be summed up by noting that any reference to behavioral regularities, whether universal or statistical, is
irrelevant in rational explanations. I know that a certain type of action is rational in certain types of circumstances irrespective of whether, or how often, such actions and circumstances have occurred in the
spatio-temporal reality, just as I know the correctness of a sentence
without having to know whether it has ever been uttered as a matter of
fact (cf. Itkonen 1978a, chaps. 6-7). In other words, I know that insofar as there are, for instance, morphological changes similar to the
one I am considering right now, they must be explainable in the same
way; but their existence or nonexistence is irrelevant to my analysis.

One qualification is in order. As, e.g., Hempel (1965:470-71)
notes in his criticism of Dray (1957), to say that C was the rational
thing for A to do does not explain, strictly speaking, why A did C *as
a matter of fact* (since one can also act irrationally). However, this
point is not very serious. Dray-type rational explanations can be made
into genuine explanations simply by adding that C was not just the rational thing for A to do, but A also planned to do C or decided to do
C, and then did C in fact. No further explanation is needed. Only if

A had *not* done C, i.e., if he had acted irrationally, *then* we would
have reason to ask for a further explanation.[7]

Coseriu (1974[1958]) presents an account of linguistic change
which is, in essence, closely similar to the one expounded in the present section. He notes that the theoretical question about why languages change cannot be answered by uncovering more and more regularities of linguistic change:

> [Die] eigentliche Fragestelling [der Veränderlichkeit der Sprache]
> gründet sich, wie es notwendigerweise in den Wissenschaften vom
> Menschen geschieht, auf das "Vorwissen" über die Sprache, das
> heisst auf die aller Wissenschaft vorausgehende Kenntnis, die der
> Mensch von sich selbst hat. Einer der Irrtümer, unter denen die
> Sprachwissenschaft am meisten leidet -- und der sowohl aus der
> Betrachtung der Sprachen als "Sachen" als auch aus der Verwechs-
> lung von Humanwissenschaften und Naturwissenschaften herrührt --
> liegt darin, die theoretischen (rationalen) Probleme auf bloss
> "generelle" Probleme reduzieren zu wollen. Im Fall des Sprach-
> wandels besteht dieser Irrtum in dem Glauben, das Problem der Ver-
> änderlichkeit der Sprachen erfahre seine Lösung durch das Auf-
> finden der "Ursache" oder aller angeblichen "Ursachen" der vielen
> einzelnen Veränderungen. (Op. cit., p. 57; cf. also pp. 158-59.[8])

As a minor point of disagreement it may be mentioned that Coseriu
(p. 170 and 194) explicitly denies the possibility of unconscious rationality. However, I do not see on what grounds, e.g., acts of adopting a linguistic innovation can be characterized as "intentional actions" (p. 195) after the possibility of unconscious intentions has
been rejected (ibid.).

My argument here is meant to show that it·is a *fundamental mistake*
to require that analogical changes, for instance, should be entirely
predictable, or could not be accepted unless backed up by corresponding regularities. Consequently, the preceding discussion would seem to
vindicate the position of those who, like Anttila (1974), have consistently emphasized the inevitable *ad hoc* character of analogical change.
-- This is not to deny that certain general limits can, and should, be
imposed upon *possible* rational behavior, for instance upon possible analogical change. The search for such limits is exemplified, in fact, by

the search for Greenberg-type linguistic universals. From the present point of view, considering new types of languages amounts to considering new *environments* of rational (linguistic) behavior.

8. LONG-TERM TELEOLOGICAL CHANGE OR DRIFT

Short-term change, as here defined, does not exhaust the domain of linguistic change. In addition to it, we have to admit long-term (teleological) change, or what Sapir (1921) calls "drift". The character of the latter will be grasped most easily by contrasting it with its short-term counterpart. A change exemplifying long-term teleology does not try to achieve some universal goal, like the principle of iso-morphism in morphology. Rather, the goals seem to be specific to in-dividual languages or language families. Moreover, as its name already indicates, long-term teleology is not just a reaction to some actual or potential disturbance; rather, it is a process extending over several generations, sometimes over several thousand years. It is this fact which makes Sapir (1921:183) admit that "these psychic undercurrents of language are exceedingly difficult to understand in terms of indivi-dual psychology, though there can be no denial of their historical re-ality". It may be admitted that individual psychology is unable to pro-vide an adequate conceptualization of the phenomenon of drift, but it is not easy to find an alternative framework that would be able to do the job. As a consequence, definitions of drift are likely to be in-coherent in one way or another. Consider Sapir's (1921:155) definition according to which "the drift of a language is constituted by the un-conscious selection on the part of its speakers of those individual variations that are cumulative in some special direction". It is ob-vious enough, however, that the selection of a given variation is an individual process while the accumulation of several such variations (which must be the result of corresponding selections) is a social pro-cess; and therefore it is difficult to see how the two can be combined in such a way that one is said to select (with an "unconscious intention") that which others will select too in the future.

Other linguists, too, have operated with a notion equivalent to
the Sapir-type drift. For instance, the universal tendency of the Indo-
European languages to reduce their inflectional system is a recurrent
theme in Meillet (1921 and 1938). More precisely, he identifies the
goal of this long-term teleological change in the following terms:

> Ce serait à peine une exagération trop forte de dire que l'his-
> toire des langues indo-européennes se résume essentiellement en
> un effort pour passer du mot-forme, existant à l'état de formes
> fléchies multiples dont chacune a une valeur particulière, au
> mot existant isolément et toujours sembable à lui-même. (Meillet
> 1921:28.)

Accordingly, individual changes -- for instance the replacement
of the simple preterite *j'aimai*, *tu aimas*, etc. by the "analytic" form
j'ai aimé, *tu as aimé*, etc. -- are explained by showing that they are
part of the universal tendency governing all of the Indo-European languages (op. cit., p. 158). This corresponds exactly to the general
rationale of teleological explanations, as defined here in Sect. 2.

On the other hand, when Meillet tries to describe the mechanism
of drift in concrete terms, his account is no more convincing than
Sapir's. Meillet (1938:110-11) notes that in the period between the
7th and the 10th centuries the Celtic languages of Great Britain and
Ireland, on the one hand, and French, on the other, had the following
sound changes in common: the change of [u:] into [y:] and the reduction and/or loss of final syllables as well as intervocalic consonants.
However, since the Celtic population of Gaul has spoken Latin since the
3rd and 4th centuries,[9] we must ask how it was possible that a drift
apparently inherent to the Celtic languages made its appearance in Old
French, without any language contact and centuries after the adoption
of Latin by the originally Celtic population. Meillet (1938:ibid.) offers the following answer:

> Comme les innovations considérées ont eu lieu longtemps après le

moment du changement de langue, on ne saurait les expliquer par
une déviation initiale qui aurait eu lieu à l'époque du changement. Dès lors on est amené à supposer que ces innovations ré-
sulteraient de tendances existant chez des sujets dont les ancêtres ont changé de langue. Hypothèse hardie qui tend à faire
croire que certaines habitudes acquises aurait pu être trans-
mises par l'hérédité. Il ne s'agirait pas de l'hérédité de ca-
ractères anatomiques acquis, mais d'une chose bien différente,
d'hérédité d'habitudes acquises. Cette hérédité serait comparable à celle qu'on observe dans des races de chiens employés à
des usages particuliers.[10]

Similarly van Ginneken (1927) can find no other explanation for
the existence of long-term sound changes or "sound laws" than that the
ability to perpetuate them must be literally hereditary. From the
methodological point of view, however, it is more commendable to postulate the existence of some relatively unfamiliar, "emergent" mechanisms, as in the general systems theory, than to use familiar concepts,
e.g., heredity, to explain something that they are obviously unable to
explain.

In recent times no one has to my knowledge presented a more forceful defense of long-term linguistic teleology than Lass (1974). He
points out (p. 337, fn. 3) that current work on diachronic linguistics
has generally avoided the investigation of long-term processes. He
tackles one such problem, viz., a series of changes concerning the
vowel length in English and Scotch, and he comes to the conclusion
that the only way to *explain* all these apparently disconnected changes
is to see them as parts of a general process towards the elimination
of phonemic vowel quantity, or the predictability of vowel length. In
other words, he justifies the use of teleology just as I did in Sect.
2 here:

The classic instance will be where a given synchronic state will
be insightfully interpretable (or interpretable at all) only as
either the aimed-at result of a series of past events, or as a
stage in the implementation of that result. And the past events
themselves -- i.e. without reference to their ultimate goal --
will be 'irrational', that is unconnected, inexplicable (p. 312).[11]

> I take it as axiomatic that attempts to organize data in some way,
> under some generalizing heading, are preferable to null hypotheses.
> ...; I am separating out a particular sequence of events from the
> (apparently) formless historical matrix they are embedded in, and
> claiming at least that I discern pattern and structure (p. 347).[12]

It needs to be pointed out, in particular, that the goals of Lass'
"orthogenetic" processes need not in themselves be good or bad, according to some universal standard. -- Lass admits that teleological explanations do not meet all of those criteria which are generally thought
to define "scientific" explanations (cf. fn. 14). Yet he does not take
this to mean that (long-term) teleology should be straightforwardly
dismissed as "unscientific" or "mystical"; and I fully agree with him.
What is or is not taken as "scientific" is an eminently time-dependent
question. For instance, most linguists seem to think that Newtonian
mechanics with its strongly deterministic assumptions provides still
today the only model of "scientific" explanation, although modern physics has several decades ago accepted the view of the *statistical* nature
of the basic physical laws. And only a tiny minority among linguists
has as yet come to see that the models of linguistic explanation need
not be taken from physics at all (cf. Itkonen 1978a, chap. 9). Therefore, when choosing our conceptual tools, we have no reason to confine
our attention to what the general opinion happens at a given moment to
consider as "scientific".

Furthermore, linguistic drifts are by no means the only examples
of long-term teleological processes resisting any attempted reduction
to individual psychology. I am thinking here of those large-scale
societal processes which made Adam Smith and Hegel coin the terms "in-
visible hand" and "cunning of reason": often when a society comes to
a new, unpredictable situation, it "responds" in a way that tends to
maintain and perhaps to enhance its "well-being". The intriguing aspect here is that the society's responses, consisting of the joint results of individual people's actions, could be characterized as "rational", although they have been intended by no one.[13]

Phenomena subsumable under long-term teleology are explained by
noting what is their goal and how they contribute to achieving it.
This is valid teleological explanation. Now, I do not wish to preclude the possibility that long-term teleology will some day be reduced to short-term teleology or to individual psychology. But neither do I wish to preclude the possibility that we have to do here
with a phenomenon *sui generis*. It is conceivable that an over-indi-
vidual system has its own "emergent" type of rationality which does
not coincide with individual rationality. The goal of such a rationality cannot be emphatically understood, as can the goal of short-term
teleology, but must be inferred from what is seen to happen in the history of a language, or of a society. It is this feature which gives
to long-term teleology its at least seemingly mysterious character.

The preceding discussion presupposes, of course, that no plausible alternative account of drifts has been proposed so far. Such an
account would apparently reinterpret a drift as a chain-reaction, i.e.,
as a series of successive changes each of which has its own (short-
term) teleological justification. This is, in essence, the research
strategy of Martinet (1955): "weak points" in a (sound) system must
be amended, and this inadvertently brings about new weak points which
again must be amended, and so on. It is to be noted, however, that
Martinet-type chain-reactions may affect different parts of the system, and therefore they seem to lack the one unchanging goal characteristic of genuine drifts. Rather, the principle of amendation of
weak points is something like a phonological counterpart of the (morphological) principle of isomorphism. -- Vennemann (1974 and 1975) has
recently proposed a Martinet-type "explanation of drift". In the remaining part of this section I shall explain why I think that Vennemann's account is a failure.

Vennemann starts from his (and Bartsch's) "principle of natural
serialization". All syntactic constructions are analyzed as asymmet-
rical relations between one "operator" and one "operand". Given the
construction XY, Y is the operand, if XY is itself of the category Y,

as, e.g., the construction ADJ + NP is itself of the category NP. From
the fact that this line of thinking applies to artificial languages,
Vennemann fallaciously infers that it also applies to natural languages
(for a discussion of similar fallacies, cf. Itkonen 1976). However,
even if Prep may be constructed as the operand of the construction Prep
+ NP, it is not an operand *in the same sense* as NP is the operand of
Adj + NP. (For one thing, the latter is self-sufficient while the former is not.) Moreover, it is simply unconvincing to say that a transitive verb V, e.g., "see", is the operand of V + NP since it combines
with NP, e.g., "dog", to form the intransitive verb V + NP, e.g., "see-
dog". It is much more natural to say, in keeping with the dependency
grammar, that a transitive verb like "see" *equally* requires a subject
and an object to form a sentence. -- The "principle of natural serialization" says that in a given language all operators either precede or
follow their respective operands.

Vennemann discusses, in particular, the change of the Indo-European word-order from SOV to SVO and separates three stages in this process (Vennemann 1975:295):

I.   phonological   →   II. morphological   →   III. word order
     reduction   reduction   change

This is of course something like a simplified version of the traditional view of the matter. What is new, perhaps, is the fact that
Vennemann relates the change SOV → SVO to ambiguities resulting from
the object-topicalization. If in a SVO language the object is topicalized, there is no ambiguity since the change is of the type NP + V + NP
→ NP + NP + V. In a SOV language without case morphology, however, the
object-topicalization results in ambiguity, since the change is of the
type NP + NP + V → NP + NP + V. This is why, according to Vennemann,
SOV languages which have lost their case morphology as the result of
phonological reduction have to change into SVO languages. -- It is clear
enough that the importance of object-topicalization has been much over-

rated here. Even in a SVO language without case morphology, where no
ambiguity can result, the cases of object-topicalization are not very
numerous. (How often do we have reason to say, for instance, "John's
new car my wife likes"?) It is natural to assume that in a SOV language without case morphology, where ambiguity would result, the cases
of object-topicalization are even less numerous. Could this tiny number of cases, with no help from any additional factors, bring about a
change of the basic word order? I cannot believe it.

   This is, however, precisely what Vennemann would have us believe.
The loss of case morphology does not make other operator-operand constructions ambiguous and hence cannot force them to change their respective word orders. At first, only the verb has changed its position
vis-à-vis its operator. Why should other operands follow suit? This
is where the "principle of natural serialization" comes into play:
This principle is psychologically valid. Therefore once the verb has
changed its position, the word orders of other operator-operand constructions are changed by analogy.

   At this moment we have to ask whether all, or anything, of this
is true. Does SOV change into SVO only after the loss of case morphology? Is the change caused by the ambiguity of object-topicalizations?
Using in part Vennemann's own data, Sasse (1977) gives negative answers
to these questions. Similarly, Leinonen (1977) offers disconfirmatory
evidence from the history of the Russian word order. For my part, I
shall mention here one rather wide-ranging counter example to Vennemann's basic assumption of a correlation between the change SOV → SVO
and the reduction/loss of case morphology.

   Proto-Uralic had the SOV order and six cases. Samoyed has retained both characteristics; some Ostyak dialects, while maintaining
the SOV order, have *reduced* the number of cases to 3. On the other
hand, Lapp and Finnish have changed SOV into SVO and, at the same time,
they have continuously *increased* the number of their cases to 8-9 and
15, respectively. To further complicate the picture, Hungarian, while
increasing the frequency of SVO, has retained the basic SOV order and

has *increased* the number of its cases to 20 (cf. Erkki Itkonen 1966: 312-13). -- These facts are diametrically opposed to Vennemann's thesis.

If Vennemann's reanalysis of drift is falsifiable, then it has been falsified. It is possible, however, that it was meant to be un- falsifiable; it is difficult to interpret the following passage in any other way:

> Where, however, a contrary development takes place, one that changes an ordering arrangement away from natural serialization, a factor other than the pressure of the principle must be respon- sible. Such a factor may be an internal one: some intrinsic communicative advantage of the deviant pattern, given the total structure of language. ... The remaining possibility is that the factor responsible for a contrary development is an external one, the primary one here being contact with a language of the oppo- site word order type (Vennemann 1974:351-52).

Vennemann enumerates here the possible interpretations of evidence contrary to his thesis. The interpretation that his thesis might be false is not among them. Therefore the thesis must be unfalsifiable.[14]

I have discussed here one recent attempt to reanalyze a drift as a series of short-term changes. From the fact that this attempt is a fail- ure I cannot conclude, of course, that any similar attempt must also be a failure. However, such attempts as are known to me at the moment are only slightly more convincing, and much less explicit, than Vennemann's. Therefore I continue to regard Lass-type teleological explanations as a legitimate type of explanation in diachronic linguistics.

9. EXAMPLES

A. *Phonology and Morphology*

As I see it, there are three principal types of phonological tele- ology: the universal tendency of the "least effort", manifested by re- ductive and assimilatory processes; the language-specific tendency to maintain a preferred surface-phonetic pattern; the universal tendency,

differently manifested in different languages, to amend weak points in
sound systems. In this context "sound system" means a system of phonemes classified in terms of Troubetzkoy-type distinctive features.
That is, I reject the interpretation of "sound system" as a generative
system of phonological *rules*. As Kisseberth (1970) and others have
pointed out, the generative rule notation is inherently atomistic and
therefore incapable of rendering the concept of teleology.[15] This concept is in turn inseparable from the concept of linguistic change. --
It is good to add that Kisseberth's (1970) notion of "conspiracy" is a
"rediscovery" of facts that have always been known. To give a random
example, consider how Meillet (1928:129) characterizes the prosody in
Proto-Indo-European:

> Le rythme résulte uniquement de la succession de syllabes longues
> et de syllabes brèves; les syllabes longues sont des sommets du
> rythme; et par suite, la succession de plus de deux brèves nuisant
> au rythme, la langue tend, par des procédés divers, à l'éviter.

In order to exemplify the types of short-term morphological change,
I shall make use of the standard notation of Anttila (1972). "I", "V".
"Λ", "II" stand, respectively, for "one meaning - one form", "two meanings - one form", "one meaning - two forms", and "two meanings - two
forms". These cases will be combined with productive action and preventive action. In connection with producing, the arrow "→" means a
change from worse to better, whereas in connection with preventing, the
opposite is the case. Now the basic types of productive change and preventive change can be represented as follows:

	a. Λ → I		a. I → Λ
I. produce		II. prevent	
	b. V → II		b. II → V

There are innumerable instances of type Ia. In the following two
examples the change concerns a stem and an ending, repectively:[16]

MHG   (ich) spranc   ⎫   NHG   │sprang│
           (wir) sprungen ⎭   →   │sprang│en

Lat.   cantámus   ⎤   It.   cant│
           tenémus   ⎬   →   ten │ iámo│
           vívimus   ⎥   viv │
           sentímus   ⎦   sent│

Type Ib occurs normally as a response to a change II → V, and will be discussed together with it.

In discussing the history of a given language it is often impossible, and also unnecessary, to distinguish between *preventing* a change and *cancelling* it. For instance, a form disturbing the regularity of a paradigm may briefly appear in the language of some speakers before they cancel it, while others prevent it from appearing in the first place. A well-known example is the Greek sound change $s → \emptyset$ /V_V, which was prevented from applying to the future tense forms (e.g., λύσω), because otherwise these would have coincided with the present tense forms (e.g., λύω). It is possible, however, that in some cases the development λύσω → λῦω → λύω took place and was cancelled afterwards. Since the principle of isomorphism constitutes the goal both of prevention and of cancellation, these two cases will be presented here together. Our four types Ia, Ib, IIa, and IIb, combined with the prevention/cancellation distinction, can be now summed up as follows:

A.   I (→ Λ) → I

B.   II (→ V) → II

Our symbols "I" etc. stand for (groups of) specific morphemes. A and B must be seen against the background of sound changes which occur elsewhere in the language and which, if unobstructed, would bring about the changes I → Λ and II → V. Let us consider A. If I → Λ does not occur, the speakers have *prevented* this change. If I → Λ occurs, then

from the standpoint of morphological teleology we do not say that the
speakers have produced this (phonological) change; rather, we say that
they have *forbeared* to prevent the change. If ʌ → I occurs next, the
speakers have *cancelled* the change I → ʌ by *producing* the change ʌ → I.
If the speakers forbear to cancel the former change, i.e., to produce
the latter change, then we have simply the sound change I → ʌ, a case
not covered by A, which is a model of (teleological) *morphological*
change. -- Perfectly analogous remarks apply to B.

First, two examples of A:

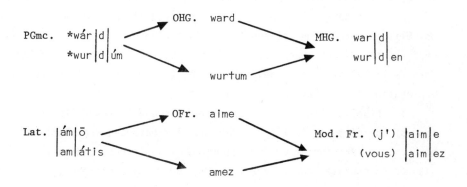

Second, two examples of B:

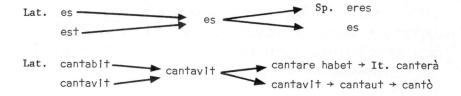

B.   Syntax

In what follows, I intend to show that our principle of isomorphism
provides a useful reinterpretation of Bever and Langendoen's (1971 and
1972) explanation of the history of the English relative clause formation.

In Old and Middle English (= OE and ME) the following types of construction were possible: "I met a boy wants to see you" (cf. "He sente after a cherle was in the toun") and "There is a boy wants to see you" (cf. "Ther was noon auditour coude on him winne"). In Modern English, however, only the following types of construction are possible: "I met a boy *who* wants to see you" and "There is a boy *who* wants to see you"). It is this change, i.e., the relative pronoun's becoming obligatory, which Bever and Langendoen set out to explain.

Bever and Langendoen note that although the change can be *described* in terms of transformational rules, these do not seem to be able to *explain* it. In particular, an apparatus of generative rules is unable to establish a connection between the obligatoriness of the relative pronoun and the disappearance of the ME case system. Yet Bever and Langendoen feel that it is precisely this connection which provides the needed explanation since they take the latter to have *caused* the former.

To establish their point, Bever and Langendoen resort to the concept of "perceptual strategy". Perceptual strategies are short-cut methods for arriving at an understanding of sentences, and they are assumed to operate independently of the "predictive grammar", i.e., the standard type of generative grammar consisting of rewrite rules. Bever and Langendoen (1972:45) propose the following two perceptual strategies for English: "(a) A string consisting of a nominal phrase followed by a finite verb whose inflection agrees with that nominal phrase is the beginning of an internal structure cluster (i.e., a sentence). (b) The verb phrase (optionally including a nominal) is the end of such a cluster". Or more formally:[17]

A. X_1 Nom V_f X_2 $\rightarrow$ $\underline{}_s X_1$ Nom V_f X_2

B. $\underline{}_s X V_f$ (Nom) $\rightarrow$ $\underline{}_s X V_f$ (Nom)$\underline{/}_s$

(A) applies before (B). If, after the application of (A) and (B), the square brackets contain a non-sentence, the (complex) sentence in question is deemed to be perceptually ambiguous. For instance, applying

(A) and (B) to the sentences "John thinks Bill is a fool" and "I met
a boy wants to see you" gives the following results:

A. $\underline{\big/}_s$ John thinks $\underline{\big/}_s$ Bill is a fool.
B. $\underline{\big/}_s$ John think$\underline{s}\big/_s$ $\underline{\big/}_s$ Bill is a foo$\underline{l}\big/_s$

A. $\underline{\big/}_s$ I met $\underline{\big/}_s$ a boy wants to see you
B. $\underline{\big/}_s$ I me$\underline{t}\big/_s$ $\underline{\big/}_s$ a boy wants to see you$\underline{\big/}_s$
            or perhaps
$\underline{\big/}_s$ I met $\underline{\big/}_s$ a bo$\underline{y}\big/_s$ wants to see you$\underline{\big/}_s$

    In other words, the first sentence is perceptually unambiguous
while the second is perceptually ambiguous. As Bever and Langendoen
see it, the reason why constructions exemplified by this second sentence were possible in Old English and Middle English, is that the
(remnants of) case endings sufficed to disambiguate them. However,
after the case endings had disappeared, the resulting sentences violated the perceptual strategies (A) and (B), and in order to disambiguate them, a relative pronoun was from now on obligatorily required.[18]
    According to Bever and Langendoen, the disappearance of existen-
tial constructions like "There is a boy wants to see you" cannot be explained in the same way, because they do not violate the principles (A)
and (B).[19] Therefore this change is explained by reference to the "predictive grammar", and not to perception. The grammar becomes simpler,
i.e., the number of the grammatical rules required to generate the sentences decreases, if the relative pronoun is made obligatory also in
sentences like "There is a boy who wants to see you", after it has been
made obligatory in sentences like "I met a boy who wants to see you".
This, then, is the explanation of the related change. -- Bever and
Langendoen view their over-all explanation as demonstrating the ("dynamic") interaction between perceptual strategies and the predictive
grammar.
    I wish to criticize Bever and Langendoen's analysis on three ac-

counts. First, their concept of "perceptual strategy" misses a significant generalization about linguistic ambiguity. Second, their
reference to grammar-simplification is not genuinely explanatory, with
the consequence that there is no interaction, dynamic or otherwise,
between perceptual strategies and the predictive grammar. Third, their
concept of "predictive grammar" is incoherent.

The avoidance of ambiguity is a general principle, which is equally operative in morphology and in syntax. It consists in producing the
change V → II or in preventing the change II → V. It is this principle
which explains the well-known "clash of homonyms" investigated by Gilliéron, on the one hand, and the changes of the English relative clause
formation investigated by Bever and Langendoen, on the other. To say
that a sentence like "I met a boy wants to see you" is perceptually ambiguous is to say that it is an instance of V; that is, the one form *a
boy* has two functions, i.e., the function of the object and that of the
subject. Therefore, it is understandable that the speakers tend to produce the change V → II by making the relative pronoun *who* obligatory.
Notice, however, that the avoidance of ambiguity is just one side of
the more general principle of isomorphism the complementary side of
which is the avoidance of synonymy, i.e., either the producing of Λ → I
or the preventing of I → Λ. Bever and Langendoen's remarkably atomistic or non-generalizing account cuts off the "perceptual strategies"
from their larger context, i.e., from Gilliéron-type clashes of homonyms, on the one hand, and from the principle of isomorphism, on the
other.

Next, consider the claim that the disappearance of existential constructions like "There is a boy wants to see you" is *explained* by showing that corresponding sentences with *who* are simpler to generate. This
cannot count as a genuine explanation since it is well known that grammars may be simplified as the result of purely technical manipulations,
i.e., manipulations that have nothing to do with the presumed psychological reality of linguistic change. However, a genuine explanation
can, again, be achieved by means of the principle of isomorphism, more

precisely by reference to the avoidance of synonymy, or of functionally identical and formally different expressions. Once the relative pronoun has been made obligatory in constructions like "I met a boy who wants to see you", this is the standard expression for relative clauses, and expressions without *who* are felt to be instances of needless formal variation.[20] Notice that this account, which was given in terms of ambiguity vs. synonymy of surface expressions is not interchangeable with an account given in terms of generative rules, in particular since the latter are not allowed to "look forward" to the surface expressions resulting from the process of generation. Notice also that the change in question, just like the change discussed in the previous paragraph, is explained, ultimately, by the principle of isomorphism. Since we do not have to switch our explanatory principle from perception to grammar, as Bever and Langendoen have to do, we again reach a generalization which Bever and Langendoen miss.

Finally, and partly as a corollary from the preceding paragraph, it is obvious enough that the term "predictive grammar" as employed by Bever and Langendoen cannot refer to any genuine or consistent entity. They postulate three components as relevant to the psychology of language, viz., mechanisms of speech production, those of speech perception, and the "predictive grammar". The data investigated by theories of speech production and perception consists in actual linguistic performance whereas the data of the predictive grammar is provided by conscious intuitive knowledge about properties of actual or potential sentences. In the case of speech production and perception, the resulting theoretical descriptions purport to refer to unconscious psychological mechanisms. By contrast, the theoretical descriptions provided by the predictive grammar have no comparable (psychological) referent; rather, they constitute just one possible way of presenting the intuitively known facts in a systematic way.[21] This is where Bever and Langendoen go astray. On the one hand, Bever and Langendoen (1972:33) claim that a predictive grammar is simply the standard type of generative grammar, that is, one that contains a base component consisting of phrase struc-

ture rules and a transformational component consisting of transforma-
tion rules. On the other hand, they claim (1972:39 and 48-49) that
predictive grammars are learned by children and are thus psychologically real in their entirety. However it is generally agreed today
that transformations possess no psychological reality from the viewpoint either of speech production or of speech perception; this is admitted even by Bever and Langendoen. But it is impossible to see what
other role transformations could play *qua* psychologically real entities,
because within the psychology of language there is simply no room for
any (unconscious) mechanisms over and above those of sentence production and perception. Therefore, as I already pointed out, a predictive grammar can at most qualify as one possible way of systematizing
intuitive linguistic knowledge. It is to be noted, however, that in
some of the most recent developments of linguistic theory transformations have been rejected, not just *qua* psychologically real entities,
but also *qua* formal means of systematization (cf. Kac 1978).

Examples of drift were not given in this section, since they were
discussed in Section 8 (cf. also Itkonen 1978b).

10.   A COMPARISON WITH ANDERSEN'S (1974) TYPOLOGY OF LINGUISTIC CHANGE

Andersen (1974) divides linguistic innovations into two main types,
viz., adaptive and evolutive, of which the former deals with the "communicative system" while the latter deals with the grammar, or "linguistic structure". Adaptive innovations are further subdivided into "accommodative", "remedial", and "contact" innovations, which are exemplified, respectively, by the creation of new vocabulary, the avoidance of
homonyms, and the spread of linguistic change. Evolutive innovations,
on the other hand, are subdivided into "abductive" and "deductive" innovations. As in Peirce's logic of science (cf. Itkonen 1978a:1.3),
abduction and deduction are closely connected. Abduction means postulating a theory from which the observed data can be deduced, and abductive
linguistic innovation means accordingly a grammatical reinterpretation

of observed linguistic data. Deductive linguistic innovation, in turn, means producing, in accordance with one's internalized grammar, forms that differ from accepted ones.

As far as I can see, it is quite easy to translate Andersen's typology into the terminology of short-term change, as it was presented in Sect. 9. In the case of accommodative innovation we have the change from "one meaning - no form" into the standard "one meaning - one form". In remedial innovation there is a change from "two meanings - one form" into "two meanings - two forms". Contact innovation, or adoption of a change, presents a teleology *sui generis*, based on the concept of linguistic solidarity and the rewards and sanctions that go with it. It is clear enough, however, that contact innovations are superimposed on the teleology explicated, in morphology, by the principle of iso-morphism; cf. Meillet (1921:73-74):

> Et quant aux sujets chez lesquels les innovations ne naissent pas spontanément, ils sont tout prêts à les accepter, parce qu'elles répondent à un besoin senti par eux.

Andersen's evolutive innovations deal not with the teleology, but with the technical aspect of linguistic change. That is, it may always be asked what is the goal of an abductive or of a deductive innovation, and *this* question can be answered, in morphology, only by reference to the principle of isomorphism. For instance, Andersen's (1974:23) ex-ample of an abductive innovation *cheris* (= sing.) → *cheris* (= pl.) fol-lowed by the deductive innovation *cheris* (= sing.) → *cheri* (= sing.) must be teleologically explained, of course, as a change from "two mean-ings (i.e., sing. and pl.) - one form" into "two meanings - two forms", or V → II.

Hence, the teleological framework introduced in Sect. 4 - 7 and 9 seems to be able to handle all (morphological) cases covered by An-dersen's typology. On the other hand, Andersen's emphasis on *innova-tion* seems to prevent him from handling cases of the prevention of change, which are part and parcel of my short-term "actionist" framework.

11. CONCLUDING REMARK

"Short-term teleology" and "long-term teleology", as here defined, represent something like ideal types, and there are certainly many intermediate cases between the two. In particular, it may be difficult to decide which long-term processes may be properly characterized as "drifts". I do think, however, that setting up a dichotomy of ideal types of this kind might serve the goal of conceptual clarification in today's diachronic linguistics.

NOTES:

1) Cf., e.g., Anttila (1972, chap. 5 and 1974); Jeffers (1974); Kiparsky (1974); Vincent (1974).

2) From a more general point of view, teleology may be viewed as just one subtype of "causality".

3) In the positivistic philosophy of science it is customary to make the further step of trying to reduce causality to functional dependence between various quantities.

4) My notion of teleology does not imply the existence of time-independent (nomic) regularities. Hence, I shall say here nothing about whether teleological regularities can or cannot be reduced to causal ones.

5) Paul adds: "Trotz allen Umgestaltungen, die auf dieses Ziel losarbeiten, bleibt es ewig unerreichbar".

6) This type of "consideration" is of course unconscious; cf. Sect. 7.

7) This account is insofar simplified as I have assumed that C is the only rational alternative. If there are more such alternatives, then it must of course be explained why A chose precisely C.

8) Coseriu's philosophical position is here practically identical with the one which, in my opinion, is presupposed by any theory of "autonomous linguistics" (cf. Itkonen 1978, chap. 2). However, sciences like socio- and psycholinguistics are based on observation of behavioral regularities in space and time, and therefore they require a more empiricist methodology, although they still *presuppose* a Coseriu-type philosophy of language.

9) Muller (1929:28) notes, however, that Celtic was sporadically spoken in Gaul still at the end of the 6th century.

10) Meillet goes on to attribute the successive consonant shifts in Proto-Germanic and Old High German as well as in Armenian to similar "hereditary tendencies".

11) The general systems theory makes use of precisely the same type of argument; cf. Laszlo (1972:11): "And the unique value of the exploration of general order is the possibility of elucidating connections between disparate types of phenomena, disjunctively treated by lower-level specialized theories. ...[The intrinsic justification of such elucidation] lies in finding order and interconnection where none had been found before: the very aim of cognitive theoretical science".

12) This is the general rationale of "pattern explanations". Diesing (1972:237-38) emphasizes the functionalist (i.e., teleological) nature of pattern explanations that make up a *holist* social or psychological theory.

13) Notice that these societal processes are different from "social selection", as this term was used in Sect. 7. Because of the therapeutical value of their goals, they also differ from Lass' orthogenetic processes.

14) Since Vennemann conceives of his theory as a set, or hierarchy, of universal statements, its unfalsifiability is really damaging. This kind of unfalsifiability must be sharply distinguished from the (relative) unfalsifiability of teleological explanations, which seems to worry Lass (1974:314 and 347), though it should not. If the data to be described has deliberately been limited, i.e., if the requirement of the time-independent universal (or statistical) validity of the description has been dropped, there sooner or later comes a moment when no genuine counter-examples can be found. In that case, a bad description or explanation is one which is not literally false, but less coherent, i.e., less simple and less general (within the limits allowed by the data), than some other (cf. Itkonen 1978a, chap. 9). As Diesing (1972:233) notes, "holist theories are not composed of universal empirical generalizations and are not tested like empirical generalizations". --Bell (1977) investigates the universality of some putative drifts or "diachronic conspiracies", e.g., the tendency of medial clusters to favor the occurrence of final ones, and he notes that in the light of statistical tests of significance the evidence is far from conclusive. Bell's results are interesting, but they are not directly relevant to the discussion of Lass-type teleological processes, because the latter imply no claim to universality.

15) T. Itkonen (1976) offers good examples of synchronic morphological and syntactic phenomena that cannot be handled by (atomistic) generative rules.

16) None of the changes to be discussed below could be characterized as a "sound change". -- "PG.", "OHG.", "MHG.", "MG.", "Lat.", "OF.", "MF.", "It.", and "Sp." stand, respectively, for "Proto-Germanic", "Old High German", "Middle High German", "Modern German", "Latin", "Old French", "Modern French", "Italian", and "Spanish".

17) These strategies are formulated incorrectly in Bever and Langendoen (1972:43-46). The correct formulation can be found in Bever and Langendoen (1971:436).

18) Paul (1975[1920]:140–41) investigates the occurrence of this
construction in Middle High German. He notes that its use *increased*
towards the end of the Middle Ages. Therefore its disappearance from
Modern German cannot be explained simply by reference to an increasing
ambiguity.
19) One might question this claim.
20) This assumes that as long as the constructions with and without *who* were equally optional, there could arise no very strong tendency to supplant the one in favor of the other.
21) This point is argued extensively in Itkonen (1978:3.6 and
passim).

REFERENCES:

Andersen, Henning. 1974. "Towards a Typology of Change: Bifurcating
      Changes and Binary Relations", in John M. Anderson and Charles
      Jones, eds., *Historical Linguistics I: Syntax, Morphology, In-
      ternal and Comparative Reconstruction*. Amsterdam: North Holland.
Anderson, John M. and Jones, Charles, eds. 1974a. *Historical Linguis-
      tics I: Syntax, Morphology, Internal and Comparative Reconstruc-
      tion*. Amsterdam: North Holland.
-------------------------------------- 1974b. *Historical Linguis-
      tics II: Theory and Description in Phonology*. Amsterdam: North
      Holland.
Anttila, Raimo. 1972. *An Introduction to Historical and Comparative
      Linguistics*. New York: Macmillan.
-------------- 1974. *Analogy*. Publications of the General Linguis-
      tics Department of the University of Helsinki, 1.
Bell, Alan. 1977. "Diachronic Conspiracies -- Some Conditions for
      Synchronic Evidence". Paper presented at the XIIth International
      Congress of Linguists in Vienna, Austria.
Bever, Thomas G., and Langendoen, Terence. 1971. "A Dynamic Model
      of the Evolution of Language", *Linguistic Inquiry*.
-------------------------------------- 1972. "The Interaction
      of Speech Perception and Grammatical Structure in the Evolution
      of Language", in R. P. Stockwell and R. K. S. Macaulay, eds.,
      Linguistic Change and Generative Theory. Bloomington: University
      of Indiana Press.
Davidson, Donald, Suppes, Patrick, and Siegel, Sidney. 1957. *Decision
      Making: An Experimental Approach*. Stanford: Stanford University
      Press.
Diesing, Paul. 1972. *Patterns of Discovery in the Social Sciences*.
      London: Routledge.
Dray, William. 1957. *Laws and Explanation in History*. Oxford: Ox-
      ford University Press.
Dressler, Wolfgang. 1977. *Grundfragen der Morphonologie*. Wien: Ver-
      lag der Österreichischen Akademie der Wissenschaften.

Friedman, Milton. 1953. *Essays in Positive Economics*. Chicago: University of Chicago Press.

Ginneken, J. van. 1927. "Die Erblichkeit der Lautgesetze", *Indogermanische Forschungen*.

Grice, H. Paul. 1975. "Logic and Conversation", in Peter Cole and Jerry L. Morgan, eds., *Syntax and Semantics III: Speech Acts*. New York: Academic Press.

Hempel, Carl G. 1965. *Aspects of Scientific Explanation and Other Essays in the Philosophy of Science*. New York: The Free Press.

Itkonen, Erkki. 1966. *Kieli ja sen tutkimus (= Language and Its Study)*. Porvoo: W. Söderström.

Itkonen, Esa. 1976. "The Use and Misuse of the Principle of Axiomatics in Linguistics", *Lingua*.

------------ 1978a. *Grammatical Theory and Metascience*. Amsterdam: Benjamins.

------------ 1978b. "The Significance of Merovingian Latin to Linguistic Theory". Publications of the General Linguistics Department of the University of Helsinki, 5.

Itkonen, Terho. 1976. "Syntaktisten vaikutusyhteyksien luonteesta" (with English summary: "Non-generative Phenomena in Finnish Morphology and Syntax"), *Virittäjä*.

Jeffers, Robert J. 1974. "On the Notion of 'Explanation' in Historical Linguistics", in John M. Anderson and Charles Jones, eds., *Historical Linguistics II: Theory and Description in Phonology*. Amsterdam: North-Holland.

Kac, Michael. 1978. *Corepresentation of Grammatical Structure*. London: Croom Helm.

Kiparsky, Paul. 1972. "Explanation in Phonology", in Stanley Peters, ed., *Goals of Linguistic Theory*. Englewood Cliffs, N.J.: Prentice-Hall.

-------------- 1974. "Remarks on Analogical Change", in John M. Anderson and Charles Jones, eds., *Historical Linguistics II: Theory and Description in Phonology*. Amsterdam: North-Holland.

Kisseberth, Charles. 1970. "On the Functional Unity of Phonological Rules", *Linguistic Inquiry*.

Lass, Roger. 1974. "Linguistic Orthogenesis? Scots Vowel Quantity and the English Length Conspiracy", in John M. Anderson and Charles Jones, eds., *Historical Linguistics II: Theory and Description in Phonology*. Amsterdam: North-Holland.

Laszlo, Ervin. 1972. *Introduction to Systems Philosophy*. New York: Harper.

Leinonen, Marja. 1977. "A Close Look at the Natural Serialization". Publications of the Linguistic Association of Finland.

Mackie, J. L. 1974. *The Cement of the Universe. A Study of Causation*. London: Oxford University Press.

Manninen, Juha and Tuomela, Raimo, eds. 1976. *Essays on Explanation and Understanding*. Dordrecht: Reidel.

Martinet, André. 1955. *Economie des changements phonétiques*. Bern: A. Francke.

Meillet, Antoine. 1921. *Linguistique historique et linguistique générale*. Paris: H. Champion.
---------------- 1928. *Esquisse d'une histoire de la langue latine*. Paris: Hachette.
---------------- 1938. *Linguistique historique et linguistique générale*. 2nd vol. Paris: C. Klincksieck.
Muller, H. F. 1929. "A Chronology of Vulgar Latin", *Beihefte zur Zeitschrift für romanische Philologie* LXXVIII.
Nagel, Ernest. 1961. *The Structure of Science*. New York: Harcourt.
Paul, Hermann. 1975[1920]. *Prinzipien der Sprachgeschichte*. Tübingen: Niemeyer.
Sapir, Edward. 1921. *Language*. New York: Harcourt.
Sasse, Hans-Jürgen. 1977. "Gedanken über Wortstellungsveränderungen", *Papiere zur Linguistik*.
Stoutland, Frederick. 1976. "The Causal Theory of Action", in Juha Manninen and Raimo Tuomela, eds., *Essays on Explanation and Understanding*. Dordrecht: Reidel.
Vennemann, Theo. 1974. "Topics, Subjects, and Word Order: From SXV to SVX via TVX", in John M. Anderson and Charles Jones, eds., *Historical Linguistics I: Syntax, Morphology, Internal and Comparative Reconstruction*. Amsterdam: North-Holland.
--------------- 1975. "An Explanation of Drift", in Charles N. Li, ed., *Word Order and Word Order Change*. Austin: University of Texas Press.
Vincent, Nigel. 1974. "Analogy Reconsidered", in John M. Anderson and Charles Jones, eds., *Historical Linguistics II: Theory and Description in Phonology*. Amsterdam: North-Holland.
Woodfield, Andrew. 1976. *Teleology*. Cambridge: Cambridge University Press.
Wright, Georg Henrik von. 1968. *An Essay in Deontic Logic and the General Theory of Action*. Amsterdam: North-Holland.
----------------------- 1971. *Explanation and Understanding*. London: Routledge.
----------------------- 1976. "Replies", in Juha Manninen and Raimo Tuomela, eds., *Essays on Explanation and Understanding*. Dordrecht: Reidel.

SOUND CHANGE AND PERCEPTUAL COMPENSATION

TORE JANSON
University of Stockholm

The work reported here started with some ideas about a well-knowr development in Late Latin. These ideas lead to a hypothesis about a general feature of sound perception, and this hypothesis was tested through an experiment. The hypothesis was confirmed and in the course of the experiment, a sound change in progress was discovered. I shall touch very briefly upon the original idea and the background for the hypothesis, concentrating upon the experiment and its results.

Classical Latin had a five-vowel system with length distinction: the system contained the vowels /ī ē ā ō ū ĭ ĕ ă ŏ ŭ/. Some time in late antiquity, the length distinction broke down. In the western part of the Empire, the substitute for the five-plus-five system was a seven-vowel system without length distinction, containing the vowels /i e ɛ a ɔ o u/. In the transition from the first system to the second one, there were two notable mergers: /ĭ ē/ merged into /e/, and /ŭ ō/ merged into /o/.[1] Now, the problem which first caught my attention was how and why these mergers came about.

This is one part of a development which has been hotly debated by Romance philologists and occasional intruders from other fields for several decades. I shall not go into this discussion here: there is ample reading for anyone who is interested.[2] As a background for the following discussion it is enough to point out a phonetical fact of obvious importance for the explanation of the merger.

From the measurements of vowel qualities in different languages it is well known that languages with vowel systems similar to the original Latin one show characteristic differences between the short and the long vowels. Typically, the short vowels are closer to the center of the vowel space: that is, they are closer to the neutral vowel [ə] and thus pronounced less distinctly than their long counterparts. An illustration is given in Figure 1, showing measured formant values for the vowels in Czech. The chart is reproduced from Lehiste (1970), where a full discussion of the length feature and its correlates is to be found.

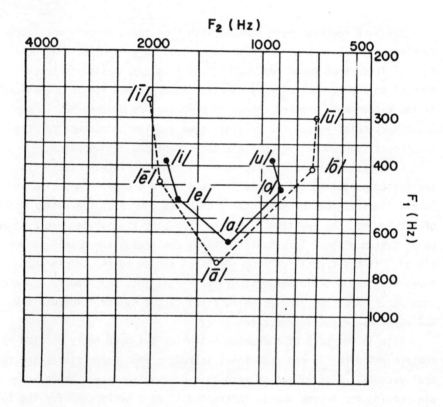

Figure 1

Formant values of Czech vowels. Reproduced from Lehiste (1970:31).

As can be seen, the short vowels tend to move toward an imaginable center fairly far down in the vowel space. The reason for this is at
least partly physiological. When vowels in any language are pronounced
without stress, they tend to be reduced in the same way as phonemically
short vowels are reduced in comparison to their long counterparts.[3]
However, it seems to me that in several languages with a length distinction this difference in quality is greater than one would expect
to result from physiological constraints.

As has first been pointed out by Straka (1959), this general tendency is important for the interpretation of the Latin development.
For in the process, short /ĭ/ and /ŭ/ may sink rather drastically, as
is seen in Figure 1, so that their qualities may become similar to
long /ē/ and /ō/, respectively. This has often been taken as *the* explanation for the mergers in Latin. In my opinion, however, that is
a little hasty.

The reason is that Figure 1 is only an illustration of how the
Czech vowels are produced, and the Latin ones may have been produced,
but it does not take account of their perception. But if we acknow-
ledge that the phonological contrast is one of length in both languages
(and I think there are very good reasons for doing so, although they
will not be discussed here), then there is a discrepancy between perception and production. Although there are considerable differences in
quality between the short and the long vowels, these are not perceived
as such. For example, although there is a great qualitative difference
between Czech [i:] and [ɪ], they are evidently perceived as qualitative-
ly similar, i.e., sharing all features except length. On the other
hand, Czech [e:] and [ɪ] are produced with almost identical qualities
but are perceived as different with regard to both length and quality.
We must assume that a similar situation also prevailed in Latin for
some time preceding the merger.

No one seems to have reflected on the question how there can be
such a systematic difference between production and perception. For
my part, I can only think of one explanation: that the listener some-

how adjusts for the measurable differences in the production, i.e.,
that he performs some kind of *perceptual compensation*. If he hears a
short vowel, he will perceive it as less central than a long vowel of
the same quality.

If this is correct, it must be applicable to the situation in
Latin. The mergers which happened there must then have been produced
by two changes: diminishing of the perceptual compensation, so that
the bonds between short and long vowels were dissolved, and elimination
of the length distinction as such. Naturally, these two changes may
have occurred in close connection with each other. The crucial point
is that the perceptual bond between short and long must have disappeared
before the merger could come about.

This leads up to the statement of a bipartite hypothesis: in languages with a length distinction, there exists a perceptual compensation which eliminates the difference in production between short and
long vowels; this compensation, however, is not a constant universal of
language perception but may take on different values at different times
or in different languages.

This hypothesis can clearly be tested. For practical reasons, the
test persons had to be mainly Swedes (Swedish has a length distinction,
but a richer vowel inventory than Latin and Czech). The compensation,
if it exists, should be most obvious among the front vowels, so these
were selected for the test. It can be seen from Figure 1 that the line
from short /i/ to short /e/ runs more or less towards the central vowel,
that is, in the direction of the reduction and opposite to that of the
supposed compensation. Somewhere along that line is the phoneme boundary between /i/ and /e/. It is possible to produce vowels of different duration that are in the neighborhood of that boundary. Now, if
people tend to hear these vowels more like /i/ when they are shorter
and more like /e/ when they are longer, that will confirm the hypothesis of perceptual compensation.

A perceptual test was arranged in accordance with these assumptions. Synthetic vowels were used as stimuli. Formant values were

selected in the following way. Average formant values for [i] and [e]
for one male speaker of the Stockholm dialect of Swedish were used to
produce the two corresponding synthetic vowels. Then, formant vowels
for five other synthetic vowels were calculated from these in such a
way that they were placed at approximately equal distances along the
line from [i] to [e] in the vowel space.

Of each of these seven vowels, ten shorter (65 msec.) and ten
longer (115 msec.) copies were produced. Even the longer ones were
judged to be heard as phonemically short. The 140 tokens were random-
ly mixed on tape. It was played to the test persons, whose task it
was to decide, for each vowel, whether they heard [i] or [e] by fil-
ling in the appropriate letter on a form.

First, 20 Swedes of different ages and with different dialects
were tested. The result can be seen in Figure 2 (top). The two curves,
for the longer vowels and the shorter vowels, fall together for the
vowel stimuli 5, 6, and 7: these are always identified as [e], regardless of duration. Likewise, stimulus vowel 1 is almost always identified as [i]. But in the intermediate region of uncertainty, represented by stimuli 2, 3, and 4, duration makes a great deal of difference.
The effect is greatest in stimulus 3, which is identified as [e] in
37 percent of the cases when shorter and in 81 percent of the cases
when longer. Thus, first part of the hypothesis was confirmed: there
is a considerable amount of perceptual compensation for vowel shortness
in Swedish.

To test the second part of the hypothesis, the simplest way seemed
to be to test persons having a native language without any length distinction. I had the opportunity to test 6 native Greeks (Modern Greek
has a simple five-vowel system). The result is shown in Figure 2 (bottom). Clearly, the difference between the two curves is very much
smaller, and they even cross each other towards the tails. However, in
the regions of maximal uncertainty (which is here around stimulus 4:
the placement of the phoneme boundary in the two languages is not identical), there is a slight difference in the same direction as for the

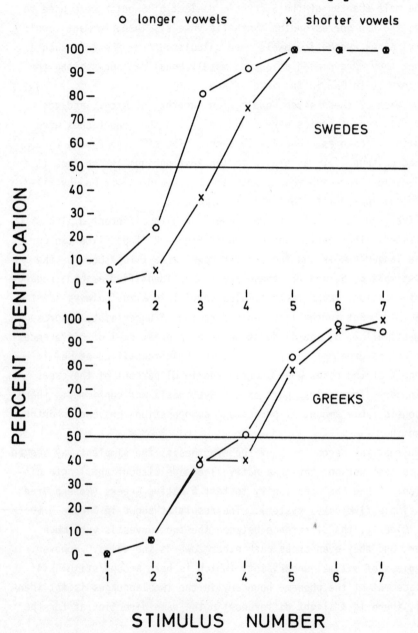

Swedes. It can be shown that it is just over the border-line for statistical significance.[4] Thus, it seems that some amount of perceptual
compensation does indeed exist in Greek too, but it is clearly much
smaller than in Swedish. A convenient way of measuring this difference
is to look at the distance between the points where the two curves
cross the 50% line. This distance is almost as much as the distance
between two stimuli for the Swedes, and less than a third of that for
the Greeks. Since the stimuli vowels are placed about 36 mels from
each other in the vowel space, the distances can be calculated as 32
mels for Swedes and 10 mels for Greeks.[5] Thus, the amount of perceptual compensation is indeed variable, and the second part of the hypothesis is also confirmed.

   However, an accidental observation during the experiment led to
an even more striking corroboration of the hypothesis. In the original
group of Swedes, there were five teenagers from Stockholm. On inspection, it seemed that the amount of perceptual compensation was considerably less for these subjects than for the rest of the group. A number of additional tests were conducted, so that two new groups could
be formed, both containing only native inhabitants of Stockholm. The
first consisted of 21 persons aged 13-16, the second of 19 persons who
were 30 years or above. The result was that the amount of compensation
was 36 mels for the older group and 20 mels for the younger group. The
difference is clearly significant.

   Two types of explanation could be thought of to account for this
difference. One line of argument is that the cause is some sound
change in progress. The other one is that there is some general difference in speech perception between younger and older people: one
may think of late learning among the younger, or conversely of impaired
hearing among the older ones, and so on.

   In order to find out which type of argument was the more probable
one, a new series of tests had to be run. Again, two groups were formed,
one consisting of youngsters and one of middle-aged people. In these
groups, all came from different parts of the country than the Stockholm

area. The values for the compensation for those groups were 26 and 28
mels respectively. This difference is well within the limits for ran-
domness. Thus it seems that there is not among Swedes any general difference between younger and older people. One can therefore hardly explain the difference between young and old Stockholmers as anything
else than a dialectal difference, that is, a sound change in progress.
Although the exact nature of this change is still to be investigated,
it seems very probable to me that what is happening right now is a
gradual disappearance of the older Stockholm dialect in favor of a
pronunciation which conforms more to the standard language of the
country.

By way of conclusion, I would like to point out two facts of a
certain interest to a conference on historical linguistics. First, in
this case a hypothesis about a historical development led to this discovery of a feature of sound perception, which means that historical
phonology can contribute to phonetics just as well as the other way
around. Secondly, in this case the salient feature of sound change
turned out to be not the change in the pronunciation, but a change of
perception. It is remarkable that Stockholm children evidently perceive some sounds in another way than their parents perceive the same
sounds. Further investigations of such variation and change of perception seem to me to be a most promising area of research.

NOTES:

1) A full account of this development can be found in any handbook
on Romance linguistics, for example, Lausberg (1969), Bec (1970-71), or
Hall (1976).

2) In addition to the handbooks mentioned in note 1, the reader is
referred to Spence (1965) for an overview of the discussion up to that
date. Additional material can be found in Spore (1972).

3) See Lindblom (1963), Gay (forthcoming).

4) See Janson (1979) for the statistical analysis and generally
for a more detailed description of the experiment and its results.

5) These values are actually calculated as the difference between mean probabilities. See Janson (1979).

REFERENCES:

Bec, P. 1970-71. *Manuel pratique de philologie romane*. Tome 1-2. Paris.
Gay, T. Forthcoming. "Effect of Speaking Rate on Vowel Formant Movement".
Hall, R. A., Jr. 1976. *Proto-Romance Phonology (= Comparative Romance Grammar, vol. 2)*. New York/Oxford/Amsterdam.
Janson, T. 1979. "Vowel Duration, Vowel Quality, and Perceptual Compensation", *Journal of Phonetics* 7.93-103.
Lausberg, H. 1969. *Romanische Sprachwissenschaft*. Part 1. Berlin.
Lehiste, I. 1970. *Suprasegmentals*. Cambridge, Mass.
Lindblom, B. 1963. "Spectographic Study of Vowel Reduction", *The Journal of the Acoustical Society of America* 42.830-43.
Spence, N. C. W. 1965. "Quantity and Quality in the Vowel-system of Vulgar Latin", *Word* 21.1-18.
Spore, P. 1972. *La diphtongaison romane*. Odense.
Straka, G. 1959. "Durée et timbre vocaliques", *Zeitschrift für Phonetik und allgemeine Sprachwissenschaft* 12.276-300.

THE NEOGRAMMARIAN DOCTRINE: BREAKTHROUGH OR EXTENSION OF THE SCHLEICHERIAN PARADIGM

A PROBLEM IN LINGUISTIC HISTORIOGRAPHY*

KONRAD KOERNER
University of Ottawa

1.0 *The Problem Defined*

It might appear that I have expounded contradictory views concerning 19th-century linguistics. According to one (Koerner 1976a[1972]), the linguistic theories advanced by August Schleicher during the 1860s provided a theoretical framework or paradigm for subsequent research in historical-comparative linguistics, which at the time was almost identical with linguistics *tout court*.[1] The other view (Koerner 1976b), enunciated somewhat later, according to which the year 1876 might be regarded as something like a turning point in linguistics, appears to conflict with the first standpoint. Indeed, most available histories of linguistics accept the view that it is with the *Junggrammatiker*, and during the later 1870s and 1880s, that a new approach to historical-comparative linguistics was initiated. On this interpretation, contemporary researchers in the field still rely heavily on the principles worked out and codified by Brugmann, Delbrück, Osthoff, Paul, Sievers, Verner, and their associates.

---

* This is a thoroughly revised and greatly extended version of a paper first presented at the Fourth International Conference on Historical Linguistics held at Stanford University, California, 26-30 March 1979. It significantly profitted from pertinent comments by Terence H. Wilbur (Los Angeles) and Michael Serwatka (Boulder) as well as an opportunity, arranged by Kurt R. Jankowsky, to present the essence of my argument at a special seminar held at Georgetown University, Washington, D.C., on 28 March 1980.

The present paper is an attempt to reconcile these two opposing points of view. First, it will investigate the epistemological basis of the *fable convenue* according to which the Neogrammarians established a new frame of reference for historical-comparative research; second, an attempt will be made to show that it was in fact Schleicher who, through his work in Indo-European phonology and morphology, in language typology, dialect study, field work, and many other areas of investigation, laid the basis for something like a 'disciplinary matrix' on which subsequent generations of linguists have built. This contradictory view can, I believe, only be resolved if appropriate consideration is given to extra-disciplinary factors, including the sociology and psychology of the community of linguists, i.e., factors which have always, in one way or another, had an impact on both the evolution of the discipline and the self-understanding of its practitioners, whether it be tacit knowledge or not.

2.0 *Theoretical Presuppositions*

In a paper published a number of years ago (Koerner 1974) I identified three common types of history writing in linguistics. These different types may be characterized by determining the motives behind their composition.

The first type may be called a Summing-Up History. A history belonging in this category is usually written by a distinguished practitioner toward the end of his scholarly career. It purports to express the feeling of the majority of his colleagues, namely, that the field has reached a stage of maturity, i.e., a state of affairs in which all that remains to be done is what Thomas S. Kuhn (1970:24) has called the 'mopping-up operations' of 'normal science'. Benfey's (1809-81) *Geschichte der Sprachwissenschaft* (1869) and Raumer's (1815-76) *Geschichte der germanischen Philologie* (1870) fit this characterization very well.[2] Their works appeared shortly after Schleicher's death and provided a summary of the achievements of Western linguistic science up to that point. Even Pedersen's frequently cited book (especially in its English translation of 1931)[3] and Vilhelm Thomsen's (1842-1922)

Sprogvidenskabens historie (1902) may be placed in this category. They simply extend the surveys of Benfey, Raumer, and others[4] to the post-1870 period which is largely associated with the *junggrammatische Richtung*. Significantly, they do not claim that this recent trend constituted a break with previous endeavours, either in methodology or in actual research. Similarly, historical accounts of the development of modern linguistics written in the 1960s, such as those by Malmberg, Ivić, Leroy and others, do no more than present the achievements of the post-Saussurean era, most of them expressing the feeling that a plateau has been reached.[5]

The second type of history-writing tends to be practiced by individual authors who are usually much younger in age than those of 'summing-up' accounts. Histories of this type put forward a forceful argument claiming that the work conducted by the contemporary generation of researchers represents something like a new departure. The writers use history for a purpose other than simply depicting the development of the discipline from earlier times to the present. In fact they use it for propagandistic, political and frequently polemic purposes, indulging in what the late Sir Henry Butterfield (1931:11) aptly described as the 'Whig interpretation of history':

> Through this system of immediate reference to the present-day, historical personages can easily be classed into the men who furthered progress and the men who tried to hinder it; so that a handy rule of thumb exists by which the historian can select and reject, and can make his points of emphasis.

The best modern example of 'Whig History' is without doubt Chomsky's *Cartesian Linguistics* (1966).[6] But his book is by no means the first history of its type. If we look into the late 19th century, for example, we will find an account by Berthold Delbrück (1842-1922), who set out to defend the particular view of linguistic science taken by his fellow-*Junggrammatiker*. Accordingly, pre-1870 linguistics was represented as an earlier phase in the development of the discipline, from which more recent doctrines marked a clear departure. Earlier tenets in linguistics were by and large associated with the name of Franz Bopp (1791-1867).[7] In his *Einleitung in das Sprachstudium* of 1880 (as well as in subsequent revised editions, including the 6th of 1919)

Delbrück depicts Schleicher's views as either fully in line with those
of Bopp (Delbrück 1882:45-46, 47, 53) or, when they differed from those
of Bopp, as falling short of the brilliance demonstrated by the Young
Grammarians (48-53 pass.). Indeed, the concluding statement (p.55) describes Schleicher as a 'philologist' together with Bopp and Grimm, Pott
and Curtius. This is quite in contrast to Schleicher's own self-con-
ception, namely, that he was a 'glottologist', a scientist of language.
Ironically enough, it was Schleicher who advocated time and again a
clear-cut division of labour between 'Philologie' and 'Sprachwissenschaft oder Glottik'(cf. Schleicher 1850:1-5; 1860:119-23), dismissing
the former as merely a historical discipline interested in language only
to the extent that it reflects the development of the culture of a given
people. (Compare also Arbuckle 1970, who depicts Schleicher as the originator of this 'gratuitous' distinction.) This philologist/linguist
dichotomy (which has a long-standing tradition ever since its first
use in the 19th century[8]) reminds us of dichotomies of comparable polemic intent,such as mechanist/mentalist, taxonomist/transformationalist
etc. in 20th-century debates.[9] I would not emphasize Delbrück's account
of Schleicher if it were not for the fact that 20th-century histories
of linguistics have tended to repeat this one-sided view of Schleicher's contribution to the field, not realizing that Delbrück was expounding an unabashedly partisan point of view. Indeed, modern accounts
have not only perpetuated this biased interpretation of Schleicher's
accomplishments, but have tended to subject Schleicher to ridicule,
particularly when he carried his teachings to their logical conclusion
by establishing a little story in Indo-European on the basis of reconstructed forms; cf. King's (1969:154-55) remark: "What can you do with
a reconstructed text but look at it? Hence our chuckling about people
who reconstruct fables in proto-Indo-European." Other scholars (e.g.,
Blumenthal 1970:3) depict Schleicher as a 'biology professor' or characterize him in a similar fashion (cf. Bronstein et al. 1977:186-87)
because of his naturalist conception of language.

     The third type of history writing concerns the not yet fully re-
cognized treatment of the development of linguistic science. It will

be employed in the present paper. This third approach, for which I chose the term 'historiography' (giving it a somewhat different meaning than it generally assumes), would require nothing less than the disinterested attempt to set the record straight. However, this 'sineira-et-studio' approach to the subject matter is in need of a methodology, and careful consideration is necessary if it is not to result in a naive 'development-by-accumulation' account. The historian Leopold von Ranke (1795-1886), a close contemporary of Bopp, may perhaps be credited with having enunciated and practiced what I have in mind (cf. Ranke 1824 and his subsequent voluminous work). Indeed, his famous dictum that it is the duty of the historian to establish "wie es eigentlich gewesen" may be taken to represent the best historiographic tradition rather than what has frequently been associated with shallow 'positivism'. The next section will therefore address itself to the question of method in linguistic historiography.

3.0 *Considerations for the Historical Argument*

Even if one disagrees with a recent statement[10] that there are few publications extant that are devoted to questions of method in the historical treatment of the science of language, it is true that much remains to be done in this area. Proposals that I have made since 1972 can only be regarded as preliminary, even though I still believe that the essence of these papers might still be valid, at least for the description of events and phases in 19th and 20th century linguistics. For example, I still regard the distinction between what I have termed, following Kuhn, 'paradigm' or probably more appropriately 'discipinary matrix' (Kuhn 1970:184)[11], on the one hand, and 'climate of opinion', *Zeitgeist* or intellectual atmosphere of a particular period under investigation, on the other, as useful. This distinction is essential in the present argument. The former term denotes intra-disciplinary organization and research practice, the latter notion refers to extra-linguistic factors, be they epistemological, psychological, socio-economic or other, which have made an (at times considerable) impact on the practioners of a particular discipline.

Kuhn's concept of 'paradigm' has been widely discussed by historians and philosophers of science as well as by scholars interested in the history of linguistics. The most cogent criticism to date seems to be Shapere's (1964) review article of the first edition of Kuhn's book. Kuhn recognized the ambiguity of the concept and, as a result, suggested in its stead the term 'disciplinary matrix' (1970:182). If we interpret it as the sum of concepts and procedures of analysis to which the student is introduced and which will permit him to account for the data that constitute the object of investigation, this concept may serve in the presentation of theories of language in the history of linguistics as well.

The concept of 'climate of opinion', which I believe to be the other aspect the historian of linguistics has to take note of, seems to be frequently overlooked by historians. Expectedly, this factor is considered irrelevant by those concerned with the day-to-day workings of the craft, though it cannot be ignored by those who wish to obtain a better understanding of their own activity. Becker (1932:26) supplied the following illustration of the notion which is also relevant to my proposition:

> Whether arguments command assent or not depends less upon the logic that conveys them than upon the climate of opinion in which they are sustained. What renders Dante's argument or St. Thomas' definition meaningless to us is not bad logic or want of intelligence, but the medieval climate of opinion — those instinctively held preconceptions, in the broad sense, that *Weltanschauung* or world pattern — which imposed on Dante and St.Thomas a peculiar use of the intelligence and a special type of logic. To understand why we cannot easily follow Dante or St. Thomas it is necessary to understand (as well as may be) the nature of this climate of opinion.

The 19th century, which concerns us here, is much closer to our present-day understanding than the medieval world. In fact, in almost every field of human endeavour the 20th century has built on what the preceding century has erected. Nevertheless, we are far removed from the mid- and late 19th-century *épistème* (Foucault) that it has in effect become difficult for us to understand certain preoccupations, and appreciate certain views shared by Schleicher and the generation of linguists

which followed him. This very difficulty is largely responsible for the
fact that 20th-century scholars dismiss the ideas of 19th-century linguists so readily. Because they do not comprehend the intellectual
climate as well as the general 'context of situation' (Firth) of the
period, modern researchers in the field often accuse earlier generations of lack of clarity, consistency, and method,even though it is
safe to say that 19th-century scholars were at least as much up to
standards of their own time as 20th-century linguists could hope to be.
In fact, a comparison between Hermann Paul's (1846-1921) *Prinzipien*,
which first appeared 100 years ago (and has been reprinted as late as
1970), and, say, Chomsky's *Aspects* of 1965,done by a disinterested historian of linguistics,might well conclude that Paul's views are much
more relevant to the understanding of the nature of language and its
development than those of Chomsky that are still championed by many
practitioners in the field.

   Therefore, if we are to do justice to 19th-century linguistic
thinkers, we must be careful not to rely on accounts of the type represented by Chomsky's *Cartesian Linguistics* (1966), where the historian
engages in 'ancestor hunting', establishing a lineage of thought that
leads directly to his own views. Such a history depicts the immediately preceding generation of scholars as not worthy of attention, or, to
cite one of the most damning judgments passed by present-day transformationalists on the ideas of others, as 'uninteresting'. Earlier historians of this type have perhaps been kinder to their predecessors. However, as we have seen from Delbrück's account of Schleicher, it is quite
hazardous to rely on their judgments of the work of those scholars who
were their immediate predecessors. We can make similar observations
about the accounts of Thomsen and Pedersen,written at the beginning of
this century,and about the many histories written during the past 25
years that have slavishly relied on these earlier evaluations for their
treatment of 19th-century linguistics.

   What is lacking in previous histories of linguistics is not so
much a positivist attitude that is concerned with relating the development
of the discipline as objectively as possible, but rather a clear dis-

tinction between what one might call, on the one hand, the intellectual
'Überbau', the 'Zeitgeist' of a particular period, and, on the other,
the 'mechanics of the trade', the intralinguistic problems and the solutions offered by linguists at different points in time. Such a distinction between what I have called 'climate of opinion' and 'disciplinary matrix' will significantly help distinguish the 'pro-domo'-type argument from the true advances made by a particular group or generation
of linguists. The next section is an attempt at demonstrating the use-
fulness of this distinction.

4.0 *'Schleicherian Paradigm' vs 'Neogrammarian Breakthrough'*

    In a recent paper Henry Hoenigswald (1980) stated emphatically
that a distinction must be made between what a linguist is saying what
he does and what he is really doing. (There may in fact be a third component that the linguist may not be aware of, namely, the epistemological part of his argument.) There is general agreement that 19th-century
linguistics, at least until the 1880s, was imbued with naturalist conceptions, both about the nature of language in general and about its
mechanism and evolution. This does not mean that there were no scholars
during that period who held different and opposing views. Linguists in
the Humboldtian tradition, for instance, tended to associate themselves
with the view that linguistic science was in fact a 'Geisteswissenschaft'
and not a 'Naturwissenschaft'. However, if the technical vocabulary of
the period as well as the concepts and methodological principles advocated by the majority of linguists, irrespective of their philosophical
allegiance, is a guide, we may note that linguistic theory and practice
were clearly marked by the natural sciences of the late 18th to the
mid-19th century, particularly botany, comparative anatomy, geology, and
evolution theory. This impact of the 'Zeitgeist' of the period can be
seen not only in the terminological kit of the 19th-century linguist
(compare terms such as 'analysis', 'assimilation', 'dissimilation',
'stem', 'root'[12], 'growth', 'decay', even the term 'linguistics' itself,
which appears to be modeled after 'physics', 'mathematics', etc.[13]), but

also in the tendency to conceive of language as an 'organism' (a term still used by Saussure in the sense of 'system') consisting of 'structure(s)' (a term figuring in the title of Bopp's comparative work of 1820 but already used by F. Schlegel in his 1808 book)[14], and in the claim that the development of language follows strict 'physical' laws.

There can be no doubt that the view of linguistics as a natural science (not so much in regard to its object of investigation but rather to its methodology) reached its peak in August Schleicher's (1821-1868) work. Even though there is no truth to the traditional claim that he developed his ideas under the deep influence of Darwin's *Origin of Species* (1859), there is every reason to believe that Schleicher introduced concepts into linguistics that he had drawn from the natural sciences, at times via Hegel's 'Naturphilosophie' (cf. Koerner 1975a:748-752, for details). For instance, there can be no doubt that the family-tree concept, which he so ardently defended from 1853 on, owes much to (probably Lamarckian) biology (and probably much less to his philological training under Friedrich Ritschl, which included the establishment of stemmata or 'Stammbäume' of manuscripts, as Hoenigswald has suggested). Indeed, we have evidence from Schleicher's own writings (cf. Schleicher 1855, 1863) that he was well acquainted with the natural sciences of his day, especially botany, and that he frequently advocated the adoption of principles of linguistic analysis that followed the lead of the natural sciences. For example, it was Schleicher who introduced the term and concept of 'morphology' into linguistic analysis and the rigorous application of a strictly formal approach to language typology (Schleicher 1859).

I have demonstrated on several occasions (cf. Koerner 1976a [1972]: 692-98; 1975a:755-58) the significance of Schleicher's contribution to linguistics: recognition of the importance of the 'sound laws' and the analogy principle in language analysis, the adoption of the systematic use of the asterisk in reconstruction (cf. Koerner 1975b), as well as the development of rigorous principles in the reconstruction of proto-stages of language in general. In his *Compendium der vergleichenden Grammatik der indogermanischen Sprachen* of 1861-62 (which served as the

basic linguistics text, until Brugmann and Delbrück began publishing
the *Grundriss* twenty-five years later (1886-1900), we have the first
attempt to analyse Indo-European in its entirety rather than treating
only one or another of its branches (as Grimm had done) or dealing with
the individual members of the family separately placing them side by
side (as Bopp had done). In the *Compendium*, Schleicher laid down the
following principles for historical-comparative linguistics, which
still today, 130 years later, have lost little of their validity:

> When comparing two linguistic forms of two related languages, I
> first try to trace the forms to be compared back to their pro-
> bable base forms, i.e., that structure [Gestalt] which they must
> have except for the sound laws [Lautgesetze] that had an impact
> on them, or at least I try to establish identical phonetic si-
> tuations in historical terms for both of them. Since even the
> oldest languages of our language family are not available in
> their oldest shape — this is also true for Sanskrit! — and
> since in addition the existing languages are known to us in very
> different stages of their development [Altersstufen], we must
> first try to remove the different ages of the languages as much
> as possible before a comparison can be made. (Cited after Schlei-
> cher 1852:iv-v; my translation: KK.)

This successful fusion of the almost ahistorical approach to language
comparison which we find in Bopp and the exclusively historical treatment of a particular language family as practiced by Grimm, together
with the particular emphasis on phonology and morphology, provided
subsequent workers in historical-comparative linguistics (which was
almost identical with linguistics *tout court* in the past century) with
a framework which I have not hesitated to call, with Kuhn, a 'paradigm'.
I see no reason for changing my viewpoint today. This entails the assumption that the so-called 'Paradigma der Junggrammatiker' (Růžička
1977:15) is essentially an extension of the 'Schleicherian Paradigm'.
Indeed, this claim was first made almost 100 years ago by Hermann Collitz
(1855-1935), when he stated that the appearance of Schleicher's Compendium (1861-62) marked the beginning of a new epoch of research in comparative grammar (and in fact the only such 'wesentliche umgestaltung'
as he asserted in 1886), especially in phonology. Collitz (1883:2)
described Schleicher's achievement as follows:

... his presentation [of comparative Indo-European grammar]
forms a unique self-contained system [ein eigenartiges, in
sich gefügtes und nach allen seiten abgeschlossenes system],
which tried to show strict lawfulness in the development of
the phonology from the proto-language down to the individual
languages, which assigned every individual phonological phenomenon its particular place, and which especially through
the manner in which it proceeded with the investigation of a
linguistic fact provided a model for the time to come. (My
translation: KK)

Collitz, it should be noted, was in many respects opposed to the neogrammarian tenets. However, it is interesting to note that no less a
scholar than Brugmann himself acknowledged in 1885 that he did not
agree with Curtius' assessment that the 'junggrammatische Richtung'
constituted a break with the past. On the contrary, he concedes (contrary to what he and Osthoff wished to make the linguistic world believe in 1878):

Ich für meine Person habe die neueren Anschauungen immer nur
für die organische und folgerechte Fortentwicklung der älteren
Bestrebungen gehalten. ... Wenn wir Jüngeren auf absolut stren-
ge Beobachtung der Lautgesetze dringen und die Aufgabe der
sprachgeschichtlichen Forschung immer erst dann für gelöst erach-
ten, wenn den lautlichen Unregelmäßigkeiten gegenüber die Ant-
wort auf das warum? gefunden ist, so ziehen wir nur die letzte
Consequenz von dem, was man schon vorher verlangt hatte und
was in Gemeinschaft mit Schleicher und Andern namentlich gegen
Bopp und Benfey erfolgreich vertreten zu haben eines der Haupt-
verdienste gerade von Curtius ist. (Brugmann 1885: 125)

In other words, Brugmann himself denies the existence of what the 65-
year-old Curtius, Brugmann's former teacher, in his critique of the
neogrammarian position (1885), *felt* to be a 'Bruch mit der Vergangen-
heit' and a mode of research along 'völlig neuen Bahnen'. Even if we
recognize Brugmann's reconciliatory gesture toward Curtius, the above
passage should be taken (as Szereményi has recently done in *Phonetica*
36.164, 1979) as important evidence pointing toward the correctness of
my claim that the year 1876, and the work of the *Junggrammatiker* after
that historic date, did not constitute a 'scientific revolution' in
(historical-comparative) linguistics. Historians of 19th-century linguistics have confirmed Collitz's and Brugmann's observations. Thus,

Brigit Beneš (1958:123), comparing the theories of the major figures
of the period, concludes: "Die junggrammatische Doktrin ... ist nur
eine konsequente Weiterführung der Schleicherischen Vorstellung von
der Sprache als eines autonomen Organismus". Not only did the metatheory not change but also — what is more important — linguistic
practice remained substantially the same. This view has been corroborated by several others in recent years. For example Putschke (1969:
21) states: "Die methodischen Grundsätze der junggrammatischen Schule
können höchstenfalls als eine Absolutsetzung der um 1870 bestehenden
Methodenpraxis angesehen werden".

Jankowsky, who treated the neogrammarian school in an important
monograph, notes (1972:126): "Their work is much more comprehensive
conclusion and selective intensification of what has been taught and
practiced — more taught than practiced though — before them." Hoenigswald (1974:351) concedes: "Until more is known we shall say that
it is in the [eighteen] sixties, and with August Schleicher, that the
great change occurred." And Christmann, in his anthology of 19th-
century linguistics, maintains (1977:3) that the doctrine of the so-
called *Junggrammatiker* "[stellt] eine direkte Fortsetzung und Weiterführung der Konzeption Schleichers dar."

This view, to which I have subscribed since 1972, however, is by
no means shared by all scholars who have written on the subject. Thus,
Benware (1974:54) for instance regards the period of 1850-1870 as marking "the culmination of the linguistic theories of Bopp", arguing that
a "new 'paradigm' was introduced into linguistics by Whitney and Scherer" (p.85). His study, however, does not go much beyond the year 1868
and supplies little evidence for the claim except for largely repeating the arguments advanced by Brugmann, Delbrück, and others.

Yet the question whether or not there was a 'breakthrough', a major shift of emphasis, in linguistics associated with the *junggrammatische Richtung* from 1876 onwards can by no means be resolved simply
on the basis of the two above quotations from Collitz and Brugmann, nor
by citing authors of historical accounts of the period. Hoenigswald
(1978:21, 22) appropriately notes:

> The great fact is not that 1876 *was* a turning point or that
> it marks one of the great 'breakthroughs' in history. ... The
> important thing is, rather, that it was immediately *felt* as a
> turning-point by both friend and foe.

While I am not so sure that this was true for the opponents of the
Young Grammarians, especially those of the same generation — we noted
above that Georg Curtius (1820-85) appears to have felt that there was
a break with previous commitments — it may well have been that the
adherents of the 'junggrammatische Richtung' felt that way. Delbrück's
account of 1880 may be taken as an expression of this feeling. However,
in the absence of sufficient evidence for this interesting claim[15], we
might cite the statement of a distinguished second-generation Young
Grammarian, namely Antoine Meillet (1866-1936). In his *Introduction
à l'étude comparative des langues indo-européennes*, first published in
1903, he stated "Après 1875, ..., la scission entre les conceptions du
XVIIIe[!] siècle et celles de la grammaire comparée est dès lors définitive".[16] This statement suggests that great linguists do not necessarily have to be discerning historians of their discipline, but it
also indicates that the mid-1870s were widely regarded as a new beginning or a turning-point by many practitioners in the field.

Indeed, the 'annus mirabilis' 1876 (Hoenigswald) did see the publication of at least six important writings that 'hang together' (Hoenigswald 1978:17)[17], namely, those by Verner, Brugmann, Osthoff, Leskien, Sievers, and Winteler (cf. Koerner 1976b, for details). These
studies helped explain a number of phenomena that had puzzled previous
generations of linguists, and broadened the scope of our understanding
of the nature and structure of the Indo-European proto-language and
its descendants. In addition, the principles advocated and/or put to
use in these and many other (cf. Koerner 1978b:xviii, note 6) 1876
publications contributed to the clarification of theoretical issues
that had been recognized since Schleicher. The result was an air of excitement which at times led to excessive claims of originality on the
part of the young scholars of Leipzig and their close allies. (That
many of their claims had to be corroborated in later research and in
ensuing controversies has been documented most carefully in Wilbur's

study of 1977.)

As noted earlier in this paper, there is evidence that most of the *Junggrammatiker* perceived a break between their work and that of their predecessors, especially Curtius and Schleicher. It could be shown that this impression was not entirely unjustified, though I believe that this has much less to do with the Neogrammarians' insistance on the infallibility of 'sound laws' (which received particular support from Karl Verner's findings) and the importance they attached to the analogy principle than with a change in the 'climate of opinion' during the 1880s and 1890s. This change in the intellectual climate may be characterized by a departure from biological conceptions in matters concerning the humanities (Geisteswissenschaften), and the emergence, during the second half of the 19th century, of psychology, sociology and political economy as autonomous disciplines. (This change in the climate coincided with a number of other socio-political factors, such as the spectacular economic growth of Germany following the Franco-Prussian war, the consolidation of the German state, and the expansion of its educational system.) Closer to the concerns of linguists of the mid-1870s, however, were ideas concerning the social and psychological nature of linguistic processes. These notions began to infiltrate their circles principally through the writings of Heymann Steinthal (1823-99), a Humboldtian linguist turned Herbartian psychologist, and of the American but largely German-trained Sanskritist and general linguist William Dwight Whitney (1827-94), who was influenced by Spencerian sociology.

However, as I have tried to document elsewhere (Koerner 1979), Whitney played a very important role, which, at least during the late 1870s, was not primarily scientific but polemic in nature. From the early 1870s onwards, Whitney attacked the theories of those scholars who were particularly influential during the second half of the 19th century, namely, Max Müller, August Schleicher, and also Steinthal, whose psychologism he found excessive. Where Germany is concerned, it appears that his attack upon Schleicher's 'physical theory of language'

(Whitney 1871) was especially effective. Owing to the prestige that
Whitney had already acquired, both as an Indic scholar and as a general linguist, it permitted the younger generation of linguists to dismiss Schleicher's ideas about the biological nature of language. This
attitude was further facilitated by the fact that Schleicher had died
several years earlier, in 1868. Interestingly enough, this overt rejection of Schleicher's biologism did not mean that earlier expressions of the 'new faith' on the part of the Young Grammarians showed
a clear rejection of language as something like an autonomous entity,
a quasi-physical organism. 1879 publications by Brugmann as well as
by Osthoff still advanced a persuasive argument in favour of a natural-
science theory of sound change.

Once raised by Whitney, however, the question whether linguistics
was a natural science or a so-called 'historical science' (historische
Wissenschaft) could no longer be avoided. For example, the French
scholar Lucien Adam (1833-1918) decided that linguistics was both:
While phonetics and morphology employed the methods of the natural
sciences, the content aspect of language was part of human intelligence
and hence had to do with the 'historical' sciences (Adam 1881:394-95).
In Germany, it appears that it was in the year 1880, with the appearance of Delbrück's *Einleitung* and, in particular, with Hermann Paul's
(1846-1921) *Prinzipien der Sprachgeschichte* — note that both scholars
had been pupils of Steinthal and not, like August Leskien (1840-1916),
of Schleicher — that the shift toward sociological and, more importantly, psychological explanations of language change began to exert its influence. Curiously enough, however, these ideas did not have a visible
impact on the actual practice of comparative-historical linguistics of
the time. We find that the other *Junggrammatiker* (as well as the majority of their contemporaries), though they officially rejected Schleicher's biologistic conceptions, continued to treat language as a
'thing' independent of the speaker and his social context. It appears
that the thoroughness of their work and its inner consistency were in
fact only possible because of this (tacitly accepted) premise. The emphasis of their research lay (as in the work of Schleicher) on phonolo-

gy and morphology, to the neglect of semantic and syntactic studies.[18]

Apart from this emphasis on the basic building blocks of language, we find that all the concepts, technical terms, and procedures of analysis employed in the work of the Neogrammarians (as well as their contemporaries) were either introduced or developed by Schleicher: 1) the family-tree model of the Indo-European languages; 2) the rigorous method of reconstruction of proto-forms based on a strict application of the 'sound laws'; 3) the use of the concept of analogy[19] in the explanation of language change; 4) the term 'morphology' (which he took from biology). Indeed, if we return to the question posed at the beginning of this paper, we soon discover that the linguistic theories and methods that we are accustomed to associate with the *Junggrammatiker* (cf. Blümel 1978) have their origin in the work of Schleicher and his generation (e.g., the work of Curtius). We are therefore justified in maintaining that, irrespective of the considerable advances in Indo-European phonology and morphology made in 1876 and subsequent decades, the 'Young Grammarians' did not provide anything like a new paradigm, a new frame of reference in comparative-historical linguistics. Instead their work was carried on within the 'disciplinary matrix' established largely by Schleicher, and what appeared to many at the time, and to later generations of linguists as well, as a 'breakthrough' was little more than a further articulation, an extension of the 'Schleicherian Paradigm'.

5.0 *Concluding Remarks*

It is worth repeating that there was, in the last quarter of the 19th century, and especially from the early 1880s onwards, a change in the intellectual climate that led scholars of the period (not only linguists!) to become more aware of the differing nature of inquiry in the natural sciences (Naturwissenschaften) and in the human sciences (Kulturwissenschaften). This is clearly argued by Wilhelm Dilthey (1833-1911) in his *Einleitung in die Geisteswissenschaften* (Leipzig, 1883). This was the period when psychology, sociology, and political economy emerged as autonomous disciplines, a development which could not remain without repercussions within neighbouring fields, including linguistics. This influence of the social and behavioural sciences is clearly evident, for example, in Philipp Wegener's (1848-1916) *Untersuchungen über die Grundfragen des Sprachlebens* (Halle, 1885) which, however, received little attention by 19th-century linguists. Indeed, I have tried to argue that the incompatibility between theoretical claims and actual practice led, during the 1890s, to a crisis (though probably not perceived by most linguists of the time themselves) out of which the 'Saussurean Paradigm' began to take shape (cf. Koerner 1975a:759ff.). The change in the 'climate of opinion' helped the *Junggrammatiker* and others to free themselves from the Schleicherian 'yoke', at least as far as the naturalist views underlying Schleicher's metatheory were concerned.[20] Yet they continued, by and large, to work within the framework established by Schleicher and others before 1870. In sum, while noting the cumulative progress and the refinement in methodology that began with the year 1876, I dare to assert that there was nothing like a revolution taking place in linguistics in the 1870s as is frequently claimed.[21] This had to wait until the reflections on the substance and methods of linguistic science which occupied much of Saussure's attention during 1891-1911 came to light with the publication of his posthumous *Cours de linguistique générale* in 1916, exactly 100 years after Bopp's *Conjugationssystem*.

NOTES

1) The 'Humboldtian trend' (cf. Koerner 1977), concerned with general problems of language, linguistic typology, non-Indo-European languages, etc., played a secondary role in the development of the discipline, though the 20th century witnessed a revival of interest in this more philosophical approach to language.

2) We may note at least in passing that these histories were written in a nationalistic atmosphere prevailing in Germany in the 19th century, especially following the defeat of the Austrian armies by the Prussians in 1866 and the movement toward unification of the German-speaking lands. This explains the depiction of linguistics as an essentially German enterprise in these accounts.

3) Note that the 1924 Danish original was preceded by two earlier
studies by Pedersen on the same subject; cf. Koerner (1978a: 16 and 19)
for details on Pedersen 1899 and 1916.

4) Many other accounts of the period in question may be found in
Koerner (1978a); they reflect by and large the same views as those by
Benfey and Raumer. I have selected the latter two titles for the pre-
sent argument because they are the best known works of the period.

5) This sentiment, if wide-spread, may of course lead to a feeling of frustration among young, theory-oriented researchers. Eventually, they may look for alternative ways of conducting research, thereby
perhaps introducing a change of emphasis and a 'revolution' in the
Kuhnian sense of the term.

6) In private conversation Chomsky has conceded that Norman Kretz-
mann's claim, according to which Chomsky used history largely for polemic purposes, was not unfounded. Curiously enough, however, it seems
that Chomsky nevertheless regards his book as a serious contribution
to the history of linguistic thought.

7) It is true, however, that Delbrück displays more 'urbanitas' in
his account than modern linguists seeking to interpret history their
way.

8) For those interested in the history of the philology/linguis-
tics debate the following references may be mentioned to which a host
of others could be added: Georg Curtius (1820-85), *Die Sprachwissenschaft in ihrem Verhältnis zur klassischen Philologie* (Berlin: W. Bes-
ser, 1845; 2nd ed., 1848); Karl Brugmann (1849-1919), "Sprachwissenschaft und Philologie: Eine akademische Antrittsvorlesung", in Brugmann's *Zum heutigen Stand der Sprachwissenschaft* (Strassburg: K. J.
Trübner, 1885), pp.1-41. That this debate is still alive may be gathered from recents discussions, such as Kurt R. Jankowsky, "Philologie-
Linguistik — Literaturwissenschaft", *Lingua Posnaniensis* 17.21-35
(1973), and Dietrich Hofmann, "Sprachimmanente Methodenorientierung —
sprachtranszendente 'Objektivierung': Zum Unterschied zwischen Linguistik und Philologie", *Zeitschrift für Dialektologie und Linguistik* 40.
295-310 (1973). Since the late 1960s, a polemic distinction between
'Sprachwissenschaft' and 'Linguistik' in Germany (and, e.g., between
'glottologia' and 'linguistica' in Italy) has been made on occasion;
cf. Reiner Hildebrandt, "Linguistik contra Sprachwissenschaft", *Neuere
Forschungen in Linguistik und Philologie: Aus dem Kreise seiner Schüler
Ludwig Erich Schmitt zum 65. Geburtstag gewidmet* (Wiesbaden: F. Steiner, 1975), pp.1-6. — Interestingly enough, Raimo Anttila, in his paper "Linguistik und Philologie", which he contributed to Renate Bartsch
and Theo Vennemann's *Linguistik und Nachbarwissenschaften* (Kronberg im
Taunus: Scriptor, 1973), 177-91, made a strong plea in favour of a
stronger philological orientation of linguistics, whereas the editors
themselves in their contribution to the volume ("Linguistik", pp.9-20),
argue that 'Linguistik' is essentially the theoretical portion of
'Sprachwissenschaft'.

9) It may be said that Delbrück describes Schleicher in a manner
reminiscent of Chomsky's depiction of Bloomfield. Indeed, it appears
that scientists eager to promote what they regard as their 'original'

views tend to be patricidal.

10) Cf. the newly created periodical "Histoire – Epistémologie – Langage", published by the Societé d'Histoire et d'Epistémologie des Sciences du Langage (Paris), vol.I, No.1 (1979), p.57.

11) Even this term cannot be transferred to the discussion of the history of linguistics without modification. Kuhn (1970: 184) seems to associate it, at least partly, with what he calls 'metaphysical paradigms' or 'metaphysical parts of paradigms'. This aspect of science I would associate with what I termed 'Überbau' and not with the mechanics of the trade.

12) It is true that the concept of 'root' was introduced into Western linguistics through Hebrew grammar, perhaps already as early as the Renaissance, cf. Johann Reuchlin's *De rudimentis hebraicis* (Pforzheim: Thomas Anshelm, 1506). It was used by Justus Georg Schottel(ius) in his 655-page *Teutsche Sprachkunst* (Braunschweig: B. Gruber, 1641). However, I am not aware of any reference to Schottelius' book or any reference to Hebrew grammar with respect to this concept in 19th-century linguistics. It seems that the term had to be re-introduced into linguistics in the 19th century, just as many other insights of earlier centuries had to be rediscovered.

13) According to Jankowsky (1972: 94, n.1) the term 'Linguistik' "is first used around 1800, coinciding with the desire to align language with natural scientific procedure". However, Jankowsky does not cite a source for this usage. The first occurrence of the term I know of is the short-lived journal edited by Johann Severin Vater and Friedrich Justin Bertuch, *Allgemeines Archiv für Ethnographie und Linguistik* (Weimar, 1808). (Note that in German botany is called 'Botanik'.) For the much earlier use of the term 'Sprachwissenschaft' Jankowsky (1972: 93, note) refers to the title of a 1721 book by Johann Georg Ansorge (pseud. Melander), *Deutscher Rath und Lehrmeister, ... ; für Studierende wie auch für alle dieser edlen Sprachwissenschaft Beflissene* (Jena).

14) Even a scholar like Jacob Grimm (1785-1863), who is usually associated with a 'romanticist' view of language, makes explicit references to the natural sciences, especially to Linné's work in botany as a model for scientific research in linguistics (cf. Koerner 1980: 216-17, for details).

15) A similar observation has been made with regard to the transformational-generative school in linguistics; cf. Stephen O. Murray's paper, "Gatekeepers and the 'Chomskyan Revolution'", *Journal of the History of the Behavioral Sciences* 16.73-88 (1980).

16) Quoted after the 8th ed. (Paris: Hachette, 1937; repr., University, Ala.: Univ. of Alabama Press, 1964), pp.468-69. In his 1925 book, *La Méthode comparative en linguistique historique* (Oslo: Aschehoug & Co.; Leipzig: O. Harrassowitz, etc.; repr., Paris: H. Champion, 1966), Meillet speaks of the "principes posés entre 1875 et 1880" (p.vi).

17) Hoenigswald may have supplied the link between many of the important 1876 studies that van der Horst (1979: 34, n.1) finds missing in Koerner 1976b (cf. Hoenigswald 1978: 17-20). As regards the latter's second criticism that the paper is based on a methodological fault

according to which I began with the assumption that the year 1876 was
an important date, and that I was trying to supply significant publications for that date after the fact, I cannot but reply that I had been
fascinated (like Hoenigswald and others) by what appeared at first
sight to be sheer coincidence until I discovered the various connections between the publications in question.

18) Even Delbrück's voluminous output can hardly be cited as a
counter-example since he advanced no syntactic theory of his own, working instead along the lines of the ancient parts-of-speech tradition
in which the centre of attention is the word rather than the sentence.

19) Although Schleicher did not assign to 'analogy' the status of a
formal principle (cf. Schleicher 1876[1860]:61–62), it should not be
forgotten that he induced his pupil Jan Baudouin de Courtenay (1845–
1929) to give monograph treatment to just this subject; cf. Baudouin's
study, "Einige Fälle der Analogie in der polnischen Deklination",
(Schleicher & Kuhn's) *Beiträge zur vergleichenden Sprachforschung* 6.19–
88 (1869), completed in Jena in June 1868, half a year before Schleicher's death. Baudouin received a doctorate from the University of Leipzig in 1870 on the basis of this work.

20) That Schleicher's theories were felt to be oppressive by members
of the younger generation of linguists may be gathered from manuscript
notes by F. de Saussure (who studied in Leipzig and Berlin for four
years, 1876–1880) which date back to 1894. Talking about linguistics
prior to the advent of the *junggrammatische Richtung*: "... lorsque cette
science semble <triompher> de sa torpeur, elle aboutisse à l'essai ri-
sible de Schleicher, qui croule sous son propre ridicule. Tel a été le
prestige de Schleicher pour avoir simplement *essayé* de dire quelque
chose générale sur la langue, qu'il semble que ce soit une figure hors
pair <encore aujourd'hui> dans l'histoire des études <linguistiques>"
(Quoted after Rudolf Engler's critical edition of the *Cours* [Wiesbaden:
O. Harrassowitz, 1968], p.8). Saussure was a much more frustrated and
also much more aggressive man than the reader of the 'vulgata' edited
by Bally and Sechehaye might suspect.

21) Something like this was implied by Meillet and his collaborator
Joseph Vendryes, when they asserted, in the Preface to their joint *Traité de grammaire comparée des langues classiques* (Paris: H. Champion,
1924; 4th ed., 1966), that there had been "depuis une vingtaine d'an-
nées [i.e., since about 1900] aucune révolution comparable à celle qui
a transformée la grammaire comparée entre 1872 et 1880". In fact, comparative-historical linguistics has only in recent years received a
new outlook owing to the introduction of structuralist principles of
language study and the admission of sociological and psychological considerations in the explanation of language evolution. (This may explain the renewed interest in Paul's *Prinzipien* of 1880, 5th ed., 1920,
which was not even mentioned once in Pedersen's (1924/1931) history of
19th-century linguistics.)

REFERENCES*

Adam, Lucien. 1881. "La linguistique, est-elle une science naturelle ou une science historique?". *Revue de linguistique et de philologie comparée* 14.373-95.

Arbuckle, John. 1970. "August Schleicher and the Linguistics/Philology Dichotomy: A chapter in the history of linguistics". *Word* 26:1.17-31.

Becker, Carl L(otus). 1932. *The Heavenly City of the Eighteenth-Century Philosophers*. New Haven, Conn.: Yale Univ. Press. (35th printing, 1971.)

Benfey, Theodor. 1869. *Geschichte der Sprachwissenschaft und orientalischen Philologie in Deutschland*. Munich: J. G. Cotta.

Benware, Wilbur A(lan). 1974. *The Study of Indo-European Vocalism in the 19th Century; from the beginnings to Whitney and Scherer: A critical-historical account*. Amsterdam: J. Benjamins.

Blümel, Wolfgang. 1978. "Zu den methodischen Grundsätzen der junggrammatischen Richtung". *Sprachwissenschaft* 3:1.83-96.

Blumenthal, Arthur L. 1970. *Language and Psychology: Historical aspects of psycholinguistics*. New York: J. Wiley & Sons.

Bronstein, Arthur J., et al. 1977. *Biographical Dictionary of the Phonetic Sciences*. New York: Press of Lehman College.

Brugmann, Karl. 1879. "Zur Geschichte der Nominalsuffixe -as-, -jas- und -vas-". (Kuhn's) *Zeitschrift für vergleichende Sprachforschung* 24.1-99.

_____. 1885. *Zum heutigen Stand der Sprachwissenschaft*. Strassburg: K. J. Trübner. (Repr. in Wilbur 1977.)

Butterfield, (Sir) Herbert. 1931. *The Whig Interpretation of History*. London: G. Bell & Sons. (Repr., 1968.)

Collitz, Hermann. 1883. "Der germanische Ablaut und sein Verhältnis zum indogermanischen Vokalismus". *Zeitschrift für deutsche Philologie* 15.1-10.

_____. 1886. *Die neueste Sprachforschung und die Erklärung des indogermanischen Ablautes*. Göttigen: Vandenhoeck & Ruprecht. (Repr. in Wilbur 1977.)

Delbrück, Berthold. 1880. *Einleitung in das Sprachstudium: Ein Beitrag zur Methodik der vergleichenden Sprachforschung*. [Later editions were titled *Einführung in das Stdium der indogermanischen Sprachen*.] Leipzig: Breitkopf & Härtel. (2nd ed., 1884; 4th ed., 1904; 6th rev. and enl. ed., 1919.)

_____. 1882. *Introduction to the Study of Language: A critical survey of the history and methods of comparative philology of Indo-European languages*. Transl. by Eva Channing. Ibid. (New ed., Amsterdam: J. Benjamins, 1974.)

Dilthey, Wilhelm. 1883. *Einleitung in die Geisteswissenschaften: Versuch einer Grundlegung für das Studium der Gesellschaft und der Geschichte*. Erster Band. Leipzig: Duncker & Humblot.

* For reasons of economy a number of well-known titles have not been included in the present bibliography; they may be found in Koerner 1978a, together with comments and references to reviews.

Hoenigswald, Henry M(ax). 1974. "Fallacies in the History of Linguistics: Notes on the appraisal of the 19th century". *Studies in the
History of Linguistics* ed. by Dell Hymes, 346-58. Bloomington & London: Indiana Univ. Press.
_____. 1978. "The *annus mirabilis* 1876 and Posterity". *Transac-
tions of the Philological Society (Commemorative volume 'The Neogrammarians') 1978*.17-35.
_____. 1980. "A Reconstruction". *First Person Singular: Papers
from the Conference on an Oral Archive for the History of American
Linguistics (Charlotte, 9-10 March 1979)*, ed. by Boyd H. Davis and
Raymond K. O'Cain, 23-28. Amsterdam: J. Benjamins.
Jankowsky, Kurt R(obert). 1972. *The Neogrammarians: A re-evaluation of
their place in the development of linguistic science*. The Hague: Mouton.
King, Robert D(esmond). 1969. *Historical Linguistics and Generative
Grammar*. Englewood Cliffs, N.J.: Prentice-Hall.
Koerner, E(rnst) F(rideryk) K(onrad). 1974. "Four Types of History-
Writing in Linguistics". *Historiographia Linguistica* 1.1-10. (Rev.
and abridged version in Koerner 1978b.53-62.)
_____. 1975a. "European Structuralism - early beginnings". *Current
Trends in Linguistics* ed. by Thomas A. Sebeok, vol.XIII: *Historiography of Linguistics*, 717-827. The Hague: Mouton.
_____. 1975b. "Zu Ursprung und Geschichte der Besternung in der
historischen Sprachwissenschaft: Eine historiographische Notiz".
(Kuhn's) *Zeitschrift für vergleichende Sprachforschung* 89:2.185-90.
(Repr. in Koerner 1978b.211-16.)
_____. 1976a[1972]. "Towards a Historiography of Linguistics: 19th
and 20th century paradigms". *History of Linguistic Thought and Contemporary Linguistics* ed. by Herman Parret, 685-718. Berlin & New
York: W. de Gruyter. (An earlier version appeared in *Anthropological
Linguistics* 14.255-80; repr. in Koerner 1978b.21-54.)
_____. 1976b. "1876 as a Turning Point in the History of Linguis-
tics". *Journal of Indo-European Studies* 4.333-53. (Repr. in Koerner
1978b.189-209.)
_____. 1977[1973]. "The Humboldtian Trend in Linguistics". *Studies
in Descriptive and Historical Linguistics: Festschrift for Winfred P.
Lehmann* ed. by Paul J. Hopper, 145-58. Amsterdam: J. Benjamins.
_____. 1978a. *Western Histories of Linguistic Thought, 1822-1976:
An annotated chronological bibliography*. Ibid.
_____. 1978b. *Toward a Historiography of Linguistics: Selected Es-
says*. Foreword by R. H. Robins. Ibid.
_____. 1979. "L'importance de William Dwight Whitney pour les
jeunes linguistes de Leipzig et pour F. de Saussure". *Studies in Diachronic, Synchronic, and Typological Linguistics: Festschrift for Oswald Szemerényi* ed. by Bela Brogyanyi, 437-54. Amsterdam: J. Benjamins.
_____. 1980. "Pilot and Parasite Disciplines in the Development of
Linguistic Science". *Folia Linguistica Historica* 1.213-24.
Kuhn, Thomas S(amuel). 1970. *The Structure of Scientific Revolutions*.
2nd enl. ed. Chicago: Univ. of Chicago Press. (1st ed., 1962.)
Osthoff, Hermann. 1879. *Das physiologische und das psychologische Mo-*

ment in der sprachlichen Formenbildung. Berlin: C. Habel.
Pedersen, Holger. 1931. *Linguistic Science in the Nineteenth Century*.
  Transl. from the Danish by John Webster Spargo. Cambridge, Mass.:
  Harvard Univ. Press. (Repr., under the new title of 'The Discovery
  of Language', Bloomington, Ind.: Indiana Univ Press, 1962.)
Putschke, Wolfgang. 1969. "Zur forschungsgeschichtlichen Stellung der
  junggrammatischen Schule". *Zeitschrift für Dialektologie und Linguis-
  tik* 36.19-48.
Ranke, Leopold von. 1824. *Zur Kritik neuerer Geschichtsschreiber; eine
  Beylage zu desselben romanischen und germanischen Geschichten*. Leipzig & Berlin: G. Reimer.
Raumer, Rudolf von. 1870. *Geschichte der germanischen Philologie*. Munich: R. Oldenbourg. (Repr., New York: Johnson, 1965.)
Růžička, Rudolf. 1977. *Historie und Historizität der Junggrammatiker*.
  Berlin: Akademie-Verlag.
Schleicher, August. 1850. *Die Sprachen Europas in systematischer Uebersicht: Linguistische Untersuchungen*. Bonn: H. B. König. (New ed., Amsterdam: J. Benjamins, 1982.)
_____. 1852. *Formenlere [sic] der kirchenslawischen Sprache, er-
  klärend und vergleichend dargestellt*. Bonn: H. B. König.
_____. 1855. "Kurzer Abriss der Geschichte der slawischen Spra-
  che". *Oesterreichische Blätter für Literatur und Kunst* No.19 (7 May
  1855). (Repr. in *Beiträge zur vergleichenden Sprachforschung* 1.1-27,
  1857.)
_____. 1856-57. *Handbuch der litauischen Sprache*. 2 vols. Prague:
  J. G. Calve.
_____. 1858. *Volkstümliches aus Sonneberg im Meininger Oberlande*.
  Weimar: H. Böhlau. (2nd ed., Sonneberg: C. Albrecht [in Commission],
  1894.)
_____. 1859. *Zur Morphologie der Sprache*. St.Petersburg: Kaiserl.
  Akad. der Wissenschaften.
_____. 1863. *Die Darwinsche Theorie und die Sprachwissenschaft*.
  Weimar: H. Böhlau.
_____. 1876[1860]. *Die deutsche Sprache*. 3rd ed. Stuttgart: J. G.
  Cotta. [2nd and 3rd ed. were prepared by Johannes Schmidt.]
_____. 1876[1861-62]. *Compendium der vergleichenden Grammatik der
  indogermanischen Sprachen*. 4th ed. prepared by Johannes Schmidt and
  August Leskien. Weimar: H. Böhlau.
Shapere, Dudley. 1964. "The Structure of Scientific Revolutions". *The
  Philosophical Review* 73.383-94.
van der Horst, J. M. 1979. "Van organisme naar mechanisme; 1870". *Taal-
  verandering in Nederlandse dialejten: Honderd jaar dialektvragenlij-
  sten 1879-1979* ed. by Marinel Gerretsen, 21-35. Muiderberg/Holland:
  D. Coutinho.
Wegener, Philipp. 1885. *Untersuchungen über die Grundfragen des Sprach-
  lebens*. Halle/S.: M. Niemeyer.
Whitney, William Dwight. 1871. "Strictures on the Views of August
  Schleicher respecting the Nature of Language and Kindred Subjects".
  Transactions of the American Philological Association 2.35-64. (Repr.,
  under the title of "August Schleicher and the Physical Theory of

Language", in Whitney *Oriental and Linguistic Studies: The Veda; the Avesta; the Science of Language*, vol.I, 298-331. New York: Scribner, Armstrong & Co., 1873 [actually already published in Oct. 1872]. Repr., Freeport, N.Y.: Books for Libraries Press, 1972.)

Wilbur, Terence H(arrison), ed. and introd., 1977. *The "Lautgesetz"-Controversy: A documentation*. Amsterdam: J. Benjamins. [Reprints the 1885-86 monographs by Curtius, Brugmann, Delbruck, and others concerning the 'neue Richtung, in historical-comparative linguistics.]

Addendum:

Christmann, Hans Helmut, ed. & introd. 1977. *Sprachwissenschaft des 19. Jahrhunderts*. Darmstadt: Wissenschaftliche Buchgesellschaft.

OBSERVATIONS ON THE SOURCES, TRANSMISSION, AND MEANING OF 'INDO-EUROPEAN' AND RELATED TERMS IN THE DEVELOPMENT OF LINGUISTICS

KONRAD KOERNER
University of Ottawa

0. *Introductory Remarks.* Almost four generations ago, Heymann Stein-thal (1823-99) tried to demonstrate to his contemporaries, in the Pre-face to his voluminous *Geschichte der Sprachwissenschaft bei den Grie-chen und Römern*, the importance of writing the history of 19th-century linguistics, citing what he believed to be a revealing example:

> Wie notwendig aber eine Geschichte der Sprachwissenschaft un-sres Jahrhunderts schon wäre, dafür will ich hier ein Beispiel geben. Woher stammt der Name "indogermanisch"? Wäre es nicht wichtig und anziehend dies zu wissen? Gruppirt sich doch, möch-te ich sagen, die ganze neuere Sprachwissenschaft um jenen Namen? (Steinthal 1890:X-XI)

Steinthal noted that accounts in linguistic books until then had been misleading on the sources of the term 'indogermanisch', and he wondered about its true origin, especially since other terms had been used to group together the family of languages for which 'Indo-European' has become the most widely accepted term. Indeed, Steinthal also wondered about the origin of the latter term, though he seems to believe that *indogermanisch* "Indo-Germanic" is the earlier coinage.[1]

Steinthal (1890:XII) believed that he had found the original source in Friedrich Schmitthenner's (1796-1850) use of 'indisch-teutsch' both in the subtitle and within the text of his *Ursprachlehre* of 1826, an observation which was soon contradicted by Gustav Meyer (1850-1900) in an article devoted to the question raised by Steinthal (Meyer 1893).[2]

Subsequent research into the question of the origin and use of the
term 'Indo-European' as well as the various related expressions such
as 'Indo-Germanic', 'Aryan', and others (e.g., Meyer 1901, Norman 1929,
Siegert 1941/42) have made it clear that we have to do with a rather
complex situation. The fact that these terms were used not only by
linguists but also by writers outside the realm of the study of language, for instance by geographers, anthropologists, and biologists,
added to the complexity.

In the present paper[3] I will first discuss the development of the
concept of 'Indo-European' and its various appellations (1.0) and subsequently trace the origin and meaning of the three most frequently
used terms in 19th-century comparative-historical works, namely, 'Indo-European' (2.0), 'Indo-Germanic' or *indogermanisch* (3.0), and 'Aryan' (4.0). In the conclusion (5.0) an argument will be presented in
favour of the universal use of 'Indo-European', not only outside German-speaking lands.

1.0 *Notes on the development of the concept of 'Indo-European'*

As is evident from the history of any discipline, whether a natural or a social science, inventions and discoveries often precede the
respective terms that are used to describe or refer to them. The history of linguistics is no exception. Although it may be important to
note when and where a particular coinage was first introduced into the
technical terminology — indeed, such coinages may signal the incep-
tion of or a particular turning-point in the professionalization of a
field — we should not be surprised to discover that the concept of a
particular observation antedates the descriptive term. Thus, we might
wish to date the beginning of linguistics as an autonomous discipline
from the early 19th century, but this would not automatically suggest
that earlier findings are necessarily erroneous and 'unscientific'.[4]

Since the Renaissance, when the educated classes turned their attention to the vernaculars of Europe, many scholars and writers have
realized that there are a number of languages which are genetically
related; cf. the works by Claude Saumaise (1588-1653), Marcus Zuerius

Boxhorn (1602-1653), and others, in which the hypothesis of a unity between certain Asian and a number of European languages was promoted (cf. Droixhe 1978:86ff., for expatiation). This proto-language from which these others were said to have derived was called 'Scythian' after the name of an ancient nomadic people of southeastern Europe and Asia of Iranian origin. From the early 18th century onwards, especially owing to Leibniz's writings on these questions, the term 'Japhetic' (in contradistinction to those languages that were later grouped together by the name 'Semitic') became general currency among scholars of language. In fact, Rasmus Kristian Rask (1787-1832) still used (Danish) *japetisk* in the sense of "Indo-European" (cf. Diderichsen 1974:303, n.6, where Rask's other appellations, e.g., *gotisk* for "Germanic", are cited).[5]   During the second half of the 19th century, after Celtic had finally been admitted as a branch of the Indo-European language family, several scholars, in recognition of the fact that the languages of this branch are the most western ones in terms of geographic distribution, suggested the term 'Indo-Celtic' (cf. Siegert 1941/42:83, for details).

    Still other terms were suggested to denote the Indo-European language family. Humboldt, in a paper read before the Berlin Academy of Sciences on 26 April 1827, suggested the term 'Sanskritisch' (Humboldt 1827:18, n. = 1963:129-30, n.2), adding the following explanation for his preference:

> Dieser Ausdruck dürfte sich für die mit dem Sanskrit zusammen-
> hängenden Sprachen, die man neuerlich auch Indo-Germanische ge-
> nannt hat, nicht bloss durch seine Kürze, sondern auch durch sei-
> ne innre Angemessenheit empfehlen, da Sanskritische Sprachen, der
> Bedeutung des Worts nach, Sprachen kunstreichen und zierlichen
> Baues sind.[6]

We may gather from this argument that the question of appropriateness was raised at a very early time in regard to the usage of 'Indo-Germanic'. We should remember, however, that Sanskrit was then still regarded by many as representing, if not the original proto-language, the language closely representing it. Franz Bopp (1791-1867), who had been teaching Sanskrit to the much older Wilhelm von Humboldt (1767-

1835), avoided a general term in his earlier writings. In the preface
to his *Vergleichende Grammatik des Sanskrit, Send, Armenischen, Griechischen ... und Deutschen* (Bopp 1833:V) he makes a passing reference
to the 'indisch-europäischer Sprachstamm' but he does not seem to use
the term in the text. In fact, in the preface to the second edition
of his Comparative Grammar, Bopp expressed himself against the use of
'Indo-Germanic', clearly favouring 'Indo-European':

> Ich nenne den Sprachstamm, dessen wichtigste Glieder in diesem
> Buche zu einem Ganzen vereinigt werden, den indoeuropäischen,
> wozu der Umstand, daß mit Ausnahme des finnischen Sprachzweigs,
> sowie des ganz vereinzelt stehenden Baskischen und des von den
> Arabern uns hinterlassenen semitischen Idioms der Insel Maltha
> alle übrigen europäischen Sprachen ... ihm angehören. (Bopp
> 1857:XXIV)

It is interesting to note that the authority of the acknowledged foun-
der of comparative-historical grammar in Europe was not sufficient to
persuade the majority of scholars in German-speaking lands to adopt
the term 'Indo-European' (rather than 'Indo-Germanic' or another term).
It appears that the (probably first) use of 'Indo-Germanic' in the tit-
le-page of a very influential book of the period, namely, August Friedrich Pott's (1802-1887) *Etymologische Forschungen auf dem Gebiete der
Indo-Germanischen[7] Sprachen* (1833-36) had a considerable impact on the
minds of Pott's contemporaries. From the mid-19th century onwards,
'Indo-Germanic' (*indogermanisch*) became the most frequently used term
in the German literature. Even 'indo-germanique' and 'Indo-Germanic'
are frequently found in the writings of Frenchmen and Englishmen respectively, though 'Indo-European' and 'indo-européen' remained by and
large the most common expressions.

However, there was yet another term which had fairly wide currency in the 19th century, namely, 'Aryan'. In fact, from the early 1860s
onwards, the Oxford professor of Sanskrit, Friedrich Max Müller (1823-
1900), used 'Aryan' in lieu of 'Indo-European', and it appears to be
owing to his very popular writings on language, philosophy, and many
other subjects that this term became widely used in the Anglo-Saxon
world. Müller justified his preference (similar to the manner in which
other scholars had justified their particular term) by saying that,

if 'Aryan' is not a better term to denote the language family in
question, it is at least the shorter one (Müller 1872:11). Compare
Heinrich Zimmer's (1851-1910) explanation for his use of the term:
"Ich bediene mich des Ausdrucks arisch statt indogermanisch oder indoeuropäisch, ohne jedoch damit sagen zu wollen, er sei richtiger als
jene; kürzer und bequemer ist er jedenfalls." (Zimmer 1876:5 note)

     Hermann Osthoff (1847-1909), commenting on Zimmer's usage, replied
to what he believed to be   'eine nicht zu billigende Laune' on the
part of the author in the following terms:

> Nach einer einheitlichen terminologie in der benennung unseres
> sprachstammes muss nachgerade gestrebt werden und da haben vor
> allen benennungen, objectiv geurteilt, doch nur entweder 'indo-
> germanisch' oder 'indoeuropäisch' aussicht auf dauer. Wem 'in-
> dogermanisch' zu lang ist, kann ja, namentlich in einem druck-
> werke, abkürzungen gebrauchen: 'indog.' oder gar 'idg.'. (Ost-
> hoff 1876:6, note)

We now know that Osthoff was entirely correct in his predictions, and
also that his suggested abbreviations, especially the second one, have
become generally adopted by historical linguists writing in German. We
will see in the following sections of this paper how these predictions
came true, not to mention other developments in the usage of certain
terms not anticipated by Osthoff.

2.0 *On the origin of 'Indo-European'*

     Although the review article of the first two volumes of Johann
Christoph Adelung's (1732-1806) largely posthumous *Mithridates, oder
Allgemeine Sprachenkunde* (Berlin: Voss, 1806-1809)[8] appeared anonym-
ously, it has been established that its author was the English natural
scientist and Egyptologist Thomas Young (1773-1829), a very close contemporary of Friedrich Schlegel (1772-1829). Apart from the ascrip-
tion, which appears to be well established (cf. Siegert 1941/42:75-76,
n.4, for details), it seems to be generally accepted in the literature (e.g., Norman 1929; Rocher 1960) that Young was in effect at the
origin of the term 'Indo-European'. Indeed, in his 43-page account
of the allegedly 'nearly five hundred languages and dialects' (which
Young [1813:254] reduces to a much smaller figure) Young adopts a much

more organized position than Adelung, "more dependent on the nature and
connection of the languages themselves" (Young 1813:253) than the more
or less haphazard collection of data displayed by the compiler of the
Mithridates.

It is when discussing the various languages of the globe (their
genetic relationship as well as their geographic distribution) that
Young introduces the term 'Indo-European':

> Another ancient and extensive class of languages, united by a
> greater number of resemblances than can well be altogether acci-
> dental, may be denominated the Indoeuropean, comprehending the
> Indian, the West Asiatic, and almost all the European languages.
> If we chose to assign a geographic situation to the common parent
> of this class, we should place it to the south and west of the
> supposed origin of the human race [i.e., southeastern Europe ac-
> cording to theories of the day]; ... (Young 1813:255)

In order to refute the suggestion found in the fourteenth edition of
the *Encyclopaedia Britannica* of 1929 (vol.12, p.262), namely, that
Young was using the term "without any remark as to its being a new
coinage", Siegert (1941/42:76) quotes several other passages from
Young's review. For instance, in the lines immediately following the
above citation, Young used the phrase 'may be called' again, indicating that he was proposing a new term or at least a particular usage:

> ... leaving the north for our third class, which we can only
> define as including all the Asiatic and European languages not
> belonging to the former; which may be called Atactic, or, per-
> haps, without much propriety, Tataric; and which may be subdiv-
> ided into five orders, Sporadic, Caucasian, Tartarian, Siberian,
> and Insular.

Indeed, Young makes use of 'Indo-European' throughout his review (e.g.,
pp.264, 270, 273, 281) in the sense of "common parent (language)" and
did not repeat Friedrich Schlegel's (1808:3) error of identifying this
proto-language with Sanskrit.[9] It is true that Young did not identify
all the languages belonging to the Indo-European family, and not all
of them correctly. However, his list is fairly complete (p.256), and
includes Celtic, for instance, which only much later was recognized as
a branch of Indo-European: "The *Celtic* family is a very extensive and
very interesting subdivision of the Indoeuropean class" (p.273). On the
other hand, Young (probably following N. B. Halhed's[10] suggestions) in-

cluded Arabic, though he further on (p.267) modified his view by stating that,

> ... though not intimately connected with the European languages, it [i.e., Arabic] is well known to have afforded some words to the Greek and Latin, and it has also some terms in common with the Sanskrit though apparently fewer than either the Greek or the German.

Young shows a similar oscillation with regard to Armenian, which he classifies (p.256), together with Ossetic and Albanian - which we now recognize as Indo-European languages, among the 'Caucausian' language family, when he concedes (p.285) that there are sufficient connections between Armenian and Sanskrit as well as Persian "that the coincidences may have been derived from a common parent."

With regard to the Balto-Slavic group, Young (p.281) affirmed: "The connexion of the Sclavonian and Lithuanian, which we have comprehended in the title of the *Sclavic* family, with the other of the Indoeuropean class, is sufficiently established." We may summarize his general views on Indo-European by quoting a longer passage from the same account (264-65):

> The Indoeuropean languages we have to referred to as a single class, because every one of them has too great a number of coincidences with some of the others, to be considered as merely accidental, and many of them in terms of relating to objects of such a nature, that they must necessarily have been original rather than adoptive. The *Sanscrit*, which is confessedly the parent language of India, may easily be shown to be intimately connected with the Greek, the Latin, and the German, although it is a great exaggeration to assert any thing like its identity with either of these languages.

Although neither cites the above statement, both Norman (1929:318) and Siegert (1941/42:76) are convinced that Young was at the origin of the term 'Indo-European'. The late Frederick Norman (1897-1968) asserted that "from the manner in which Young introduces the word it is tolerably certain that he coined the expression."

In view of what we will gather from the next section of the present paper, it is interesting to note that Siegert (1941/42), who, without having seen Norman's article, was convinced of Young's authorship of the term,[11] asserted (p.77): "Eine Entlehnung des Ausdrucks [i.e.,

the German equivalent 'Indo-Europäisch', as found in Pott 1833:XXX]
aus dem Englischen halte ich allerdings für unwahrscheinlich, da die
Abhandlung YOUNGs in Deutschland kaum bekannt war." If this is so,
it would mean that the German 'indo-europäisch' as well as the French
'indo-européen' have other sources than Young's 'Indoeuropean'.[12]

3.0 *On the origin of 'Indo-Germanic'*

Following Steinthal's (1890:X-XII) efforts to trace the source of
the term 'indogermanisch', several scholars have further investigated
the subject. G. Meyer (1893:127-28) quoted various passages from Julius (Heinrich von) Klaproth (1783-1835), a German scholar who had been
associated with the Academy of Sciences at St.Petersburg for a number
of years. He used both 'Indo-Germanen' and 'Indo-Germanisch' quite frequently in his voluminous survey of the languages of Asia (and also of
other continents, notably Europe), *Asia Polyglotta*, written in German,
but published in Paris in 1823 (cf. Klaproth 1823a:42,43,56,62,74,75,
84,97,108,210,244). However, G. Meyer (p.128) doubted that Klaproth
was in effect the coiner of these terms, and Leo Meyer (1830-1910), cov-
ering roughly the same ground, noted several years later: "Klaproth
gebraucht ... den Namen 'Indo-Germanisch' wie einen ganz bekannten"
(Meyer 1901:455-56).

In view of these doubts cast upon the authorship of Klaproth, it
is interesting to note, as Siegert in his well-informed article of 1941
does, that Klaproth spoke, in the first (and only) volume of the *Archiv
für asiatische Litteratur, Geschichte und Sprachenkunde* (St.Petersburg,
1810) of a "großen *Indisch-Medisch-Sclavisch-Germanischen* Völkerkette"
(p.81; Meyer 1893:128). This reference to a 'large chain of peoples'
suggested to Siegert (1941/42:80): "Was liegt da näher als die Annahme,
KLAPROTH habe selbst ein solches Kompositum an dieser Stelle [i.e., in
Asia Polygotta] zum ersten Male gekürzt."

If Siegert's hypothesis is correct, it would mean that Klaproth
used the two endpoints of the above concatenation to embrace the large
language family, and to render the rather unwieldy expression somewhat
more manageable. This suggestion would also refute another hypothesis

according to which Klaproth was merely contracting an ad-hoc compound suggested by Friedrich Schlegel in his review of Johann Gottlieb Rhode's (1762-1827) 78-page booklet, *Über den Anfang unserer Geschichte* (Schlegel 1819:456, note = 1975:516, note), namely "indisch-lateinisch-persisch-germanische Sprachfamilie", which Schlegel reduced also to 'indisch-lateinisch-germanisch' in the same footnote (cf. Meyer 1893:125-126; Siegert 1941/42:79). Indeed, despite the impact of Schlegel's *Ueber die Sprache und Weisheit der Indier* (1808) on linguistic scholarship at the beginning of the 19th century, it is doubtful that Klaproth would have taken note of Schlegel's review article devoted to a subject which has little to do with language — not to mention the fact that, following his conversion to Catholicism in 1808, Schlegel had abandoned linguistic investigations altogether.

Before suggesting another source for 'Indo-Germanic', let us cite the first instance in Klaproth's book in which the term is used. In his proposed survey of the peoples of Asia according to the languages they speak, Klaproth starts with the 'Indo-Germanen'[13], describing the members of this family in the following terms:

> Dieses ist der am weitesten verbreitete Stamm in der Welt, denn seine Wohnsitze fangen in Zeilon an, gehen über Vorder-Indien und Persien, über den Kaukasus, nach Europa, welchen Erdtheil er fast ganz inne hat, bis zu den Shetlandinseln, dem Nord-Kap und Island. Zu ihm gehören Indier, Perser, Afgᶜanen, Kurden, Meder, Osseten, Armenier, Slawen, Deutsche, Dänen, Schweden, Normänner, Engländer, Griechen, Lateiner und alle von Lateinern abstammenden Völker Europas. (Klaproth 1823a:42)

Published seven years after Bopp's *Conjugationssystem* (1816), Klaproth's list constitutes a noticeable improvement over the one supplied by Young ten years earlier, though Klaproth appears to exclude Celtic (cf. p.43), which Young (1813:256) did count among the Indo-European languages. Interestingly enough, in the French translation of his *Reise in den Kaukasus* (Halle, 1812-14), which Klaproth published in Paris in the same year as *Asia Polyglotta*, Celtic is compared with Ossetic and other Indo-European languages (Klaproth 1823b II, 469ff.)

More importantly perhaps, in the linguistic portion of his *Voyage au Mont Caucase* Klaproth (1823b II, 437) states: "Les Ossètes ... ap-

partiennent à la souche des nations indo-germaniques en Asie." And
on page 440, he affirms that "la langue des Ossètes prouve ... qu'ils
appartiennent à la même souche que les Mèdes et les Perses, c'est-à-
dire, à l'indo-germanique." Siegert (1941/42:80), who quotes these
and other passages (especially one, p.449, which demonstrates beyond
any doubt that Klaproth meant "Indo-European" by *indogermanique*), is
persuaded to believe that all "diese Tatsachen deuten ... darauf hin,
daß die Bezeichnung von KLAPROTH 1823 geschaffen worden ist."

We have noted earlier that other scholars (G. Meyer 1893; Leo
Meyer 1901) doubted Klaproth's authorship of the term. Also Norman
(1929:314) suggested that the fact that Klaproth "who constantly employs 'Indogermanen' and 'indogermanisch' without explaining his terminology", might have "either used the term in earlier work where he
explained it or ... found it in the writings of another philologist:
no such reference has as yet appeared."

With respect to the first conjecture, we may safely assume that
Klaproth did not use 'Indo-Germanisch' in his pre-1823 publications;
this possibility has already been thoroughly investigated by G. Meyer
(1893) and confirmed by research undertaken by Siegert (1941/42). Norman's second suggestion that Klaproth took the term from another philologist must remain an open question until all relevant writings of
the period have been inspected. I, for one, doubt it, especially ·in
view of Shapiro's recent findings, which suggest quite another source
from which Klaproth might have drawn. In what follows, pertinent information has been taken from this paper (Shapiro 1981), though the
suggested connections are all my own.

In his review of Rhode (1819), F. Schlegel refers to the 'mosai-
sche Weltkarte' in the Atlas of the 'berühmte Geograph' Malte-Brun
(Schlegel 1975:480, n.*). It is true that Rhode's book has to do with
historical-geological and geographic speculations which explain Schlegel's reference to such a work. However, this mention also suggests
that the geographer in question, the Danish-born Frenchman Conrad Malte-Brun (1775-1826), was indeed a well-known figure at the time. He
had settled in Paris soon after his banishment from Denmark in 1800,

founded the *Annales des Voyages* (1808-1814), and was one of the co-foun-
ders of the Société de Géographie de Paris. (It may be that Schlegel,
who spent several years in Paris between 1802 and 1806, knew Malte-Brun
personally, as he was acquainted with Georges Cuvier (1769-1832).)

Klaproth, the Berlin-born traveller and Orientalist, had settled in
Paris in 1815. He received, owing to an intervention of Wilhelm von
Humboldt, the title and salary of professor of Asiatic languages and
literature from the King of Prussia, with permission to remain in
Paris as long as he required for the publication of his works. (As a
matter of fact, Klaproth died in Paris in 1835.) I do not know whether
Klaproth made Malte-Brun's personal acquaintance, but there is no doubt
in my mind that Klaproth consulted the voluminous *Précis de la géographie universelle*, which appeared in Paris from 1810 onwards (and was
completed by others in 1829), when revising the French version of his
1812-14 report on his travels to the Caucasus and Georgia, namely, the
Voyage au Mont Caucase et en Géorgie (Paris, 1823; new ed., 1836). As
we have noted above, Klaproth used the term 'indogermanique' quite
frequently, a term not found in the German original. We may presume
that, if Klaproth did not coin the terms 'Indo-Germanisch' and 'indo-
germanique' himself, he must have come across them after his departure
from Berlin in 1815.[14]

In this connection, it is interesting to note (as Shapiro has recently done) that in the second volume of Malte-Brun's *Précis de la
géographie universelle* (Paris, 1810), in which the author attempts a general overview of the world's languages, we find the statement: "Nous
nommerons en premier lieu la famille des *langues indo-germaniques*, qui
règnent depuis les bords du Gange jusqu'aux rivages de l'Islande" (Malte-Brun 1810:577). (This statement is repeated in the 1812 edition.)

Proceeding in the (at least since Schlegel's book of 1808) 'traditional' fashion, Malte-Brun, in the 'livre quarante-cinquième' of
his work, begins his enumeration with Sanskrit in the east, and ends
with the 'langues germaniques' in the west, with Persian, Greek, Latin, and 'les langues slavonnes' (and their various modern daughter
languages) in between (Malte-Brun 1810:577-78). Like Young (1813:256),

he excludes Armenian and, like Klaproth (1823:43), the Celtic languages from the 'langues indo-germaniques' (p.579). There is no hint
in Malte-Brun's *Précis* that he was introducing a new term. Indeed, it
would be injustifiable to expect the geographer to invent such an expression. Rather, it must be assumed that Malte-Brun drew this information from another, possibly linguistic, source.

It seems likely that Klaproth took the term from the *Précis*, but
the question remains where did Malte-Brun take his term from? To this
question, it appears, an answer could be found by establishing Malte-
Brun's sources, perhaps his personal library and other books generally
accessible to someone working in Paris during the early 1800s.

The later history of the use of 'Indo-Germanic' by 19th-century
and early 20th-century linguists is well established. It seems clear
to me that Humboldt, in his 1827 paper "Ueber den Dualis", was referring to (his beneficiary) Klaproth when he made a reference to the new
appellation 'Indo-Germanisch' (cf. the quotation, p.161 supra). Similarly, I am inclined to believe that Pott, in the preface to his *Etymologische Forschungen* (1833:XXX), was thinking of Humboldt's (and probably also to his former teacher Bopp's) objection to this term, when
he spoke of "Der Sanskritsprachstamm, — oder mag man, ihn den Indo-
Europäischen, Indo-Germanischen zu benennen, vorziehen, — ...", though
in effect he was opting for the last of the three terms.

In 1840, Pott contributed a 112-page article on 'indogermanischer
Sprachstamm' to Joh. Samuel Ersch (1766-1828) and Joh. Gottfried Gruber's
(1774-1851) *Allgemeine Encyclopädie der Wissenschaften*, in which he
sets out to justify his choice:

> Verschiedene Benennungen jenes Stammes. Die Verlegenheit, für
> Völker und Sprachen passende Collectivbenennungen aufzufinden,
> zeigt sich in vollem Masse auch bei dem hier in Frage kommenden
> Sprachstamm, dessen von uns gewählter Name (Indogermanisch), so
> viel sonst gegen seine Zweckmässigkeit einwenden lässt, wenig-
> stens sehr gangbar und allgemein verständlich geworden ist. (Pott
> 1840:1)

Somewhat later (on the same page), he expresses himself against 'Indo-
European' in the following terms:

> Der von Andern in Anwendung gebrachte Ausdruck: 'Indo-Europäisch'

hält vor einer mürrischen Kritik noch weniger Stich: weitgefehlt
nämlich, daß in Ostindien (nicht einmal die diesseitige Halbinsel
hat lauter sanskritische Idiome) und in Europa sämmtliche Sprachen verwandtschaftlich unter einander und mit dem von uns be-
sprochenen Stamme verbunden wären, zählt vielmehr jenes Land ...
in gleicher Weise als unser Erdteil, nicht wenig Sprachen völlig
anderen Ursprungs und Wesens, als die sind, welche man unter obi-
gem Ausdrucke befaßt.[15]

Although 'Indo-Germanic' continued to be used in the English-speaking

world until the end of the 19th century by several scholars (cf. Norman

1929:320, for relevant references)[16] there can be no doubt that either

'Indo-European' or, following Max Müller's usage, 'Aryan' were the most

frequently employed terms. It is interesting to note that Leo Meyer

(1901:451) argued that indeed 'Indo-Germanic' is older than 'Indo-Euro-

pean', especially in view of Shapiro's (1981) findings:

> Die Benennung "indogermanisch" ist eben die erste, die als zu-
> sammenfassende für den als nah zusammengehörig und wirklich ver-
> wandt erkannten Sprachstamm gebraucht worden ist und sie faßt auch
> in sehr zweckmäßiger Weise die Sprache des im fernen Osten weit-
> ausgedehnten indischen Gebietes und der gerade in der Mitte Euro-
> pas weitausgedehnten Germanen zusammen, um ein großes Ganzes zu
> bezeichnen, das man doch nicht wohl mit Aufzählung aller seiner
> Hauptteile bequem nennen konnte.

Indeed, it could have been argued, at least until Celtic had (by the

mid-19th century) become generally recognized as a branch of Indo-Euro-

pean, that 'Germanic' represents the group of languages which is the

extreme western distribution of the Indo-European language family —

something which is evident in Malte-Brun's enumeration (supra), for in-

stance. By 1857, when Bopp wrote the preface to the second edition of

his *Vergleichende Grammatik*, the situation had changed, thus lending

particular support to his argument in favour of the use of 'Indo-Euro-

pean':

> Die häufig gebrauchte Benennung "indogermanisch" kann ich nicht
> billigen, weil ich keinen Grund kenne, warum in dem Namen des um-
> fassendsten Sprachstammes gerade die Germanen als Vertreter der
> urverwandten Völker unsers Erdtheils, sowohl der Vorzeit, als der
> Gegenwart, hervorzuheben. (Bopp 1857:XXIX)

Instead, Bopp would prefer either 'indo-classisch', because Latin and

Greek had conserved the basic type of the language family much better

than any other European language, or, following Humboldt, 'sanskritisch', since it does not emphasize a particular nationality but a (linguistic) characteristic shared by all members of this 'most perfect' language family.[17]

Outside German-speaking countries Bopp's plea did not remain un-heard, and the French Swiss Adolphe Pictet (1799-1875) made 'Indo-Eu-ropean' a viable competitor to 'Indo-Germanic' by using it in the title of his influential work, *Les Origines indo-européennes, ou les Aryas primitifs* (Paris, 1859-63). However, among German linguists of the 19th century the term 'indogermanisch' became the customary one (cf. Siegert 1941/42:78-79, for exceptions). Neither Bopp's authority - toward the end of his 1857 preface he had argued "Für jetzt ziehe ich ... die Bennennung INDO-EUROPÄISCH (oder INDISCH-EUROPÄISCH) vor, die auch bereits, sowie die entsprechende im Englischen und Französischen eine große Verbreitung gewonnen hat" - nor the popularity of Count Gobineau's 4-volume *Essai sur l'inégalité des races humaines* (Paris, 1853-55), who criticized the appellation 'indo-germanique', appear to have had much effect on this development. In the second volume of his *Essai* (p.105), Gobineau (1816-82) argued against the term as follows:

> Si l'on voulait absolument appliquer aux groupes des langues des noms de nations, il serait plus raisonnable pourtant de qualifier le rameau arien d'*hindou-celtique*. On aurait du moins ainsi la désignation des deux extrêmes géographiques, et on indiquerait les deux faces les plus différentes du système; mais, pour mille causes, cette dénomination serait encore détestable.

In fact, even in Germany several scholars suggested 'Indo-Celtic' (*in-dokeltisch*) in lieu of 'indogermanisch' (cf. already Pott 1840:1) in an attempt to designate the two extreme branches of the large Indo-European family tree (cf. Siegert 1941/42:83), but with little success. Gobineau, for his part, used 'Aryan'; he was promoting a 'white' or Indo-European 'supremicist' view which had dear consequences (cf. Poli-akov 1974:233-37), regardless of Pott's (1856) efforts in countering Go-bineau's outrageous speculations.[18]

In his *Die Sprachen Europas*, August Schleicher (1821-68), probably the most influential mid-19th-century linguist, expressed himself in favour of the use of 'indogermanisch' because it is the most frequently

used term, even though he concedes (p.123) that it is 'nicht bezeich-
nend'. He rejected not only 'Indo-European', but also 'Aryan', 'Sans-
kritic', and 'Japhetic', terms also current in the past century, plead-
ing (p.124):

> ... gönne man den germanischen Nationen die Ehre diesem Sprach-
> stamme theilweise den Namen gegeben zu haben, in der dankbaren
> Erinnerung, daß Deutsche es waren, welche die Zusammengehörig-
> keit der betreffenden Sprachen zuerst methodisch erwiesen und
> dadurch für die Sprachwissenschaft überhaupt eine neue Aera her-
> beigeführt haben.

Schleicher might have had a good argument, but already his own association (if not latent identification) of 'germanisch' with 'deutsch',
which in English is still much closer, namely, 'Germanic' and 'German',
might already have led to an opposition even on the part of scholars
whose Anglo-Saxon background would have included them among the Germanic branch. Thus, the American Sanskrit scholar and general linguist
William Dwight Whitney (1827-94) noted:

> ... a few still employ the term 'Indo-Germanic', which seems to
> savour of national prepossession, since no good reason can be
> given why, among the western branches, the Germanic should be
> singled out for representation in the general title of the fam-
> ily. (Whitney 1867:193; similarly also Whitney 1875:180)

Julius Jolly (1849-1932), the German translator of Whitney's *Language
and the Study of Language*, tried to counter Whitney's criticism with
an argument reminiscent of Schleicher's when he stated, after having
referred to other German scholars who had in his view refuted Whitney's
objection:

> ... obschon auch noch daran zu erinnern wäre, dass es von allen
> Völkern unseres Stammes gerade die Jnder und die Germanen sind,
> die am meisten zur Entdeckung desselben beigetragen haben: die-
> ses Verdienst also in dem Namen des Stammes zu verewigen, wäre
> kein Unrecht, wenn dies auch, wie im Texte erwähnt, keineswegs
> in der Absicht der Namensschöpfer lag. Das Entscheidende aber
> bleibt, dass die Benennung "indogermanisch" nun einmal allgemein
> in Deutschland recipirt ist, ... (Whitney 1874:283, note)

Whatever the argument in favour of the use of 'indogermanisch', the
fact remains that, from the last quarter of the 19th century onwards,
this term has been the regular one in German-speaking countries. Thus,
beginning with volume XXIII (1875-77), Adalbert Kuhn's (1812-81) in-

fluential, if not the leading journal of the period, "Zeitschrift für vergleichende Sprachforschung" changed its subtitle from "auf dem Gebiete des Deutschen, Griechischen und Lateinischen" into "auf dem Gebiete der indogermanischen Sprachen". At about the same time, in 1876, a year which appears to have been crucial in the development of linguistics (Koerner 1976), Adalbert Bezzenberger (1851-1922) founded the "Beiträge zur Kunde der indogermanischen Sprachen" (which thirty years later merged into Kuhn's Journal). Finally, in 1891, on the occasion of the 100th anniversary of Franz Bopp's birth, Karl Brugmann (1849-1919) and Wilhelm Streitberg (1864-1925) founded the journal "Indogermanische Forschungen" bearing the subtitle "Zeitschrift für indogermanische Sprach- und Alterthumskunde".

In this manner, we may say that the usage 'indogermanisch' over and above any other term was cemented once and for all, irrespective of the nationalistic or other connections that some might have associated with 'Indo-Germanic', especially following the founding of the German state in 1871 and during and, in effect, preceding the Third Reich. The post-World War II period has witnessed, especially in the western part of Germany, a restoration of the historical-comparative tradition in Indo-European studies, and despite the propagandistic misuse made of terms such as 'germanisch' and 'indogermanisch' in the past, there exists to my knowledge no proposal to adopt 'indoeuropäisch' in lieu of the 'traditional' term, even if it were to simply follow the general usage outside German-speaking countries.

4.0 *On the origin, uses and abuses of 'Aryan'*

It must have been an act of courage to write an article, as Hans Siegert did, devoted to the history, uses and misuses of the concept and term 'Aryan' at the height of Nazi-German power. As was typical of the period, the subtitle of the journal "Wörter und Sachen", founded in 1909 by the Viennese Rudolf Meringer (1859-1931), had been changed from the neutral "Kulturhistorische Zeitschrift für Sprach- und Sachforschung" to the much more 'tinged' "Zeitschrift für indogermanische Sprachwissenschaft, Volksforschung und Kulturgeschichte". The present section is much indebted to Siegert's (1941/42:84-99) research.

In contrast to 'Indo-European' and 'Indo-Germanic' the term 'Aryan' has the advantage of having been an actual name for a people or a group of people. Apart from that, some scholars, notably Max Müller, argued that it was much shorter. On the other hand, however, the fact that it had previously been used with a precise meaning made its application to a different context at best problematical. Originally, it was the word that Indo-Iranian tribes used to characterize and to distinguish themselves from other tribes not related to them in terms of language; in fact, this is the only sense in which 'Aryan' is still employed today by historical linguists, namely, as a cover term for the Indo-Iranian branch of Indo-European.

It appears that, as a technical term, it was introduced into European scholarship by Hyacinthe Anquetil-Duperron (1731-1805), with whose work F. Schlegel obviously was familiar. Thus, in his review of Rhode (1819), when speaking of the Zend-Avesta, Schlegel (1975:515, 518) refers to Anquetil's authority. Indeed, it is there (but also p.527) that he speaks of the 'Aryans' arguing that the language should be called by the name of the people, not by any other appellation; for instance, the Greek in which the New Testament has been written should not be called 'language of the gospels' (Evangeliumsprache). Thus it would appear that the particular use of 'Aryan' for a language group was promoted by Friedrich Schlegel. The transfer of the term to denote the entire language family, however, does not have its source in Schlegel's argument; it must be found in later 19th-century linguistic scholarship.

Much ink has been spilled on the etymology of 'Aryan', which originally meant "rightful, honourable, noble" and, as we may note, contained already the germ of racism which was later exploited by 19th and 20th century ideologists of various kinds. The etymological connection that 19th-century scholars tried to establish between 'Aryan' and 'Eire' (Ireland) turned out to be spurious, but it served to promote the argument that 'Aryan' could be employed to refer to 'Indo-European' and, as Zimmer (1879:150) would have it, as the only correct designation (die allein richtige Bezeichnung), a view which, according to Siegert (p.89), was already present in Schlegel's interpretation of the term. However, we are less interested in the various etymologies advanced by 19th-century philologists (cf. Siegert, pp.84-89 passim, for details) than in the technical use made of 'Aryan'.

In the development of 'Aryan' in the sense of "Indo-European" it appears that the Norwegian-born Indo-Iranist and pupil of August Wilhelm Schlegel (1767-1845) at Bonn, Christian Lassen (1800-1876), played a seminal role. In a detailed footnote to a polemics against Bopp's 'System der Sanskritsprache', Lassen made a deliberate transfer of the term from its original, restricted application to the entire language family, with a prominent position among the European branches assigned to the Germanic group. This was based, ironically enough, on an etymological misreading of a classical text:

> Die Inder und die Altpersischen Völker nannten sich mit demselben Namen, dem der Arier, der auch bei den kriegerischen Deutschen seiner ehrenden Bedeutung nicht unwürdig erscheint: Tacit. Germ. XLIII: Ceterum Arii [*recte*: Harii] super vires, quibus enumeratos paullo ante populos antecedunt, truces, insitae feritati arte et tempore lenonciantur ... (Lassen 1830:71 note)

Pictet in 1837 and Pott in 1840 refer to Lassen's proposal, though Pott did not approve of the expansion of the original application, whereas Pictet, especially in his *Les Origines indo-européennes* (1859-63), adopted the suggested usage. It is on the authority of Pictet that Max Müller began promoting the special use of 'Aryan' in the sense of "Indo-European" from the first volume of his *Lectures on the Science of Language* (1861) onwards (cf. Müller 1875; 1888). However, even though he was instrumental in making the term very popular in the Anglo-Saxon world, he is not guilty of racism of any kind, regardless of Poliakov's (1974:213f.) accusation. For Müller, for his part, wished to have nothing to do with what ethnologists of his time made of the term and concept. For him, 'Aryan' was to be regarded as a strictly linguistic term:

> To me an ethnologist who speaks of Aryan race, Aryan blood, Aryan eyes and hair, is as great a sinner as a linguist who speaks of a dolichocephalic dictionary or a brachycephalic grammar. It

is worse than a Babylonian confusion of tongues — it is down-
right theft. We have our own terminology for the classification of languages: let the ethnologists make their own classification of skull, and hair, and blood. (Müller 1888:120)

Pictet, for his part, made the term 'arien' (as well as 'indo-europé-
en') widely known in the French-speaking lands (cf. Siegert 1941/42:77,
n.2 and 95-96), and this with the latent association between people
and language.   This connection, it appears, was exploited by ethnologists who had leanings toward Aryan supremacy, the best-known of
which was undoubtedly Gobineau. However, since racist prejudice and,
worse, the persecution of those not belonging to the 'Aryan' family of
peoples is generally associated with Germany (and Austria), I would like
to mention at least two 19th-century authors, both of them Americans,
who reflect quite nicely the ideology of 'Indo-European' (white) supremacy, namely, Albert Pike's (1809-1891) *Lectures of the Arya* (1873) and
Charles Morris' (1833-1922) *The Aryan Race* (1888).[19]   Still in 1926 V.
G. Childe (1892-1957) felt justified to use the term 'Aryan' to refer
to the Indo-European peoples, although he notes: "As a racial designation it is peculiar to the Indo-Iranians" (p.95).

     Yet by the time Siegert (1941/42) was writing his account of the
semantic evolution of the term, 'Aryan' had become almost exclusively
a term with racial connotations. 'Aryan' in the sense of "Caucasian
of non-Jewish decent" was a central part of Nazi-ideology. This concept
was soon extended, as we know, to other minorities, including the gypsies,
who by the 1840s had become recognized as being of Indo-European, if
not Aryan, origin. When Siegert (p.99) suggested that, because of its
confusing usages, the term 'Aryan' should be abandoned altogether, he
was making a daring statement if we consider the historical circumstances
by which he was surrounded: at that time, the persecution of so-called
'Non-Aryans' (Nicht-Arier) was growing fiercer and fiercer day by day.

     Today, 'Aryan' is used, if at all, only to designate the Indo-Iran-
ian branch of the Indo-European language family. Honoré Chavée's suggestion made in 1867 (and implemented by him in subsequent publications)
to use 'aryaque' in referring to the 'langue indo-germanique primitive'
or *indo-germanische Grundsprache* - in contradistinction to 'arien' -

was unsuccessful, for various reasons. First, Chavée (1815-77) was
considered as an 'érudit éclairé' (Meillet) but not as a professional
linguist; second, he was writing in the "Revue de Linguistique" (Paris,
1867-1916), which was shunned by many scholars of the period, in France
as well as abroad, because of its open subscription to Comtean positivism (cf. Koerner 1981); and third, because it was based on an incorrect
etymology (cf. supra).

Similarly, the use of 'Ario-European', recommended by Graziadio
Isaia Ascoli (1829-1907) already in 1854 (cf. Siegert 1941/42:93, n.1),
was not taken up by many scholars. The Pole Jan Baudouin de Courtenay
(1845-1929) appears to have been an exception (1884). In fact, at least
among linguists, the term 'Aryan' in the sense of "Indo-European" (cf.
Bradke 1890) became rarely used by the end of the 19th century, and
there were even fewer scholars at the beginning of the 20th century
who used the term in this sense (e.g., Jacobsohn 1922).[20]

5.0 *Concluding Remarks*

By 1861, when Schleicher's *Compendium der vergleichenden Grammatik
der indogermanischen Sprachen* began appearing, the majority of scholars
in the German-speaking lands employed 'indogermanisch' rather than 'indoeuropäisch'. Karl Moritz Rapp (1803-1883), a pupil of Bopp like his
very close contemporary A. F. Pott, was one of the few scholars of the
period who consistently used 'Indo-European' ('indisch-europäisch' or
'indoeuropäisch') in his writings; consider his 4-volume *Grundriss der
Grammatik des indisch-europäischen Stammes* (1853-55). Already by 1880,
before Brugmann had even begun working on his *Grundriss*, Rapp's work was
no longer referred to even in the annals of the discipline (cf. Delbrück
1882:62, where he is simply mentioned by name together with a few others
as expounding an evolutionist theory of language).

Owing to the prestige of German scholarship in comparative-historical linguistics (which included, for reasons of national pride and, I
presume, simply by habit, the regular use of 'indogermanisch' so dearly
cherished by the *Junggrammatiker*), the term 'Indo-Germanic' was used
even by foreign scholars. C. C. Uhlenbeck (1866-1951), for example,

still employed 'Indogermanic' in 1937, whereas, by 1941, the second-
generation Neogrammarian, Holger Pedersen (1867-1953), preferred 'indoeuropäisch'. By that time, Germany was at war with almost every
European country, and there was no reason for a Dane to identify with
the 'Germanic' part of the term, especially since it was clearly tinged
with Teutonic overtones.

One might have thought that, with German minds having sobered from
past experience, which included the misuse of linguistic terminology,
'indogermanisch' would have become more and more obsolete. But perhaps
this is asking too much from a branch of linguistic research which is
as tradition-laden as *Indogermanistik*. As a historian of linguistics,
I would regret it if the term were to be discontinued in the titles of
periodicals which have served many generations of researchers under
this name. But as someone aware of historical events in general, I see
no particular reasons for clinging to 'Indo-Germanic' and related
terms in present-day publications.

The pros and cons of the use of 'Indo-European' have, in a way,
already been discussed in the preceding survey. We may summarize the
reasons why this term is preferable to 'Indo-Germanic' in the following points:[21] (1) It is used regularly (and unambiguously) by all scholars outside the German-speaking area; (2) it is probably more vague in
its original meaning and, as a result, more easily amenable to a precise scientific definition, and (3) 'Germanic' is too close to 'German'
not to lead to possible confusion in the minds of some people, if not
to irritation that one particular branch of the European branches of
this large 'family tree' should be given prominence over and above all
the others (i.e., Celtic, Romance, Slavic, etc.).

To the explanation that 'indogermanisch' describes the most southern (Indian) and the most northern (Germanic) branch of the Indo-European family of language, an explanation that I was given as a student
in Germany some fifteen years ago (cf. also Sowinski 1974:100), I cannot but reply with Norman's (1929:313) cogent remark that it "merely
attempts to define an antiquated term in the light of present knowledge."

NOTES

1) Thus Steinthal (1890:XI), with reference to the phrase "indo-germanique ou mieux indo-européen" found in Emile Egger's (1813-85) *Notions élémentaires de grammaire comparée*, 4th ed. (Paris: A. Durand, 1854), p.6, surmised that the latter term had been created "zur Beruhigung patriotischer Beklemmungen von einem Franzosen".

2) Delbrück, who had earlier suggested that Klaproth might be the originator of the term 'indogermanisch' (cf. Delbrück 1882:2, n.1), says little else in his (1894) note than defend his reliance on Steinthal's (1890) suggestions in the 3rd ed. of his *Einleitung in das Sprachstudium* (Leipzig: Breitkopf & Härtel, 1893), and that he had not been aware of Meyer's (1893) findings.

3) The present article has little in common with my paper, "The Sources, Development and Meaning of the Term 'Indo-European'", presented at the Third International Conference on Historical Linguistics (Hamburg, 22-26 Aug. 1977), though its essential findings have been incorporated here.

4) We know from the history of any discipline (not only from 20th-century linguistics!) that the understanding of 'scientific' and, of course, 'unscientific', has been changing together with the real or alleged 'progress' having been made at given points in time.

5) The term 'Japhetic', so popular in the 18th and early 19th century (cf. Klaproth 1812-14), appears to have been discredited once for all by the absurd theories of Nikolaj Jakovlevič Marr (1865-1934) and the disasterous consequences of their adoption as the official 'Marxist' doctrine in Stalinist Russia (until its debunking by Stalin himself in 1950).

6) Earlier, in the same paper, Humboldt, when speaking about the concept of language relationship (Verwandtschaft), refers to *Asia Polyglotta*, p.43 (Humboldt 1827:9 = 1963:119, n.2), to exactly the same page on which Klaproth introduces the term 'Indo-Germanisch' for the first time in his book.

7) Norman (1929:315, n.1) writes 'indogermanisch' when referring to the title of Pott's *Etymologische Forschungen* (1833-36), where in fact Pott used, in full agreement with Klaproth's orthography, 'Indo-Germanisch'. By contrast, when referring to Young's term, Norman (p.317, and note 2 on p.318) cites 'Indo-European', where in fact Young was using the term without a hyphen. It appears that he was relying heavily on secondary sources (notably Meyer 1893). Norman committed a number of other orthographic errors that seem to support this. For instance, instead of 'J. G. Rhode' he writes 'R. Kodes' (p.314, n.7), and the name of his countryman Robert Gordon Latham (1812-88) is constantly misspelt 'Lathom', in fact 7 times on pages 318-20.

8) I take this from Young's (1813:254) remark, made in reference to Adelung's claim that nearly 500 languages and dialects had been treated in his *Mithridates*, that "a number of which the publishers *have promised to complete in the third volume*" (emphasis mine), that Young had not yet seen the third volume which appeared in 1812.

9) F. Schlegel (1819:454 = 1975:514) said later: "was ich in der an-

gebenenen früheren Schrift über Indien [i.e., Schlegel 1808] vom Samskrit [*sic*] gesagt, gegen meine Absicht ist mißverstanden worden".

10) Nathaniel Brassey Halhed (1751-1830), in the preface to his *Grammar of the Bengal Language* (1778), had spoken of the "similitude of Shanscrit with those of Persian and Arabic, and even Latin and Greek". — On Halhed's importance for Sir William Jones' (1746-94), ideas about the Indo-European language family, s. now Rocher (1980).

11) Cf. Siegert (1941/42:76): "Dieser ganze Zusammenhang deutet darauf hin, daß hier der Terminus *"Indoeuropean"* bewußt geschaffen und nicht etwa von einem anderen übernommen wurde."

12) Norman, as we have already pointed out above (note 7) gives the (nowadays more usual) hyphenated form instead of Young's 'Indoeuropean'.

13) The fact that 'Indo-Germanen' is misspelt 'Indo-Germanien' in the chapter heading may suggest that it was a compound of a fairly recent origin. (The 'Inhaltsverzeichnis', p.1, gives 'Indo-Germanen'.)

14) It is perhaps an indication that Klaproth might well have had personal contacts with Malte-Brun, if we note that, following Malte-Brun's death in 1826, the second series of the "Annales des Voyages, de la géographie, de l'histoire et de l'archéologie" (Paris, 1819-70), was continued, during 1827-35 - i.e., until Klaproth's death - under the co-editorship of Klaproth. - The title of the first series was, quite revealing, I believe, in view of Klaproth's important travels, "Annales des voyages, de la géographie et de l'histoire, ou, Collection des voyages nouveaux les plus estimés, traduits de toutes les langues européennes" (Paris, 1809-1814).

15) The same argument was made by Leo Meyer (1901:451): "Wenn Bopp der Benennung 'indoeuropäisch' einen gewissen Vorzug geben will, wie es außerhalb Deutschlands überhaupt zu geschehen pflegt, so ist dagegen immer wieder und gar nicht genug zu betonen, daß die Europäer ganz und gar nicht alle zu dem selben Sprachstamm gehören; es werden bei solchem Gebrauch von 'indoeuropäisch' namentlich die ugrofinnischen Sprachen in ganz ungehöriger Weise einfach bei Seite geschoben."

16) Henry Sweet (1845-1912), for instance, used 'Indogermanic' in the title to his review of F. de Saussure's *Mémoire* and Friedrich Kluge's (1856-1926) *Beiträge zur Geschichte der germanischen Conjugation* (Strassburg: K. J. Trübner, 1879); see Sweet (1880). - As a matter of fact, 'Indo-Germanic' was used in the English translation of C. Malte-Brun's *Précis*, *Universal Geography*, vol.I (Edinburgh: A. Black, 1822; Boston: Wells & Lilly, 1824), i.e., 8 years before the usage attested by Norman (1929:318), where reference is made to an anonymous review in the *Edinburgh Review* 51.529ff. (July 1830).

17) It appears that Bopp used 'indo-germanisch' only once, namely, in a paper read before the Berlin Academy in 1842; there, he was directly referring to Klaproth (Siegert 1941/42:78).

18) I believe that Poliakov (1974:197) is quite unfair to Pott when he associates him with racist views, surmising that he had helped to promote Gobineau's views (p.259). Cf. also Joan Leopold's review of Poliakov's book in *Historiographia Linguistica* 4.401-406 (1977), esp. p.404.

19) Interestingly enough, Poliakov, in his biased account of the German Romanticist tradition from Herder onwards, does not mention

either of the two American ethnologists.

20) Forty years ago, Siegert (1941/42:99, n.1), noting the 'Sprach-verwirrung' in the use of 'Aryan' and the many terms offered for 'in-dogermanisch' (e.g., "japhetisch, indoeuropäisch, indogermanisch, sanskritisch, indokeltisch, arisch, mittelländisch, europäisch, sar-tisch, kaukasisch, indisch-deutsch, ario-europäisch", a list to which other terms, for instance 'thrakisch' could be added, cf. Johann Seve-rin Vater's (1771-1826) translation from Rask (1822)), suggested the creation of an historical dictionary of linguistic terminology, a pro-posal which I would like to repeat here, since it appears that, on the basis of such a dictionary it would be possible to delineate much of the development of linguistic thought. – Thus, it is curious to see that, where the term 'Semitic' is concerned, so many scholars in the 19th century believed that Johann Gottfried Eichhorn (1752-1827) was the creator (cf. Pott 1840:1; Westphal 1873:IX; Steinthal 1890:XII). It appears to have been Leo Meyer (1901:457), who was the first to es-tablish once for all that the coiner was in effect August Ludwig von Schlözer (1735-1809) in 1781. In an article, "Von den Chaldäern", pub-lished in part VIII of the *Repertorium für biblische und morgenländi-sche Litteratur* ed. by Eichhorn – hence the confusion, I presume – pp. 113-76, Schlözer stated: "Vom Mittelländischen Meer an bis zum Eufrat hinein, und von Mesopotamien bis nach Arabien hinunter, herrschte be-kanntlich nur Eine Sprache. Also Syrier, Babylonier, Hebräer und Ara-ber, waren Ein Volk. Auch Phönicier (Hamiten) redeten diese Sprache, die ich die Semitische nennen möchte; sie hatten aber solche erst auf der Gränze gelernt." (Op. cit., p.161). On the history of 'Hamitic', see Knappert (1976).

21) Drobin's recent article (1980) does not add anything to the dis-cussion; it is concerned with the reality behind the concept of 'Indo-European' (indogermanisch), not the appropriateness of the term.

REFERENCES

Baudouin de Courtenay, Jan. 1884. *Uebersicht der slavischen Sprachen-welt im Zusammenhang mit den anderen ario-europäischen (indogermani-schen) Sprachen*. Leipzig: T. O. Weigel.

Bopp, Franz. 1833. *Vergleichende Grammatik des Sanskrit, Send, Armeni-schen, Griechischen, Lateinischen, Littauischen, Altslawischen, Go-thischen und Deutschen*. Berlin: F. Dümmler.

––––––––––. 1857. *Vergleichende Grammatik* ... . 2nd rev. ed., vol.I. Ibid.

Bradke, Peter von. 1890. *Ueber Methode und Ergebnisse der arischen (in-dogermanischen) Altertumswissenschaft*. Giessen: J. Ricker.

Chavée, Honoré. 1867. "La science positive des langues indo-européennes, son présent, son avenir". *Revue de Linguistique et de Philologie com-parée* 1.1-35.

Childe, Vere Gordon. 1926. *The Aryans: A study of Indo-European ori-gins*. London: K. Paul, Trench, Trübner & Co.; New York: A. A. Knopf.

Delbrück, Berthold. 1882. *Introduction to the Study of Language: A cri-tical survey of the history and methods of comparative philology of Indo-European languages*. Transl. by Eva Channing. Leipzig: Breitkopf

& Härtel. (New ed., with a foreword by E. F. K. Koerner, Amsterdam: J. Benjamins, 1974.)

Delbrück, Berthold. 1894. "Noch einmal 'indogermanisch'". *Anzeiger für indogermanische Sprach- und Altertumswissenschaft* 3.267-68.

Diderichsen, Paul. 1974. "The Foundation of Comparative Linguistics: Revolution or continuation?". *Studies in the History of Linguistics* ed. by Dell Hymes, 277-306. Bloomington & London: Indiana Univ. Press.

Droixhe, Daniel. 1978. *La Linguistique et l'appel de l'histoire (1600-1800)*. Geneva: Droz.

Drobin, Ulf. 1980. *Indogermanische Religion und Kultur? Eine Analyse des Begriffes Indogermanisch*. Stockholm: Inst. for Comparative Religion, Univ. of Stockholm.

Gobineau, Joseph Arthur, comte de. 1853-55. *Essai sur l'inégalité des races humaines*. 4 vols. Paris: F. Didot.

Humboldt, Wilhelm, Freiherr von. 1827. *Ueber den Dualis*. Berlin: Akademie der Wissenschaften, 1828. (Repr. in W. von Humboldt, *Schriften zur Sprachphilosophie* ed. by Andreas Flitner and Klaus Giel, 113-43. Darmstadt: Wissenschaftliche Buchgesellschaft, 1963.)

Jacobsohn, Hermann. 1922. *Arier und Ugrofinnen*. Göttingen: Vandenhoeck & Ruprecht.

Klaproth, Julius Heinrich. 1810. *Archiv für asiatische Litteratur, Geschichte und Sprachenkunde*. Erster Band. St.Petersburg: Im Academischen Verlage. [No more published]

----------. 1812-14. *Reise in den Kaukasus und Georgien in den Jahren 1807 und 1808, auf Veranstaltung der Kaiserlichen Akademie der Wissenschaften zu St.Petersburg*. 2 vols. Halle/S.: Waisenhaus.

----------. 1823a. *Asia Polyglotta*. Paris: A. Schubart. (2nd ed., Paris: Heidelhoff & Campe, 1831; repr., Leipzig: Zentralantiquariat, 1970.)

----------. 1823b. *Voyage au Mont Caucase et en Géorgie*. 2 vols. Paris: C. Gosselin. [Rev. French version of Klaproth 1812-14; the second vol. deals with Caucasian languages.]

Knappert, Jan. 1976. "Origin and Development of the Concept of Hamitic: The first sixty years, 1851-1911". *Orientalia Lovaniensia Periodica* 6/7.303-320.

Koerner, E. F. Konrad. 1976. "1876 as a Turning Point in the History of Linguistics". *Journal of Indo-European Studies* 4.333-53. (Repr. in Koerner, *Toward a Historiography of Linguistics*, 189-209. Amsterdam: J. Benjamins, 1978.)

----------. 1981. "Positivism in 19th-Century Linguistics". *Rivista di Filosofia* (in press).

Lassen, Christian. 1830. "Über Herrn Professor Bopps System der Sanskritsprache". *Indische Bibliothek* ed. by A. W. Schlegel, 3.1-113. Bonn: E. Weber.

Malte-Brun, Conrad. 1810-29. *Précis de la géographie universelle, ou, Description de toutes les parties du monde, sur un plan nouveau, d'après les grandes divisions naturelles du globe, ... 8 vols. Paris: F. Buisson.

----------. 1812. *Précis de la geographie universelle*. Vol.II, 2e édition. Ibid. (First ed., 1810.)

Meyer, Gustav. 1893. "Von wem stammt die Bezeichnung Indogermanen?".
Anzeiger für indogermanische Sprach- und Altertumswissenschaft 2.125-
130.
Meyer, Leo. 1901. "Über den Ursprung der Namen Indogermanen, Semiten
und Ugrofinnen". *Göttingische gelehrte Nachrichten* 1901, Phil.-hist.
Klasse, 448-59. Göttingen: Vandenhoeck & Ruprecht.
Müller, F(riedrich) Max. 1861. *Lectures on the Science of Language;
delivered at the Royal Institution of Great Britain in April, May,
and June 1861*. London: Longman, Green, Longman & Roberts.
----------. 1872. *Über die Resultate der Sprachwissenschaft*. 3rd. ed.
Strassburg: K. J. Trübner.
----------. 1875. "Aryans". *Encyclopaedia Britannica*, 9th ed., vol.2,
p.672. Edinburgh: C. & A. Black.
----------. 1888. *Biographies of Words and the Home of the Aryas*. London: Longmans, Green & Co.
Morris, Charles. 1888. *The Aryan Race: Its origin and its achievements*.
Chicago: S. C. Griggs & Co.
Norman, Frederick. 1929. "'Indo-European' and 'Indo-Germanic'". *Modern
Language Review* 24.313-21.
Osthoff, Hermann. 1876. "Zur frage des ursprungs der germanischen N-de-
clination (Nebst einer theorie über die ursprüngliche unterscheidung
starker und schwacher casus im indogermanischen)". *Beiträge zur Ge-
schichte der deutschen Sprache und Literatur* 3.1-82 (Nachwort, 82-89).
Pedersen, Holger. 1941. *Tocharisch vom Gesichtspunkt der indoeuropäi-
schen Sprachvergleichung*. Copenhagen: E. Munksgaard.
Pictet, Adolphe. 1859-63. *Les Origines indo-européennes, ou, les Aryas
primitifs*. 2 vols. J. Cherbuliez. (2nd rev. and enl. ed., Geneva:
Sandoz & Fischbacher, 1877.)
Pike, Albert. 1873. *Lectures of the Arya*. Louisville, Kentucky: The
Standard Printing Company.
Poliakov, Léon. 1974. *The Aryan Myth: A history of racist and nation-
alist ideas in Europe*. Transl. from the French by Edmund Howard.
London: Chatto & Heinemann for Sussex Univ. Press.
Pott, August Friedrich. 1833-36. *Etymologische Forschungen auf dem Gebiete der Indo-Germanischen Sprachen*. 2 vols. Lemgo: Meyer.
----------. 1840. "Indogermanischer Sprachstamm". *Allgemeine Encyclo-
pädie der Wissenschaften und Künste in alphabetischer Folge* ed. by
Johann Samuel Ersch and Johann Gottfried Gruber, zweite Section (H-
N), 18. Theil, 1-112. Leipzig: F. Gleditsch.
----------. 1856. *Die Ungleichheit menschlicher Rassen, hauptsächlich
vom sprachwissenschaftlichen Standpunkte, unter besonderer Berück-
sichtigung von des Grafen Gobineau gleichnamigen Werke, mit einem
Überblick über die Sprachverhältnisse der Völker: Ein ethnologischer
Versuch*. Lemgo & Detmold: Meyer.
Rapp, Karl Moritz. 1853-55. *Grundriss der Grammatik des indisch-europä-
ischen Stammes*. 4 vols. Stuttgart: J. G. Cotta.
Rask, Rasmus Kristian. 1822. "Über die Thrakische Sprachclasse". *Ver-
gleichstafeln der Europäischen Stamm-Sprachen und Süd-, West-Asiati-
scher* ed. by Johann Severin Vater, 3-182. Halle/S.: Renger.
Rhode, Johann Gottlieb. 1819. *Ueber den Anfang unserer Geschichte und*

die letzte Revolution der Erde, als wahrscheinliche Wirkung eines Kometen. Breslau: W. A. Holäufer.

Rocher, Ludo. 1960. "Enkele aantekeningen bij het begrip *het Indo-Europees*". *Tijschrift van de Vrije Universiteit van Brussel* 3.14-33.

Rocher, Rosane. 1980. "Nathaniel Brassey Halhed, Sir William Jones, and Comparative Indo-European Linguistics". *Recherches de Linguistique: Hommages à Maurice Leroy* ed. by Jean Bingen et al., 173-80. Brussels: Editions de l'Univ. de Bruxelles.

Schlegel, Friedrich. 1808. *Ueber die Sprache und Weisheit der Indier: Ein Beitrag zur Begründung der Alterthumskunde.* Heidelberg: Mohr & Zimmer. (Repr., with an introductory article by Sebastiano Timpanaro, Amsterdam: J. Benjamins, 1977.)

----------. 1819. Review article on Rhode 1819. *Wiener Jahrbücher der Litteratur* 8.413-68. (Repr. in *Kritische Friedrich-Schlegel-Ausgabe* ed. by Ernst Behler et al., vol.8.474-528. Munich-Paderborn-Vienna: F. Schöningh.)

Schleicher, August. 1850. *Die Sprachen Europas in systematischer Uebersicht: Linguistische Untersuchungen.* Bonn: H. B. König. (New ed., with an introductory article by Konrad Koerner, Amsterdam: J. Benjamins, 1982.)

----------. 1861-62. *Compendium der vergleichenden Grammatik der indogermanischen Sprachen: Kurzer Abriss einer Laut- und Formenlehre der indogermanischen Ursprache.* 2 vols. Weimar: H. Böhlau. (4th ed., prepared by Johannes Schmidt and August Leskien, 1876.)

Schmitthenner, Friedrich. 1826. *Ursprachlehre: Entwurf zu einem System der Grammatik mit besonderer Rücksicht auf die Sprachen des indischdeutschen Stammes.* Frankfurt/M.: J. C. Hermann. (New ed., with an introduction by Herbert E. Brekle, Stuttgart-Bad Cannstatt: Frommann-Holzboog, 1976.)

Shapiro, Fred R. 1981. "On the Origin of the Term 'Indo-Germanic'". *Historiographia Linguistica* 8.165-70.

Siegert, Hans. 1941/42. "Zur Geschichte der Begriffe 'Arier' und 'arisch'". *Wörter und Sachen: Zeitschrift für indogermanische Sprachwissenschaft, Volksforschung und Kulturgeschichte* 22 (= N.F. 4), 73-99.

Sowinski, Bernhard. 1974. *Grundlagen des Studiums der Germanistik.* 2nd rev. ed. Cologne & Vienna: H. Böhlau.

Steinthal, Heymann. 1890. "Vorwort zur zweiten Auflage". *Geschichte der Sprachwissenschaft bei den Griechen und Römern, mit besonderer Rücksicht auf die Logik.* 2nd enlarged and rev. ed., vol.I, IX-XIII. Berlin: F. Dümmler. (Repr., Bonn: F. Dümmler, 1961.)

Sweet, Henry. 1880. "Recent Investigations of the Indogermanic Vowel-System". *Transactions of the Philological Society 1880-81.*155-62.

Uhlenbeck, Christianus Cornelis. 1937. "The Indogermanic Mother Language and Mother Tribes Complex". *American Anthropologist* 39.385-93.

Whitney, William Dwight. 1867. *Language and the Study of Language.* New York: Scribner, Armstrong & Co.; London: Trübner & Co. (3rd ed., augmented by an analysis, 1870.)

----------. 1874. *Die Sprachwissenschaft: W. D. Whitney's Vorlesungen über die Prinzipien der vergleichenden Sprachforschung, für das deut-*

sche Publikum bearbeitet und erweitert. By Julius Jolly. Munich: Th.
Ackermann. (Repr., Hildesheim: G. Olms, 1974.)
----------. 1875. *The Life and Growth of Language: An outline of linguistic science.* New York: D. Appleton & Co.; London: H. S. King. (Repr., with an introduction by Charles F. Hockett, New York: Dover
Publications, 1979.)
[Young, Thomas]. 1813. Review article on Johann Christoph Adelung, *Mithridates, oder, Allgemeine Sprachenkunde*, vols.1-2 (Berlin: Voss,
1806-1809). *The Quarterly Review* 10 [No.19], 250-92 (Oct. 1813).
Zimmer, Heinrich. 1876. *Die Nominalsuffixe a und ā in den germanischen
Sprachen.* Strassburg: K. J. Trübner.
----------. 1879. "Arisch". *Beiträge zur Kunde der indogermanischen
Sprachen* 3.137-51.

*Addenda:**

Halhed, Nathaniel Brassey. 1778. *A Grammar of the Bengal Language.* Bengal: Printed at Hoogly.
Schlözer, August Ludwig von. 1781. "Von den Chaldäern". *Repertorium
für biblische und morgenländische Litteratur* ed. by Johann Gottfried
Eichhorn, Part 8, 113-76. Leipzig: Weidmanns Erben & Reich.

*A paper listed in Shapiro (1981:169), not seen by the present writer
is that by the distinguished American Indo-Europeanist Carl Darling
Buck (1866-1955), "'Indo-European' or 'Indo-Germanic'?", *Classical
Review* 18.399-401 (1904).

SEMANTIC INVESTITURE OF UNDERSPECIFIED UNITS IN SYNTAX

STEPHAN LANGHOFF
University of Hamburg

1. THE "PROBLEM": INFINITIVAL POSTMODIFIERS

This article can be called a "paper to read" -- a syntagma which consists only of a noun and an infinitival postmodifier, and which is highly underspecified with regard to modality. It is typically found in distribution with "have/be" or related verbs:

    (1a) This is a paper to read

    (1b) There is a paper to read

or somewhat more personal:

    (1c) I have a paper to read.

The characteristic features of infinitival postmodifiers become evident as soon as we try to paraphrase them in order to elucidate the nature of underspecified modality here:

    (2a) I am allowed to read a paper

is certainly a part of its meaning. It furthermore carries some connotations of moral obligation, since I decided to read this paper during the third ICHL and also told everybody that I would, which we can capture in the paraphrase:

(2b)   I have to read a paper.

We can also focus on the lexical meaning of "have" and "be" here expressing "existence" of sorts; what is existent and visible to you is
a *modified paper*, namely

(3a)   a paper that can be read
(3b)   a paper that should be read
(3c)   a paper that must be read.

Paraphrases of this kind characterize many a grammar of English,
and I could go on to present them -- but I believe this to be sufficient to show that we cannot explain the essence of underspecified
modality by concentrating on its particular aspects signalled by the
respective modal verbs. We have to look at the functioning whole instead, that is, language in use, and accept that language as a means
of communication is of necessity both *unspecific and underspecified*.

    I will show that the "missing meaning" cannot be treated as being
explicit in some kind of deep-structure with the context only disam-
biguating and ruling out. The full meaning is not there in deep-structure! The "missing meaning" is rather added by the hearer who always
has his personal and sociological background and who always receives
a signal embedded in the here and now of his experience, which he
shares with his interlocutor in many senses, even if not in all regards.

2.   DEMONSTRATION OF UNDERSPECIFIED MODALITY

    Let us now consider some examples from my own contrastive corpus
of as yet around 5,000 entries from books and newspapers. I have to
restrict myself to presenting only one single type of modal postmodifiers, namely, those that bear a resemblance to the passive: This paper does not read itself but *it is to be read*. As opposed to the other

West-European languages, English has developed a passive form for these (Jespersen 1937:60, 62). In my example

> (4)   The lady was very serious, ritualistic almost, in her
>   pleasures, and *was not to be hurried*

the underspecified modality lies in "be" + infinitive. This is a case of grammatical meaning corresponding to German "sein" + infinitive, which, however, only occurs in the active.

It is crucial to realize that in distribution with "there is" and German "es gibt" we find no clear-cut borderline between the grammatical meaning and the rest of lexical meaning still to be found in "be" and "sein". Whereas grammatical meaning is still prevailing in

> (5)   The money would be out of my hands, in the baggage compart-
>   ment, while we crossed the Atlantic, but *there is nothing
>   to be done* about it

we have a hybrid of *ability* (grammatical meaning) and *existence* (lexical meaning) in sentences like this:

> (6)   The others came back an hour later with dates and coffee.
>   They said that *there was nothing* else *to be had* in the
>   village, and grumbled that what they had bought had been
>   expensive.

Probably some of you have been asked by German customs officers:

> (7a) Haben Sie etwas zu verzollen?

This can be treated as a blend of two unmarked structures which are reflected by the marked English equivalents

> (7b) Have you got anything to declare?

> (7c) Have you got to declare anything?

The moral obligation "haben zu" here overlaps with "haben" in the
sense of *something is with you* -- in your suit-case or pockets, for
example -- because it is not just *something*, but a modified something
that is to be declared. Whereas in German this blend exists in syntax and semantics, the two readings are distinguished in English syntactically, since the infinitival postmodifier must of necessity *fol-*
low the noun modified (Pence/Emery 1963:89). But on a semantic level
we can find precisely this kind of blend in English, too:

> (8) But before I could cross the ocean, I *had a few things to*
>   *do* closer to home. First I would *have to get* a passport.

Here "I had things to do" explicitly means "I had to do them".

Already these examples show that -- at least in connection with
underspecified modality -- there is no clear line between "be/have"
and "be to/have to", and we see that this applies to their contrastive
counterparts, too. We do not have to go so far to say that the readings become identical, but they surely approach each other enough to
serve the purpose of the communicative situations in which they occur.
Their similarity can be labeled "partial identity". The "ambiguity"
is at best *vagueness*, or better *underspecification*.

The description of "social games", as it were, -- the verbaliza-
tion of socially expected actions -- strikingly demonstrates that you
only have to hint at the modality, and that explicit modality (modal
verbs, etc.) can become an obstacle in conversation. We find a bun-
dle of moral constituents in

> (9a) I *have a bone to pick* with you.
> (9b) Ich *habe ein Hühnchen* mit dir *zu rupfen*.
> (10) Wenn Bürger *etwas zu fragen haben*, dann sollen sie ihre
>   Antwort erhalten, und zwar von zuständiger Stelle.

"Suggestive speech" which is disapproved by puritanical souls shows
the same (Maher 1977a). K. O. Erdmann calls it "absichtlich unbe-

stimmter Wortgebrauch" (Erdmann 1925:47).

3. EXPLANATIONS

Explanation of these phenomena requires a closer look at all factors involved and at their interrelations.

3.1. Nature of Language as a Means of Communication

Theorists should always remember that natural languages are
ill-defined (Hockett 1968; Wandruszka 1971:219). Oppositions in
language are largely *inclusive*, whereas logical ones are *exclusive* (Coseriu 1971:138, 151). "'Tag' bezeichnet das Gegenteil
von 'Nacht' aber auch 'Tag und Nacht'" (Coseriu 1971:139).

Panchronic work shows that language is "jerry-built", to
use Bolinger's term; we constantly find, to use an image, build-
ings still under construction next to ruins, remainders from the
past (Maher 1977b). Bolinger (1973:23) also shows that speakers
are often haphazard in the way they throw a modifier into a sentence in an "illogical" manner, which, at first glance, seems
paradox, since in most cases speakers communicate to coordinate
their actions in a precise and meaningful way -- but knowing that
speech acts are not separable from their situational contexts,
we come to the conclusion that natural languages must of necessity be unspecific and underspecified, as partners always already
share a common knowledge to begin with which does not need to become verbalized. In fact, it could not even be verbalized.

Hearers easily infer missing elements into the received signal, uniting what they are actually perceiving with memory, their
knowledge about things absent but relevant. This is analogous to
visual perception: Our sensory organization adds to the received
signal in a dynamic mode of "completion figures" as Slagles's
work shows.

H. Brinkmann calls this "Reduktion", and stresses the dynamic aspects when he says,

> jede sprachliche Aufnahme ist mehr als ein einfacher Nachvollzug dessen, was der Sender anbietet...[es ist] eine Übersetzung des Angebotenen in den eigenen sprachlichen Horizont. (Brinkmann 1974:159.)

We find the same thing in Jespersen's terms "expression, impression, suppression" which are to be found, he says in all speech-activity (Jespersen 1925:809).

I will use Collins' term *"semantic investiture"* for this Gestalt completion (Maher 1977a). When I called this "a paper to read", I only had to hint at the modality or futurity by using nothing more than an infinitival postmodification; your knowledge about conferences and papers enabled you to perceive the *whole Gestalt*. It is precisely this unified perception -- Kronasser's "Ganzheit des Erlebens" (1968:65) -- that causes "haben zu" and "haben" to blend and to form an inseparable whole, e.g. when the officer asks you "Haben Sie etwas zu verzollen?" What you *have to* declare, you *have with* you; what *is to be* declared, *is* actually *with you*. Contrastive lexicology captured this similarity long ago (Russian, Irish, Latin, Arabic, and other languages use no "have"-words as do English and German, but use instead "be" or "with").

3.2. Perception

Let me be brief here and just give a survey. Perception is organized. *Context* and *memory* complete unfinished Gestalten. Kronasser (1968:68) means this when he speaks of

> Kontextbedeutungen: Tätigkeit und Ort, die oft gekoppelt vorkommen, verschmelzen vorstellungsmässig zu einer Einheit,

so dass zur Bezeichnung des einen auch die Bedeutung des
anderen treten kann.

In this light the particular modalities "obligation, necessity, ability", etc. are nothing more and nothing less than different aspects of the same thing: *futurity*. And just as in
visual perception we can focus our awareness on one particular
aspect, which is then foregrounded, while the others form the
background without, however, being ruled out; they cannot be regarded as being ruled out simply because *fore- and background presuppose each other* -- they are relative. Static theories as the
generative models cannot cope with these dynamics of figure-ground
differentiation and change in awareness or attention.

3.3. Nature of the Infinitive

The high degree of underspecified modality found in the example sentences can be explained by the characteristics of the
infinitival form, which includes panchronic and contrastive view-
points.

Half verb and half substantive, the infinitive is a hybrid
(Pence/Emery 1963:65). Morphologically it is the most recent
verbal form in Indo-European languages (Bréal 1900:79). Its function is to express an action in the most indefinite manner (Onions
1965:121), which is also shown by its connotations of futurity
(Mincoff 1958:222); it thus allows very short forms of locutions
(Pence/Emery 1963:67, 74) and structures of high flexibility
(Quirk 1972:881). Bolinger (1961:377) speaks of its "hypothetical
character" as opposed to the "concrete" character of the Gerund,
but he takes care not to become too specific, which again shows
how difficult this form is to handle.

To close the circle, let us bear in mind that the old term
"infinitive" describes exactly this underspecifying quality; it

is not limited in form as to *person* or *number*, and does not represent *time* in the same way as the finite verb does (Pence/Emery 1963:58; Hirt/Arntz 1939:78).

3.4. Underspecified Modality

We see that the infinitive is an excellent means to achieve suppression of specific modality as found in the modals etc. But like so many others, modality is a concept which soon turns out to be harder to handle the more one learns about it. We have only seen so far that it is an unspecified semantic relation between a noun, for example, "a paper", and an infinitive, "to read", for example. The achievement of the process "to read a paper", however, is blocked -- *it is not factual.* Let us therefore take modality and futurity as the same thing.

The syntagmata under discussion furthermore show that modal verbs are *not necessary* for modality and *too specific* for underspecified modality. Matters are complicated by the fact that "have to/be to" are also unnecessary for expression of modality: "be" and "sein" can serve the same purpose in suitable contexts, for example, in laws:

(11a) Die Bundesrepublik Deutschland *ist* ein Rechtsstaat.

This cannot be *meant* to be a fact. Nor can it be *understood* as describing a fact since the hearer knows that laws can easily be infringed. He completes the unfinished Gestalt:

(11b) Die Bundesrepublik Deutschland *soll* ein Rechtsstaat *sein.*

Bolinger (1961) speaks of "ambiguity in the infinitive", but, as outlined above, I prefer to take it as underspecification

of modality. We do not have here ambiguous readings, but holistic dynamic modal elements back- and foregrounding according to
speakers' and hearers' views. This is most clearly seen in the already mentioned "social games" in 9a, b, and 10. These are not at
all describable in terms of modals; we need a Gestalt approach to
organize our own findings and others into a meaningful, realistic
whole.[1] I hope to have made clear, so far, that first of all we
have to replace dualistic *either-or* approaches by the *as-well-as*
concept. We can concentrate on one element, but we cannot explain
it without considering the other parts of the whole field.

3.5. Nature of "have/be" as Underspecified Elements

Let us now for a moment take a closer look at "have/be" as
full verbs. In English as well as in German they are so unspecific that they often have more grammatical then lexical meaning;
they serve mainly as concatenators. Thus sentences like 12a

(12a)   Haben Sie Maultiere?

is just bound to get an infinitival postmodification

(12b)   Haben Sie Maultiere zu verkaufen?

adding modality to the very often non-modal "Haben-perspektive"
(a useful term taken from H. Brinkmann). The minimal amount of
lexical meaning made it easy for "have/be" to join the group of
phrasal verbs, and this also explains our difficulty to elucidate
the meaning of "a paper to read" by completing the syntagma with
these verbs (sentences 1a, b, c). We can assume that such highly
underspecified units can only develop in situational contexts
with a very high frequency (Maher 1977b).
We can take it for granted, however, that language largely

deals with things absent; if things are present, there is usually
no need to verbalize them. Consider the deictic

(13)   There is still a lot of work to do.

In speech-act theory we would have to decide whether to call this
a declarative sentence or an indirect speech act uttered to make
the hearers work harder. But is underspecified modality really
fully explicit -- just waiting to be disambiguated? Again it is
more appropriate not to postulate so many different readings but
to treat this as underspecification. Then these different readings are no longer mutually exclusive; they are just different
aspects of the same thing. This, I think, takes into consideration the sociological reality and does not twist the obvious facts.

4.   CONCLUSIONS

The foregoing descriptions (part 2) and explanations (part 3)
teach us that linguistic research has to center on the following points.

4.1. The Perceptual Basis of Grammatical Theory

Grammatical theory has to deal with language in use. Any
kind of grammar that explains structure without taking into consideration the obvious -- people who use language in a given here
and now situation with all its various and varying conditions --
must necessarily fail to provide any profound insight. Labov's
work is a good start. Taking perception as the innate basis of
speech accounts for the interplay between "here and now" and memory, things perceived and those absent or remote, but relevant
for the communicational topic. Explanation of the *means* of speech
is not enough; we have to consider the relation of those means to
the *ends* they serve, as Hymes (1975:372) puts it. First we have

to work on a phenomenological basis, on on-going processes of the
present. We then see that the principle of perception is also
the adequate basis for describing diachronic change (see below
4.4). Thus we can overcome the synchrony-diachrony *dichotomy* by
panchronic *as-well-as*.

4.2. Findings and Principles of Gestalt Psychology

The Gestalt psychologists' insight that perception is more
than mere *re*ception is not only useful but necessary for linguistics as the work of Anttila, Maher, Slagle, and others show.[2] It
is fairly obvious, as List (1973:16) points out

> dass die Suche nach fest umschriebenen sprachlichen Einhei-
> ten als solchen müssig bleiben muss, wenn nicht gleichzeitig
> die Gesetzmässigkeiten ihrer Vorkommens- und Funktionszu-
> sammenhänge aufgesucht werden....Der umfassendste Funktions-
> zusammenhang heisst ohne Zweifel Kommunikation.

The principle of figure-ground differentiation and our ability to fore- and background features at will by focusing our awareness I find methodologically very important for any kind of research. Many problems can be solved as soon as we are willing to
change the point of view "je nach Bedarf" as Kronasser (1968:73)
convincingly describes. This procedure does not only capture best
the dynamics of synchrony but also diachronic change. But let me
first outline the advantages of a contrastive approach.

4.3. The Contrastive Approach

A contrastive basis can clarify blends, different readings
and overlaps in an uncomplicated way by using a natural language
as a meta-language as has been shown by examples 7a, b, and 10.
It furthermore demonstrates that underspecification in general and

underspecified modality in particular as well as the principle of
semantic investiture are by no means confined to particular languages or certain structures; they are part of communication. It
moreover shows what makes a good translation in our context. Take
the modality in

> (14a)   ...wo es zweifelhaft wird, in welche Klasse ein be-
>   stimmter Typ von Begriffen *einzuordnen ist*.
>
> (14b)   ...and we may well be in doubt as to *how to group* a
>   given set of concepts.

A good translation has to keep the same amount of underspecification, which is the case here.

The infinitive is, says Bréal (1900:79), the first form to
be learnt by children in Indo-European languages, and the first
to pass between two peoples, when they come into contact and try
to understand each other. In many languages we use infinitives
for giving orders, which may well be one of the reasons why it
is the first form to be learnt by children. This ties in with
the fact that foreign workers in Germany pick up infinitives
quickly, and it would be worth while to continue Meisel's work on
their communicative surroundings and contacts with Germans -- the
overwhelming part of which is connected with their jobs, where
they receive orders.

Let us also bear in mind that the contrastive approach is not
confined to synchrony (cf. Bolinger 1973).

4.4.   Panchrony: Dynamic Synchrony as a Basis for Diachronic
         Change

The synchronic dynamics of focusing on a particular aspect
of a Gestalt while the others are backgrounded, can be observed
from a diachronic viewpoint, too -- and precisely here can we
re-integrate synchrony and diachrony to form panchrony. The

unity of perception relates temporal sequence, space, and causality, as pointed out by Quirk (1972:352), Slagle, Kronasser, and
others. Kronasser (1968:158) calls this "Erlebenseinheit":

> [es ist der] Zusammenhang zwischen Raum, Zeit und Kausalität
> nach denen wir unser Denken zu ordnen gewohnt sind.

Thus in many languages the same expressions are used for spacio-
temporal and logical relations. But only in theory, Kronasser
(ibid.) reminds us, can we isolate *space* from *time*. Only then
are we led to postulate a natural, linear, or even irreversible
development from *space* to *time* to *logical relations* in prepositions, for example. It is like that very often, it is true, but
there is a lot of counter-evidence.[3] Moreover this isolated,
static view neglects influences from other languages; there is
evidence that German "seit" gains back its former causal function
under the impact of English "since" which has been temporal and
causal throughout time (Carstensen 1965:69; Grimm 1905:10/372).
Here we have *not a linear* development *but a dynamic, unforeseeable*
reaction: "seit" lost its logical relation (counterevidence to
irreversibility) and then regained it under the impact of translations aided by the hearers' ability to infer causality immediately ("Erlebenseinheit")! We can say with Coseriu (1971:50),

> Jedes einzelne Wort besitzt eine höchst komplexe Geschichte,
> die nicht linear, sondern im Zickzack verläuft, aufgrund von
> lautlichen und semantischen Gleichheiten, Kreuzungen und Zu-
> sammenstössen mit anderen Wörtern.

From a perceptual basis we can understand how each aspect,
be it space, time, or inferred causality, can be brought to the
foreground. *Change* in this light is a change in foregrounding,
in focusing awareness on another aspect. Neglect of this renders
many a description of change unrealistic. Of course, a holistic

approach has to look at both sides of the coin: We have to consider the *changing* as well as the stable, the *unchanging* parts of
the whole, which is also neglected by many linguists.

4.5. Synthesis vs. Analysis

I will finish by calling your attention to a very important
point which I consider to be crucial, and this paper was intended
to make this clear.

Rigid either-or dichotomies, disjunctive rules, that is, tax-
onomies seldom capture reality; they more often obscure the facts
and thus add to the problem rather than to its solution. We can
say they themselves become the problem. Gestalt linguistics can
solve the problem -- a Gestalt is a whole, a complete in itself;
but when we cut it up to "explain" its structure, we end up having bits and pieces and not a whole anymore (Perls 1973:121).
When analyzing, we are often no longer able to look at the whole,
because we concentrate too much on the particular parts "bei denen
dann oft das Wesentliche der Sprache aus den Augen verloren wird",
to quote Coseriu (1971:149) again. Thus we get less essential
information about the matter the more we divide it up and cut it
down -- until understanding and insight are effectively blocked.

But what is "das Wesentliche der Sprache"? I believe, as
Hockett does, that it is the "ill-definedness" and its dynamic
character.

NOTES:

1) Between presenting this paper and publishing it this has been
achieved by Langhoff 1980 including contrastive and panchronic levels.
2) Developed in detail in a broader perspective by Langhoff 1980.
3) German "um", for example, has kept its local (and temporal)
meaning throughout time, whereas its side-development *final* and *causal*
"um" clearly decreased during the last centuries (cf. Grimm's *Wörterbuch* 11:761, 773, 777).

REFERENCES:

Anttila, R. 1979. "Language and Semiotics of Perception". Manuscript.
Bolinger, D. 1961. "Syntactic Blends and Other Matters", *Language* 37.
---------- 1973. "John's *Easyness to Please", *IRAL*.
Bréal, J. 1900. *Semantics*.
Brinkmann, H. 1959. "Die 'haben'-Perspektive im Deutschen", *Sprache-Schlüssel zur Welt*.
---------- 1974. "Reduktion in gesprochener und geschriebener Sprache", *Sprache der Gegenwart* 26.
Carstensen, B. 1965. *Englische Einflüsse auf die deutsche Sprache nach 1945*.
Coseriu, E. 1971. *Sprache -- Strukturen und Funktionen*.
Erdmann, K. O. 1925. *Die Bedeutung des Wortes*.
Grimm, J. 1905. *Deutsches Wörterbuch*. Bd. 10.
Hirt, H. and Arntz, H. 1939. *Haupt-probleme der indogermanischen Sprachwissenschaft*.
Hockett, C. F. 1969. *The State of the Art*.
Hymes, D. 1975. "The Pre-war Prague School and Post-war American Anthropological Linguistics", *CILT*. Volume 1.
Jespersen, O. 1970. *A Modern English Grammar II*.
---------- 1925. *The Philosophy of Grammar*.
---------- 1937. *Analytic Syntax*.
Kronasser, H. 1968. *Handbuch der Semasiologie*.
Labov, W. 1974. "The Boundaries of Words and Their Meaning", in Bailey, C. and Shuy, R. W., eds., *New Ways of Analyzing Variation*.
Langhoff, S. 1980. *Gestaltlinguistik -- eine ganzheitliche Beschreibung syntaktisch-semantischer Sprachfunktionen am Beispiel Modaler Infinitivkonstruktionen des Deutschen und Englischen*.
---------- Forthcoming. "Underspecified Modality in 'Have to/Be to' -- A Contrastive Study on Semantic Investiture".
List, G. 1973. *Psycholinguistik -- Eine Einführung*.
Maher, J. P. 1977a. "The Semantics and Perception of IC Structure: A Gestalt Approach to Color Terms: Green", *LACUS 3*.
---------- 1977b. *Papers on Language Theory and History I*. Amsterdam Studies in the Theory and History of Linguistic Science. Volume 3.
Meisel, J. M. 1975. "Ausländerdeutsch und Deutsch ausländischer Arbeiter", *Zeitschrift für Literaturwissenschaft und Linguistik* 18.
Mincoff, M. 1958. *An English Grammar*.
Onions, C. T. 1965. *An Advanced English Syntax*.
Pence, R. W. and Emery, D. W. 1963. *A Grammar of Present-day English*.
Perls, F. 1973. *The Gestalt Approach and Eye Witness to Therapy*.
Quirk, R. et al. 1972. *A Grammar of Contemporary English*.
Wandruszka, M. 1971. "Gedanken zu einer deutsch-französischen Intergrammatik", *Sprache der Gegenwart* 17.

THE PHONETIC NATURE OF THE NEO-ŠTOKAVIAN
ACCENT SHIFT IN SERBO-CROATIAN

ILSE LEHISTE and PAVLE IVIĆ
Ohio State   *Serbian Academy*
University   *of Sciences*

The Neo-Štokavian accent shift is generally assumed to have taken
place in the course of the 15th century. It consisted of moving the
word accent toward the beginning of the word by one syllable. New
tonal oppositions arose as a result of the accent shift: an original
accent on the first syllable of a word, which could not be moved further forward, is now phonetically and phonemically distinct from the
accent that appears on the first syllable as a result of being shifted
there from its original position on the second syllable. Since quantity remains distinctive in the dialects in which the accent shift took
place, those dialects now have four accents, traditionally referred to
as short falling, short rising, long falling, and long rising. In a
sequence of studies (Ivić 1958; Lehiste and Ivić 1963; Ivić and Lehiste
1963, 1965, 1967, 1969, 1970, 1972 Lehiste and Ivić 1972, 1973), we
have established the phonetic and perceptual characteristics of these
four accents in standard Serbo-Croatian, which is based on dialects in
which the accent shift was fully carried through. These phonetic characteristics involve four features: duration, fundamental frequency,
intensity, and vowel quality.

Greater duration, higher pitch, greater intensity, and unreduced
vowel quality are ordinarily considered features of stress. We prefer
to use the term "accent" to refer to perceptual prominence which may
involve any or all of these factors. There is no doubt that the syl-

lable now considered accented (and provided with an accent mark in
transcriptions) is perceived as the most prominent syllable of a word
or close-knit phrase consisting of a word and preposition. In many
Indo-European languages, the most prominent syllable (usually called
the stressed syllable) is characterized by all four above-mentioned
phonetic features: it has relatively higher pitch and greater length
than other syllables in the word, it possesses higher intensity and
contains a fully articulated vowel. Unstressed syllables lack one or
more of these characteristics.

In dialects in which the Neo-Štokavian accent shift has taken
place, syllables now perceived as accented derive from two sources.
There are originally accented syllables still bearing accent; these
syllables occur only as first syllables of a word. There are also
formerly pretonic syllables that now carry a shifted accent. Shifted
accents are found on any syllable of a word except the last. The
Neo-Štokavian accent shift moved the accent toward the beginning of
a word by one syllable; this, however, could not happen in cases in
which the accent was originally on the first syllable. One possible
outcome of the Neo-Štokavian accent shift could have been merger of
shifted accents with original accents on the first syllable. But the
merger did not take place. Words of two or more syllables, accented
on the first syllable, have different phonetic realizations depending
on whether the accent on the first syllable is an original first-syl-
lable accent or a shifted accent.

In words containing originally accented first syllables that still
carry accent, these accented syllables possess all four phonetic characteristics of stressedness: greater duration, higher pitch, greater intensity, and unreduced vowels. In such words there are no other syllables possessing these same features. In words in which the first
syllable carries a shifted accent, that first syllable likewise possesses the four characteristics of stressedness; however, the accented
syllable is not the only syllable with high pitch and high intensity.
The formerly stressed syllable -- now posttonic -- still carries high

pitch and high intensity. To establish the presence of accent on a
given syllable, high pitch and high intensity are not sufficient clues:
these features are shared by the two kinds of accented syllables, but
they are also shared by posttonic syllables following one kind of accented syllables (those bearing shifted accents).

Two features are shared by accented syllables alone: greater duration and unreduced vowel quality. These two features suffice to distinguish the syllables bearing a shifted accent from posttonic syllables following a shifted accent; however, they do not distinguish between the two kinds of accented syllables. Furthermore, both features
are somewhat unreliable for bearing the main burden of identifying the
presence of an accented syllable. One problem is that duration is independently contrastive: the opposition between long and short vowels
does not depend on the place of the accent, and is found in words with
both accent types. We have found that the duration of an unaccented
long vowel differs but little from the duration of an accented short
vowel. Duration may indeed serve as a strong stress cue, but in languages in which duration is independently contrastive, the importance
of duration as a stress cue is likely to be limited. The second problem is that vowel quality depends to a considerable extent on duration.
There is extensive allophonic variation in the quality of both stressed
and unstressed vowels depending on whether the vowel is phonemically
short or long. Again, if vowel length is contrastive and not confined
to stressed syllables, and if vowel quality is dependent on length, the
feature of vowel quality cannot serve as a primary cue to the presence
of stress.

Basically, then, differences in the type of accent cannot be con-
clusively identified on the basis of properties of the stressed syllable alone. The phonetic reasons have just been outlined; and there is
decisive confirmation from the fact that there are no accent differences in monosyllabic words. All monosyllabic words bear only one kind
of accent, which is conventionally identified with, and phonetically
similar to, the old unshifted accent on the first syllable of polysyl-

labic words -- the accent traditionally called falling.

But since the shift of the accent from the second syllable of a
word to the first did not result in a merger with words already bearing an accent on the first syllable, there must exist phonetic features
that make it possible to distinguish between old falling accents and
the new rising accents. Our descriptive studies show that the main difference between falling accents and rising accents lies in the relationship between the accented syllable and the posttonic syllable. We have
shown with experiments using synthetic speech that listeners are able
to identify the presence of one of the two accents on the first syllable of a disyllabic word if the relationship between the two syllables
possesses the following characteristics: the word is identified as
carrying the falling accent, when the posttonic syllable has a low fundamental frequency, and it is identified as carrying the rising accent,
when the posttonic syllable has a fundamental frequency that is approximately as high as or higher than that of the first syllable.

The Neo-Štokavian accent shift appears to have involved a number
of steps, both phonetic and interpretative. As the first step, pretonic syllables appear to have acquired higher fundamental frequency
and higher intensity than before -- possibly by a kind of anticipatory
assimilation. It was not a shift of high fundamental frequency and intensity from the accented syllable to the pretonic syllable; if it had
been, no tonal differences are likely to have resulted. Higher pitch
and higher intensity are, however, stress cues; the presence of these
two stress cues on the formerly pretonic syllable appears to have attracted to that syllable two further characteristics associated with
stress: greater length generally associated with a stressed syllable,
and the change from reduced vowel quality to unreduced quality. The
need to distinguish between original accents on the first syllable and
shifted accents on the first syllable then caused a major change in the
suprasegmental system of the language: the domain of accent changed
from a single syllable to a disyllabic sequence. Instead of identifying an accented syllable by properties of that syllable itself, speak-

ers now identify an accented syllable on the basis of the relationship
between the accented syllable and the posttonic syllable. There are
many possible reasons why fundamental frequency constitutes the main
basis for determining this relationship. It is well known that different syllable nuclei have different intrinsic intensities; thus intensity could serve a decisive role only if the vowels of the two syllables were identical, so that the difference in intrinsic intensities
could not interfere. Intensity differences may also result from such
nonlinguistic factors as changing distance between speakers or even a
casual turning of the head. The human ear appears to be relatively
more sensitive to fundamental frequency differences than to intensity
differences, even though it is difficult to compare sensitivities in
the two different sensory modalities. The reinterpretation of disyllabic sequences originally differing in the placement of stress as disyllabic sequences differing in the distribution of the fundamental
frequency contour thus seems quite plausible.

We have carried through extensive analyses of two dialects with
unshifted accents, one Čakavian dialect and one Kajkavian dialect
(Lehiste and Ivić 1973), and one Slavonian dialect in which the Neo-
Štokavian accent shift appears to be in progress (Lehiste and Ivić
1976). Our studies of Čakavian and Kajkavian accents show what the
accentual system of the Štokavian dialects may have been like before
the accent shift; the Slavonian dialect provides evidence for intermediate stages. The Čakavian and Kajkavian accentual systems involve two
long accents and one short accent. There exists a quantity opposition,
free stress, and a tonal opposition on stressed long vowels. The tonal
opposition on stressed long vowels is realized as a difference in the
fundamental frequency movement: the so-called long falling accent has
a rising-falling or falling fundamental frequency movement, while the
so-called neoacute accent has a relatively level fundamental frequency
contour. The two long accents may contrast on monosyllabic words as
well as on any syllable of a polysyllabic word. There are no systematic fundamental frequency differences associated with posttonic syllables.

In the Slavonian dialect, vowel length is likewise contrastive.
There are two short accents -- the short unshifted accent, called the
short falling accent, and the Neo-Štokavian short rising accent, but
the short falling accent is not restricted to the first syllable.
There are three long accents; the two old accents, long falling and
neoacute, and the Neo-Štokavian long rising accent. The distribution
of the two old accents resembles that found in Čakavian and Kajkavian
dialects with the old accentual system. Shifted long rising accents
have been moved toward the beginning of the word by one syllable. The
two old accents (falling and neoacute) differ among themselves with regard to the fundamental frequency movement on the accented long syllable itself. The long falling accent has a slight rise in the beginning, a peak close to the beginning, and a considerable fall toward the
termination of the syllable nucleus. The neoacute has either a mono-
tone fundamental frequency pattern or a rising-falling pattern with a
late peak. Both old accents are followed by posttonic syllables with
low fundamental frequency. The two old accents also contrast on monosyllabic words. The fundamental frequency curves of the neoacute and
the Neo-Štokavian long rising accent are practically identical on the
accented syllable; the old neoacute, however, is followed by a posttonic syllable with a low fundamental frequency, while the Neo-Štokavian long rising accent is followed by a syllable with a fundamental frequency that is on the average as high as the fundamental frequency on
the accented syllable. The Neo-Štokavian long rising accent never occurs on monosyllabic words. It would be impossible to distinguish it
from the neoacute (the old rising accent) on the basis of the phonetic
characteristics of the accented syllable itself.

These are observations made on the basis of words whose accents
are clearly identifiable. However, the four speakers who produced our
test materials (described in Lehiste and Ivić 1976) also produced
many words whose accentual patterns were not clearly identifiable
with any of the five standard patterns just described. We did not include the unstable productions in the article in which we described the

Slavonian accentual system. They were, however, transcribed and analyzed in the same manner as the other test materials, and provide crucial evidence for the accent shift in progress.

To change from the old unshifted system (as found in the Čakavian
and Kajkavian dialects) to the Neo-Štokavian system, several steps are
necessary. The opposition between the old falling accent and the neoacute has to be eliminated. Both old accents on the first syllable
have to acquire the phonetic shape of the long falling accent. Accents
occurring on non-first syllables have to be moved toward the beginning
of the word by one syllable; disyllabic sequences have to be created
with high pitch and intensity on both the formerly pretonic syllable
and the formerly accented syllable. Our four informants produced instances of all these steps, several of them having preferred patterns.
Speaker 2, for example, produced long falling accents on the first syllable in six out of 21 words in which speakers 3 and 4 had the neoacute on the first syllable. All speakers produced instances of incomplete shifts, in which the pretonic syllable has already acquired relatively high pitch and intensity, but the posttonic syllable is still
carrying its original pattern, including duration appropriate to a
stressed syllable. Often a different stage of the accent shift was
found in the productions of the same word by different speakers. For
example, the word *voda* "water" was produced by speaker 4 with its original accentual pattern -- short falling accent on the second syllable,
/vodà/; speakers 2 and 3 produced versions with incomplete shift (/vòdà/)
and speaker 1 had the Neo-Štokavian shifted form, with a short rising
accent on the first syllable, /vòda/. Exactly the same distribution of
stages was found for *koza* "goat"; other words showed variations of this
pattern. The word *igla* "needle", for example, was produced with the
original unshifted pattern (/iglà/) by speakers 2 and 4, with an incomplete shift (/ìglà/) by speaker 3, and with a complete shift by speaker
1 (/ìgla/).

The phonetic analysis of incomplete shifts suggest that the first
step in the accent shift does indeed involve anticipation of high funda-

mental frequency and intensity on the pretonic syllable. Completed
shift involves an additional durational change, relatively greater
length being shifted from the originally accented syllable to the originally pretonic syllable. There is no direct way to establish whether
the change in the domain of accentual pattern from the accented syllable to the disyllabic sequence has already taken place in the systems
of any of the speakers; indirectly, one might conclude that as soon as
minimal pairs arise in the language involving disyllabic words with the
neoacute (or falling) accent on the first syllable on the one hand, and
the Neo-Štokavian long rising on the first syllable on the other hand,
the relationship between the accented and posttonic syllables must have
become the crucial distinguishing factor. We did not include minimal
pairs in our test materials, but they contain a fair number of instances in which the accentual patterns are minimally contrastive, e.g.,
svȋla "silk" vs. strĩna "wife of father's brother"; trȃva "grass" vs.
šȃtra "tent"; etc.

It is an interesting question how the neutralization of the opposition between the old falling and the old rising accent (neoacute) relates to the development of the Neo-Štokavian accent shift. In the
dialects with shifted accents, there is no obvious trace of a possibly
different treatment of the two old accents during the accent shift:
both yield the Neo-Štokavian rising accents on the formerly pretonic
syllable, and both yield long falling accents on the first syllable.
The Slavonian situation suggests that speakers may have followed different paths in eliminating the opposition between the two old accents.
One of our speakers (speaker 2) appears to have advanced much farther
than the others in neutralizing this opposition and replacing the old
rising (neoacute) accent with the phonetic pattern characteristic of
the long falling accent. However, in our materials he only does this
in the first syllable. Clearly much more information is needed to
solve this problem; the observations based on four speakers each producing 216 test utterances can only serve to point out directions further research might take.

The presentation in this paper has been purposely kept on a very general and rather abstract level. There are many details that deserve separate presentation and discussion, for example, the differences between long and short accents, the ways in which word accents are modified in various sentence contexts, the extent to which word accents can be neutralized, the ways in which other features besides fundamental frequency may influence the perception of word accents, etc., etc. And we make no assumptions as to what might have prompted the accent shift in the first place. We do, however, offer the following tentative model for the process referred to as the Neo-Štokavian accent shift.

1. Acquisition of relatively high pitch and intensity by pretonic syllables, possibly through the mechanism of anticipatory assimilation, with retention of high pitch and intensity on the originally accented syllable.

2. Acquisition of relatively greater duration and unreduced vowel quality by the pretonic syllables.

3. Loss of relatively greater duration by formerly accented syllables, and gradual reduction of their vowel quality.

4. Reinterpretation of the phonetic characteristics of accentedness, involving the change of the domain of accent from a single syllable to a disyllabic sequence.

The accent shift was accompanied by neutralization of the opposition between long falling and neoacute accents, and by the phonetic merger of neoacute with the long falling accent on the first syllable of polysyllabic words and on monosyllabic words. Dialects differ as to whether this neutralization preceded the accent shift or took place in parallel with the steps outlined above. There is, however, no difference in the final outcome: in dialects in which the Neo-Štokavian accent shift has been completed, the opposition between the long falling and neoacute accents has been neutralized.

REFERENCES:

Ivić, Pavle. 1958. *Die serbokroatischen Dialekte*. The Hague: Mouton.
Ivić, Pavle and Lehiste, Ilse. 1963-72. "Prilozi ispitivanju fonetske i fonološke prirode akcenata u savremenom srpskohrvatskom književnom jeziku", Matica srpska, Novi Sad, *Zbornik za filologiju i lingvistiku*. Part I: VI (1963), pp. 31-71; Part II: VIII (1965), pp. 75-117; Part III: X (1967), pp. 55-93; Part IV: XII (1969), pp. 115-66; Part V: XIII (1970), pp. 225-46; Part VI: XV (1972), pp. 95-133.
Lehiste, Ilse and Ivić, Pavle. 1963. *Accent in Serbocroatian: An Experimental Study* (= *Michigan Slavic Materials, No. 4*). Ann Arbor: Michigan.
Lehiste, Ilse and Ivić, Pavle. 1972. "Experiments with Synthesized Serbocroatian Tones", *Phonetica* 26.1-15.
Lehiste, Ilse and Ivić, Pavle. 1973a. "Interaction between Tone and Quantity in Serbocroatian", *Phonetica* 28.182-90.
Lehiste, Ilse and Ivić, Pavle. 1973b. "Akustički opis akcenatskog sistema jednog čakavskog govora", *Naučni sastanak slavista u Vukove dane* 3.159-70.
Lehiste, Ilse and Ivić, Pavle. 1976. "Fonetska analisa jedne slavonske akcentuacije", *Naučni sastanak slavista u Vukove dane* 6.67-83.

HOMO : HVMVS AND THE SEMITIC COUNTERPARTS:
THE OLDEST CULTURALLY SIGNIFICANT ETYMOLOGY?

SAUL LEVIN
State University of New York at Binghamton

The main facts that I am going to cite are so widely known that a
connection between them might well have been perceived long ago. Actually it was noted by Brunner 1969:175.[1] Among the ancient Indo-European languages Latin is the most familiar to Occidentals, and among the
Semitic languages Hebrew. These two exhibit most clearly the pair of
words meaning 'man' and 'the ground': *homō, humus;* אָדָ֛ם {ʔɔðɔ́m}, אֲדָמָ֖ה
{ʔăðɔmɔ́ħ}. I intend to show the cultural import of having the words
for 'man' and 'the ground' formed from the same root. I will also explore the phonetic similarity of the Indo-European root to the Semitic.

There are many Indo-European cognates of *homō,* and even more of
humus. But they are unevenly distributed. Coexisting, like *homō* and
humus in Latin, are *žmuõ* and *žēmė* in Lithuanian. *Humus* and *žēmė,* however, are in quite different declensions, although their gender is feminine. For *humus,* in the Latin "second declension," the gender is a
significant anomaly, because most nouns of that declension are masculine. A more precise correspondence is between the locative *humī* 'on
the ground' and the adverb *žemaī* 'low' (Frankel 1965:1299,1320). The
Greek χαμαί means the same as *humī,* but Greek has no cognate to *homō.*

Duine, the Irish word for 'man,' has been analyzed as a derivative
from *dú,* whose genitive is *don* and which means 'a place'; only vestiges
are left in Old Irish of the earlier sense, 'the ground' (Vendryes
1923:437-441). The formation of *duine* is unlike *homō* and *žmuõ;* but it
recalls the Greek χθόνιος (vocative χθόνιε), which is manifestly

derived from χθών, χθον- 'the earth, the ground.' χθόνιος is accordingly an adjective that means 'pertaining to the ground, arising
from the ground'; but it has no particular reference to man and sometimes designates an infernal god (e.g., Aeschylus, *Cho*. 1).[2]

Homō and *žmuõ* are derivatives too, in a way, with something suffixed after the consonant *m* at the end of the root. Outside of the
nominative singular their stem is *homin-*, *žmon-* or *žmūn-*. The morphological process was prehistoric and archaic; no such nouns were still
being added to the Latin or the Lithuanian vocabulary from other roots
in the historical period. The root itself is nominal, rather than
verbal, and appears with no suffix at all in the Greek χθών, besides
being evinced by the Sanskrit case-forms {kṣámi} (locative) and {jmáḥ,
gmáḥ, kṣmáḥ} (genitive).

For my inquiry it is unnecessary to cite all the diverse Indo-
European evidence. Most pertinent are these generalizations:
(1) From no other word for 'the ground' -- no matter from what root --
is there a derivative that designates 'man.'
(2) Such words for 'man' are found only in certain languages that have
a related word for 'the ground.' But the Germanic group constitutes a
notable or at least an apparent exception: Gothic and Old English *guma*,
Old Norse *gumi*, Old High German *gomo*.

At this point it becomes more than a coincidence that these Germanic languages show, instead of any cognate of *humus*, a feminine noun
similar to the other Semitic word nearly synonymous with {ʔăḏɔmɔ́ɦ} --
namely, one similar to the Hebrew אֶרֶץ {ʔέrɛc}, Arabic أَرْضٌ {ʔard|un},
etc. Only Akkadian among the Semitic languages has a feminine suffix:
{arsatu(m)} or {erṣetu(m)}, whereas in Germanic it is either "strong"
as in Old Norse *jǫrð* or "weak" as in Old English *eorþe*, or mixed as in
the oblique cases of Old High German *erda*. The feminine gender is constant in both words for 'earth,' with or without a suffix, throughout
their Indo-European and Semitic range.[3]

Since Moeller (1909:34, 1911:72) pointed out the Semitic connections of the important Germanic word *jǫrð*, *eorþe*, *erda* (*earth* in modern

English), there has been no reason to ignore such an evident etymology,
whether or not we think it substantiates his theory of an ancestral
language earlier than Indo-European and Semitic. He cited also the Homeric Greek ἔραζε 'on (to) the ground.' There is, besides, a gloss of
Hesychius, ἐρεσιμήτρην· τὴν γεωμετρίαν -- i.e., 'ground-measure-
ment,' presumably drawn from an early text in the Ionic dialect. It
would be wrong to overlook these occurrences in Greek and imagine a total blank between Asia Minor and northern Europe.[4] But now we have to
consider together the two competing words for 'earth.' Not only are
they unequally distributed, one predominating in Indo-European, the
other in Semitic; but the adverb which means 'on the ground' is more
strikingly restricted.

The only clear Semitic cognate of the Hebrew {ʔăḏɔmɔ̄ħ} is the
post-Biblical Aramaic אַדְמְתָא {ʔₑḏæmtɔ̄(ʔ)}, with the suffixed article
{-ɔ(ʔ)}.[5] And not even in Hebrew is there anything from this root like
the Greek adverb χαμαί 'on the ground' or the Latin *humī*. On the
other hand Hebrew does express this meaning by אַרְצָה {ʔárˠcɔħ} or, at a
terminus, אָרְצָה {ʔɔ́rˠcɔħ} (e.g., Gen. 18:2, 24:52). An exact cognate
{arṣh} occurs in the brief Ugaritic corpus (Virolleaud 1936:34-35 and
pl. 1,3). Furthermore, Homeric Greek (as mentioned above) has ἔραζε
besides the more frequent χαμαί. ἔραζε is found nine times in all,
invariably at the end of a verse; it never reappears in subsequent
Greek literature. But a sort of hybrid, χαμᾶζε as if the end of
ἔραζε were attached to χαμαί, serves for a metrical alternant at
the end of a verse when preceded by a word with a final short vowel;
e.g., ἆλτο χαμᾶζε 'he jumped onto the ground' *(Il.* 3.29, etc.; cf.
Aristophanes, *Ach.* 341, 344).[6]

The unsuffixed {ʔɔḏɔ̄m} 'man' is most prominent in Hebrew, but also
common -- not surprisingly -- in Phoenician, a neighboring dialect, and
in Ugaritic. The cognate {ʔdm} in ancient South Arabian means 'a man'
in a special sense, a vassal or attendant. We leave aside the later
diffusion of the Hebrew word as a proper noun 'Adam' in Aramaic, Arabic, and Ethiopic, no less than in European languages.

Scientific linguistics cannot derive the unsuffixed masculine
{ʔɔdɔ́m} from the suffixed feminine {ʔădɔmɔ́ħ} as the Bible says that
{ʔɔdɔ́m} was fashioned (Gen. 2:7): "And the LORD God shaped man, dust
from the ground." However, in a few passages {ʔɔdɔ́m} itself stands as
an explicit or probable synonym for {ʔέrɛc} 'earth' (Baumgartner 1967:
14). The clearest is Proverbs 30:14, with its parallelism so typical
of Hebrew poetry: "to eat wretches off the earth (מֵאֶרֶץ {meʔέrɛc}) and
needy ones off the ground (or, from mankind, מֵאָדָם {meʔɔdɔ́m})." At
any rate מֵאָדָם in this verse is virtually equivalent to 'everywhere.'
Man was perceived to extend as far and wide as the earth does.

There is a Semitic root with the same three consonants {ʔ-d-m},
meaning 'red'; and Semitic etymologists, medieval and modern, have
tried to connect {ʔădɔmɔ́ħ} 'the ground' with it, and even {ʔɔdɔ́m}
'man.' I would not rule out the possibility of paronomasia, especially since {ʔɔdɔ́m} and {ʔădɔmɔ́ħ} are far from being pan-Semitic. Most
probably an Indo-European word, something like the Greek χθών, pene-
trated prehistorically into a part of the Semitic territory.

If we compare the Hebrew pair {ʔɔdɔ́m} and {ʔădɔmɔ́ħ} phonetically
with the Latin pair *homō* and *humus,* all that they share is [-ɔm].[7]
But the two prior consonants in Hebrew [ʔ-d] correspond better to an
Indo-European consonant group represented in Greek by χθ- [kʰtʰ].
The Indo-Europeanists have reconstructed the prehistoric source of it
as $*g^h\bar{d}$- or something just as unwieldy.[8] The actual Indo-European
languages show various simplifications of this theoretical complex
sound. We have only to posit that when it came into the forerunner of
Hebrew, the first component of it was reduced to a mere glottal stop.
For that is homorganic with any voiced consonant.[9]

Part of my theory is that the word carried an association with
'man,' as no other word for 'earth' did. The association, far from
being universal, is peculiar to certain cultures. In Latin of the
classical period, it remained only as a scholarly guess, for lack of
any clear morphological relation of *homō* to *humus;* and it was among
the many etymologies ridiculed by Quintilian (1.6.34); *etiamne hominem*

appellari [sc. *sinemus*] *quia sit humo natus, quasi uero non omnibus animalibus eadem origo, aut illi primi mortales ante nomen imposuerint terrae quam sibi* 'Shall we also allow man to be so called because he is born of the ground, as though all animals had not the same source or those first mortals set up a name for the earth before one for themselves?'

The modern Indo-Europeanists have, in effect, answered Quintilian's challenge by contrasting earthly man not with other earthly beings but with the heavenly gods -- *diut* or *di* in Latin.[10] The Sanskrit cognate {dēváḥ, dēvébhyaḥ}, etc., is indeed transparently formed from the root {div-} 'the sky' (genitive {diváḥ}); but none of the terms for 'man' in Sanskrit connects him with the earth. Greek has no cognate either of *homō* or of *diuus;* yet the adjective ἐπιχθόνιος 'on earth,' characterizing ἀνήρ 'a man,' is in obvious opposition to ἐπουράνιος 'in heaven,' characterizing θεός 'god' (*Il.* 2.553, *Od.* 18.484). In this vestigial way the sense of man's earthliness lingered among the Greeks.[11]

From Hebrew we get a different view of the relation between {ʔɔd͡ɔ́m} 'man' and the ground, and the contrast between man and other beings. At the beginning of creation, according to Genesis 2:5, "the LORD God had not made rain upon the earth (עַל־הָאָרֶץ { əal-hɔʔɔ́rɛc}), and there was no man to tend the ground (וְאָדָם אַיִן לַעֲבֹד אֶת־הָאֲדָמָה: {wᵛʔɔd͡ɔ́m ʔáyin laəðɓód ʔɛꟳ-hɔʔɔ̆d͡ɔmɔ́ħ})." The earth as something to tend is {ʔɔ̆d͡ɔmɔ́ħ}, not {ʔɛ́rɛc} (cf. Gen. 4:2, Zech. 13:5, Pr. 12:11, 28:19; Is. 30:24); and {ʔɔd͡ɔ́m} is man in the role of tending it, as a husbandman rather than a hunter.

{ʔɔd͡ɔ́m}, furthermore, is often contrasted with אֱלֹהִים {ʔĕlohíym} 'God' or 'gods,' and God's abode is in the sky (e.g., Ps. 14:2, 115:16). But when the immediate contrast is between sky and earth, the expression is שָׁמַיִם וָאָרֶץ {sɔmáyim wɔʔɔ́rɛc}, never *{sɔmáyim waʔɔ̆d͡ɔmɔ́ħ}. As the ordinary Hebrew word for 'mankind,' {ʔɔd͡ɔ́m} contrasts man's habitat with that of the birds and the fish. Hence man's paradoxical mastery over these is emphasized in the powerful verse, Genesis 1:26,

"And God said, 'Let's make mankind {ʔɔdɔ́m} in our image, by our like-
ness; and let them dominate the fish of the sea and the fowl of the
sky, and the beasts and all the earth {hɔʔɔ́rɛc}, and all the reptiles
crawling upon the earth (again {hɔʔɔ́rɛc}).'" Man's superiority to the
creatures <u>outside</u> of his own element is mentioned first; and their element -- the sea or the sky -- is expressed.

Even the other terrestrial animals, in Hebrew, are less associated
with {ʔǎdɔmɔ́ɦ} than man is. The wild beasts are חַיַּת הָאָרֶץ {xay·áꝷ
hɔʔɔ́rɛc} (Gen. 1:25,30, etc.) or in the more archaic form חַיְתוֹ־אֶרֶץ
{xay⌣ꝷow⌣ʔɛ́rɛc} (1:24, Ps. 79:2), or alternatively חַיַּת הַשָּׂדֶה {xay·áꝷ
haś·ɔdɛ́ɦ} (Gen. 2:19,20, etc.), חַיְתוֹ שָׂדָי {xay⌣ꝷow śɔdɔ̄́y} (Is. 56:9, Ps.
104:11), literally 'the beast of the field,' חַיְתוֹ־יָעַר {xay⌣ꝷow⌣yɔ̄ʿar}
(Ps. 50:10, 104:20) 'the beast of the wood.' Similarly, when the tame
beasts are included, בְּהֱמַת הָאָרֶץ {b·ɛhɛ̆máꝷ hɔʔɔ́rɛc} (Is. 18:6, etc.)
with the collective singular like {xay·áꝷ}, or the plural בַּהֲמוֹת שָׂדָי
{b·ahǎmówꝷ śɔdɔ̄́y} (Ps. 8:8, Joel 2:22). Only the crawlers are mentioned along with either word for 'earth': רֶמֶשׂ הָאֲדָמָה {rɛ́mɛś
hɔʔǎdɔmɔ́ɦ} (Gen. 1:25, etc.), or {hɔrɛ́mɛś hɔromɛ́ś ʿal⌣hɔʔɔ́rɛc} 'the
reptiles crawling upon the earth' (quoted above; cf. Ezek. 38:20). Man
and the reptiles, including the worms, are most intimate with the soil;
and man gets it on his head purposely in token of grief (וַאֲדָמָה עַל־רֹאשׁוֹ:
{waʔǎdɔmɔ́ɦ ʿal⌣roʔśów}, I Sam. 4:12; cf. Neh. 9:1).

The occurrences of the Ugaritic cognate of {ʔɔdɔ́m} are datable ar-
chaeologically from the second millennium B.C. Beyond that, the distribution of forms that mean 'man' and forms that mean 'ground' or
'earth' in ancient Semitic and Indo-European languages suggests a considerable prehistory. Other items of vocabulary that are well repre-
sented in both groups, such as the Arabic ﺛَﻮْﺭًﺍ {θawr|an} 'a bull' (ac-
cusative) : ταῦρον, Latin *taurum*, etc. (Pokorny 1959:1083), prove
some common experience in an early period; but it may have been merely
the clear observation of something naturally conspicuous. It need not
constitute proof that both groups, for example, had already <u>tamed</u> the
bull. The words that associate 'man' with 'the ground' are more in-

triguing, in that they attach him intimately to something particular
in his surroundings and reveal his mind swaying his perceptions.

That this came about pretty early in Indo-European prehistory is
likely, because of the unusual or anomalous formation of *homō* (and its
case-forms) from the root. The recurrences in Hebrew and some related
Semitic languages do not, in my opinion, point to a pre-Indo-European
and pre-Semitic origin, but rather to diffusion -- diffusion, however,
from an Indo-European source which unlike Latin preserved a complex
initial consonant. Reciprocal diffusion would account for the distribution of the other word for 'earth,' well-nigh universal in Semitic, found also in some European languages -- notably the Germanic.

Any etymology, if valid, shows that the speakers of a certain
language were aware of such-and-such, and it bears upon their culture
to that extent. But the etymologies I would single out show something
more special than that. They uncover influences of which there is
otherwise not a trace.

NOTES

1) I came upon it independently (Levin 1971:735), but of course I
give him credit for priority.

2) Also the Sanskrit {ksámyah} (genitive {ksámyasya}, RV. 2.14.
11, 7.46.2) simply means 'earthly,' in contrast to {divyáḥ} 'heavenly.' In Tocharian A {śom} 'youth,' B {śaumo} 'man' (pl. {śāmna}) may
be from the same root as A {tkam} (genitive {tkanis}), B {kem}
'earth'; but opinion is divided -- see Schulze 1931:80. At best the
speakers of the language could hardly have sensed any etymological
connection, as was more palpable in Latin.

3) The Germanic word represented by *ground* in modern English
(< OE. *grund)* is considered to have no Indo-European cognates -- *grunt*
in certain Slavic languages and *grunt-* in the Baltic languages being
simply a loan-word from High German. But I suggest that it may reflect the root $*g^h\overline{a}$-m + a suffix (whereas *guma, gumi, gomo* 'man' reflects the root with the initial consonant-group simplified). In most
Germanic languages it is <u>masculine</u>, but feminine in Old Norse and usually in Middle Low German as well as some modern dialects (Grimm, s.v.
"Grund").

4) The Germanic languages stand out also in having the number
'seven' without -*t-*, unlike the rest of Indo-European but like Semitic
(Levin 1975:202-203). It is no accident that 'six' and 'seven' are

the numbers manifestly cognate; for they were of the utmost importance
in Mesopotamian and Hebrew civilization, the influence of which is
known to have been immense in historical times. That it began still
earlier, appears quite probable from these numerals and some other
items of vocabulary.

5) The Syriac (Christian) writing agrees approximately with the
Jewish אַהְמְרָא or אַמְרָא. The {-mt-} right before the suffixed article is reminiscent of the consonants at the end of the Germanic noun
grund (above, note 3).

6) In the *Iliad* it is limited to the final position -- 23 times
out of 24; and the lone instance of
Τυδεΐδης δὲ χαμᾶζε θορὼν ἔναρα βροτόεντα (*Il.* 10.528)
comes in the lay of Dolon, which is recognised to be in a quite different and presumably later style (cf. *Od.* 16.191, 22.84). χαμᾶζε
was preferred to ἔραζε; for where they would be metrically interchangeable -- after a verb in -ε(ν) -- it is χαμᾶζε, except in
χεῦεν ἔραζε 'he poured on the ground' (*Il.* 17.619, *Od.* 15.527,
etc.), where *χεῦε χαμᾶζε would have entailed a repetition of [k^h].

The morphology of ἔραζε is dubious, because the phonetic value
of the letter Z is not established, and neither is that of the Hebrew
צ. In spite of θύραζε 'out of doors' (*Il.* 18.416, etc.), which
could well be taken for the accusative plural θύρᾱς (cf. 6.89,298,
etc.) + -δε (as in οἴκαδε 'home(ward),' φύγαδε 'to flight,'
etc.), there is a strong argument against positing a morpheme boundary
within the ζ ([éras-] or [éraz-] + [-de]): τέλοσδε 'goal-ward' (*Il.*
9.411, 13.602), Θήβασδ' ἦλθε 'he went to Thebes' (23.679, with elision of -ε), and ἔρεβόσδε 'westward' or 'to the darkness' (*Od.* 20.
356) show that -δε added to a base in σ did not produce -ζε in Homeric Greek (contrary to the Attic Θήβαζε, 'Αθήναζε). So it is
quite possible that ἔραζε was not formed within Greek, but merely adapted from a Semitic source not unlike what is found in Hebrew.

7) The nominative ending of *hum|us* is possibly cognate to the He-
brew "construct" {ʔaďˇmaŧ, ʔaďˇmoŧ-} '(someone's) ground.' But on the
whole the "construct" feminine {-aŧ, -ɔŧ-} of Hebrew corresponds rather
to the "third declension" neuter -*us* (-ος in Greek, {-aḥ} in Sanskrit). See Levin 1971:254-255.

8) Pokorny 1959:414 symbolizes it *$gh\bar{d}$-. The Hittite word for
'earth,' variously transcribed {te-e-kan, tegan, tēkan}, is regarded as
cognate by some but not all Indo-Europeanists; besides Pokorny, p. 416,
see Friedrich 1952:220. The dental consonant comes before the velar,
as in Tocharian A {tkam̐} (see above, note 2); but in Hittite a vowel
intervenes. In the light of general phonology, a metathesis from
dental + velar to velar + dental is more likely, given a non-initial
cluster of consonants; but it is hard to gauge whether the Greek χθ-
or the Tocharian {tk-} reflects a more ancient sequence.

9) The vowel [-ɔ-] between these two consonants in {ʔɔďɔm} is conditioned in Hebrew by the accent on the syllable immediately following.
The [-ǎ-] in {ʔǎďɔmɔ́ḥ} is, on the other hand, a minimal transition between the consonants; and it is similar in Aramaic.

10) Meillet 1920:255: "Quand . . . on recourt à des expressions
telles que 'mortel' . . . ou que 'terrestre,' comme il arrive dans
lat. *homō*, got. *guma*; lit. *žmogùs* (pl. *žmônês*ჟ et qu'on oppose ainsi
les 'hommes' aux dieux 'immortels' et 'célestes,' on se sert d'un vocabulaire d'origine religieuse." Cf. Porzig 1954:208.

11) ἐπίγειος, a synonym of ἐπιχθόνιος, does not appear until much later and refers to man only in an epitaph found at Rome *(IG*
14.1571.4).

REFERENCES

Baumgartner, Walter. 1967. *Hebräisches und aramäisches Lexikon zum
Alten Testament.* 2d ed. Leiden: E. J. Brill.
Brunner, Linus. [1969]. *Die gemeinsamen Wurzeln des semitischen und
indogermanischen Wortschatzes.* Bern: Francke.
Fraenkel, Ernst. 1965. *Litauisches etymologisches Wörterbuch.* Vol. II.
Heidelberg: C. Winter.
Friedrich, Johannes. 1952. *Hethitisches Wörterbuch.* Heidelberg: C. Win-
ter.
Grimm, Jacob und Wilhelm [et al.]. 1854-1954. *Deutsches Wörterbuch.*
Leipzig: S. Hirzel.
Levin, Saul. 1971. *The Indo-European and Semitic Languages: An Explora-
tion of Structural Similarities Related to Accent, Chiefly in Greek,
Sanskrit, and Hebrew.* Albany: State University of New York Press.
_____. 1975. "The Indo-European and Semitic Languages: A Reply to
Oswald Szemerényi". *General Linguistics* 15.197-205.
Meillet, A. 1920. "Les noms du 'feu' et de l' 'eau'". *Mémoires de la
Société de Linguistique de Paris* 21.249-266.
Moeller, Hermann. 1909. *Indoeuropaeisk-semitisk sammelignende Glossari-
um.* Kjøbenhavn: G. H. Schultz.
_____. 1911. *Vergleichendes indogermanisch-semitisches Wörterbuch.*
Göttingen: Vandenhoeck & Ruprecht.
Pokorny, Julius. 1959. *Indogermanisches etymologisches Wörterbuch.* Vol.
I. Bern: Francke.
Porzig, Walter. 1954. *Die Gliederung des indogermanischen Sprach-
gebiets.* Heidelberg: C. Winter.
Schulze, Wilhelm, Emil Sieg, and Wilhelm Siegling. 1931. *Tocharische
Grammatik.* Göttingen: Vandenhoeck & Ruprecht.
Vendryes, J. 1923. "Sur quelques faits de vocabulaire". *Revue celtique.*
40.428-441.
Virolleaud, Charles. 1936. *La légende de Keret.* (Mission de Ras-Sharma,
vol. II) Paris: P. Geuthner.

LA DESINENCE FEMININE *-esse*

LEENA LÖFSTEDT
University of Helsinki

La désinence *-(e)sse* < *-issa* désigne une personne féminine dans des mots remontant au grec par l'intermédiaire du latin, p.ex.:

afr. *abbeesse, abbesse* < *abbatissa*
    diaconisse (XIVe s.) < *diaconissa*, etc.

et dans des néologismes romans ou français:

    comte - comtesse (à partir de la Chanson de Roland)

    prestre - prestresse (1190-1718; significations principales "femme attachée au culte d'une des anciennes divinités"; "concubine de prêtre", FEW IX, p. 358a)

    prince - princesse (à partir de 1320 "fille ou femme de prince", FEW IX, p. 390a)

    aprentif/s - apresntisse (p. ex. EBoilLMest.36,8 se auc. vent s'aprentisse), etc.

En raison de l'emploi fréquent du résultat du lat. *-issa*, le lat. *-trix* n'a guère survécu en français.[1]

Parfois il y a de la redondance. Si *maistresse* a été utile pour distinguer le *maistre* (< *magister*) masc. (v. T-L *maistre* col. 904 sqq.) de la *maistre* (< *magistra*) féminine (v. T-L col. 912 sq.), les deux termes, distincts en latin, étant confondus en français, le terme *compagnesse* est superflu à côté de *compagne* qui, appliqué à des êtres humains est exclusivement du féminin, ainsi que *louvesse* à côté de *louve*,

servesse à côté de *serve*, etc.; de même *damesse*, hapax, qui peut être
dû à des nécessités métriques.[2]

Parfois on peut observer une certaine hésitation quant au radical
utilisé: au XIVe s. *diaconisse* est concurrencé par *diacresse* formé par
le masc. correspondant (*diacre* < *diaconus*), p. ex. - L'*s* flexionnel du
c.-s. masc. ne s'est conservé, sauf erreur, que dans le fêm. correspondant à *senechal* : *senechaucesse*, *senechalcesce* (aflandr. XIIIe s., cf.
T-L s.v. et FEW XVII p. 70a), ces deux à côté de *senescalesse* (FEW
ibid.) - Un cas spécial est également *sachesse* qui fait concurrence à
sachete (T-L "religieuse de l'Ordre du sac ou de la pénitence de Jésus-
Christ"); le masc. correspondant est le dim. *sachet*.

Ajoutons que les types tirés d'un adj. (substantivé) sont récents:
borgnesse noté par le FEW dès 1613 (I 569 b) semble remonter à Michel
d'Amboise et à Rabelais (v. Huguet s.v.); *pauvresse* (FEW VIII p. 58 a :
1788) et *sauvagesse* (FEW XI, p. 618 a) datent de l'époque moderne.

Certains sous-groupes se détachent d'entre les fêm. en -*esse*. Les
masc. en -*e(s)/-on* forment leurs féminins en -*(on)nesse*: dans ce cas,
la nasale du c.-r. masc. fait partie du dérivé féminin: *baron - bar-
(on)nesse*:

<blockquote>

Guil Brit. 135 a　　virago: barenesse
G. Coinci 185, 231　　Et des mesons lors leur barnesses
　　　　　　　　　　　Seur leurs barons se font mestresses
　　　　　　　　　　　　　　(T-L s.v. *barnesse*),

</blockquote>

de même *vignon - vignonnesse* (Godefroy) et les termes péjoratifs *larron
- larronesse*, *larenesse*, *larnesse* et *felon - felonesse*, *felenesse*, ce
dernier ayant donné naissance à un nouveau masc. *felonés* (T-L *felon*,
col. 1696 sq.). Ajoutons l'adv. *glotonessement* (du XVe s., FEW IV p.
173 a) correspondant à *gloton* dont le fêm. normal est *glote*.

Les formes awallon. *mienesse*, correspondant à l'afr. (en part.
pic., flandr., hain.) *mie*, et *mirjenesse*, correspondant à l'anorm. *mi-
rie*, *mirje* (cf. FEW VI:I, p. 604 a-b, tous dérivés de *medicus*) montrent
que -*(on)nesse* peut être utilisé en dehors de son champ d'emploi primi-
tif.

Un autre sous-groupe est formé de termes en -*erresse* (-*eresse* dans
les documents récents) correspondant aux masc. du type -*er(r)e(s)/-eor*
(lat. -*ator/-atorem*), plus proches ceux-ci, du c.-s. que c.-r. masc.
Ce groupe est largement majoritaire: en effet de 194 noms féminins en
-*esse* que j'ai tirés du T-L (A-S inclusivement), 159 appartienent au
type -*er(r)esse*, soit plus de 75%. Ces termes désignent le plus souvent des artisanes. On a l'impression qu'il s'agit d'une création
facile et spontanée: le verbe dont on peut tirer un nomen agentis en
-*erre(s)/-eor*, se prête également à la formation d'un équivalent féminin en -*er(r)esse*. Dans la plupart des cas, le masc. en -*erre(s)/-eor*
est effectivement attesté. Cependant *chevaleresse* (XIVe - XVIe s.)
correspond à *chevalier*, et -*er(r)esse* empiète également sur le domaine
d'-*esse*: à côté de *miresse* (de *mire* "médecin") on trouve les formes
mireresse, *mirreresse*, à côté de *clergesse* (correspondant à *clerc*) on
a la variante *clergerasse* (de Metz, cf. ci-dessous).[3]
     Le même suffixe fém. a été utilisé, dès l'afr., pour des forma-
tions (semi-)érudites, basées sur un radical latin: le masc. correspondant est en -*or*, -*eur* ou fait défaut:

> *curator* (T-L XIIe s.) - *curaterresse* (Godefroy, de 1359),
> *predecesseur* (fin XIIIe s.) - *predecesseresse* (XIVe s.,
>   v. FEW IX, p. 287 b),
> *successeur, successour* (XIIIe s.) - *successeresse* (XIVe s.,
>   v. FEW XII, p. 379 b),
> *testamenteur* (FEW XIII:I, p. 283 a: 1200-1631) - *testa-
>   menteresse* (Godefroy, fin XIIIe s.),
> *testateur* (XIIIe s.) - *testateresse* (XIVe s., v. FEW XIII:I,
>   p. 283 b),
> *tuteur* (XIIIe s.) - *tuterresse* (début XIVe s., v. FEW
>   XIII:2, p. 450 b),
> *usufruiteresse* (1303), *usufrutueresse* (1498); pas de masc.
>   correspondant. Pour le masc., on se sert du terme
>   *usefructuaire* (hapax XIIIe s.), *usufructuaire* (à par-
>   tir de 1328, v. FEW XIV, p. 86 a),
> *succederesse* (1382) est sans masc., le terme est probable-
>   ment fait sur *demanderesse* (FEW XII, p. 379 b et note 6),
> *mineresse* "une fille mineure qui approche de la majorité"
>   terme dialectal propre à l'Est et au Nord-Est, fém.
>   de *mineur*, appartient à ce même type semi-érudit (v.
>   FEW VI:2, p. 125 a).

Il n'est donc pas étonnant que *-er(r)esse* ait résisté beaucoup plus longtemps que son partenaire morphologique, le c.-s. masc. *-e(r)re(s)* et que plusieurs termes datent d'une époque où l'ancien c.-r. était la seule forme du masc. Huguet donne p. ex. les paires suivantes: *chicaneur - chicanneresse, colporteur - colporteresse* (d'un texte de l'an 1533), *controuveur - controuveresse*, etc.

Le troisième type, *-euresse*, est assez rare. Il est tiré du masc. en *-eur* (< *-orem*), soit directement, soit par l'intermédiaire d'un fém. en *-eure* (v. ci-dessous), ou bien il est emprunté au provençal *-oressa*: *freremenouresse*, hapax anglonormand (FEW VI:2, p. 125 a); *menouresse* à côté de *menourete* appartient au dial. béarn. (ibid.); mfr. *segnieuresse* peut provenir du provençal (FEW XI, p. 451 b), de même *mayeuresse* (FEW VI:I, p. 56 b).

Les paires presentées par Rabelais (v. Huguet s.v. *abbegesse*)

> V 2   Les masles il nommoit...Abbegaux, Evesgaux, Cardin-
>   gaux...Les femelles il nommoit Abbegesses, Evesges-
>   gesses, Cardingesses,

relevant du type *-al/-esse*, n'ont pas de parallèles ailleurs (v. pourtant p. 228).

Fréquent et productif au moyen âge, *-esse* désignant des êtres féminins est un suffix plutôt rare de nos jours.[4] Les néologismes sont rare (p. ex. *félibresse*, FEW III, p. 446 b, qui est resté un terme livresque) et plusieurs termes anciens luttent pour leur existence: *ministresse*, qui a signifié "servante" (XIVe s. - XVIIe s.), "femme d'un ministre protestant" (1623); "femme d'un ministre", cède la place à *Madame* dans cette dernière acception: le Ministre et Madame X (Stehli, p. 105). De même, ce terme, lorsqu'il désigne une "femme ministre" (Lar 1949 cité par FEW VI:2, p. 116 b) doit subir la concurrence plus heureuse de *ministre* (cf. Stehli, p. 94 et p. 100). Seul, *maire* peut désigner "femme maire" à côté de *mairesse* qui, dès le moyen âge, a désigné "femme d'un maire" (FEW VI:I, p. 56 b); aujourd'hui on appelle le plus souvent *Madame* la femme d'un maire

Les femmes exerçant une profession traditionnellement masculine pré-
fèrent donc en général utiliser le titre de leurs confrères, et les
épouses de ces confrères portent le titre *Madame*: les deux groupes
évitent les titres spécifiquement féminins devenus équivoques.

Les titres univoques ont mieux résisté (*abbesse*; *princesse*). Les
termes *typesse*, *piffresse*, *chéfesse* appartiennent au langage populaire,
de même *pastoresse* (Stehli, p. 28). L'influence de l'anglais supporte
certains termes: *hôtesse (de l'air)* est étayé par *(air) hostess*; le
récent *stewardesse* est un anglicisme (Grevisse §244).

C'est surtout le type *-er(r)esse* qui est rare aujourd'hui. Notons
quakeresse (1755, v. FEW XVIII, p. 100 b) qui correspond à l'anglais
quakeress (attesté 1764, cf. *A Dict. of Amer. Engl.*); et les termes
juridiques *bailleresse* "qui baille à ferme ou à loyer", *défenderesse*
"à qui on fait une demande en justice, partie à laquelle le procès est
intenté", *demanderesse* et *venderesse*, ces deux derniers ayant les équi-
valents *demandeuse*, *vendeuse* dans l'emploi ordinaire; *chasseresse* qui
est poétique et cède la place à *chasseuse* dans le langage ordinaire;
charmeresse qui est vieilli; *pécheresse* qui est un terme de culte; en
dehors de ces termes spéciaux il en restent *devineresse*, *enchanteresse*
et *vengeresse* dont on peut dire pour le moins qu'ils n'appartiennent
pas au vocabulaire de base, encore que ces deux derniers soient assez
fréquents, comme adj., en littérature.[5]

La première étape dans la lente disparition du type *-er(r)esse*
est sans doute la perte du c.-s. masc. *-e(r)re(s)*, c.-à-d. de la base
morphologique du type fém. La seconde étape est la naissance de deux
nouvelles formes féminines qui remplacent *-er(r)esse*: *-euse* d'origine
populaire, et *-atrice* d'origine savante.

En choisissant un nouveau féminin pour *-eur* la langue a hésité
entre l'addition d'un *e* féminin (p. ex. *successeurs et successeures*,
Godefroy; *possessoure*, FEW IX, p. 238 a, Grevisse §347 b rem.), moyen
phonétiquement peu sûr à cause de l'amuïssement de l'*e* final; et l'emploi du suffixe adjectival *-euse* (*heureux - heureuse*). Ce dernier rem-
porte la victoire définitive au XVIe s., car la désinence *-eur* s'était

confondu avec *-eux* en raison de l'amuïssement· des consonnes: des consonnes finales selon Meyer-Lübke (*Hist. Gr.* II §50) ou des consonnes
préconsonantiques selon Fouché, p. 669, rem. Celui-ci soutient que
la perte temporaire de l'*r* final est due à l'analogie du pl.: *men-*
teu(r)s avec l'amuïssement d'un *-r-* préconsonantique ayant déterminé
menteu(r). Quoi qu'il en soit, le nomen agentis en *-eur* se confond
ainsi avec l'adj. en *-eux* et on relève, aux XVIe - XVIIe s., bon nom-
bre de graphies du type *chasseux, contreroleux* pour *chasseur, contre-*
roleur; citons de Huguet

> M. de la Porte, *Epithètes*, 288 r°. Oiseleur. Cauteleux
> ou caut, patient chasseux (Huguet, s.v. *chasseux*),

> Aubigné, Miss. et Disc. mil. 24 (I 191) que le Marechal...
> se face contrerolleux du General des vivres (Huguet
> s.v. *contreroleux*, cf. également Fouché l.c.)

A cette même époque deviennent fréquents les féminins du type
chasseuse, contreroleuse (v. Huguet) et les auteurs commencent à hé-
siter entre *-euse* et *-eresse*, p. ex.

> M. de la Porte, *Epithètes* 259 r° et v° Medee: Colchide,
> sorciere... empoisonneuse ou empoisonneresse (Huguet,
> s.v. *empoisonneresse*)

La forme *-eresse* est pendant longtemps soutenue par la tradition:
l'existence d'un terme en *-euse* n'exclut pas la création d'un synonyme
en *-eresse*: *causeuse* est daté déjà en 1534 alors que *causeresse* n'est
attesté q'en 1580 (FEW II:I, p. 543 b et 544 a).

Le type *-eur/-euse*, toujours productif à l'époque moderne (*appre-*
teur - appreteuse) est le continuateur le plus important du type médi-
éval *-erre(s)/-er(r)esse*. En partie, la paire médiévale a délégué ses
fonctions à la paire *-ateur/-atrice* qui également reste productive (p.
ex. *agitateur - agitatrice*, v. Stehli, p. 138).

Parfois le développement *-er(r)esse > -atrice* a été sinon tout à

fait mécanique, au moins facilité par un développement phonétique:
l'amuïssement de l'*e* intertonique. A côté des formations semi-latines
en *er(r)esse* (p. 219): *curaterresse*, *testateresse*, *tuterresse*, on observe les graphies *curatresse* (Godefroy, de l'an 1424), *testatresse*
(FEW XIII:I, p. 283 b: utilisé entre 1400-1565), *tutreisse* (Godefroy,
déjà 1301). La prononciation n'a guère changé lorsqu'on a latinisé
ou italianisé la graphie en *curatrice* (FEW II:2, p. 1562 a, de l'an
1478), etc.

La graphie *testaresse* (Godefroy, 1412) qui pour le FEW XIII:I,
p. 284, note 4, semble être une faute de copie ou de lecture, peut
être étayée par *debellaresse* (Huguet) et considérée, elle aussi, comme
témoin d'une fusion entre -*atrice* (dont elle conserve la voyelle de
liaison[7]) et -*er(r)esse* (dont elle conserve la désinence).

S'il règne en maître pendant la période de l'afr., le suffixe
-*er(r)esse* se trouve donc en rivalité avec deux autres suffixes impor-
tants dès le mfr. Dans le même temps, à partir de l'époque de l'afr.,
s'opère un autre développement lexicographique: la modification du
sens et de l'emploi d'-*er(r)esse*.

Un nomen agentis latin peut être utilisé comme adj., lorsque
l'adj. correspondant fait défaut (*Creator Spiritus*, etc. v. Hofmann-
Szantyr §92; Cic. ad Quint. I 1,19 *in tam corruptrice* provincia, v.
Wackernagel, p. 54); cela vaut également pour le type en -*o(n-)* désignant des êtres vivants (*exercitus tiro*; Plaut. Aul. 562 *magis curi-
onem*, v. Hofmann-Szantyr, l.c.). La paire fr. -*erre(s)*, -*eor* / -*er(r)-
esse* connaît le même emploi:

> Dial. Gr. 19,7 par ars enchanteresses,
> JM *Veg.* 4,37 nex espiarresses, etc.,[8]

et il est fréquent pour le type -*on/-(on)nesse*:

> JM *Veg.* 4,39 une tres felonnesse estoile,
> Jub. N. Rec. II,114 et si estoit si larronnesse, que...
>   (T-L s.v. *larronesse*),
> Joufr. 3777 Puis fu haute dame barnesse (T-L s.v. *barnesse*).

A l'époque de l'afr. *felon/felonnesse* est presque uniquement adj.; de
même à l'époque moderne, le survivant de ce groupe, le terme *patronnesse*
(*dame patronnesse*), tandis que la forme ordinaire du fém. de *patron* est
patronne (Grevisse §244 2, 4).

L'emploi adjectival d'-*er(r)esse* a été favorisé par la collision
de ce suffixe avec -*erece*. Les suffixe afr. -*erez*, -*eret/-erece* résultats d'-*ariciu(s)/-aricia* (cf. Meyer-Lübke, *Hist. Gr.* §133) servent à
former des adj. dénominals et, plus tard, déverbals, qui désignent
quelque chose qui appartient au nom principal ou qui exécute l'acitivi-
té exprimée par le verbe:

> (*celle*) *vineresse* (S. Bern. *serm.*, Godefroy) est dérivé de
> *vin*,
>
> (*kien*) *cacheret* (Gl. Lille, T-L *chacerez*) peut être tiré
> de *chasse* ou de *chasser*,
>
> (*annel*) *esposeret* (1484) appartient au verbe *espouser* (FEW
> XII, p. 211 a).

A l'exception du picard et du normand, les résultats du lat. -*icia* et
du lat. -*issa* sont identiques dans les dialectes de la Gaule du Nord:
ainsi *chevaleresse* "femme, fille d'un chevalier" est devenu homophone
avec *chevalerece* "appartenant à un cheval" (p. ex. *biere chevalerece*)
et ce dernier terme est souvent même écrit *chevaleresse* (v. T-L); de
même le fém. de *chasserez* "appartenant à la chasse", "propre à faire la
chasse" est homophone, plus tard homonyme, du fém. de *chasserre(s)*
"chasser". Un terme en -*er(r)esse* représente donc aussi bien un adj.
(-*erez*) qu'un nomen agentis (-*erre[s]*). Cependant, au fur et à mesure
que le masc. -*erre(s)* tombe en désuétude, l'emploi adjectival devient
de plus en plus fréquent. Sémantiquement, au lieu de désigner "quel-
qu'un qui exerce telle activité, qui a telle activité pour métier", le
suffixe -*er(r)esse* revêt fréquemment un sens plus vague "(personne, être
ou chose) capable de qch", "susceptible de telle activité", "en ayant
l'habitude", ce qui perment à un poète médiocre de remplacer les verbes

finals qui ne riment pas par deux tours du type *être + er(r)esse* qui
riment toujours, p. ex.

<blockquote>
Peler. v. 5553 N'estes que embabilleresse
de gent e enveloperesse
(T-L s.v. *embabilleresse*)

v. 9510 Ceste main est pertuiseresse
de maisons et descouverresse
(T-L *descouverresse*)
</blockquote>

ou aux écrivains de la renaissance d'utiliser les termes en *-er(r)esse*
surtout comme épithètes, se rapportant aussi bien à des choses qu'à des
êtres humains :

<blockquote>
p. ex. *levres baiseresses, affaires chicanneresses.*
qualités comanderesses; voix flateresse,
langues flateresses, flateresse grace, chançon
flateresse, Muse flateresse, tourbe flateresse
(Huguet s. les lemmata en *-esse*),
</blockquote>

ou équivalant souvent à un participe

<blockquote>
Gringore, *Les folles entreprises*, 1,25 langues serpen-
tines, decepvantes, flateresses (Huguet s.v. *fla-*
teresse),
</blockquote>

ou suivis de compléments d'adverbe

<blockquote>
Ambr. *Guerre* 3540 Une i ot (sc. perriere) si jeteresse /
que trop estoit damajeresse (T-L s.v. *damageresse*)

Anc. *Poés. franç.* II 189 elles sont si malles / Plus
jangleresses que sigalles (Huguet s.v. *jangleresse*)

Montaigne I,40 une loyauté messagere et aucunement pi-
peresse (Huguet s.v. *pipeur*)
</blockquote>

En raison de ce développement le type *-er(r)esse* avait perdu sa

précision lexicographique. Toujours préférée du point de vue stylis-
tique, la désinence n'avait plus aucun avantage sémantique sur *-euse*:
les deux servaient former des nomina agentis et des adjectifs.

Non seulement les termes en *-er(r)esse* et *-(on)nesse*, mais les
autres mots en *-esse* aussi sont parfois utilisés comme épithètes:

> Dial. Gr. 214,3 sa compagnesse disciple (condiscipula,
>   v. T-L s.v. *compagnesse*)
>
> (Passim:)   galère capitainesse (Huguet, s.v. *capitaine*),

maîtresse et *traîtresse* connaissent toujours cet emploi,[9] cf. Grevisse
§349. A l'époque moderne on laisse pourtant souvent les formes *maître*
et *traître* se rapporter à des termes féminins; les autres termes en
-esse qui sont restés assez fréquents aujourd'hui ne connaissent guère
l'emploi adjectival: on dit *une drôlesse*, *Suissesse*, *duchesse*, *com-
tesse*, *nègresse*, *pauvresse*, etc., mais *une histoire drôle*, *une femme
suisse*, p. ex.,[10], cf. Grevisse l.c.

Ce sont donc les termes en *-esse* grammaticalement univoques (seulement noms) qui ont le mieux résisté. On est amené à en conclure que le
double rôle joué par les fém. en *-er(r)esse* au moyen âge et pendant la
renaissance a diminué les chances de survie du nomen agentis. A mon
avis cet emploi adjectival d'*-er(r)esse* a causé plus de dommage que le
développement sémantique de certains nomina agentis qui finissent par
désigner des instruments (Meyer-Lübke, *Hist. Gr.* §52 et 65 et *Gr. d.
rom. Spr.* II §490, p. ex. *écumeresse* "écumoire"), ou le sens particulier qu'on reçu certains représentants isolés de l'ancienne dérivation
par le suffixe *-erece* (*sécheresse*, *forteresse*, cf. Meyer-Lübke, *Hist.
Gr.* §133). En effet, *-eur* et *-euse* peuvent eux aussi désigner des ma-
chines (*projecteur*, *veilleuse*, cf. en outre Stehli, p. 111) et une poly-
valence du même type que *forteresse*, *chanteresse* gêne d'autres suffixes
également (cf. *travailleur* - *honneur* et tous les fém. en *-eur*; *richesse*,
bassesse - *pauvresse*).

Il y a pourtant une ressemblance phonétique qui a pu effectivement

nuire à la survie du fém. -esse. Il est heureux pour -esse que le suffixe -asse augmentatif - péjoratif ne soit devenu fréquent et productif
qu'au XVIe s. (Meyer-Lübke, Hist. Gr. §173) et que ce développement
n'ait guère eu lieu que dans les dialectes méridionaux du domaine français, où il est dû à l'influence des langues limitrophes (Gamillscheg-
Spitzer, p. 44 sq.).

Cependant /asse/ péjoratif n'est pas tout à fait inconnu de l'ancien fr. non plus: riace "qui rit trop ou mal à propos" (XIIIe s. -
Pathelin) semble être tiré du verbe rire (FEW X, p. 397 b,p. 400 a,
note 4):

> Du clerc qui fame espousa, 583: Tant par iert fox
> qu'il n'avoit mie/ Seulement une seule amie/
> Ainz en avoit .II. a sa sele:/ L'une estoit josne
> jouvencele,/ Et l'autre estoit vielle riace/
> Plus que l'aiole saint Pancrace, etc.

Pigace (pica + agaza, cf. FEW VIII, p. 421 a et 424, notes 4,6)
s'applique à une femme qui se pare vaniteusement, dans un texte agn.
de l'an 1285 (v. Grisay-Lavis-Dubois-Stasse, p. 199).

Cependant ni riace ni pigace ne peuvent être confondus avec des
termes en -esse (*riesse et *pigesse n'existent pas). Cette confusion
des désinences existe pour l'afr. baiasse/baiesse (< bacassa, cf. FEW
I, p. 196 b) "servante". Le terme n'est pas expressément péjoratif en
afr.: ce n'est qu'au XVIe s. que bagasse adopte le sens "prostituée"
sous l'influence du provençal, changement dont a pris son essor l'emploi très fréquent du suffixe péjoratif -asse.[12] Cependant, comparé
à des titres afr. comme princesse, duchesse, chevaleresse, etc., bai-
asse/baiesse désignait une personne de rang inférieur et on imagine
facilement que, même avant la modification sémantique, le terme a pu
être utilisé comme invective.

Alors que baiasse/baiesse ne sont que variantes d'un seul terme,
les deux dérivés d'homme, hommesse et hommasse, désignant des femmes
les deux, sont à l'origine du mois, deux mots distincts l'un de l'autre.

Hommesse relevé aux XIVe - XVIIe s., *hommesse* "vassale" (1340, v. Godefroy s.v.), *hommesse lige* "femme qui doit hommage à un suzerain" (FEW
IV, p. 456 b), et *hommassement* dans le Ménagier de Paris:

> 1, p. 14 (Femmes)...qui ne tiennent compte de leur honneur
> ne de l'onnesteté de leur estat...et marchent hommas-
> sement et se maintiennent laidement...,

semble indiquer que le terme péjoratif *hommasse* "(femme) virile, qui
tient moins de la femme que d'un homme" (FEW IV, p. 454 b) date d'avant
ce texte (1393). *Hommace* n'est attesté qu'au XVIe s.; il est notamment
utilisé comme traduction du lat. *virago*:

> Du Moulin, *Chirom.*, p. 133   Celles auxquelles croist
> la barbe sont appelees viragines ou hommasses
> (Grissay-Levis-Dubois-Stasse, p. 195).

> Calvin, *Bible fr.*, Genèse 2, Lors Adam dit: A ceste fois
> il y a os de mes os, chair de ma chair: on appellera
> icelle hommace, car elle a esté prise de l'homme (Hu-
> guet, s.v. *hommasse*),

Chez Cotgrave *hommesse* signifie "femme virile":

> Hommesse, a manly or stout woman (Godefroy s.v.).

Devenu synonyme avec *hommasse*, *hommesse* est sorti de l'usage: seul
hommasse est resté vivace.

   Parmi les termes péjoratifs en -*asse* relevés des dialectes du Sud-
Ouest par Gamillscheg-Spitzer, p. 45, le poitev. *boitrasse* "femme boi-
teuse" et *pétrasse* propre aux dial. vend. et angev., s'expliquent à mon
avis[13] par une confusion d'-*er(r)esse* et d'-*asse*: en effet, l'-*r*- fai-
sant partie de ces dérivés de *boiter*, *péter* doit être attribué à l'influence d'-*er(r)esse*.

   La désinence féminine des paires rabelaisiennes du type *abbegal* -
abbegesse est-elle hypercorrecte? La forme fém. phonétiquement la plus

proche d'*abbegal* est *abbegasse* -- la valeur de /ga/ reste intacte. Rabelais connaissait la terminaison -*asse* et savait également qu'à son
époque elle n'était pas courante à Paris. L'aurait-il supplantée par
-*esse*?

Dans l'Est de la France, la confusion des suffixes -*esse* et -*asse*
était inévitable à cause de la palatalisation d'*a* et de la confusion
d'*a* et d'*e* qui en résulte. La graphie -*asse* est souvent utilisée au
lieu d'-*esse*: notons *contasse* (alorr., cf. FEW II:2, p. 940 b), *clergerasse* (Metz, de l'an 1345, v. Godefroy) et *leivres beserasses* (Greg.
Ez. 92,10, teste bourg. du XIIe s.). Un texte champenois (Aube) de
1305 donne *Adine la mirause*, exemple que le FEW VI:I, p. 604 b range
parmi ceux du type *miresse*. La graphie *au* indique-t-elle que l'*a* était
vélarisé (cf. lorr. *tauble*, Pope §1322 XVI, Wilmotte, p. 257) et non
pas palatalisé, c.-à-d. que la terminaison (hypercorrecte?) était défi-
nitivement un -*asse*, non pas un -*esse*? On imagine facilement que cette
désinence féminine des dialectes de l'Est, instable du moins graphique-
ment, s'est confondue avec le nouveau suffixe -*asse* et que cette confusion avec un suffixe péjoratif était nuisible à la survie de la désinence fém., et l'on s'attend par conséquent plutôt à trouver des restes
de ce type dans des dialectes septentrionaux du domaine où le suffixe
péjoratif n'avait pas pénétré. Cela semble être le cas, cf. FEW III,
p. 214 a: wallon *eleresse*, lièg. *èléresse* "éplucheuse"; ibid. VII, p.
403 a lièg. *ourdiherèsse* "femme qui ourdit la toile"; de même, à côté
du terme juridique *trève pecheresse* qui remonte probablement au moyen
âge, on trouve le lièg. *vèdje pèh'rèce* "ligne à pêcher", les deux termes
représentant l'adj. *pesceret*, -*ece* "propre à la pêche" (FEW VIII, p.
579 a).

Un cas particulier est constitué par la paire *bêta*, *bétasse* du fr.
populaire: la nuance péjorative du suffixe fém. est superflue dans
cette combinaison (redondance péjorative: le sémème *bête* + le suffixe
-*asse*, cf. Trésor de la langue fr. s.v. *bétasse*). Cf. *putasse* qui est
dialectal (v. note 12).

Nous avons déjà constaté que les femmes exerçant une profession

traditionnellement masculine portent volontiers le titre de leurs confrères (*poète, professeur, docteur*,[14] *pasteur, dentiste*,[15] etc.). Le
titre masculin est plus général: "Mlle X est une célèbre poètesse"
semble indiquer que, pour n'être qu'une femme, elle ne rime pas mal,
tandis que "Mlle X est un célèbre poète" égale la dame à tous les po-
ètes contemporains, hommes et femmes. En plus, on a vu que certains
titres féminins peuvent prêter à équivoque désignant traditionnellement
non (seulement) la femme qui exerce telle fonction, mais (aussi) l'é-
pouse de son confrère[16]: *Mme l'amirale, Mme la ministresse*, etc.

L'emploi du masc. pour désigner une femme n'est pourtant pas une
innovation de notre temps. Etayée par un usage latin,[17] cette substitution est pratiquée déjà au moyen âge lorsque la situation rend clair
le sens de l'énoncé:

> Ménag. 1, p. 6 (adressé à une femme) Le quart
> article est que vous comme souverain maistre
> de vostre hostel, sachiez ordonner disners, etc.

parfois d'entre plusieurs termes, un seul est au fém.:

> ibid. 2, p. 59 Aprés, chere seur, sachiez que
> sur elles, aprés vostre mary, vous devez estre
> maistresse de l'ostel, commandeur, visiteur,
> gouverneur et souverain administrateur.

> St. Francois de Sales, *Sermons recueillis*, 34
> (IX, 341) Moyse entonna son beau cantique...
> en ce mesme temps Marie sa soeur chantoit...
> avec celles de son sexe, comme capitainesse
> et chef d'iceluy (Huguet, s.v. *capitaine*).

Dans l'exemple suivant, réduplication synonymique d'un type unique, le
terme fém. semble désigner les travaux féminins de servante dont se
charge la dame, et le terme masculin l'état social auquel elle descend.
Le terme masc. est donc plus général:

Ménag. 1, p. 83 Sarre...en laissa son lit et le
soulas de son mary, et lui bailla Agar sa
chambriere et la fist dame, et elle tres
humblement devint serviteresse et humble
servant.

NOTES :

1) Cf. les restes *fausseriz*, *genitris*, *miautriz*; au sujet de nouveaux emprunts v. ci-dessous. - On a parfois *duchoise* (< -*ense* ?) en
afr.; c'est la variante en -*esse* qui l'a emporté.

2) Enéas 6987 *quant poingneient a els damesses / cuidoient que
fussent deesses*; selon l'apparat de Salverda de Grave, *damesses* est la
leçon du ms. D seulement.

3) Encore au XVIe s. *capitenneresse* (hapax au lieu de *capitainesse*;
Huguet, s.v. *capitaine*) et à l'époque moderne *droleresse* (Neufch., Belgique) à côté de *drolesse* (FEW III, p. 161 a; cf. ci-dessous p. 226).

4) Grevisse §244,2 et §245 en énumère une soixantaine dont plusieurs n'appartiennent pas au langage quotidien.

5) Le type -*er(r)esse* a pourtant mieux résisté dans certains dialectes (cf. p. 229).

6) Ce développement s'annonce peut-être déjà dans *prieus* (dès
1170) / *prieuse* (dès Chrétien de Troyes, cf. FEW IX, p. 394 a), où le
changement de suffixe (*prior* > *prieus* ou déjà lat. *prior* > *priosus*) ne
semble pas être expliqué. Parmi les dictionnaires latins, seul Du
Cange connaît *priosa*, et ce terme est expliqué comme un emprunt au français. Par analogie *sousprieus/supprieuse* (hain., ca 1350, cf. T-L s.v.
sosprior et *sospriose*). Cf. aussi T-L s.v. *tuëor*. - La prononciation
indiquée est restée jusqu'à nos jours dans *monsieur*.

7) A moins qu'il ne s'agisse d'une simple confusion d'*er* et d'*ar*
(cf. Fouché, p. 349).

8) Cf. l'emploi des suffixes prov. et portug. -*aire* et -*ador* qui
forment des adj. verbaux (portug. *abridor* "qui ouvre", *accusador* "accu-
sant", v. Meyer-Lübke, *Gr. d. rom. Spr.* II, §490).

9) T-L a plusieurs exemples de *traistresse* adj. et FEW XIII, p.
153 a, donne *traistressement* à partir du XIIIe s.; *maistresse* est attesté comme épithète au XVe s., v. FEW VI:I, p. 41 a.

10) De même *princesse* ne semble pas connaître l'emploi adjectival:
amendes princesses et *haricots princesses*, donnés comme exemples de
l'emploi adjectival de *princesse* chez Littré s'expliquent plutôt comme
mot principal + apposition: sg. *haricot* (masc. !) *princesse*, pl. *haricots princesses* par attraction.

11) Cf. p. 44: "Von einer wirklich pejorativen Form des Suffixes
kann im eigentlichen Norden Frankreichs nicht gesprochen werden, da
hier das Suffix an Bezeichnungen von Einzelwesen nicht antritt".

12) Surtout dans les dialectes mériodionaux du domaine fr., pour
désigner une personne du sexe fém.: *pétrasse* (angev., vend.), *pétasse*

(vend.), *putasse* (Anjou), *boitrasse* (poitev.); c'est Joubert, *Erreurs populaires au fait de la médicine* (1578), qui a introduit le terme *fillasse* dans la litt. fr. (Gamillscheg-Spitzer, p. 45). - Le terme *bécasse* appliqué à des femmes (à partir du XVIe s., v. Trésor de la langue fr.) diffère de *pigasse* en ce que l'oiseau n'a rien de péjoratif; *bécasse* péj. semble plutôt s'expliquer comme une récomposition: *bec* + *-asse*.

13) Gamillscheg-Spitzer l.c. supposent, pour *pétrasse*, la fusion de *putasse* avec *péter*.

14) Le terme *doctoresse*, assez vivace, peut désigner une "femme médecin" tandis qu'une femme promue dans une université au grade le plus élevé est *docteur* (Stehli, p. 37 et Grevisse, §245 rem. 3): en s'adressant à ces dames on emploie *docteur* invariablement.

15) Dans les termes en *-e*, l'article peut désigner le sexe: *une dentiste*, *une architecte* (mais *un poète*).

16) Ambivalence qui n'a gêné les titres des artisanes qu'à un moindre degré. Dans la société de nos ancêtres la femme d'un artisan participait au travail de son mari que celui-ci exécutait au domicile (cf. EBoil. *LMest.* XXXVII, 3 *Se un home est Crespiniers et sa fame Crespiniere*; ibid. LXXXVII, 17 *se valet du mestier prent fame qui ne soit du mestier, il ne puet pas a sa fame aprendre le mestier devant qu'il ait son ovrooir tenu an et jour*), en effet le métier dont la veuve héritait et qu'elle était capable de continuer était la base de sa sécurité sociale (ibid. XL, 11 *Item, chascune fame de cy en avant qui aura esté fame de mestre ouvrier juré...pourra ouvrer et faire ouvrer en toute sa veveté ou dit mestier*; LIII, 5; LXX, 6; LXXXVII, 9).

17) Cf. B. Löfstedt, *Symbolae Osloenses*, 38/1963, pp. 47 sqq., en part. p. 49, note 8.

ABREVIATIONS:

A.   Dictionnaires Utilisés:

A *Dictionary of American English on Hist. Principles*, compiled at the University of Chicago under the editorship of Sir William A. Craigie and James R. Hulbert. 1938-1944. Chicago: University of Chicago Press.

Du Cange = *Glossarium mediae et infimae Latinitatis conditum a C. du Fresne*, domino Du Cange, editio nova a L. Fabre. 1-10, 1883-1887. Niort.

FEW = Wartburg, Walter v., *Französisches etymologisches Wörterbuch*. 1922. Tübingen: J. C. B. Mohr.

Godefroy, F. *Dictionnaire de l'ancienne langue française*. 1-10. 1880-1902. Paris: F. Wieweg.

Huguet, E. *Dictionnaire de la langue française du seizième siècle*. 1925-1967. Paris: H. Champion.

Lar 1949 = *Nouveau Larousse Universel*. 2 vol. s.d. (1948-1949). Paris: Larousse.

T-L = *Altfranzösisches Wörterbuch*. 1925- Adolf Toblers nachgelassene Materialien bearbeitet und mit Unterstützung der preuss. Akademie der Wiss., von der 25. Lieferung an mit Unterstützung der Akademie der Wiss. und der Lit. (Mainz) hg. von E. Lommatzsch. Berlin-Wiesbaden.

Trésor de la langue française, dictionnaire de la langue du XIXe et du XXe s., publié sous la direction de P. Imbs. 1971- . Paris: Editions du centre national de la recherche scientifique.

B. Textes:

EBoil *LMest*. = *Livre des mestiers d'Etienne Boileau*, p. p. R. de Lespinasse et F. Bonnardot, 1879. Paris: Impr. Nationale, sous les auspices de l'Edilité parisienne.

JM *Veg* = *Vegesce*...traduction par Jean de Meun, p. p. L. Löfstedt, 1977, Helsinki: Annales Acad. Scient. Fennicae.

Ménag. = *Le Ménagier de Paris*, traité de morale et d'économie domestique, composé vers 1393 par un bourgeois parisien, p. p. J. Pichon. 1846-1847. Paris: Société des Bibliophiles Français.

(Pour d'autres textes v. les bibliographies du T-L et du FEW.)

OUVRAGES CONSULTÉS:

Fouché, P. 1966-1973. *Phonétique historique du fr*. 1-3. 2e éd. Paris: Klincksieck.

Gamillscheg, E. - Spitzer, L. 1921. *Beitr. zur rom. Wortbildungslehre*. Génève: I.S. Olschki. (Contenu: Grundzüge der gallorom. Wortbildung par E. G., Über Ausbildung...von Gegensinn par L. S.)

Grevisse, M. 1964. *Le bon usage*. 8e éd. Gembloux (Belgique)-Paris: Ed. Duculot-Libr. Hatier.

Grisay, A. - Lavis, G. - Dubois - Stasse, M. 1969. *Les dénominations de la femme*. Gembloux: J. Duculot.

Hofmann - Szantyr = (Leumann, M. -) Hofmann, J. B. - Szantyr, A. 1972. *Lateinische Grammatik II*. München: Beck.

Meyer-Lübke, *Hist. Gr.* = Meyer-Lübke, W. 1921. *Historische Grammatik der französischen Sprache*. 2. Teil. Wortbildungslehre. Heidelberg: C. Winter.

Meyer-Lübke, W. 1890-1902. *Grammatik der romanischen Sprachen*. 1-4. Leipzig: Reisland.

Pope, M. K. 1966. *From Latin to Modern French*. Réimpr. de l'éd. rév. 1934. Manchester: University Press.

Stehli, W.   1949.   *Die Fem.-bildung von Personennamen im neuesten Französisch.*   Bern: A. Francke.
Wackernagel, J.   1957.   *Vorlesungen über Syntax II.*   2e éd.   Basel: Birkhäuser.
Wilmotte, M.   1932.   *Etudes de philologie wallonne.*   Paris-Liège: Libr. Droz.

BETWEEN MONOGENESIS AND POLYGENESIS

YAKOV MALKIEL
University of California, Berkeley

I.

In our culture, *mono-* and *poly-* have become neatly contoured,
sharply polarized prefixes, entering into a number of words familiar
not only to specialists but also to educated laymen. To be sure,
there are situations in which only the formation displaying *mono-*
has attained importance -- let me remind you of *monolith*, *monologue*,
monomania, and *monopoly*, and the reverse also happens: *Polyglot* is
a far more common word than *monoglot*. Occasionally, the element of
contrast is lost: For most speakers, a *monograph* is not at all asso-
ciable with a *polygraph*. But the normal state of affairs presupposes,
it is almost idle to insist, some sort of polarization: *monogamy* vs.
polygamy, *monotheism* vs. *polytheism*, *monomorphism* vs. *polymorphism*,
and the like. Within this majority group, one can, at first glance,
safely place *monogenesis* vs. *polygenesis*, two parallel terms which
were made famous, in the past century, particularly by research in
folklore, to say nothing of their role in theology, but which also
served as key terms in glottogenetic research, including the sensa-
tional turn-of-the-century studies by Alfredo Trombetti, especially
his provocatively titled 1905 book, *L'unità d'origine del linguaggio*.

In today's biological and physical sciences, *mono-* and *poly-*
also enjoy considerable currency, but the polarization seems distinctly
less dramatic. Very often, the rapidly expanding highly technical ter-

minologies of these sciences offer whole clusters of tags, involving
mono-, *di-* (or *bi-*), *tri-*, and, upon occasion, even higher numbers,
so that *poly-* appears only at the end of a series, implying some such
message as "more than three", or "more than four", or even "more than
five". Examples can be culled from any up-to-date encyclopedia, e.g.,
monophiletic, *diphiletic*, *polyphiletic*; *mononuclear*, *binuclear*, *tri-*
nuclear, *polynuclear*. This sort of specialization has spilled over
into linguistics: *mono-*, *bi-* (or *di-*), *tri-syllabic*; *mono-*, *di-*, *tri-*
phthong; and the like. The modern languages are sometimes divided in
their respective preferences for the Latin or the Greek numerals, so
that one finds *mono-* and *poly-* pitted against *uni-* and *multi-*, but
this is a side-issue of very small relevance. Truly important is the
fact that *mono-* and *poly-* are not, inescapably, subject to polarization the way *in* and *out*, *before* and *after*, *up* and *down*, *cis-* and *trans-*,
endo- and *exo-* seem to be in ordinary or scientific discourse. Could
there be some middle ground between monogenesis and polygenesis, the
way these labels are used in linguistic analysis?

Today's paper is purely exploratory and does not aspire to any
Yes-or-No decision on this score. Its aim will be amply fulfilled if
we can end the discussion on some such conciliatory note as: "Perhaps". Moreover, to get the discussion off the ground, I have avoided
tackling grandiose problems, such as the origin of speech, of a specific language family, or even of a concrete language, and have limited myself to tidily circumscribed lexical problems, among which the
simplest could pass off as blends or mergers. You may reject as far
too pompous the appeal to mono- or poly-genesis in contexts where individual word origins, however complicated, are involved. At least, I
have circumnavigated the hazard of improper sensationalism by refrain-
ing from the use of any such alternative title as "Words of Dubious
Paternity".

I propose to examine, in different depths of detail, all in all
four lexical situations, where close inspection cautions us against the
assumption of a simple, rectilinear descent from a single source. In

certain contexts we shall witness not only conflations of the ordinary type, but genuine instances of protracted symbiosis. The last example to be examined transcends by a wide margin even the boldest definitions of lexical contamination.

II.

By way of opening illustration, let me present to you the case history of the Romance family to which E. *desire* (verb and noun) clearly pertains. On the surface, everything seems to be smooth, but this smoothness, as you will see before long, is deceptive. *Desire*, of course, reflects Fr. *désirer* and *désir*, which, a hunch tells us, somehow belong to Lat. dēsīderāre and dēsīderium. The first proposition is (*grosso modo*) accurate; the second -- as we shall at once discover -- is, to a considerable extent, untenable. But, before plunging into the maze of seemingly self-contradictory Romance data, let us closely inspect the underlying Latin family.

Experienced Latinists, such as A. Ernout, report that dēsīderāre and its partner cōnsīderāre are both based on sīdus, -eris "star"; better still, on the far more common plural, sīdera "configuration of stars, constellation". Both verbs have a long record;[1] on indirect evidence one assumes that cōnsīderāre was the first to be coined, initially perhaps in the language of augurs or mariners, in which it may have meant *"to gaze at constellations". Soon cōnsīderāre, in the company of its near-synonym contemplāre, acquired a lay meaning and infiltrated into everyday speech, with the broader and paler connotation of "examining carefully and with proper respect". Dēsīderāre, patterned on this older verb on the model of dēserere "to desert, forsake" vs. cōnserere "to join, fit", at the outset no doubt meant "to cease seeing, to notice -- as a rule, regretfully -- the absence of...", whence soon thereafter the more familiar "to search for, desire". A matter of major importance -- and one, unfortunately, neglected by generations of researchers -- is the fact that in Antiquity scholars were well aware

of the links tying sīdus to cōnsīderāre and dēsīderāre, as can be inferred from statements by the lexicographer Paulus ex Festo and the
grammarian Priscian; uneducated laymen, however, were quick to forget
about sīdus and sīdera, judging from the strikingly meager progeny of
these words in the Romance vernaculars,[2] even though the subfamilies
of cōn- and dē-sīderāre demonstrably continued to be mutually associated.[3] The consequence of this wide-reaching decay of sīdus in folk
speech was that cōn- and dē-sīderāre became hollow words -- after peel-
ing off the transparent prefixes one was left with nothing, as in E.
be-reave or Fr. *re-cevoir*.

   In medieval glossaries, such correspondences as Lat. *desidero* =
OSp. *desear*, or OPtg. *desejar*, or OFr. *desirer* were routinely established;[4] true, those were mere glosses, not by any chance formal pronouncements on genetic descent; but, as long as scholars remain human,
glosses, inevitably, will have half-hidden etymological implications.
With the advent of Renaissance, Neoclassicism, and Enlightenment in
the Romance countries, more explicit etymological commitments will be
found, seeking to connect both dēsīderāre with, say, Sp. *desear* and,
worse, dēsīderium with *deseo* -- worse because the mechanism of the ex-
traction of postverbal nouns from given verbs simply was not properly
understood before 1800.[5] Where pioneering etymologists and lexicogra-
phers omitted this word-family altogether or skipped the expected genetic comment, the chances are that they did so in a spirit of selec-
tivity, because the derivation seemed too obvious to deserve mention.[6]

   The situation changed abruptly in the mid-19th century, with the
flourishing of a historically oriented comparatism. Diez recognized
that, whatever the status of Fr. *désirer* and *désir* and of transparently
learnèd It. *desiderare* and *desiderio*, those among their counterparts
and rivals which lacked a consonant ordinarily as stable as *r* invited
a different approach. Thus he brought together a sharply profiled
group of nouns, namely, It. *disio*, Sp. *deseo*, Ptg. *desejo*, Prov. *desig*,
Cat. *desitj* (French was consipicuously unrepresented, he felt), endowed
them with the semantic common denominator "nostalgia", placed them hier-

archically ahead of the corresponding verbs (*disiare*, *desear*, etc.),
and proposed dissĭdium "separation" -- a fairly infrequent word, perhaps even a false reading for discĭdium, as the etymon (1853:125).[7]
Diez's idea was accepted *in nuce* by some immediate followers and found
supporters -- including a Menéndez Pidal -- even at much later dates,
when powerful alternatives had already been proposed.[8] Interestingly,
it ran very soon into stiff resistance in certain quarters. Thus, W.
Foerster (1879:511, n. 2) disliked the older scholar's semantic analysis
and, moreover, groped for a base with an open *e*, rather than a closed
i, in an effort to do justice to an OProv. variant, heretofore neglected, namely, *deşieg*. He reverted to Lat. dēsīderiu, but traced all
Romance forms to an assumed variant shorn of the *r*, thus: *desideiu,
a reconstruction which, granted its credibility, was indeed a help in
dealing with Provençal, Italian, and Spanish, but, as we now realize,
was irreconcilable with the /ž/ of Ptg. *desejo*.[9] Meyer-Lübke, on the
other hand, starting with his doctoral dissertation (1883:155) and
until the bitter end, defended a different conjecture: He was willing
to go along with Diez's dissĭdiu on the assumption that, through false
regression or rather recomposition -- on the model of sĕdēre "to sit"
beside assiduus --, a new lexical type, namely, *dissĕdiu, had arisen
in folk speech.[10] As if these three explanations were insufficient,
two more "theories" were launched in quick succession. Almost simultaneously with the appearance of Meyer-Lübke's thesis, an, all told,
less than prestigious etymologist, namely, F. Settegast, ventilated a
possibility (1883:244) which, though initially brushed off -- e.g., by
an almost sarcastic Gaston Paris (1883:133) -- or merely listed without
approval, as was done by A. Scheler, in the end, to everyone's surprise,
almost won out. According to Settegast's view, the starting point was
not the marginally recorded dissĭdium, but a very familiar abstract,
dēsĭdia, literally "a sitting long, remaining in a place", then, figur-
atively, "a sitting idle, idleness, inactivity, slothfulness", a derivative from the adj. dēses, -idis "indolent" and, like its primitive,
a member of the far-flung sedēre family. True, this supposition re-

quired some semantic legerdemain; but Settegast, for once, turned out
to be an astonishingly adroit juggler, and his partisans, half a century later, accomplished even more in keeping this explanation afloat.
Finally, a scholar of the first magnitude, and a spokesman, from the
start, for provincial Latinity, namely, H. Schuchardt, came up with a
fifth explanation, whose chief characteristic is that its advocate had
abandoned all hope of offering a single base for all Romance offshoots
(1889:533). In Schuchardt's estimate, dēsīderiu should never have been
completely dumped; comparison of Sp. *impropério* "insult" with It. *rim-
provero* "reproach" prompts one to allow, on purely accentual grounds,
for *dēsīd(e)ru as a regional variant of dēsīderiu, a conjecture which
accounts for Fr. *désir*, It. *disio*, while Sp. *deseo* and Ptg. *desejo* postulate another, more innovative variant, *dēsīdiu, for which analogy,
one way or the other, will do the trick.[11]

Compared to the liveliness of discussions in the period between
1853 and 1889, which produced five independent hypotheses in thirty-six
years, the following decades may be described as uneventful, even dull.
To be sure, the assiduity of certain scholars yielded commendable results; thus, the Old French gap pointed out by Diez -- that language
seemed to lack an exact counterpart of It. *disio*, Prov. *desieg*, etc.
-- by dint of philological effort was eventually filled.[12] But, otherwise, even reputable specialists were willing to settle on various
sorts of unexciting compromises. Let me cite just two illustrations.
After fifteen years of intensive thinking about the vicissitudes of
Old Spanish sibilants, J. D. M. Ford hit upon the idea that either
Diez's solution ("'separation, lack, want', therefore 'wish, desire'")
or Foerster's alternative -- i.e., Conjectures 1 or 2, may be accepted
(1911:210a).[13] On the opposite side of the Atlantic, a Romanist as
many-sided and well-informed as W. von Wartburg, in Fasc. 12 of his
dictionary, which was distributed in 1928, at least, tried to amalga-
mate into a single composite hypothesis the separate solutions previously advocated by Settegast, in 1883, and by Meyer-Lübke, on several
occasions (1934:52-53). It is difficult to avoid the impression of a

spell of doldrums, if not of a certain stagnancy.

Though there has occurred, I repeat, no genuine breakthrough over the last few decades, Settegast's once weakly-argued thesis has been gradually reinforced by better-prepared and more highly qualified sympathizers. In the mid 'forties, J. Corominas produced such examples of the use of dēsidia by Plautus, of dēsidiōsus by Cicero, and, above all, of V. Lat. desideus in a glossary, whose compiler equated it with amor and libīdō, as to leave little doubt about the step-by-step rapprochement of dēsīderium and dēsidia. In a comment on this note, Corominas' mentor and senior friend, Leo Spitzer, by focusing attention on a characteristic Arthurian passage in Hartmann von der Aue and a parallel passage in Hartmann's model, Chrétien de Troyes, made it clear that in medieval thinking, inactivity, refusal to take risks, do battle, and engage in chivalrous pursuits, was held to be at the root of spells of languor and sensuality. Soon after, in preparing the entry *deseo* for his ambitious dictionary, Corominas threw in for good measure a few more illustrations of semantically fluid dēsidia from late Antiquity and the Middle Ages and reaffirmed his earlier thinking to the effect that a moralist world view tended to recognize in leisure a dangerous incentive to voluptuousness.[14]

With so much and such strong support flowing of late in the direction of the Settegast hypothesis, I incline to join the trend and credit the Romance phase of the development, at its most original, to convergence of dēsīderium and dēsidia. But, in so doing, I cannot help making three important reservations, of which the last bears directly on the issue of mono- vs. poly-genesis.

First, the way all scholars have described the events, dēsīderium and the correlated verb played a passive role in the process of this merger, whereas the distinction of having acted as the successful aggressor has been unanimously bestowed on dēsidia. We have been given to understand that dēsidia underwent a radical change of meaning, under a set of identifiable cultural conditions, then moved closer to dēsīderium (on a kind of chessboard), besieged it, pierced its defenses,

and consummated the blend. I submit that this course of events, as
usually pieced together (if you discount my mild exaggeration), hardly
contains a plausible account of the presumable interplay of causes.
Why not assume, with Ernout, that the initial gambit was the semantic,
pictorial erosion of cōn- and dē-sīderāre? Then, through the agency
of a *horror vacui*, so to speak, a single attempt was made -- or were
there several attempts and, if so, were they parallel or consecutive?
-- to fill the semantic empty space and, by so doing, to replenish the
sagging strength of the twin verbs. Dēsidia offered one such remedy;
the assumption that it injected its substance into the empty shell of
dēsīderāre certainly provides most of the answers that a student of
Hispano-Latin may want to raise. However, allying oneself with Schuchardt in preference to Settegast, one need not categorically discard
the possibility that in the remaining provincial varieties of colloquial Latin other remedies were tried out to energize ailing dēsīderāre.

My second qualification concerns the process of collision -- the
prelude to the merger. The traditional view in all similar situations
has been that the heads or centers of the lexical families under scrutiny clash and that the reverberations of this coming-together gradually spread over the limbs of the respective word families. This sequence of events may indeed hold in many instances, but must not be
taken for granted and can sometimes be proven wrong: The incipient
stage of the collision may, probably by way of exception, very well occur at the edges or fringes of two given word families. This is what
I have good reason to believe in fact happened in the case under study.
While we tend to focus attention on dēsidia "sloth" rather than on the
hierarchically subordinate adjective dēsidiōsus "slothful", a profusion
of medieval Latin glossaries, including those of the bilingual type,
carry dēsidiōsus, which looks and sounds remarkably, suspiciously similar to dēsīderōsus.[15] The initial contact between the two families
could perfectly well have been established at this point, lying on the
periphery, with everything else -- including the much-vaunted semantic
expansion of dēsidia -- ensuing rather than preceding this imbroglio,

or, at least, approximately coinciding with it.

My last point is the issue of polygenesis. For the sake of classificatory tidiness, we may prefer to separate, in our dictionary listings, the various lexical groups that the pioneers indiscriminately lumped together. Thus, in Migliorini-Duro's practical and, at the same time, scholarly *Prontuario* (1964:164ab), you will find, with few if any cross-references, (1) one cluster of straight Latinisms: *desiderabile* alongside *indesiderabile*, *desiderare*, *desiderio*, etc.; then, (2) two strings of words involving a vernacular blend of dēsīderium and dēsidia, namely, (a) *desio*, *desioso*, *desiare*, *desiabile* and (b) *disio*, *disioso*, *disiare*, *disianza*; then (3) another group of synonyms, traceable to Old Provençal: the verb *desirare* and the noun *desire* (beside such variants as *desiro*, *disire*, *disiro*); and, finally, (4) the straight Latinism *desidia*. I submit that, for all its enviable neatness on the descriptive plateau, such a rigid division masks a process that hovered between mono- and poly-genesis, as do all blends, up to a certain point.

III.

An educated polyglot, upon learning that the verbs E. *gain*, Fr. *gagner*, Sp. *ganar*, and Ptg. *ganhar* all have almost exactly the same meaning, will entertain few doubts as to their common descent, and even upon acquainting himself with such a tidbit as their Italian equivalent, namely, *guadagnare*, will be unlikely to change his mind at once. After all, against such a reassuring background of complete synonymy, one can adduce hundreds upon hundreds of recognized cognates which are not more radically different on the formal side, e.g., *tenir*, *tener*, *ter*, *tenere* "to hold, have". And yet, today's advanced scholars admit -- I believe without a single exception -- that Sp. *ganar* and Ptg. *ganhar* (to limit myself at the outset to one particularly striking pair) are not genetically related, even though they mean the same thing and are entirely comparable in conjugation, grammatical construction, phraseology, and other relevant respects. The demonstration

of their different ancestries was the triumph of late-19th and early-
20th-century scholarship, whose findings need not be challenged. The
question before us is, rather, whether these generations of trail-bla-
zers, in their eagerness to separate certain interwoven strains, did
not go too far. Can one seriously maintain that two verbs as similar
in appearance, service, and behavior as Sp. *ganar* and Ptg. *ganhar* were
totally independent of each other, even if one can individuate two separate etyma?

First let us quickly recapitulate how scholars, after 1850, went
about cutting a path through this jungle.[16] One of their earliest and
most lasting accomplishments was a feat of surgery -- the elimination,
through deftly-executed cuts, of three small lexical clusters which,
first impressions to the contrary, invite separate treatments, involving as they do entirely unrelated words or, in the last instance, at
least a sharply silhouetted morphological variant.

There exists, first, a word moored to rural life, namely, Sp.
gañán, Ptg. *ganhão* "farm hand", fig. "rough, husky fellow", already
absorbed into one of Nebrija's dictionaries. Diez traced it, from
the start, to Arab. gannâm, professional Orientalists concurred --
witness the Dozy-Engelmann team (1869:119) and, twenty years later,
Eguílaz y Yanguas (1886:408) --, Meyer-Lübke unhesitatingly endorsed
this derivation and, of the major 20th-century figures, only Menéndez
Pidal, to the end, insisted on interpreting it as a borrowing from Old
French, namely, *gaaignant* "gaining, winning" (1941:24). The French
connection has a single minor advantage over its rival: The Spanish
and the Portuguese forms can each be directly linked to *gaaignant*.
Those supporting the Arabism must, in deference to an elementary sound
correspondence, allow for the eventual migration of the Castilian form
to the Atlantic Coast. In terms of *realia*, the Arabic hypothesis is
incomparably stronger: Names of sheepherders junior in rank, farm
hands, and the like were frequently borrowed from Arabic -- cf. *zagal*
"shepherd's helper" -- and do not fit in the least the pattern of
French-Hispanic cultural relations in the Middle Ages.[17]

Our next deduction involves a very familiar cluster of words, referring to "deceit", initially to "mockery". There exist two parallel
series, one nominal: It. *inganno*, Sp. *engaño*, Ptg. *engano*, Occ. *engan*;
the other verbal: *ingannare*, *engañar*, *enganar*, OFr. *enganer*, Rum. în-
gînà. Diez was very much aware of the importance and relative autonomy
of this family,[18] discovered a few scattered vestiges of prototypes:
gannat, gannum, gannatura in glosses and other Low Latin texts, unwa-
veringly rejected any connection with Lat. ingenium, or with a Celtic
base appealed to by an unnamed fellow-worker or with OHG geinôn "to yawn"
but was willing to toy with the possibility of a link to OHG gaman "play,
joke", OE gamen "joke, foolery, amusement, diversion, mockery": cf., let
me add, Mod. E. game (Onions 1966:388a). Hermann Rönsch, an excellent
connoisseur of Folk Latin and early Church Latin, enriched Diez's collection of examples, chiefly from Graeco-Latin glossaries, and pleaded
for intra-Latin derivation. I find his hint of sanna "mimicking grim-
ace" -- structured along parallel lines -- very enlightened and am prepared to go along with Rönsch's postulate of a bifurcation of gannīre
"to yelp, bark, snarl" into two branches: gannīre and precariously
documented gannāre.[19] In any event, the hazardous tangle of "deceit"
and "gain" was henceforth cut, like a Gordian knot.

The third deduction may appear minor as to size, having a bearing
only on Gallo-Romance, but involves an astonishingly skillful application of a well-honed technique. The French word for "aftermath", *regain*, looks like a diaphanous combination of the prefix *re-* plus *gain*,
the familiar postverbal extracted from *gagner*; but this transparency is
deceptive. The medieval texts -- many of them metrical and rhymed --
disclose beyond the shadow of a doubt that the original form of the
word for "aftermath" was *gaïn*, making it neatly distinguishable from
gaain(g) "gain"; in fact, the ultimate threat of their homonymic collision was the reason for the "therapeutic" addition of *re-*. So *gaïn*
stands somewhat apart; A. Thomas, in a masterly note feeding on his
combined philological and dialectological prowess (1896:86-9), demonstrated over eighty years ago that *gaïn* was a hybrid, in which a Ger-

manic stem -- *waiþa* "pasturage", as in G. *Weide* -- was welded on to the
Latin suffix -īmen; and Meyer-Lübke, in an equally sparkling, construc-
tive comment on that note, specified why *waiþa* -- apparently an -*n* stem
-- and -īmen attracted each other, citing Fr. *jardin* from Goth. garda
as a close parallel (1897:154). A side-issue was thus satisfactorily
clarified.

The main thrust of Diez's effort, however, was directed at the
bold reconstruction of a widely-scattered Germanic family in Romance,
a task complicated by not a few semantic surprises (1853:185). The
chief representatives, in the ranks of the verbs, were, according to
him -- and we tend to agree with his judgment almost exactly a century
and a quarter later -- It. *guadagnare*, Romaunsch *gudoignar*, OProv. *ga-
zanhar*, OFr. *gaa(i)gner* (later *gagner*), all of them meaning "to gain,
acquire" and the OFr. member sometimes denoting "to till the field",
plus older Sp. *guadañar* "to mow", most of them accompanied by postverbal nouns -- abstract when masculine, e.g., It. *guadagno*, Fr. *gain*,
but concrete when feminine, e.g., Sp. *guadaña* "scythe, sickle".

So far, so good. Historically, it made excellent sense that Germanic occupants of Roman provinces should have devoted themselves to
agriculture -- and Diez had at his fingertips noteworthy bits of evidence to this effect, such as OFr. *gaagnage, gaaignerie* "ausgestellter
Acker, Ertrag desselben". He left considerable leeway as to the choice
of the specific etymon,[20] as long as it was in the vicinity of OHG
weida "hunt, pasturage", -- *weidanôn, weidanjan?* -- arguing thus: "Der
Begriff konnte sich von dem Jagd- und Hirtenleben auf den Ackerbau er-
strecken" (1853:185). Moreover, Diez's analysis was impeccable when he
cautiously ("vermutlich") subsumed Ptg. *ganhar*, OGal.-Ptg. *guanhar* beside *gaanhar*, OCat.-Val. *guanhar*, all of them sharing the same expected
meaning of "gaining, acquiring", under the identical Germanic base, on
the assumption of a loss of -*d*- and subsequent tendential contraction
of the newly adjacent homogeneous vowels. All of this is unassailable
from today's vantage point, as is the preservation of intervocalic -*d*-
in Eastern Castile and the Navarro-Aragonese zone. And now comes the

clinching proof of Diez's mastery: He knew, as did few of his peers,
where to stop, how to bridle his imagination. Remembering Sp. *ganar*,
of which he claimed to have found traces in Old Portuguese as well, he
balked at the tempting idea of combining it with *g(u)anhar*, to the West
and to the East, from older *guadañar*: "*Ganar* ist schwerlich daraus syn-
kopiert, da seine Form durch sehr alte Zeugnisse gestützt wird" -- and
he went on to cite samples of those testimonies. Then, brushing aside
an unwelcome Arabic base (gania "to derive profit"), Diez offered --
not as the only conceivable, but as, under the circumstances, the most
suitable etymological solution -- the noun *gana* "eagerness, desire,
appetite", another Gothic word in Spanish, "denn das Ziel des Begehrens
ist das Erreichen". Finally, the pioneer recognized (and nothing characterizes better his sophisticated realism) a certain penumbra or twi-
light zone between the domains of weida and *gan-*: In Sp. *ganancia*
"profit", contracted in Ptg. to *gança*, which is flanked in turn by a
newly-coined verb *gançar* "to gain", he saw the extension of *ganar*,
while in OPtg. *guaançar* he dimly recognized a certain approximation
to *guadañar*.

Having learned from Diez that *ganar* and *gañar*, all appearances to
the contrary, do not belong genetically together, and that *ganar* is,
rather, a verbal offshoot of the noun *gana*, used mostly in the plural
(*ganas*), one is curious to learn from what source that noun, which
Diez glosses by "heftige Begier", descended. Grammatically, one reads
(1853:163), it fits best OHG *geinōn* (i.e., mod. *gähnen*, E. *yawn*); the
transition from "wide opening of one's mouth" to "coveting" would have
been smooth. As for semantic parallels, Diez is prepared to cite OProv.
badar, Lat. *hiāre*, Gk. χαύνειν, all three of which straddled the primary (anatomical) and the derivative meanings. And Sp. *ganado*, Ptg.
gado "herd"? These, Diez hastens to explain in a separate entry (1853:
494), are simply substantivated past participles, and the semantic
shift is, once more, made plausible by isolated parallels with comparable developments in Old Provençal, in modern Occitan, and even in
the Romance ingredients of Basque.

Modern research has approved an astonishing percentage of Diez's cautious dissections -- of course, not everything.[20] One detects a number of factual errors -- thus, *gana* "desire" eked out only a precarious existence in Italian (chiefly in the stereotyped adverbial phrases *di gana* "willingly" and *di mala gana* "unwillingly") and is a transparent Hispanism, becoming consequently useless for the reconstruction of early stages. Similarly, Ptg. *gana* could be a Castilianism, though it displays a certain independence on the semantic side, meaning -- among less startling things -- "grudge". Then again, Sp. *ganado* does not at all mean "herd" (a concept for which there exists a finely-graded profusion of words in Hispano-Romance), but "cattle, livestock". However, such frills seem unworthy of further elaboration.

What eluded the attention of Diez and of his followers was, I submit, a package of more serious matters. For instance, having avoided the pitfall -- fatal to Körting -- of classing the offshoots of V. Lat. ingannāre "to mock, deceive" with the Germanic families at issue, Diez and his school refrained from asking themselves whether there was, conceivably, some causal connection between the distribution of *enganar* but *ganhar* in the West of the Peninsula, and conversely, of *engañar* but *ganar* in the Center. Speakers apparently selected the Germanic families with remarkable sophistication, so as to avoid almost at any price the hazard of too close proximity between "gaining, earning", on the one hand, and, on the other, "cheating".

The closer we look at the picture that thus unfolds, the clearer the long-drawn-out symbiosis of *waidanjan* and *gan-* appears to us. Thus, OPtg. *guanhar* should not normally have lost its /w/ element before the central vowel; witness such verbs of comparable background as *guardar* "to guard, protect", OPtg. *guarir/-ecer* observable through the prism of *guarida* "den, shelter, refuge", and *guarnecer* "to garrison, garnish, trim, furnish". The fact that, unlike Italian, Portuguese before long lost this ingredient becomes understandable on the assumption of early association of *gan-* and *waidanjan*; so does the crystallization of *gado* "cattle", the counterpart of Sp. *ganado*. Then why did any such verb as

*gar, the theoretically conceivable equivalent of Sp. *ganar*, fall short
of jelling? The answer seems to be that a new influx of uniconsonantal
verbal radicals was unwelcome -- the speakers of Portuguese had enough
trouble with the older crop: *rir* "to laugh", *vir* "to come", *pôr* "to
put", etc.

It would seem, then, that, despite the basic soundness of 19th-
century research and Diez's personal levelheadedness, things were far
more complicated than any pioneer could have imagined. A word meaning
"avid desire" does not, through some kind of spontaneous evolution,
become the equivalent of "acquiring, earning, gaining".

For such close symbiosis between two Germanic verbs to have developed relatively shortly after their absorption by two neighboring
Romance languages, several intermediate steps were doubtless necessary.
Originally, weidanjan and ganon were not at all strikingly similar in
terms of syllabic structure, conjugation class, distribution of phonemes in key positions, etc. It took the early loss of intervocalic
-d-, characteristic of Atlantic Coast Hispano-Romance, plus the subsequent contraction of adjacent vowels, plus the substitution of /gw/
for /w/ to bring together these candidates for symbiosis. Their gradual coalescence was bidirectional: *guañar* tended to lose its /w/ under pressure from *gãar*, which, in turn, extended its meaning under the
influence of its new partner.

The next important step, and one which decisively sets apart Portuguese from Spanish, was the loss of intervocalic *n*, probably in the
9th or 10th century -- a loss which presupposes earlier nasalization
of the preceding word -- something like *gãar*. From this crucially
important stage speakers could arrive at *gar* (a solution which, we
recall, they rejected on account of *gar*'s ultra-brevity, though certain derivatives, such as the nouns *gado* "livestock" and *gança* "gain"
the latter a hybrid involving the vernacular outcome of the Latin derivational suffix -antia, were tolerated). However, there were alternatives to the standard development: The restoration of the -n- was not
unattainable in a climate of multidialectalism, through contact with

neighboring Spanish; or else tentative denasalization coincided with
the introduction of a /ɲ/ sound, cf. the Latin relational suffix -īnu,
which in Romance became a diminutive or hypocoristic suffix and, in
Portuguese, developed via -ĩu into -inho. Of these two marginal possibilities, the first may have been briefly tried out, but was before
long abandoned, in view of the most unwelcome adjacency of enganar "to
cheat". Ganhar, however, as a peripheral phonological development of
gãar, coincided most opportunely with g(u)anhar, the cognate of It.
guadagnare, and thus easily won out.

The interlocking records of *waidanjan -- the substitute word for
lucrāre -- and of *gainon or *ganan thus sensitize us to the heightened
possibility of all sorts of symbiotic lexical relationships within the
Germanic layer of Romance. Further search in this domain seems to be
very promising: in fact, one discerns two mutually complementary pros-
pects: either

a.   two or more Germanic words, in a general atmosphere of tur-
     moil conducive to fluctuations, establish a kind of symbio-
     sis upon having been absorbed, or in the very course of their
     absorption, into a Romance lexicon; or

b.   a measure of interdependence develops between a Germanic
     guest and a Romance host of similar outward appearance and
     resemblant meaning.

To start out with the latter situation: Lat. sēnsu -- whose semantic range Ernout and Meillet define thus: "sens (organe; faculté
de sentir); sensibilité; sentiment, façon de sentir; pensée, signifi-
cation (d'un mot, etc.)", "(en rhétorique) 'phrase, période'" (1959-
60:614) -- was transmitted into Romance on two levels: as a learnèd
word, with retention of n before s (as in It. senso, Fr. sens; cf. E.
sense), and as a vernacular word, with expected loss of the n and a
coarsening of the meaning in the directions of "brain" or "brains",
understood not only as the seat of intelligence, but, plainly, as a
food item -- witness OProv. ses, Sp. seso(s), Ptg. siso (Meyer-Lübke

1930-35:§7822). For the more refined reference, Spanish uses the substantivated arrhizotonic past participle of the correlated verb, namely, *sentido*. Interestingly, Irish here exhibits perfect parallelism,
with the borrowings *seis* and *sians* exemplifying the very same con-
duits of transmission.

Over against the progeny of sēnsus and sentīre stands the galaxy
of Romance reflexes of Gmc. sinn, a lexical unit familiar to Germanists
from the traces it has left in Old and Middle High German, in Middle
Low German, in Middle and New Netherlandish, in Old Frisian, in Danish
(*sind*) and in Swedish (*sinne*), apparently to the exclusion of Old English (Kluge-Mitzka 1957:710a). This noun -- though not, significantly, the corresponding verb[22] -- has also left numerous vestiges in Romance, e.g., It. *senno*; Romaunsch, Friulano, OFr., OProv. *sen*; Cat.
seny, whose meanings Meyer-Lübke subsumes under the formula "Sinn, Ver-
stand, Richtung" (1930-35:7948a). There is more to report about the
deep roots that this Germanic word has struck in various Romance ter-
ritories. Thus alone in Standard Italian, i.e., literary Tuscan, one
encounters, in addition to *senno*, all sorts of derivatives and compounds, e.g., *assennato* "wise, sensible, judicious, wary, discreet"
and the corresponding abstract *assennatezza*; *dissennare* "to deprive
of sense, drive mad", flanked by self-explanatory *dissennato* and *dis-
sennatezza*; *forsennato*, extracted from the stereotyped phrase *fuori
senno* "frantic, beside oneself, delirious", accompanied in turn by
forsennatezza; also the hilarious compounds *sputasenno* "pompous person" and *cacasenno* "conceited individual, know-all" (recorded in Migliorini and Duro's highly selective *Prontuario*, consequently not devoid of importance). The dialects go even further, cf. Abruzz. *abbo-
nesinnu*, *abburisinne* "certain, accurate" placed on record by Salvioni;
cognate languages betoken the same vitality, witness OFr. *assener* "to
aim, assign, determine", which lingers on in the modern fixed phrase
asséner un coup "to strike (lit. aim) a blow". Finally, late medieval
Spanish and Portuguese, as vehicles of poetry, imported *sen*, for spar-
ing use, from Old French or Old Provençal, or from both.

From this description of the bare facts, it follows that the Latin
tradition of sē(n)su/sentīre has been at its strongest in Hispano-Romance; that the impact of *sinn* has been most powerful in Italy and the
adjoining Rhaeto-Romance zones; while in French territory sinn was so
lightly superimposed on sēnsu as to have allowed a state of thorough
interpenetration to ensue. When Francophones use *sens* for "meaning",
they perpetuate a Latin tradition, but once they press into service
the same word for "direction" (e.g., in reference to traffic), they
walk in the footsteps of their Frankish ancestors. Fr. *sens* has thus
become what certain German scholars, in discussing lexical monstrosi-
ties of their own language, call "Zwitter-" or "Mischbildung".

One could, for a fleeting moment, wonder whether the segment common to sē(n)su and sin(n) was sufficient, after the attrition of *n* before *s*, to justify the contact and partial amalgam here adumbrated.
But this loss of n -- as in mēnsa "table" > Sp. *mesa*, mēnse "month" >
It. *mese*, Fr. *mois* -- was in many places tendential rather than sweeping. Remember the recurrent medieval graphies *occansio* and *thensaurus*,
which point to wavering and occasional hypercorrection, as does OSp.
fonsado "garrison, detachment of soldiers" < fossātu (lit. "dug in")
in the company of dial. (Arag.) *onso* "bear" < ursu (through false re-
stitution of a dwindling consonant before s) and against the background of blends such as q(u)assāre "to shake repeatedly, break" X
campsāre "to circumnavigate, shirt, shun" > Sp. *cansar* "to wear out,
tire". Cf. also the aforementioned Irish reflexes *seis* and *sians*.

Of the alternative situation hinted at, only the sketchiest outline can here be drawn. From late Antiquity until the Middle Ages,
the majority of Romance languages (least of all those pertaining to
the Balkan peninsula) absorbed, in the wake of tidal waves and through
tremors, a total of four Germanic verbal bases of conspicuous outward
similarity: three of them can, experts report, be credited to Germanic
as a whole, namely, *wardôn "to observe", *warnjan "to warn", and *warôn "to watch, preserve", while the fourth has been specifically assigned
to Old North Frankish and to Gothic, namely, *warjan "to ward off".

These four verbs and their offshoots are certainly no unknowns to students of Romano-Germanic symbiosis; but earlier generations of scholars
would select now the one, now the other for microscopic inspection --
as is true, for instance, of Hugo Styff's Lund dissertation, whereas
the thing to do at this point, one feels, is to engage in a sharply
silhouetted comparative study, as can indeed at present be accomplished
at relatively low cost with the help of Wartburg's massive entries in
one of the concluding volumes of his monumental dictionary.[23] The
areas, periods, and semantic shades that Wartburg succeeded in setting
off should alert us to the high probability of symbiotic processes.
Thus *warnjan lost no time in shedding its traditional meaning ("to
warn"), to acquire instead those of "keeping, protecting" (witness
the military term *garnison* "garrison", which eventually percolated
into German) and, ultimately, that of "equipping, decorating, decking
out" (as is shown by *garnir* "to garnish").   Since *warôn and *wardôn
likewise referred to "keeping, guarding, preserving", it is almost
inconceivable that there should not have ensued in due time processes
already familiar to us from earlier exposure to the dēsīderium/dēsidia
and the *waidanjan/gan- imbroglios.   To cite just one particularly seductive possibility in this direction: All students of Old French
have encountered in their readings the form *gar*, interpreted now as
a straight interjection (e.g., by Hans Espe 1908:52), now as a kind
of contextually motivated "Kurzform" or allegro variant of *garder*
(e.g., by E. Lommatzsch in his masterly revision of A. Tobler's dictionary [1960:97a-99a], who furnishes a goodly assortment of telling
glosses: "schau, sieh, gib acht!").   Both judgments may well be correct in part; but, viewed in the historical perspective, the erratic
form could easily, one feels, at bottom, represent a member of the
original paradigm either of *warjan or of *warôn, a member which span
off or split off, achieved a measure of independence by virtue of its
interjectional status, and was ultimately attracted into the orbit
of *garder*, from *wardôn, by way of saltatory transfer from one word
family to another, so to speak.   Or, for that matter, contrast Mod. G.

ab-wehren with its exact contemporary E. equivalent (*to*) *ward off*, a
group in which *ward*, transparently, acts as a doublet of *guard*, hence
constitutes an offshoot of *wardôn, but paradoxically matches a German
representative of *warjan. Or else compare Fr. *regarder* "to look",
regard "look", plus its kin *égard* (deferential) "consideration" (strikingly reminiscent of G. *Rück-sicht*), all three assignable to the fief
of *wardôn, to such lexical units as OProv. *esgar* and *regarar*, whose
messages Meyer-Lübke rendered by "Anblick, Urteil" and "anblicken",
respectively, noun and verb being both clearly traceable to *warôn.
Then again, take the Hispano-Romance development of *warjan, not in
the semantic direction of "healing", as in Fr. *guérir* (at the outset
preponderantly *garir*), but rather headed toward such nuances as "to
give shelter or protection to"; "to keep, preserve, guard, lead to a
pasturage", where early contact with *guardar* "to keep, guard" and *res-
guardar* "to protect, shield" was practically unavoidable -- small wonder that, before long, *guarecer* became dispensable and that its use
declined, except in certain conservative varieties of rural speech.[24]
Incidentally, the conspicuous delay of the triumph of *guérir* over *garir*
in French -- Wartburg records the fact without concealing his own surprise -- becomes less startling once we recall the almost equally late
spread of *égarer* (from Normandy via Paris all over Northern France)
and, to add another dimension to the knotty state of affairs, the be-
lated loss of final -*d* in the actual pronunciation of *regard*. *Garir*,
égarer, *regard*, all three descendants of different Germanic words in
Gallo-Romance, were in each other's way, so one of them, namely, *garir*,
was allowed to yield to its variant *guérir*, fortunately available at
the critical moment as if to disencumber the situation. So within this
thick underbrush, one is left wondering to which ancestral family each
ultimately belongs -- so heavily entwined have the branches of the four
trees become with the passage of time. A major contingent of words appears here to stand at or near the midpoint between monogenesis and
polygenesis.

IV.

The last problem before us suffers from such a degree of intricacy and has entailed such sharp disagreements among scholars of high repute that I can undertake to offer little more than a thumbnail sketch. Essentially the questions involve a tightly-arranged cluster of demonstrative particles typical of racy colloquial Latin, starting with such archaic texts as the Plautine comedies.[25] If the pithiest among these particles were em and ēn,[26] the one best-known was, in all likelihood, ecce, which came astonishingly close, in regard to its semantic range, to Fr. *voici*, but, grammatically, above all qualified for ushering in demonstratives, thus: ecce istam and, through further compression, eccistam. Where a demonstrative heralded by h was involved, that h- was sloughed off in the process of amalgamation, e.g., eccum, eccam, eccos.

Eccum, in fact, eventually congealed into a variant, indeed a rival, of ecce. Their further vicissitudes in folk speech can, for the most part, be easily kept apart, inasmuch as, at the Romance stage, the /k·/ of ecce, representing a lengthened velar stationed before a front vowel, fell prey to assibilation, whereas the /k/ of eccum, placed in a halfway different environment, remained exempt from any such mutation. Hence, in the last analysis, the contrast between, say, Fr. *celui*, *cette*, *ici*, *-ci*, and It. *colui*, *questo*, *quella*, etc. Individual compounds displaying the bound form ec- and serving as vehicles for "interrogatives of impatience and insistence" began to fall into desuetude in Imperial Latin and may thus, rightly or wrongly, appear to be of scant concern to the Romanist (e.g., ecquis "is there anybody?" or ecquandō "but when...?"), but the binuclear ecce/eccum kernel, or at least some of its scattered splinters, outlived this attrition and apparently established contact with another string of particles comprising the items at, atque, ac, ast, which were, at the outset, tantamount to "on the other hand". This secondary rapprochement caused the crystallization, by way of compromise, of an *accu

element, clearly discernible in a number of geographically widespread
pronouns, adjectives, adverbs, and prepositions, witness Sp. *aquí* alongside *ahí* "here", *acá* beside differently nuanced *allá* and *allí* "there"
(whereas Portuguese contrasts apheresized *cá* with *lá*); also, to revert
to Spanish, *aquel* "you that...there" (flanked in the Golden Age vocabulary by *aqueste* and *aquese* "that...here"), and obsolete *acullá*, plus
numerous counterparts in Portuguese, Provençal, Catalan, conceivably
in Italian (where *quello*, *questo*, *coloro*, as a result of a contour
blurring apheresis, are indiscriminately traceable either to eccu or
to *accu) and even in far-off Rumanian (e.g., [m.] *acest*, [f.] *aceas-
ta*).[27] Moreover, the vitality of eccum is vouched for by Sard. (Logud.)
ekku, by OMil. *eca*, and, according to W. Schulze's authoritative verdict, even by OHG *eggo* (for bibliographic details see Meyer-Lübke 1930-
35:§2824). By the same token, the situation in Old French has gradually become translucid: The three scholars -- through an amusing coincidence, all three Americans -- who, over the years, have sunk their
teeth into OFr. *ez* and its profusion of variants are, understandably,
agreed that *ez* represents the normal outgrowth of ecce.[28] The sole
objection that might be raised against their broadly concurrent ver-
dicts is that, by dint of concentrating on style, syntax, and semantics
they have fallen short of exploiting the evidence of certain medieval
variants heralded by *a-* rather than *e-* (even though Godefroy's late-
19th-century dictionary records *a*, *aite*, *athe*, *ast*, *aste*, *aates*, i.e.,
variants which could very well be symptomatic of the protracted coexistence of ecce and *acce in Gallo-Romance).

So Old French and Tuscan bits of evidence harmonize in all essentials and felicitously complement each other. Spanish, conversely,
for once acts like an obnoxious trouble-maker. For the corresponding
formula in that language is, to this day, *he aquí* "there is": in older
usage *he(vos)*, *fe(vos)*, *afé(vos)*... beside *he(te) aquí*. While the
sheer proliferation of minor variants is a feature shared by all three
traditions of provincial Latin, one distinctive trait of the formula's
record to the south of the Pyrenees is, aside from its unimpaired sur-

vival, also its splendid representation in oft-recited memorable passages of famous epics and ballads (e.g., *Hete, hete, don Rodrigo*).

This conspicuousness on the literary scene has led, in turn, to
an early arousal of scholarly curiosity as to the particle's origin.
One initial -- all told, timid -- attempt to grapple with OFr. *ez* was
made by Oliver Johnston, around the year 1905; in significant contrast, K. Pietsch's lavish inventory, presented practically that same
year, of conjectures previously advanced to explain, in a Hispanic
framework, the rise of *(a)fé* and *he* ran to almost thirty pages bristling with bibliographic detail: Neither those pioneering inquiries
pervading the entire 19th century, nor such as were to follow upon
them down to our own days, have, alas, yielded any consensus of etymological judgment.

There had accumulated, at the threshold of World War I, all in
all five major hypotheses -- discrete to the point of irreconcilabil-
ity -- on the background of Sp. *he aquí*, its Ptg. counterpart *eis aquí*,
and the medieval formulas *he vos, (a)fé vos*.

(a) While the Spanish American trail-blazer Andrés Bello wavered
between Lat. sg. habē "have (thou)!" and pl. habēte "have (ye)!", the
starting point, in his view, had to be, under any circumstances, an
imperative form of the verb habēre, on the order of "Have it!, Take
it from me!" (cf. the polite modern conversational phrase *aquí lo tiene
usted* "here it is"). The loose thread of the habēte conjecture was,
decades later, picked up by Ford, who defended it with decreasing conviction on, at least, two occasions. The point of departure was at
this point elaborately redefined as habēte vōs, at the cost of a tor-
tured explanation of the underlying sound development.[29] Conversely,
though the main thrust of Pietsch's aforementioned unwieldy digest was
critical, not to say polemic, he himself leaned toward habē!, a decision which, despite sharp disagreements on details, places his own position in the vicinity of that taken by Ford.

(b) Diez, as a comparatist, was both aided and hampered by his
foreknowledge of the transparent descent of Fr. *voici, voilà* -- two

obvious functional (though not necessarily genetic) analogues of OSp.
(a)févos, etc. -- from vidē "see!" plus the respective adverb of place.
His stumbling block in trying to assign the same origin to (a)févos
as to voici was the absence of any well-defined transition from word-
initial ancestral v to f-/h-. (Fr. fois "time" [in iteration] < vice,
as against Sp. vez, OSp. vegada, is by no means a comparable isolate.[30])

(c) Ascoli was, I suppose, the ground-breaking scholar who, in a
crisply-phrased side-remark, selected the (a)fé variant as the smooth-
est avenue of approach, by linking the fe ingredient with fide "faith".[31]
This conjecture has subsequently been again and again reiterated, with
numerous languages providing seemingly seductive near-parallels, e.g.,
Lat. hercle!, Fr. ma foi!, E. forsooth!, and the like.

(d) Meyer-Lübke temporarily toyed with the possibility of burden-
ing the Latin deictic particle ēn with full responsibility for having
sparked the entire development (1911-20:§2866). Later, in revising his
dictionary, he withdrew that daring interpretation (1930-35:§4089a), a
volteface which did not elude the attention and approval of Corominas

(e) After at first criticizing and rejecting Ford's intolerably
artificial proposal, Menéndez Pidal, in an admirably vigorous counter
analysis of his own, declared himself a supporter of Arabic exclamatory
hâ! as the sole sought-for etymon.[32] Among Menéndez Pidal's followers,
R. Lapesa, as the author of an oft-reprinted, widely-consulted manual,
and Corominas, through a substantial entry in his etymological dictionary (2.894a-895a), both rallied to the support of the Madrid scholar's
Orientalist thesis, and the Academy Dictionary followed suit (1970:697a).

Which of these five divergent explanations deserves to be adopted?
Some of them, at first glance, look uncannily persuasive. The fact that
Portuguese matches Sp. he by eis in a stereotyped phrase and that, further, even within the mainstream of the Spanish tradition certain 16th-
and 17th-century classics had recourse to hes or heis in lieu of he, at
first seems to underscore the advantage of a verbal base,[33] be it vidēre
or habēre. Having granted that much, consider next the fact that this
welding-on of -s or -is demonstrably constitutes a distinctly late usage,

from which no overconfident inferences ought to be drawn; make further
allowances for the tell-tale circumstance that OFr. *ez*, indisputably a
straight product of the particle ecce, at a given juncture sporadically
acquired verbal endings, as is patent in its variant *estes*; and you
will, I trust, agree that we have, in all probability, slipped under
our lens not some relic of a primeval verb, but rather a form of entirely different background, which has secondarily (or, if you wish,
obliquely) acquired certain verbal characteristics, apt to mislead even
a seasoned geneticist. Cf., on the typological side, the "personal infinitive" in Portuguese and the Italian personal pronouns equipped with
verbal endings *eglino, elleno*.

If we now switch our attention to the *fide* hypothesis and remember
the ubiquitous asseverative formulas Fr. *ma foi*, G. *fürwahr*, R. *наверно*,
and the like, it will prove difficult for us to rule out categorically
the presence -- in a principal or an accessory role -- of *fe(e)* "faith"
in sentences such as these, extracted from the *Mio Cid* epic: *¡Fevos
aquí las señas!* "here indeed are the standards!", *afé dos cavalleros
entraron* "lo and behold, two knights suddenly entered", *afélos en Valencia* "here they are in Valencia". But then skeptics are in a position
to quote equally archaic passages involving *he* rather than *fe* from venerable texts such as the *Auto de los Reyes Magos*: *Henos venidos* "finally we have arrived"; or as a religious poem by Berceo: *He aquí la
reýna, desto seý segura* "here is the [celestial] queen, be [thou] as-
sured of this". In these counterexamples, little if anything is lost
of the apparent expressivity of *fe/he* as a result of the preference
given to the *h-* variant, which obviously cannot be connected, directly
or obliquely, with *fe(e)* "faith". Returning at this point to *Mio Cid*'s
(a)fé, we can now affirm that deictic *fe/he*'s association with *fe*
"faith" need not counter-intuitively be denied, nor is it mandatory
to declare such a link indispensable. The safest modus operandi is
henceforth to shunt off the part once played in reconstruction by *fide*
from center-stage to the wings; that part, our safest guess would be,
involved a supervenient optional elaboration, of minor relevancy to

the main thrust of our etymological quest.

This gradual reduction of exciting probabilities via defensible possibilities to residual implausibilities leaves us, in the end, saddled with the choice between Arab. hâ, in Maghrebî pronunciation hê (through the agency of 'imâla), and some such archaic Latin base as well-attested ēn or em, or perhaps *ec, which may have spun off ecce, cf. the aforementioned ec-quis and ec-quandō. Were our material limited to the Hispanic corpus, we would, at first, be hard-pressed to reach a fair decision on this score, but might in the end incline to adopt Menéndez Pidal's powerfully argued preference. But since our corpus happens not to be so confined, it is incumbent upon us to reconcile OSp. *fe*, *afé*, *he*, first with Plautine usage; second with OFr. *ez/estes*; and, third, with It. *ecco*, including their respective branches and twigs, all of which, unmistakably, display an identical basic design of word order, syntactic construction (with accusative-case nouns or pronouns often accompanied by dative-case pronouns), and stylistic level.

Against a backdrop of such specificity, I venture to think that, despite Meyer-Lübke's second thought in the definitive version of his dictionary, his fine flair, in 1911, had not led him completely astray. If it is correct that exact parallelism of architectural detail remains our safest circumstantial clue to common descent, then It. *ecco*, OFr. *ez*, and OSp. *(a)fé*, *he* belong genetically together. We are thus forced to conclude that archaic Latin bases like ēn, em, and *ec -- assuming the Hispano-Romans had preferred them to ecce and eccum as part of their long-familiar general lexical conservatism -- were gradually becoming so isolated in Proto-Spanish (just imagine the grotesqueness of such words as *yen or, worse, *yec!) that speakers all over the Peninsula tended to replace them by more suitable substitutes,[34] here by exclamatory or asseverative fide "[by my] faith", there by the Arabic interjection hâ!, to say nothing of the supervenient adjustments of its final element to certain appropriate conjugational patterns. Thus Ford was, after all, well-advised in 1911 to allege the chosen

problem's essential lack of clarity, even though he was unable to lay
his finger on any specific reason for such a "messy" state of affairs;
while Menéndez Pidal, judged in retrospect, was overoptimistic in assuming that his innovative idea, for all its originality, could supersede the aggregate of earlier proposals.

Today's worker, with his firmer grasp of the difference between
primary and secondary etymologies, is just beginning to realize that
there indeed need not have existed any single "simple source" for a
cluster of words such as OSp. *fe*, *afé*, mod. *he*. A primary structure
no longer amenable to leisurely direct observation -- namely, the
link to the close-knit group of the Latin monosyllabic deictics, had
here, we cautiously infer, been eroded at an early date and was subsequently replaced in the late Middle Ages by a new network of secondary associations with a number of unrelated, but highly suggestive
words, one of them Oriental (namely, the Arabic interjection), the
others Hispano-Latin (e.g., *fe*, the organic outgrowth of fidēs). As
etymologists, we find ourselves once more marooned in the quicksands
of a no man's land, between monogenesis and polygenesis.

To sum up the entire communication: We started out by examining
a number of cases which, if an older terminology were to be enforced,
could pass off as unusually "tricky" instances of lexical blends. Thus,
the Romance reflexes of Gmc. *waidanjan and *ganon must be assumed to
have coexisted for centuries, slowly influencing each other's form
and meaning, until a homonymic clash with the locally varying descendants of Folk Lat. *ingannāre "to cheat", on account of the latter's
intrinsic semantic incompatibility with the aforementioned rivals,
finally led to a disentanglement, resulting in the paradoxical triumph
of *ganhar* in Portuguese and *ganar* in Spanish. Thus, both *ganhar* and
ganar, in a way, are each heir to the form or content of two totally
unrelated prototypes.

We advanced one step further in connection with the controversy
that has surrounded for a century OSp. (*a*)*fé*, mod. *he* (*aquí*), Ptg. *eis*
aquí, concluding from Republican Latin, Old French, Italian, and Sar-

dinian evidence that the Iberian peninsula could very well have inherited from Latin some such deictic as ēn, em, or *ec, accompanied by sets of characteristic constructions. This legacy, we argued, was apt to be eroded, at the normal rate of attrition, prompting the speakers to appeal to an assortment of substitute words, with faithful preservation of the immediately recognizable original syntactic framework. Here, then, one may legitimately invoke not mere "digenesis", but full-fledged "polygenesis", which can then be effectively pitted against the earlier explorers' crude monogenetic presuppositions.

NOTES:

1) A third offshoot, praesīderāre (Paulus ex Festo), apparently assignable to rustic parlances (A. Ernout and A. Meillet [1959-60:624b] liken it to προχειμάζω), lacks any representation in the daughter languages. Crucially important is the circumstance that no such "simple" verb as *sīderāre ever came into existence.
2) Meyer-Lübke (1930-35:§7902) gives a few scattered clues to Old Italian, for sīdus, and (in the wake of C. Michaëlis de Vasconcelos) to Old Portuguese and Modern Galician, for sīdera.
3) The proof lies in OProv. cosier "worry", for which A. Thomas, persuasively, reconstructed the base *cō(n)sīderium, which clearly echoes dēsīderium (1904:226); endorsed by Meyer-Lübke.
4) Cf. the material assembled by A. Castro (1936:205a), with the mutually corroborative data desiderium = deseo and desidero = desear extracted from the Toledo and the Escorial glossaries; by H. H. Carter (1952-53:82), with desidero flanked by the gloss desejar (though in other passages desejar corresponds to (ad)opto, affecto, capto, and even spiro); and by M. Roques (1938:102), where the alphabetic AALMA glossary (Paris, Bibl. Nat., Lat. 13033) not only explains desidero, -as by vernacular desirer, but also coins semi-learned desideratiz to do justice to the grammatical term desiderativus, and, for good measure, adds the equation Desiderius = Didier.
5) The etymology was more or less specifically supplied, in 1601, by Francisco del Rosal (S. Gili Gaya, 1947-57:762b); in 1611, by S. de Covarrubias [H]orozco (1943:457b), through mention of desiderable; and twice, in 1732, by the Real Academia Española in its dictionary (3.150a, 167b); also, R. Bluteau's glosses (e.g., Ptg. desejável = Lat. desiderabilis) speak an eloquent language.
6) Conspicuous through their discreet silence were Gilles Ménage, in 1650; and Ramón Cabrera (†1833), in his posthumous 1837 dictionary.
7) The Danish classicist J. N. Madvig, in commenting on a Ciceronian passage, had already declared dissīdium spurious, a conjecture

later endorsed by Schuchardt (1889:533). In advancing his hypothesis
Diez was admittedly influenced by the vicissitudes of Ptg. *saudade*
"nostalgia", which indeed perpetuates OPtg. *soidade* "lonesomeness"
("eig. 'Trennung', zunächst das davon hervorgehende Verlangen nach
Wiedervereinigung"), although the alleged parallelism was imperfect
(see Schuchardt, loc. cit.), quite apart from the fact that *saudade*,
over the years, absorbed other ingredients, as C. Michaëlis de Vasconcelos later disclosed in her well-known book-length monograph (1914,
rev. 1922).

   8) The ranks of immediate adherents included C. Michaëlis (1876:
262b, 285b). P. F. Monlau's reaction, presumably as early as 1865,
was typical of that period's climate of opinion: Though he cautiously
listed dēsīderāre as being, until recently, the consensus of etymologists, he added an excursus on Diez's revolutionary idea, to which he
virtually surrendered. R. Menéndez Pidal's support (1908-11:625)
hinged on the frequency of the spelling *dessear*, etc. in medieval
texts and even Golden Age printings, a factor which to the Madrid scholar apparently outweighed the cumulative evidence to the contrary of
Modern Judeo-Spanish in SE Europe, of several medieval MSS (including
those transmitting Berceo), of an early and otherwise reliable rhyming dictionary (and, let me add on my own, of the aggregate of Portuguese sources). What seems to be actually involved is the encroach-
ment, sometimes merely orthographic, of the aggressive and highly successful prefix *des-* on the crumbling domain of *de-*; cf. OSp. *des-ende*
"thereupon" in lieu of deinde. H. B. Richardson, though helpless on
the side of independent etymological analysis (1930:80), confirmed
the occurrence -- perhaps even preponderance -- of *des(s)ear*, *des(s)eo*,
and *des(s)eoso* in Juan Ruiz MSS.

   9) Foerster's formulation was criticized by Meyer-Lübke (1883:155),
who leaned in the direction of a modified Diezian thesis, but was en-
thusiastically if naïvely defended by G. Körting (s.v. dēsīderium)
throughout the three successive editions (1891, 1901, 1907) of his
ill-fated dictionary.

   10) For mature re-statements of this almost juvenile formulation,
see the author's comparative phonology (1890:§115) and, above all, the
two versions of his dictionary (1911-20 and 1930-35), of which the
earlier offers more options. Meyer-Lübke was not disinclined to accept Settegast's dēsidia, but still insisted on the need to presuppose
the agency of recomposition to arrive at ĕ as well as the pressure of
dissidium to justify the switch to the masculine-neuter, unless one
preferred to admit the primacy of the verb. He worried about the emerging possibility of categorizing It. *disio* as a Provençalism. Unlike
some of his predecessors, Meyer-Lübke analyzed the Sardinian reflexes
(Logud. *diẕidẕu*, Campid. *diẕiǧu*) as transmitted through Catalan.

   11) For the felicity of Schuchardt's ideas, somewhat inflated
claims were made by Körting. The irony or paradox consists in that
Settegast, who generally ranked as a mediocre scholar, on this occasion
hit the jackpot, while Schuchardt's thinking almost sank into oblivion.

   12) The spade work was carried out by A. Tobler, in his magisterial
review of W. Cloetta's edition of *Poème moral* (1886), and by his prize

pupil G. Cohn, in the latter's expanded doctoral dissertation (1891: 289). Tobler established *desirrer* as the OFr. standard form; he also discriminated between the straight postverbal *desir* and bi- or tri-syllabic *desi(i)er*, which qualified as an organic descendant of dēsīderium.

13) Ford's earliest gropings go back to his Harvard dissertation on Old Spanish sibilants, submitted in 1897 and published three years later; see Menéndez Pidal's hint (1908-11:625).

14) Corominas' final sizing-up of his thinking is not entirely satisfactory. He refers the reader again and again to his earlier note, neglecting any mention of Spitzer's pointed comment, which contained a number of valid corrections and qualifications. Wartburg's *Stellungnahme* is likewise omitted. The author cited R. J. Cuervo's extensive discussion of *desear*, *deseo*, and *deseoso* (1893:1042-43, 1063-65, 1065-66), without making it clear that the Colombian's etymological statement (1064b-1065a) was little more than a scrupulous, but noncommittal inventory of opinions voiced by other scholars, including J. Cornu (1888:748; cf. 1904-06:960), plus a candid admission of the enormous inherent difficulty of a deceptively simple problem. Concerning the once widespread spelling *dessear*, Corominas reaches a verdict diametrically opposed to the opinion held by Menéndez Pidal, whose name he is careful to leave unmentioned.

Despite these flaws, Corominas' treatment towers over the analysis supplied by V. García de Diego (1954:224b, 225a, §2212), who operates with the base *dēsĕdium -- an oblique reflex of dēsīderium, deflected from the straight path through influence of other words, such as dēsidia; dēsīder-āre, -ium, -ōsus are reported to have been transmitted, through regular channels, solely in Old Catalan (§§2215-17). The ultimate in conservatism prevails in the 17th ed. (1947:434c, 438a) of the Academy Dictionary, which traces the noun *deseo* to the verb *desear*, and the latter, unflinchingly, to dēsīderāre.

15) To be specific, Roques cites *deses* = *desidiosus* "perecheus" and *desidia* "pereche" from ABAVUS Douai 62 and *deses* = *desidiosus* "paraceus", *desidia* "parace, paresce" from ABAVUS Vatic. Lat. 2748 (1938: 1.20, 143); also *dese(n)s* = *decidiosus* "pereceus", *decidia* "peresce", and adv. *decidiose* "perecheusement" from ABAVUS B. N. 7692 (1936:1.309). In Castro's kaleidoscope *desidia* "pereza" (T669) and *desidiosus* "cosa perezosa" (T1522), foreseeably, reappear (1936:205a).

16) Since much of the material was paleo-Germanic, the oldest scholars engaged in sheer guesswork, as when a humanist of the caliber of Francisco Sánchez de las Brozas ("El Brocense", 1523-1601) presumed to have hit upon the Hebrew ancestry of *ganar*. The first Academy dictionary tacitly recorded this wild conjecture, as it did S. de Covarrubias' far more conservative idea that *ganar* was genetically related to *ganado*.

17) One finds some pertinent observations to this effect in M. L. Wagner's concluding stratificational study of the Hispanic lexicon (1953:347-91).

18) Not one whit less arresting than his successive dictionary entries were the comments on Med. Lat. *de-*, *en-ganare* (glosses of Reichenau) that he made in his fine monograph on paleo-Romance glossaries (1865:45).

19) Significantly, sanna may well have left its imprint on the vernacular lexicon, via a blend with saniēs "bad blood" and (īn)sānia "madness, craze"; see Y. Malkiel (1974:1-32). Rönsch's suspicion that v. gannīre may have suffered from an excess of polysemy (cf. the gloss "gannit 'latrat vel inridet'"), with the mintage of gannāre producing a certain relief, should be weighed against the circumstances responsible for the cleavage of -ātu into -ado/-ido, resulting in the coexistence of *ladrar* "to bark" and *ladrido* "bark(ing)"; see Craddock and Georges (1963:87-107).

20) If one were to reconstruct the ancestral Germanic basis from its Romance offshoots alone, one would incline to posit an initial *wad- segment in preference to the usually favored *weid- or *waid-, which have been pieced together from the evidence of sister- rather than daughter-languages. Diez's conjecture, incidentally, provoked a certain restlessness among Germanists (he himself referred to such controversies, focusing on the conjugation class of *weidanjan), while a still young and inexperienced C. Michaëlis (1874:204) somewhat rashly proposed a different, less persuasive interpretation of Sp. *guadaña* "sickle, scythe", *guadañar* "to mow".

21) I cannot go here into any detailed assessment of later research, which was to take a meandering course. Of great value is the material assembled from miscellaneous, in part not readily accessible sources by Menéndez Pidal: on *ganado* beside *gañado*, including certain passages where it corresponds to *ganancia* rather than being an equivalent of "livestock"; on the rivalry between *ganar* and *gañar* and their occasional use for the conquest of a beleaguered fortress; on a lone trace of the archaic postverbal *gaano*, the exact equivalent of It. *guadagno* and Fr. *gain* (1908-11:700-02). Menéndez Pidal's healthy realism prompted him to rebel against the Diezian view (espoused by Körting and, let me add, eventually by most Romanists) that *ganar* and *gañar*, genetically, pertained to two different worlds: "En vista de casos como los arriba apuntados, no puede separarse la etimología de *ganar* de la del it. *guadagnare*, etc., como indica Diez..., y mucho menos teniendo en cuenta la forma con ñ, *gañar*". C. Michaëlis de Vasconcelos, who prepared the *Cancioneiro da Ajuda* glossary at the peak of her career (ca. 1905), was more restrained, limiting herself to the listing of a wealth of competing variants: *gãar*, *gaanar*, *gaañar*, *guaanhar*, plus *gaança* "paga, proveito", which was the vernacular Western counterpart of learnèd Central *ganancia* (1920:41b, 43b). How deeply troubling the coexistence of these seemingly self-contradictory forms could be follows from a despondent remark of A. Steiger's (1932:87), who despaired of reconciling *gado* with *guaanhar*. Meyer-Lübke's simplified matters by omitting *gana*, *ganar*, and *ganancia* from the first version of his etymological dictionary (1911-20).

From later pronouncements let me select for brief mention just the following comments. Meyer-Lübke restated his opinion toward the end of his career (1930-35:§3637 and §9483), bracketing Sp. *ganar*, OPtg. *gãar* with, on the one hand, Sp. *ganado*, Ptg. *gado* and, on the other, Sp. *gana(s)*; he credited Sp. *guadañar* to learnèd transmission

(!); and admitted that the two families had partially conflated. S. Feist (1939:186a) recorded *gaírns* "Wunsch, Begehr, Habsucht" (plus three compounds) and *gaírnjan* "begehren, gelüsten", both related to G. *gern*, *Gier*, and *gierig*, but made no mention of gainon "gähnen, nach etwas happen", which I therefore, Meyer-Lübke's inexplicitness notwithstanding, take to be a putative form. Corominas preferred to operate with *ganan "to covet", which he had arrived at by starting out from Frisian and Scandinavian and which indeed carries with it the advantage of offering a clear-cut *a* rather than an unwelcome diphthong in the stressed syllable. He fell short of convincing W. von Wartburg (1966:467b-468a) -- so did, independently, B. Pottier as an advocate for *waidanôn --, thus leaving the Swiss etymologist in Menéndez Pidal's camp: "Wenn auch der Wechsel zwischen -ñ- und -n- im Altspanischen noch der Aufklärung harrt, so ist doch die Zusammengehörigkeit von *ganar* und *gañar* kaum zu bezweifeln". However, through a further comedy of errors, Wartburg, in lending his support to the Madrid scholar, was unaware of the latter's definitive "prise de position" (1930:413-14), where he rejected De Forest's and W. Bruckner's separate, and diversely-argued, attempts to trace the sporadic traces of OSp. *gañar* to Old French, adduced unusual archaic graphies from charters and city ordinances (*guadanare*, hypercorrect *guataniagare*), placed heavy emphasis on vestiges of broad meaning ("to acquire") in *guadañar*'s record, and drew attention to Mod. Ast. *guañar* "to germinate", *guañu* "sprout", and *guañín* "mower".

22) The existence of the verb (mod. *sinnen* "to meditate", orig. *sinnan* "to travel, strive, go", then "to perceive") has, in fact, been used by Germanists -- including Kluge and Mitzka -- to separate genetically *Sinn* from *sēnsus*. In the last analysis, however, such congeners of *sinnan* as *sinþa "travel, way" (cf. *senden*, *Gesinde*) disclose the family's relationship to OIr. *sēt* "way" and Lat. sentīre "to feel", lit. "to follow a direction". Interestingly, dial. *sinnen* (traceable to SW Germany) is a local reflex of signāre, just as its synonym in the standard, *eichen* "to gauge", mirrors (ad)aequāre (see Frings 1932:59 and in the posthumous edition revised by Gertraud Müller 1968:2.238-41).

23) Cf. 1966:510a-525a, 526a-528a, 529a-533b, 533b-540a -- matching, in Meyer-Lübke's dictionary, 1930-35:§§9502, 9504, 9507, 9508. Wartburg reproached Styff with supplying a logical string of denotations rather than unfolding a genuinely historical panorama of semantic growth.

24) Corominas (1955:817b-818a) was, I suppose, right in arguing for the direct transmission of Gmc. *warjan into Hispano-Romance, where Gamillscheg had previously interpreted OSp. *guarir/-ecer* as, by and large, a borrowing of an OFr. rendition of a Frankish word (1934-36:1.384, 2.176).

25) Small wonder that much of the trail-blazing research on these particles was conducted by students of the ancient Roman theater; cf. Sonnenschein (1891:187-90).

26) Em figured prominently in the thinking of a mature G. I. Ascoli (1901:308), who treated it on a par with ecce/eccum.

27) Most Romanists (including Gartner, Puşcariu, Tiktin, Appel, Hanssen, Menéndez Pidal), in an effort to explain *aqu-*, etc., have pleaded in favor of eccu+; Meyer-Lübke, in his comparative grammar, and Weerenbeck preferred to operate with atque; still others, among them Rydberg, granted to atque a margin of influence on eccu; a scattering of amateurs appealed to Greek or Ligurian models. For full bibliographic details up to the cut-off point, see B. H. J. Weerenbeck (1937:47-66).

28) See Oliver M. Johnston (1905:131-34); Diana Teresa Mériz (1974:533-43); Minnette H. Grunmann (1977:262-69).

Mériz's note is particularly rich in fresh insights. Of the two model sentences, *ez vos le chevalier* and *es vos li poeples*, she declares the latter rare and possibly spurious. *Estes* emerges from her analysis as much less common than *ez*. The basic meaning or function is an invitation to the audience to focus on a detail. The technical literature assessed includes fleeting references in handbooks (Brunot, Bruneau, Nyrop, Meyer-Lübke, Alessio, Greimas, Ménard) and more probing analyses in an occasional monograph (Moignet, Imbs). The date of appearance is early (*Alexis, Gormont et Isembart*), so that a long stretch of pretextual use can be safely extrapolated; extinction: 14th century. Range of use: restricted to narrative genres (common in epics, not uncommon in romances and chronicles), except for Biblical passages in literalistic translation. Classification: neither an adverb nor an interjection, nor indeed a presentative, deictic, demonstrative, or exclamatory particle, still less an apodictic particle functioning occasionally as a verb, but, on syntactic grounds (word order, government, coöccurrences), strictly an impersonal verb, stricken by a maximum of defectivity, devoid of aspectual, modal, temporal, and personal inflection, but endowed with considerable expressivity (originally an imperative).

Grunmann pursues more modest aims in examining those contexts in which *ez vos* occurs, as well as the phrase's structural variations, on the basis of an admittedly random sample: two epics and eight romances. The formula coöccurs with *(par)venir, assener*; also *errant, poignant, monté*; is often preceded by *atant*. All in all, Grunmann sets off six recurrent patterns of combination, e.g., with a substantive, often followed by a subordinate adjectival clause; with a substantive and a prepositional phrase or adverbial location; with a present participle and a noun, their succession being reversible, etc. -- neither scholar refers to It. *ecco*, still less to OSp. *(a)fé*.

29) In the Glossary of his *Readings*, Ford, by way of final pronouncement (1911:228b, 238b), distinguishes between *fe* < fide and *he*, for which he proposed three equipollent solutions: (a) ha(b)ē (impt.), (b) habēte, or (c) vidē "see now", ending the discussion on a note of candor and resignation: "The etymology is not clear". Ford's original presentation of his ideas (1903-04:49-51) ran into stiff resistance on the part of Menéndez Pidal and Pietsch; he reiterated his conjecture and offered his rebuttal of such criticism as had been leveled at him in the Notes entering into his Chrestomathy (1911:108-09), ar-

guing that habḗte vōs could have yielded *avedvos*, which in turn, first
through assimilation of *-d-* to the following *-v-*, later through dissi-
milatory elimination of the first *-v-* (supported by eventual association with *fe* "faith"), produced *ahevos* and, in the end, *afévos*. Ford
judiciously remarked: "In all this there is much assumption and mere
suggestion". On Bello's gropings and Cuervo's criticism, see Menéndez
Pidal 1908-11, s.v.

30) Although Diez's conjecture, of late, has had no supporters,
note that Meyer-Lübke went along with his predecessor in tracing OFr.
vez to a blend of ecce and vidēre and, on his own, explained OProv.
vec as a merger of vidē and eccum (1930-35:§§2822, 2824).

31) As early as 1879 he declared in overt criticism of Diez, à
propos of *afé*: "Vi veggo io un'affermazione sacramentale che si è
ridotta a mera espressione resolutiva o eccitativa, cf. il lat. hercle
o l'it. *gnaffe miafé*" (see 1886-88:7n).

32) Consistently, he made two separate entries in his tone-set-
ting glossary, one for the demonstrative adv. *fe₁*, *afé* "[Sp.] he", of
which he counted 32 occurrences in the *Mio Cid* epic; the other, much
shorter, for the noun *fe₂* "promesa de fidelidad". Menéndez Pidal carefully, if unostentatiously, surveyed the existing literature on *fe*,
he, but not on OFr. *ez* (thus, Johnston's pioneering note eluded his
watchfulness); gave a succinct description of the attachment of the
direct object (*afelo, afelos moros, affé dos cavalleros, fe·m ante
uós yo e vuestras fijas*) and of the pronominal ethical dative, suppres-
sing any hint of practically identical constructions in Ennius and in
OFr. narrative texts, whether epics or romances; offered syntactic and
phonological arguments for preferring his own Arabic theory; and very
briefly stated his reasons for repudiating the three rival explanations
which by then had come to his attention.

33) *Hes* was peculiar to, e.g., Juan del Encina and Salazar; *heis*
to Timoneda (*Dixo el caminante: "Heis aquí donde..."*) and Lope de
Vega; for illustrations see Corominas. If, with *hes*, one can attempt
to explain away the *-s* as adverbial, the more advanced form *heis* shows
undeniable adaptation to the verbal paradigm.

34) Old Aragonese, however, followed a separate course, and there
ayec (its *a-* reminiscent of the opening segment of *a-yer* "yesterday"
< heri) indeed crystallized. In 16th-century Judeo-Spanish Bible
translations colored by that dialect, one finds *ek* (in Hebrew script)
or the alternation *(h)ec ∿ (h)e*, as equivalents of Hebr. הנה /hinnē/
"lo and behold". See the notes by G. Tilander (1936:193-97) and G.
Sachs (1936:292-93).

REFERENCES:

Academia Española, Real. 1732. *Diccionario de la lengua castellana*. Vol. 3. Madrid: Viuda de Francisco del Hierro.
---------------------- 1947. *Diccionario de la lengua española*. 17th ed. Madrid.
---------------------- 1970. *Diccionario de la lengua española*. 19th ed. Madrid.
Ascoli, Graziadio Isaia. 1886-88 (earliest publication: 1879). "Di un filone italico, diverso dal romano, che si avverta nel campo neolatino: Lettera glottologica a Napoleone Caix", *Archivio glottologico italiano* 10.1-17.
---------------------- 1901. "Intorno ai continuatori neolatini del lat. ipsu-", *Archivio glottologico italiano* 15.303-16.
Bluteau, Rafael. 1712-21. *Vocabulário português et latino*. 8 vols. Coimbra: Colégio das Artes da Companhia de Jesú.
Cabrera, Ramón. 1837. *Diccionario de etimologías de la lengua castellana*, ed. J. P. Ayegui. Madrid: Marcelino Calero.
Carter, Henry H., ed. 1952-53. "A Fourteenth-Century Latin-Old Portuguese Verb Dictionary", *Romance Philology* 6.71-103.
Castro, Américo, ed. 1936. *Glosarios latino-españoles de la Edad Media*. Suppl. 22 to *Revista de Filología Española*. Madrid: Centro de Estudios Históricos.
Cohn, Georg. 1891. *Die Suffixwandlungen im Vulgärlatein und im vorliterarischen Französisch nach ihren Spuren im Neufranzösischen*. Halle: M. Niemeyer.
Cornu, Jules. 1888. "Die portugiesische Sprache", *Grundriss der romanischen Philologie* (ed. G. Gröber) 1.715-803. Strassburg: Karl J. Trübner.
----------- 1904-06. "Die portugiesische Sprache", *Grundriss der romanischen Philologie* 1.916-1037. Rev. 2nd ed.
Corominas, Juan (or Joan). 1941-42. "Nuevas etimologías españolas: *allende, aquende*", *Anales del Instituto de Lingüística de Cuyo* 1.119-29.
---------------------- 1942-44. "Espigueo de latín vulgar", *Anales del Instituto de Lingüística de Cuyo* 2.128-54.
---------------------- 1955. *Diccionario crítico-etimológico de la lengua castellana*. Vol. 2. Bern: Francke, and Madrid: Gredos.
Covarrubias, [H]orozco, Sebastián de. 1943. *Tesoro de la lengua castellana o española (1611)*, ed. Martín de Riquer. Barcelona: S. A. Horta.
Craddock, Jerry R., and Georges, Emanuel S. 1963. "The Hispanic Sound Suffix *-ido*", *Romance Philology* 17:1.87-107.
Cuervo, Rufino José. 1886-93. *Diccionario de construcción y régimen de la lengua castellana*. 2 vols. (A-D). Paris: A. Roger and F. Chernoviz.
Diez, Friedrich. 1853. *Etymologisches Wörterbuch der romanischen Sprachen*. Bonn: Adolph Marcus.

-------------- 1865. *Altromanische Glossare*. Bonn: Eduard Weber.

Dozy, R. and Englemann, W. H. 1869. *Glossaire des mots espagnols et portugais dérivés de l'arabe*. Rev. 2nd ed. Leyde: E. J. Brill.

Eguílaz y Yanguas, Leopoldo. 1886. *Glosario etimológico de las palabras españoles...de origen oriental*. Granada: Imprenta "La Lealtad".

Ernout, A. and Meillet, A. 1959-60. *Dictionnaire étymologique de la langue latine*. 4th ed. Paris: Klincksieck.

Espe, Hans. 1908. *Die Interjektionen im Altfranzösischen*. Diss. Königsberg.

Feist, Sigmund. 1939. *Vergleichendes Wörterbuch der gotischen Sprache*. Rev. 3rd ed. Leiden: E. J. Brill.

Foerster, Wendelin. 1879. "Beiträge zur romanischen Lautlehre: Umlaut (eigentlich Vokalsteigerung) im Romanischen", *Zeitschrift für romanische Philologie* 3.481-517.

Ford, J. D. M. 1903-04. "Old Spanish Etymologies", *Modern Philology* 1.49-55.

------------- 1911. *Old Spanish Readings, Selected on the Basis of Critically Edited Texts*. 2nd ed. Boston: Ginn.

Frings, Theodor. 1932. *Germania Romana*. *Teuthonista* (= *Zeitschrift für deutsche Dialektforschung und Sprachgeschichte*, Suppl. 4). Halle: M. Niemeyer.

--------------- 1966-68. *Germania Romana*. 2nd ed., 2 vols. Revised by Gertraud Müller. *Mitteldeutsche Studien 19*. Halle: M. Niemeyer.

Gamillscheg, Ernst. 1934-36. *Romania Germanica*. 3 vols. Berlin: W. de Gruyter.

----------------- 1970. *Romania Germanica*. 2nd ed. of Vol. I. Berlin.

García de Diego, Vicente. [1955]. *Diccionario etimológico español e hispánico*. Madrid: S.A.E.T.A.

Gili y Gaya, Samuel, ed. 1947-57. *Tesoro lexicográfico 1492-1726, 1 (A-E)*. Madrid: CSIC.

Grunmann, Minnette H. 1977. "The Old French Formula *ez vos*", *Romance Philology* 31/2.262-69.

Johnston, Oliver M. 1905. "Use of the French Equivalents of Latin *em*, *ēn*, and *ecce*", *Modern Language Notes* 30.131-34.

Kluge, Friedrich and Mitzka, Walther. 1960. *Etymologisches Wörterbuch der deutschen Sprache*. 18th ed. Berlin: W. de Gruyter. (The 17th ed. [1957] and the 20th ed. [1967] were also consulted.)

Körting, Gustav. 1891. *Lateinisch-romanisches Wörterbuch*. Paderborn: F. Schöningh. (1901: Rev. 2nd ed.; 1907: Rev. 3rd ed.)

Malkiel, Yakov. 1974. "Primary, Secondary, and Tertiary etymologies: The Three Lexical Kernels of Hispanic *saña, ensañar, sañudo*", *Hispanic Review* 42.1-32.

Ménage, Gilles. 1650. *Les origines de la langue françoise*. Paris: Auguste Courbé.

Menéndez Pidal, Ramón, ed. 1908-11. *Cantar de Mio Cid*. Texto, gramática y vocabulario. 3 vols. Madrid.

------------------- 1930. "Etimologías españolas", *Modern Philology*
27/4.411-14.
------------------- 1941. *Manual de gramática histórica española*.
6th ed. Madrid: Espasa-Calpe.
Mériz, Diana Teresa. 1974. "A propos du classement d'ancien français
es (< ecce)", *Romania* 95.533-43.
Meyer[-Lübke], Wilhelm. 1883. *Die Schicksale des lateinischen Neu-
trums im Romanischen*. Halle: M. Niemeyer.
-------------------- 1890. *Grammatik der romanischen Sprachen:
Lautlehre*. Leipzig: Fues's Verlag (R. Reisland).
-------------------- 1897. Review of A. Thomas, *Regain, Zeitschrift für romanische Philologie* 21.154.
-------------------- 1911-20. *Romanisches etymologisches Wörterbuch*. Heidelberg: Carl Winter. (Rev. 3rd ed., 1930-35.)
Michaëlis [de Vasconcelos], Carolina. 1874. "Etymologisches", *Jahr-
buch für romanische und englische Sprachen und Literatur* 13.204.
------------------------------------ 1876. *Studien zur romanischen
Wortschöpfung*. Leipzig: F. A. Brockhaus.
------------------------------------ [1914]. *A saudade portuguesa;
divagações filológicas e literar-históricas*...Porto: Renascença
portuguesa. (Rev. 2nd ed., [1922].)
------------------------------------ 1920. "Glossário do *Cancioneiro
da Ajuda*", *Revista Lusitana* 23.1-95.
Migliorini, Bruno and Duro, Aldo. 1964. *Prontuario etimologico della
lingua italiana*. 4th ed. Torino, etc.: G. B. Paravia & Co.
Moignet, Gérard. 1969. "Le verbe *voici* -- *voilà*", *Travaux de linguistique et de littérature publiés par le Centre de Philologie et de
Littérature Romanes (Strasbourg)* 7/1.189-202.
Monlau, Pedro Felipe. 1941. *Diccionario etimológico de la lengua cas-
tellana*. Buenos Aires: El Ateneo. (Reprint of the revised 2nd
ed. [1883], posthumous.)
Onions, C. T. (et al.). 1966. *The Oxford Dictionary of English Ety-
mology*. Oxford: at the Clarendon Press.
Paris, Gaston. 1883. Review of Settegast, "Romanische Etymologien",
Romania 12.133.
Pietsch, Karl. 1904-05. "The Spanish Particle *he*", *Modern Philology*
2.197-224.
Richardson, Henry B. 1930. *An Etymological Vocabulary to the* Libro
de Buen Amor.... London and New Haven: Yale University Press.
Rönsch, Hermann. 1879. "Romanische Etymologien, 2", *Zeitschrift für
romanische Philologie* 3.102-04.
Roques, Mario, ed. 1936-38. *Recueil général des lexiques français du
Moyen Age*. 2 vols. Paris: H. Champion.
Rosal, Francisco del. ca. 1601. *Origen y etimología de todos los vo-
cablos originales de la lengua castellana*. Bibl. Nac., MS 6.929.
Unpublished; cited via S. Gili y Gaya.
Sachs, Georg. 1936. "*Ek*", *Revista de filología española* 23.292-93.
Scheler, August. 1887. Suppl. to Diez, *EWRS*, 5th ed. Bonn: A. Mar-
cus.

Schuchardt, Hugo. 1889. "Romanische Etymologien", *Zeitschrift für romanische Philologie* 13.525-33.

Settegast, F. 1883. "Romanische Etymologien", *Romanische Forschungen* 1.237-55.

Sonnenschein, Edward A., ed. 1891. *T. Macci Plauti "Rudens"*. Oxford: at the Clarendon Press.

Spitzer, Leo. 1943-45. "Adiciones y enmiendas", *Anales del Instituto de Lingüística de Cuyo* 3.212-14.

Steiger, Arnald. 1932. *Contribución a la fonética del hispano-árabe* ... Madrid: Centro de estudios históricos.

Styff, Hugo. 1923. *Etude sur l'évolution sémantique du radical* ward- *dans les langues romanes*. Thèse de Lund.

Thomas, Antoine. 1896. "Etymologies françaises", *Romania* 25.80-97.

---------------- 1904. *Nouveaux essais de philologie française*. Paris: E. Bouillon.

Tilander, Gunnar. 1936. "*Ayec*", *Revista de filología española* 23. 193-97.

Tobler, Adolf. 1886. Review, *Poème moral*, ed. Wilhelm Cloetta, *Literaturblatt für germanische und romanische Philologie* 7.364-67.

------------- and Lommatzsch, Erhard. 1960. *Altfranzösisches Wörterbuch*. Vol. 4 (G-I). Wiesbaden: Franz Steiner.

Wagner, Max Leopold. 1953. "Etymologische Randbemerkungen zu neueren iberoromanischen Dialektarbeiten und Wörterbüchern", *Zeitschrift für romanische Philologie* 69.347-91.

Wartburg, Walther von. 1934. *Französisches etymologisches Wörterbuch; eine Darstellung des galloromanischen Sprachschatzes*. Vol. 3. Leipzig: B. G. Teubner.

-------------------- 1960. *Französisches etymologisches Wörterbuch*. Vol. 17: Germanische Elemente S-Z. Basel: R. G. Zbinden.

Weerenbeck, B. H. J. 1937. "*Aqui*, etc., en provençal, en catalan, en espagnol et en portugais", *Revue de linguistique romane* 13.47-66.

ON COMPARATIVE SYNTAX

MARIANNE MITHUN and LYLE CAMPBELL
SUNY, Albany   *SUNY, Albany*

0. INTRODUCTION:

The recent flurry of studies in diachronic syntax is most welcome, since it has brought attention to important and fertile areas of investigation. Nevertheless, the enthusiasm for such studies has not been matched by equal success, especially in syntactic reconstruction. The purpose of this paper is to examine the underlying assumptions of several approaches to syntactic reconstruction, to identify obstacles to greater accomplishment, and to suggest some priorities for future research.

1. THE COMPARATIVE METHOD:

Since it has often been hoped that principles of diachronic phonology could be transferred to diachronic syntax, we begin by considering why phonology and lexical reconstruction have been more successful than the reconstruction of grammar. Phonological reconstruction owes much of its success to the Neogrammarian hypothesis of the regularity of sound change and to observations about preferred directionality of specific changes. Syntactic change has no direct analogue of either. In the following sections we will outline the benefits accrued to diachronic phonology from these assumptions, demonstrate why they have no counterparts in syntax, and consider the significance of this lack of syntactic reconstruction.

1.1. *Regularity in Sound Change:*

The confidence that sounds do not change in random or inexplicable ways permits several crucial steps in the application of the comparative method. First, it provides a basis for the selection of comparable entities from a set of languages, i.e., cognate material. It serves as a means of distinguishing formal similarities among languages which may be due to chance, borrowing, or universals, from those due to common ancestry.

Second, the capacity to distinguish cognate material provides a basis for observing which kinds of sound changes occur the most frequently and their normal direction. Many sound changes are more likely to occur in one direction than another. The intervocalic voicing of originally voiceless stops, for example, has a much greater frequency of occurrence than the same change in the opposite direction. Such directionality provides a principled reason for choosing one reconstruction over another. If L_1 has intervocalic voiced stops corresponding to L_2 intervocalic voiceless stops, it is more likely, all else being equal, that L_1 changed in accordance with the more frequent direction of voicelessness to voicing in this position, and that L_2 then reflects the older state.

Third, the assumption of regularity of sound change permits the reconstruction of many lexical items from the postulation of a finite number of proto sounds. Once sound correspondences are established among daughter languages and proto forms posited for each correspondence, these same hypotheses may be used over and over in the reconstruction of different lexical items.

1.2. *Regularity in Syntactic Change:*

Sounds always occur in combination with other sounds and are as-

sociated with semantic or grammatical meaning to form morphemes and
words. The sound itself can be seen as a type and its various occurrences in different morphemes as multiple tokens of the single type.
The regularity hypothesis refers to the fact that the same sound may
be observed to change in the same way in different morphemes. When
the type changes, each of the multiple tokens exemplifies the change
in a regular way.

It might seem at first that the same kind of regularity should
be observable in syntactic change. Syntax simply governs larger chunks
of language than phonology. The deletion of the relative pronoun could
be observable in many different sentences, just as the palatalization
of *t before y might be exemplified by many different words in a language. There is a crucial difference, however, in the acquisition of
these two kinds of patterns. Sounds are acquired not independently,
but as parts of words in which form and meaning are linked. Unlike
words, sentences are not learned as wholes. The form and substance
are acquired separately. Sentences can be generated each time a speaker speaks, from general syntactic rules and appropriate entries from
the lexicon. A syntactic pattern is not learned anew for each sentence
which exemplifies it. A speaker may utter many passive voice sentences,
but need not have learned the sentences independently as he must learn
words. Learning the passivization rules once is sufficient for the
production of an infinite number of passive sentences. It is because
of this single acquisition of syntactic rules that there can be no equivalent to the regularity hypothesis in diachronic syntax. In syntax,
the type has only one token, the general rule, making regularity trivial.

Because of the substanceless acquisition of most syntactic rules,
sentences cannot really be cognate across languages the way words can.
They are not passed down as wholes from specific proto sentences originally uttered by speakers of the parent language.

1.3. *Further Complicating Factors:*

If there are no such things as cognate sentences, how are we to

identify comparable syntactic material? Functional or semantic equiv-
alence in formal description is not sufficient to render entities genetically comparable, since chance, borrowing, and universals may account
for similarities as well as common ancestry. This would be equivalent
to granting cognate status to *all* words with the same glosses. Furthermore, the relative role of chance similarity in syntax is much greater
than in phonology. That the form and meaning of some particular word
in two languages might be similar by chance is usually unlikely. But
the range of possible variation among many functionally equivalent syntactic patterns is so narrow that the probability of chance similarity
is correspondingly greater. If, for example, there are two possible
orders of constituents in comparative constructions, standard-pivot-
adjective and adjective-pivot-standard, then any two languages selected
at random have a high probability of sharing the same order.

The limits of our understanding of interrelationships among alternative syntactic patterns handicap us seriously in syntactic reconstruction. Given the Romance correspondence $k/\check{c}/\check{s}$, we posit $*k$ for the phonetic value of the proto sound because of our knowledge of common types
of sound shift. If, however, we observe that one daughter language exhibits SVO order, another SOV, and a third VSO, in the absence of principles of directionality, we have no indication of the word order of
their parent.

1.4. *Priorities:*

If syntactic reconstruction is to be carried out without the benefit of a regularity principle and hypothesis of preferred directionality,
other sources of information about syntactic change must be sought. One
source which has been utilized in phonological reconstruction involves
implicational universals.

Consider the relation in phonology between glottalized and plain
obstruents. The presence of glottalized obstrucents (C') in a language
implies the presence of their plain, non-glottalized counterparts (C).

The marked relationship between (C') and (C) insures that under normal conditions $C' > C$ but that $C > C'$ is not likely. This directionality is useful in reconstruction: given two languages where $L_1 C'$ corresponds to $L_2 C$, all else being equal we reconstruct $*C'$. Should we be possessed to choose $*C$ as the probable proto form, then we must at the same time present strong evidence explaining the unexpected, such as areal diffusion.

Some implicational universals involve a mutual dependency rather than implying a directionality of change. These can be utilized in reconstruction in a different way. Given the aspiration of /p^h/ in some languages, for example, we expect /t^h/, and given /t^h/ we expect /p^h/. If, however, we find correspondences suggesting that a proto language had $*$/p^h/, then we suspect that it also had $*$/t^h/ and search for evidence supporting $*$/t^h/.

Syntactic universals could provide similar clues to patterns especially likely to be found in a proto-language. If we know that all languages which can relativize off direct objects can also relativize off subjects, and we find relative clauses modifying higher direct objects in the daughter languages, then we search for relatives modifying subjects. A similar example can be drawn from word order universals. It has been observed that VOS languages have an alternative order VSO whenever the subject is "heavy", i.e., contains conjoined noun phrases or relative clauses. If this putative universal should hold true under subsequent investigation, then whenever we can reconstruct $*$VOS order for the parent, we seek evidence of $*$VSO with heavy objects. To take another example, it has been supposed that ergative languages characteristically posses rules of antipassive (cf. Johnson 1976). If this holds true, then evidence of ergativity in a proto language, such as ergative morphology, would further prompt us to seek evidence for reconstructing a rule of antipassive. The more we know about all kinds of implicational universals and the interrelationships among parts of grammatical systems, the better our chances for reconstruction.

Finally, a knowledge of the interrelationships among the various parts of grammar can allow us to benefit from some of the rigor of the comparative method. It is often possible to reconstruct inflectional and derivational morphology using the techniques of lexical reconstruction. To the extent that morphologically complex cognates bear regularly corresponding sounds, that the cognate morphemes appear in the same position in the words, and that they have not undergone substantial functional shifts, we can reconstruct morphologically complex words with the normal techniques of lexical reconstruction. Morphological analysis of these proto forms provides us with some of the proto morphology. We can reconstruct morphology by the comparative method precisely because the patterns are linked to the substance they govern. Unlike syntax, much of morphology is not regenerated anew each time a morphologically complex word is used.

Because there is no clear absolute boundary between morphological and syntactic functions and many syntactic rules are at least partially signalled on the surface by bound morphemes, reconstruction of morphology can suggest much about syntax. The reconstruction of passive, causative, instrumental, nominalizing, or infinitive morphemes, for example, suggest the existence of related syntactic rules in the proto language. Examples of this technique can be found in Norman and Campbell (1976), where the relationship between ergative morphology and rules of antipassive are discussed, and in Jeffers (1976), who notes the coincidence of VSO order and embedding nominalization.

The potential contribution of this technique to syntactic reconstruction is of course limited by the nature of morphological change. Such events as loss of morphemes, analogical change in the shape of morphemes, and shifts in their functions, are irrecoverable by the comparative method alone. Consider how much of the inflectional morphology of Latin could be recovered from the Romance languages with only this technique.

2.   WORD ORDER TYPOLOGIES:

Investigation into the interrelationships among different parts

of grammar has led to the development of one technique of syntactic
reconstruction considered by many of its proponents to be akin to the
method of internal reconstruction in phonology. A cohesiveness is
noted among certain sets of syntactic characteristics. Lehmann (1972,
1974), following Greenberg (1966), notes a tendency for languages with
principle constituent order VO to have prepositions, exhibit the order
adjective-pivot-standard in comparative constructions, and place modifiers (relative clauses, adjectives, and genitives) after nominals.
OV languages tend to have postpositions, the order standard-pivot-ad-
jective, and modifiers preceding the nouns they modify.

Just as in internal reconstruction, modern alternations provide
the basis for postulating non-alternating, unique forms in the past,
so deviation from typological consistency is used as an indicator of
an earlier consistency of a different type. Scattered OV characteristics in a primarily VO type language, for example, are taken as indications of an earlier OV type. Inherent in the method is the assumption that the history of the language can be unraveled back to some
earlier consistency. This assumption bears closer examination.

2.1. *Contradiction in the Method:*

In its strong form, the assumption of typological consistency in
proto languages leads to internal, factual, and general methodological
contradictions. First, the method itself assumes inconsistency in
daughter languages as a starting point for its application. Second,
numerous modern languages exhibit inconsistency with respect to the
Greenberg-Lehmann typologies. The postulation of a synchronically untenable restriction on proto languages violates basic axioms of diachronic linguistics. If consistent modern languages exist it is counter-intuitive to assume that inconsistency could not have existed in
the proto language.

A weaker form of the assumption leads to a paradox. This version
postulates a natural tendency inherent in all language systems to deve-

lop toward typological consistency. It does admit the existence of conflicting factors moving languages away from consistency. Consider the value to be derived from this method under the weaker form of the assumption in each of the following cases:

A. Two daughter languages are typologically consistent in the same way ($C_1 C_1$). According to this model of change, there are two plausible origins for this situation:

    1. $*C_1$: The consistency of the daughters could be a common inheritance from a parent with the same consistency.

    2. $*I$: The parent language could have been inconsistent but both daughters became consistent under the natural tendency to develop consistency.

In this case, the method does not provide strong support for choosing either alternative over the other.

B. Both daughter languages are consistent but in different ways ($C_1 C_2$). In the absence of theories about the direction of typological change, there is no clear basis for choosing either language over the other as reflecting the older state. Reasonable proto states could be the following:

    1. $*C_1$: A separate force could have brought L_2 out of alignment, then the natural force toward consistency moved it along to its current C_2 consistency.

    2. $*C_2$: Some event disrupted the consistency of L_1, then the natural tendency moved along to C_1.

    3. $*I$: The parent language was originally midway between C_1 and C_2, and a natural tendency toward consistency pushed each daughter language in a different direction.

The method rules out none of these possibilities but does prompt the search for the disruptive force required for (1) or (2). If we could rule out the existence of such a force, the method would indicate (3). Unfortunately, we have no procedure for doing so.

C. One daughter language is consistent and one inconsistent ($C_1 I_1$). Possible antecedents are the following:

1. $*I$: The parent language may have been inconsistent in
    the same way as its inconsistent daughter. The other
    daughter could have become consistent under the natural
    tendency in this direction.

2. $*C_1$: The parent could have been consistent in the same
    way as its consistent daughter. Another factor inter-
    fered with the consistency of the other daughter.

The method again prompts us to search for a disruptive force.
As above, the method would indicate $*I$ only if we could rule
out the existence of such a force.

D. Both daughters are inconsistent in different ways ($I_1 I_2$).
    Again, in this case, the method alone does not provide a
    sufficient basis for reconstructing the typological state
    of the parent. Possible reconstructions are the following:

    1. $*I_{12}$: If I_1 and I_2 are different points along the same
        path, say between C_1 and C_2, the parent could have been
        inconsistent in a way equidistant from both C_1 and C_2.
        L_1 and L_2 could both be developing naturally toward
        different consistencies.

    2. $*I_1$ or $*I_2$: Some factor could have radically altered
        the original inconsistent state of one daughter to a
        new inconsistent state. The tendency toward consis-
        tency does not enter at all here.

    3. $*C_{12}$: If C_{12} represents the consistent state between
        the two states of the daughter languages, both languages
        could have undergone change away from consistency due
        to outside factors counteracting the natural tendency
        toward consistency.

E. Both daughters are inconsistent in the same way ($I_1 I_1$). To
    say that the parent was consistent and that both languages
    spontaneously developed inconsistency goes against the assump-
    tion of a natural tendency toward consistency. That they
    both borrowed the same inconsistency is unlikely. The most
    probable explanation is that they both reflect the inconsis-
    tent state of their ancestor. In this case, then, typologi-
    cal considerations do provide a basis for choosing one proto
    system over the others.

The paradox of the word-order approach to diachronic syntax is
that the method provides results *only* when the underlying assumption,

that languages change toward consistency, fails. Furthermore, the contribution of this approach is not as significant as it may at first
seem. The method does not guarantee the validity of its result. It
only says that in this single case, typological considerations do not
invalidate the comparative method. In syntax, however, where the comparative method is without rigor unless form is attached to substance,
such guidance is of little value.

2.2. *Priorities for Research:*

If the only natural tendency in syntactic change were toward typological consistency, all languages should be consistent by now. Unfortunately, noticeable opposing shifts have too often been attributed to
the borrowing of inconsistent features without supporting evidence. If
typological considerations are to contribute to syntactic reconstruction, certain questions must be resolved.

2.2.1. *The Borrowability of Typological Characteristics:*

The relative borrowability of typological features must be
more carefully investigated. Perhaps some characteristics are
easily borrowed, because they are peripheral to the type, while
others are virtually unborrowable by languages in certain states
because to acquire them would throw the language intolerably out
of typological kilter. Such knowledge would helpfully constrain
excessive recourse to borrowing as a wild card in reconstruction.
Furthermore, if borrowing is used as an explanation of typological inconsistency, criteria for the demonstration of actual
borrowing must be developed, as in Hashimoto (1975) and Tai (1976)
for Altaic influences on Chinese.

2.2.2. *The Relative Power of Individual Shifts:*

Just as typological characteristics may vary in their borrowability at certain times, so might they vary in their capacity to
set typological shifts in motion. Perhaps languages tolerate certain inconsistencies more easily than others, perhaps some indef-
initely, others not at all. This information is essential to an
understanding of cause and effect in typological shift.

2.2.3. *The Relative Chronology of Changes in Shifts:*

It would be especially useful to discover whether typological
characteristics change in a specific order in the course of typological shift. If so, it would become possible to identify the
direction of a change in progress and so infer characteristics of
the proto language. Of course a given syntactic change may spread
to some parts of the system earlier than to others, and the specification of this order is extremely valuable. Remnants of old OV
order are claimed to be visible in French pronouns but not full
nominals and in German subordinate clauses but not main clauses.
If a precise and reliable scale could be set up of the order in
which features change in the course of a typological shift, the
direction of changes in progress could be charted, providing crucial information for reconstruction.

2.2.4. *Internal Counter-consistent Tendencies:*

If the method is to be rigorous, other demonstrable factors
undermining consistency must be identified as well. The degree
to which phonological decay and analogical restructuring, for
example, can effect typological shifts by altering crucial typological characteristics must be examined.

These priorities point to a specific goal: the explanation of
typological cohesion and dissolution rather than simple description.

At this stage, typological considerations cannot provide a rigorous
technique for syntactic reconstruction. With appropriate care, however, notions of typologically probable and improbable states can provide guidelines for the reconstruction of language systems which are
not typologically possible.

3.   EXPLANATION IN SYNTACTIC CHANGE:

It has been shown that because there is no counterpart to the
regularity hypothesis in syntax, there is no rigorous technique analogous to the comparative method for identifying cognate syntactic
patterns across languages. In fact, syntactic structures usually are
the result of the types of development which the comparative method
cannot trace on any level: those involving analogical remodeling,
reanalysis, and replacement. Without the establishment of cognate
relationships, it is difficult to amass data for the formation of
hypotheses about the preferred directionality of specific changes.
Typological considerations offer little assistance in this area.

In diachronic phonology, we can often establish directionality
by explaining what could have caused a change. If some physical factor such as muscle control accounts for the tendency toward the continued vibration of the vocal cords during the production of intervocalic stops, then this in a sense "explains" the direction of the
frequent change of stops from voicelessness to voicing between vowels.
If we understood why grammars change, we could search for the known
causes of effects observed in related languages. An understanding of
causation could also yield motivation for choosing certain reconstructions over others. In this section, several proposed explanations of
syntactic change will be evaluated in terms of their potential useful-
ness in syntactic reconstruction.

3.1.   *Internal Causes:*

Languages seem to strive for communicative efficiency, toward a

balance in the requirements for efficient production, and learnability.
This tendency toward systematic equilibrium necessitates a holistic
approach to language reconstruction. The parts of language are inter-
related with different processes working in concert. Some processes
naturally co-occur with others within syntactic subsystems. When it
becomes possible to determine the normal or the expected way in which
a language welds these into a functional unit, we can then search for
the pieces and relationships in syntactic reconstruction.

A holistic approach also provides criteria in choosing among
competing reconstructions. Alternative hypotheses can be evaluated
by considering the degree to which they fit into the framework of a
more comprehensive phenomenon (grammatical system) and to the extent
to which the reconstruction is compatible with language universals
(Dressler 1971).

Many changes are brought about by disruptions in other parts of
the grammar, putting the functional equilibrium of the language as a
communicative system under stress. Compensatory changes bring the system into a new balance. One clear example found in several modern
Indo-European languages, including English, Spanish, and others, is
compensation for lost case endings by stricter word order to signal
grammatical relationships among constituents, especially subjects, pre-
dicates, and objects. Another example is from Lapp: as sound change
eliminated certain final consonants which were the only formal means
of signaling certain case endings, consonant-gradation of stems was
extended to consonants and environments to which it had formerly not
applied. Consonant gradation thus became the formal marker of these
cases (Anttila 1972). Mithun (1976) illustrates a similar therapeutic
change in Iroquoian, where various nominalization markers were introduced to identify syntactic functions of constituents obscured by optional focus fronting rules. Kuno (1974) has proposed several universals relating various kinds of word order, based on the difficulties
of decoding which they present.

A particularly instructive example is that of Bever and Langen-

doen (1972) which illustrates the interplay between perceptual and production needs. They show that in the history of English, as a result
of the disappearance of nominal inflections between the 11th and 15th
centuries, constructions with relative clauses became perceptually complex. This perceptual complexity was counteracted by changes in the
restrictions on relative clause markers, which complicated the grammar
per se, but removed many of the perceptually difficult cases (1972:77).
A perceptually complex sentence such as: *The secretary discouraged
the man wanted to see the boss* was grammatical in this earlier period.
A complication in the grammar requiring an overt relative marker eliminated the difficulty in interpretation.

Misinterpretations or incorrect abductions in cases of surface
structure ambiguity may account for changes in related parts of the
grammar. Anttila (1972:102-04) presents several examples. To consider
just one, Greek had infinitive phrases such as θέλω γραφεῖν "I want to
write" and θέλει γραφεῖν "he wants to write", but when final -ν was
lost, the surface forms of the third person singular and the infinitive became identical. At some later time, the infinitives were rein-
terpreted as third person singular forms (θέλει γράφει "he wants he
writes") and extended to other persons (θέλω γράφω "I want I write").
For other samples of the appearance of a new construction as a reanalysis of another surface structure type, see Ebert 1976:vii-xi, Jamison
1976, and Breckenridge and Hakulinen 1976.

We do not have as our goal in this section to survey exhaustively
the internal causes of syntactic change. Rather we intend to illustrate the potential contribution of such considerations and to call
for a holistic approach to the investigation of causes of language
change. Until considerable progress is made in understanding the interrelationships among the parts of grammar, functional explanations
will be weak. In causal explanations, it can be too easy to find what
one is looking for. Even if a known cause can be found in an earlier
stage of a language for later effects, there is no guarantee that this
was the crucial cause. Criteria must be established for demonstrating

that specific causes were indeed the prime factors in proposed changes. The rewards of investigation into functional factors in linguistic change can be important, particularly given the lack of a syntactic counterpart to the comparative method and the current restrictions on the contribution of typological considerations. A holistic understanding of causes could point to hypothetical proto forms, and provide a means of distinguishing innovations from archaisms.

3.2. *External Causes:*

Syntactic borrowing is an important external cause of syntactic change. Unfortunately, it has been both underused and abused as an explanatory factor. Until recently some denied even the possibility of syntactic borrowing and still many are reluctant to accept a number of probable cases of syntactic borrowing. On the other hand, many others have indiscriminately used borrowing (substrata) to explain the origin of any otherwise unexplained data. To achieve the necessary balance between these two extremes, it is mandatory to discover which aspects of syntax are borrowable and under what conditions they may be borrowed. Criteria must also be established for adequate demonstration of actual borrowing.

A step toward definitions of conditions under which borrowing takes place is Hale's (1971) treatment of gaps in grammars and cultures. He suggests that a language lacking embedded relatives suffers from an accidental gap that it would be likely to fill given the chance, a chance such as contact with a language possessing them. Such an approach to borrowability entails, again, a holistic knowledge of language systems.

One way of constraining indiscriminate appeal to borrowing is to amass as much data as possible on clear cases of syntactic borrowing, along the lines of Thomason and Kaufman (1976). From this, probability levels for various kinds of syntactic borrowing might be established and conditions favorable or necessary specified.

Some convincing cases of syntactic borrowing are Silverstein 1974, Nadkarni 1975, Sapir 1907:533-44, Gumperz 1964, 1969, 1971, Hyman 1975, and Tai 1976. A promising type of argument involves syntactic variation in dialects of one language which correspond to syntactic phenomena of contact languages. Silverstein (1974), for example, demonstrates the existence of grammatical borrowing in Chinookan by tracing a dialect continuum, juxtaposing simple tense and aspect distinctions on the Pacific Coast (Lower Chinook, corresponding to neighboring Salishan languages), with multitense distinctions in the southern Plateau (Kiksht Chinook, corresponding to neighboring Sahaptian languages).

The sociolinguistic context of speech often accounts for syntactic changes, and these should not be neglected. Some are code-switching, stylistic variants, conversational implicature, honorifics and reverentials, etc. To take just one example, consider the development of reverentials and their impact on grammar. They have such varied results as turning third person verb forms into second (Spanish, German, Quiché), turning plural forms into singular (Mam, English, Finnish), and converting reflexives and applicatives into third person singular actives (Nahuatl). The royal *we* of medieval European languages is another case. Ritual speech generally can influence syntactic pattern to change. Finally, rules of oral literature, poetry, translation of sacred texts, etc. can all influence syntactic changes.

4.   CONCLUSIONS:

Syntactic reconstruction can be exciting, but must be confronted with a sober realization of both its potentials and limitations. In considering various methods employed for syntactic reconstruction, we have concluded that the comparative method is at present largely unproductive because of the lack of an analogue to phonological regularity and directionality. These, being bound to a theory of sound change, might be partially compensated for if we had detailed knowledge of the implicational relationships which hold among the various parts of gram-

matical systems. In particular, much can be learned about syntactic
change from proto morphology discovered via the normal techniques of
lexical reconstruction.

At present, contradictions inherent in the assumptions behind typologically based reconstructions limit the application of this technique.
With a more comprehensive knowledge of factors which counteract the tendency toward typological consistency, the method could provide a valuable check on the plausibility of reconstructed proto systems.

REFERENCES:

Andersen, H. 1974. "Toward a Typology of Change: Bifurcating Changes
    and Binary Relations", J. Anderson and C. Jones, eds., *Historical
    Linguistics: Proceedings of the First International Conference
    on Historical Linguistics*. Pp. 18-60. Amsterdam: North Holland.
Anttila, R. 1972. *An Introduction to Historical and Comparative Lin-
    guistics*. New York: Macmillan.
Bever, T. and Langendoen, T. 1972. "The Interaction of Speech Percep-
    tion and Grammatical Structure in the Evolution of Language", R.
    Stockwell and R. MacCauley, eds., *Linguistic Change and Generative
    Grammar*. Pp. 32-95. Bloomington: Indiana University Press.
Breckenridge, J. and Hakulinen, A. 1976. "Cycle and After", S. Steever
    et al., eds., *Papers from the Parasession on Diachronic Syntax*.
    Pp. 50-68. Chicago: Chicago Linguistic Society.
Campbell, L. 1974. "On Conditions of Sound Change", J. Anderson and
    C. Jones, edd., *Historical Linguistics: Proceedings of the First
    International Conference on Historical Linguistics*. Pp. 88-96.
    Amsterdam: North Holland.
---------- 1976. "Language Contact and Sound Change", W. Christie,
    ed., *Proceedings of the Second International Conference on Histor-
    ical Linguistics*. Pp. 181-94. Amsterdam: North Holland.
---------- 1977. *Quichean Linguistic Prehistory* (= *University of
    California Publications in Linguistics, 81*). Los Angeles: Uni-
    versity of California Press.
Dressler, W. 1971. "Über die Rekonstruktion der indogermanischen Syn-
    tax", *Zeitschrift für vergleichende Sprachforschung* 85.5-22. (Not
    seen.)
Ebert, A. 1976. "Introduction", S. Steever et al., eds., *Papers from
    the Parasession on Diachronic Syntax*. Pp. vii-xviii. Chicago:
    Chicago Linguistic Society.
Greenberg, J. 1964. "Hindi-Punjabi Code-switching in Delhi", H. Lunt,
    ed., *Proceedings of the Nineth International Congress of Linguists*.
    Pp. 1115-24. The Hague: Mouton.

------------ 1969. "Communication in Multilingual Societies", S.
    Tyler, ed., *Cognitive Anthropology*. Pp. 435-48. New York: Holt,
    Rinehart and Winston.
Gumperz, J. and Wilson, R. 1971. "Convergence and Creolization: A
    Case from the Indo-Aryan/Dravidian Border in India", D. Hymes, ed.,
    Pidginization and Creolization. Pp. 151-67. London: Cambridge
    University Press.
Hale, K. 1971. *Gaps in Grammars and Cultures*. Unpublished manuscript.
    M.I.T.
Hashimoto, J. 1975. "Language Diffusion on the Asian Continent".
    Paper presented at the 8th International Conference of Sino-Ti-
    betan Linguistics, Berkeley, California. (Not seen.)
Hyman, L. 1976. "On the Change from SOV to SVO: Evidence from Niger-
    Congo", C. Li, ed., *Word Order and Word Order Change*. Pp. 113-47.
    Austin: University of Texas Press.
Jamison, S. 1976. "Functional Ambiguity and Syntactic Change: the
    Sanskrit Accusative", S. Steever et al., eds., *Papers from the
    Parasession on Diachronic Syntax*. Pp. 126-35. Chicago: Chicago
    Linguistic Society.
Jeffers, R. 1976. "Typological Shift and Change in Complex Sentence
    Structure", S. Steever et al., eds., *Papers from the Parasession
    on Diachronic Syntax*. Pp. 136-49. Chicago: Chicago Linguistic
    Society.
Johnson, D. 1976. *Ergativity in Universal Grammar*. Unpublished manu-
    script.
Kiparsky, P. 1972. "Explanation in Phonology", S. Peters, ed., *Goals
    of Linguistic Theory*. Pp. 189-227. Englewood Cliffs: Prentice
    Hall.
Kisseberth, C. 1972. *The Interaction of Phonological Rules and the
    Polarity of Language*. Indiana University Linguistics Club, xerox.
Kuno, S. 1974. "The Position of Relative Clauses and Conjunctions",
    Linguistic Inquiry 5.117-36.
Lehmann, W. 1973. "A Structural Principle of Language and its Impli-
    cations", *Language* 49.47-66.
---------- 1974. *Proto-Indo-European Syntax*. Austin: University of
    Texas Press.
Meillet, A. 1937. *Introduction à l'étude comparative des langues indo-
    européennes*. 8th ed. Paris: Hachett.
Mithun, M. 1976. "Topic, Focus, and Syntactic Drift in Northern Iro-
    quoian". Paper read at the 1976 annual meeting of the American
    Anthropological Association, Washington, D.C.
Nadkarni, M. 1975. "Bilingualism and Syntactic Change in Konkani",
    Language 51.672-83.
Norman, W. and Campbell, L. 1977. "Toward a Proto-Mayan Syntax: A
    Comparative Perspective on Grammar", N. England, ed., *Mayan Lin-
    guistics 2*. Los Angeles: University of California Press.
Ohala, J. 1974a. "Experimental Historical Phonology", J. Anderson and
    C. Jones, edd., *Historical Linguistics: Proceedings of the First
    International Conference on Historical Linguistics*. Pp. 353-89.
    Amsterdam: North Holland.

-------- 1974b. "Phonetic Explanation in Phonology", A. Bruck, R.
  Fox, M. LaGaly, eds., *Papers from the Parasession on Natural Pho-
  nology*. Pp. 251-74. Chicago: Chicago Linguistic Society.
Robertson, J. 1976. *The Structure of Pronoun Incorporation in the
  Mayan Verbal Complex*. Unpublished Harvard University Ph.D. Disser-
  tation.
Sapir, E. 1907. "Preliminary Report on the Language and Mythology of
  the Upper Chinook", *American Anthropologist* 9.533-44.
Silverstein, M. 1974. *Dialectal Developments in Chinook Tense-Aspect
  Systems: An Areal-Historical Analysis* (= *IJAL Memoir 29*).
Steever, S., Walker, C., and Mufwene, S., eds. 1976. *Papers from the
  Parasession on Diachronic Syntax*. Chicago: Chicago Linguistic
  Society.
Tai, J. 1976. "On the Change from SVO to SOV in Chinese", S. Steever
  et al., edd., *Papers from the Parasession on Diachronic Syntax*.
  Pp. 291-304. Chicago: Chicago Linguistic Society.
Thomason, S. and Kaufman, T. 1976. *Toward an Adequate Definition of
  Creolization*. Unpublished manuscript.

A SYNTACTIC CORRELATE OF STYLE SWITCHING
IN THE CANTERBURY TALES

LYNN NESS and CAROLINE DUNCAN-ROSE
California State   *California State*
University   *University*

I.

One feature of Chaucer's language in the *Canterbury Tales*, his
abrupt shifting from preterit to present and back again, has been mis-
interpreted both by literary scholars and by linguists. Most literary
scholars either ignore it or consider it an oversight on the part of
the poet, an imperfection that surely would have been "corrected" with
further proofreading. Some consider it merely a stylistic device for
lending vividness or the impression of suddenness or unexpectedness to
the account of an incident. At least one scholar maintains that these
present forms are intended to convey a durative implication, whereas
another claims that their occurrence in Middle English literature is
attributable solely to the exigencies of rhyme and meter.

Such misinterpretations are at least partly due to -- and are probably an inevitable consequence of -- failure to reconstruct the Sprachgefühl of the Middle English audience. Sprachgefühl, as we use the
term, is a speaker's feel for the rightness of a linguistic form in its
total cultural context -- which is just another way of saying that it
is that supra-grammar that governs the selection of sets of rules and
formatives which co-vary with style, dialect, and other parameters.
Though many speakers may never incorporate the whole range of these
sets of rules and formatives into their productive grammars, most are

able to interpret correctly the structures that result from their selection. That ability is part of their total linguistic competence -- their Sprachgefühl.

One of the results of the pervasiveness, during the last thirty years or so, of the historical method in humanistic studies has been, as one Chaucer critic (Economou 1965:7) puts it, a revival of interest in hermeneutics -- defined, in its literary application, "as the art of rediscovering the authentic thought of the author". The reconstruction of Sprachgefühl, as Anttila (1976) observes, is a hermeneutic endeavor. This paper will demonstrate that even when the goal is linguistic rather than literary, the reconstruction of Sprachgefühl may not and sometimes cannot be accomplished without an analysis of its exploitation in literature.

Let us consider first the status of tense-switching in Modern English and its exploitation by modern authors.

II.

One of the features of Modern Literary English, which includes both Standard Written English toward the plus pole of the formality scale and its imitative spoken counterpart, is absolute tense consistency. In the narration of past events, the preterit is normally used except in a few rigidly defined types of statement such as summaries, chronological tables, references to past writings or sayings, and so on. Another exception is what is traditionally called the "historical present", which does not violate the consistency rule because, characteristically, it is used consistently throughout the recounting of an incident.

The preterit is also the predominant form for narrating past events in Standard English outside of the formal literary style; here, though, sprinkled among and equivalent to the preterits, some present forms may occur when a speaker becomes so involved in the story he is telling that the action seems to be taking place at that moment.

When narration is simultaneous with the events spoken about, the
tense-marking rules normally produce present forms of the verbs that
describe the events:

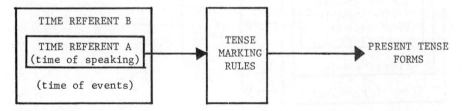

The historical present is the result, at least with respect to tense
marking, of a "recreation" of this situation in which the narrator deliberately overrides, throughout the recounting of an episode, his objective perception of the temporal relationships that would trigger
preterit forms.

When the time of narration is objectively perceived as subsequent
to the time of events narrated, the tense-marking rules produce preterit forms of the verbs that describe the events:

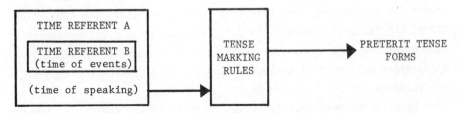

But a speaker's involvement in the narration of past events can
result in a subjective recreation of the simultaneity of events and
narration that triggers the tense-marking rules to produce present
forms. This subjective simultaneity, however, does not completely
override the speaker's objective preception of the temporal relationships that trigger preterit forms. The conflict between subjective
and objective input to the tense-marking rules shows up on the surface
as a mixture of present and preterit forms -- that is, it produces
tense switching:

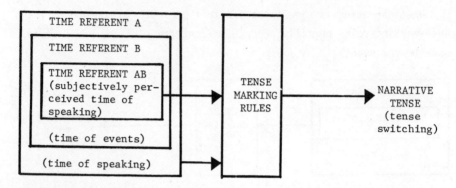

When we use the term "Narrative Tense", we are not proposing for English a third tense distinct from present and preterit; this is merely a convenient term to refer to the use of tense in spoken narrative, with its *potential* of tense switching.

The introduction of Narrative Tense is governed by extra-linguistic features such as the speaker's involvement in his narrative, the importance of the details to the plot, and the excitement of the incident being related. The presence of any of these features seems to increase the probability that Narrative Tense will occur; the subjectivity of the factors, however, all but precludes their precise quantification for use in a Labov-type variable rule -- short of monitoring vital signs with such an array of hardware as to destroy all hope of eliciting unselfconscious speech.

Despite the myth that tense switching in Modern English is limited to nonstandard speech, it can be heard in almost every natural conversation that includes narrative. Examples are appended from *The White House Transcripts* (Gold 1974; it is not surprising, in view of their purpose, that these interviews contain so few narrative passages and thus so little potential for tense switching). The speakers in the passages quoted in the Appendix are a former President of the United States (P), a White House Chief of Staff (H), and a legal adviser to the President (D).

A second handy source of corroborating evidence is the one from
which Martin Joos (1964) took his data for *The English Verb* -- Sybille
Bedford's (1958) *The Trial of Dr. Adams*. One of the passages cited by
Joos (1964:126) to illustrate tense switching in spontaneous, semi-for-
mal Standard British English is given in the Appendix. After citing
this and another passage, Joos remarks that this tense switching

> is what we get from two educated and urbane British physicians
> when either of them is "at ease" and speaking "almost with ani-
> mation" or "lively" [*sic*].

Later (1964:131) he refers to the citations again as evidence

> that the narrative actual [= present] tense for past events
> comes naturally to the lips of a man who gets himself involved
> in what he is talking about.

Tense switching comes in, according to Joos, because

> that man will *always* [emphasis his] use enough past-tense
> forms, mixed in with his actual-tense forms, to reassure
> the listener that he is 'keeping his feet on the ground'
> -- something that has a high value in English-speaking cul-
> tures.

Though Joos's explanation erroneously imparts conscious monitoring to
the "emotionally involved" speaker, it seems to capture the notion that
tense switching results from conflicting inputs to the tense-marking
rules.

Since the dialogue in *Trial* carefully follows the transcript of
the actual proceedings, it -- like *The White House Transcripts* -- is
very reliable as a source of data for spoken English. For the same
reason, however, neither reveals what, if anything, tense switching
"conveys". It might be possible and perhaps very useful to devise
Labov-like Subjective Reaction Tests for this purpose, but in fact we
have a more convenient alternative because literature exploits the

Sprachgefühl of its audience: it assumes the ability of speaker-read-
ers to match -- some more accurately and some more subtly than others,
of course -- stylistic and dialectal variants with nonlinguistic information. And the more skillfully an author exploits the Sprachgefühl
of his readers, the more his writing reveals about that Sprachgefühl.

If skillful writers exploit tense switching in narration as a marker of informality, spontaneity, or emotional involvement when it co-
occurs with features of Standard English, then we can assume that the
knowledge -- whether or not it is conscious knowledge -- that under-
lies such predictable reader response is part of the reader's total
linguistic competence.

For examples of such exploitation, we scanned the bookshelf for
a modern novel written unquestionably in Standard English and likely
to contain narrative passages spoken by emotionally involved characters
intended to be speakers of Standard English. The first one for which
we reached, Josephine Tey's *The Daughter of Time*, illustrates our
point. There is no tense switching at all in the first 89 pages;
there has been little "emotional involvement" in the dialogue. The
hospitalized protagonist, Alan Grant of Scotland Yard, intrigued by
certain discrepancies in accounts of Richard III's alleged murder of
the princes in the Tower, has been fighting boredom by investigating
that four-hundred-year-old homicide case. On page 90, Grant receives
a visit from a prominent actress who is described as "full of wrath"
against a certain playwright; her tense-switching tirade is given in
the Appendix.

The next passage in which tense switching occurs begins on page
92. Playing a rather staid and scholarly Archie Goodwin to Grant's
Nero Wolfe is an impeccably educated young upper-class American described as shy and rather formal. Before volunteering to help Grant,
he had been doing historical research of his own at the British Museum.
The extent to which the young man has been caught up in the investigation is conveyed largely by tense switching in the dialogue, in which he
is reporting his latest findings to Grant. See the Appendix. The young

researcher is also the speaker in the passage from page 121.

Tense switching occurs in Grant's speech, too, as illustrated in the dialogue from page 141.

This author clearly assumes that the rules governing narrative tense switching are part of her readers' competence, which she exploits to elicit just the response she wants. There is no reason to believe that this kind of exploitation is unique to modern literature. It is therefore obvious not only that present-day aficionados of earlier literatures can achieve a response that approximates that of the original audience only in proportion to the degree to which the total linguistic competence of that audience can be reconstructed, but also that a linguist must look to what earlier literature reveals about the assumptions of authors.

Now let us turn to Middle English and review the consequences of failure to reconstruct the Sprachgefühl that Chaucer must have assumed.

III.

The effects of gross ignorance of Middle English led to the well-known misunderstandings of the seventeenth and eighteenth centuries, during which the so-called shortcomings noted in Chaucer's work were attributed either to the "barbarousness" of the language with which he was compelled to struggle (Warton 1781:10) or, indeed, to lack of poetic skill. Dryden, for example, in the preface to his *Fables* of 1700 (Ker 1961), explains that he omits from his translation what he deems unnecessary or insufficiently dignified and adds where he thinks Chaucer deficient "for want of words in the beginning of our language" (1961:265). Though he praises Chaucer's power of description and his comprehensive nature and even finds in his verse a certain "rude sweetness...which is natural and pleasing", he "cannot go so far as [Speght], who...would make us believe that the fault is in our ears, and that there were really ten syllables in a verse where we find but nine....It were an easy matter to produce some thousands of his verses, which are

ıame for want of half a foot, and sometimes a whole one, and which no
pronunciation can make otherwise" (1961:258-59). Dryden, of course,
was unaware of the Old English sources of the inflections that were
reduced in Middle English and later dropped, of the rôles of elision
and caesura, and of the variable accentuation of French-derived words
in Chaucer's poetry.

The general critical opinion of Chaucer's work that had been characteristic of the seventeenth and eighteenth centuries is summed up by
Professor Thomas Lounsbury (1892:247):

> Warton's words make upon the mind the impression that he admired
> Chaucer greatly and was ashamed of himself for having been caught
> in the act.

Continuing progress in linguistic research, coupled with the fruits
of research on the world in which Chaucer and his audience lived and
their conception of it, has steadily added to our knowledge of Middle
English. As increased knowledge has approached more and more nearly
the fullness of Sprachgefühl, the tenor of Chaucer criticism has correspondingly reflected a response more and more closely approximating, at
least in the degree of its acclaim, that of the original audience.

But reconstruction of the Sprachgefühl of Chaucer's audience is
not yet complete, and the rules governing tense switching have proved
to be as elusive as the Pimpernel. Sometimes ignored in descriptions
of Chaucer's language (French 1929; Robinson 1933), tense switching is
sometimes mentioned in passing with the implication that it is a minor
flaw, an oversight on the part of the poet (Baugh 1963). Other scholars
(Graef 1889; Roloff 1921) have claimed that present tense forms in the
midst of preterits were used in Middle English to convey vividness or
unexpectedness. Benson (1961) tries to show that insistence on vividness as the primary quality of the historical present forces one to explain the abrupt transition from one tense to another by "lack of sequence of tense", whereas excluding vividness from the definition allows
one "to consider both an entire scene in the present (e.g., the tourna-

ment in *The Knight's Tale*), and a single line containing a lone present, manifestations of the same phenomenon" (1961:68).   In both manifestations, according to Benson, the present verbs are used to convey a "durative implication" or a "connotation of continuing action" rather than vividness (1961:69).

Visser (1966:710-11) rejects both the vividness and durative hypotheses and takes their proponents to task for not having specified the conditions under which tense switching occurred in Middle English. After deftly disposing of the opposition, Visser presents his own hypothesis: since "this interchange of tenses exclusively occurred in the poetry", and "two of the main features by which Middle English poetry distinguished itself from prose [are] rhyme and metre, [then] it is these that must have been the determinative factors in the choice of verb form" (1966:711). Visser supports his argument with an awesome arsenal of evidence whose weaknesses are not immediately apparent. They do, however, add up.

In an earlier section, Visser (1966:707) himself cites (in a footnote) examples from Chaucer's *Boece* and "Melibee".   Evidence in *Boece* must of course be used cautiously, since Chaucer was working with both the Latin original and a French translation, and we do not have access to the latter. Two occurrences of tense switching in *Boece* (I prosa 3, III metrum 12) merely translate the Latin of Boethius. In the quotation (see Appendix) from *Boece* III metrum 12, *despyseth...to drynken* translates *spernit...flumina*. The other occurrences seem to be more suggestive; in these passages the original Latin has been considerably rephrased. In *Boece* I prosa 6, for example, Boethius has an infinitive construction where Chaucer has *falleth*. In the second passage from III metrum 12 (which immediately follows the first), the whole passage renders Boethius's *vultur dum satur est modis, non traxit Tityi jecur*. The passage from *Boece* IV metrum 7 is so completely recast that no particular verb exactly corresponds to another, but the Latin verb closest in the sense of the passage to Chaucer's *yeveth* is a pluperfect.

Though we cannot discount possible influence of the French translation that Chaucer was working with, neither can we discount the possibility that these instances of tense switching were Chaucer's innovations. If so, they do constitute examples of tense switching in prose.

In the "Melibee", which is not so much a narrative as a moral debate within the meagerest of narrative frames, one would not expect to find any instances of tense switching. Indeed the one cited by Visser, unique in the "Melibee", is questionable. The verb is *answereth* only in the Ellesmere manuscript, *answerede* in all the others. Moreover, this "present" form may, as who knows how many others may also, be the graphemic result of a highly probable allophonic relationship of dental fricatives and stops in some dialects (see Visser 1966:716 for evidence).

Though we cannot deny that very few if any instances of tense switching can be found in extant Middle English prose, this fact does not seem to us to support Visser's rhyme/meter hypothesis to the extent that he claims that it does. It should be recalled that in Middle English times verse was still the normal medium for literature. There just wasn't much narrative prose being written -- at least very little has been preserved.

There was still, however, considerable use of an older verse form in which rhyme plays no systematic part and there is no fixed number of syllables to a line; clear instances of tense switching are to be found in alliterative poetry. Between lines 100 and 200 of *Sir Gawain and the Green Knight*, for example, there are seven instances -- even omitting from the count all occurrences within the rhymed bob-and-wheel pentastichs, also omitting all presents that state "timeless truths", and counting a sequence of several presents framed by preterits as a single instance.

The *Alliterative Morte Arthure* provides further examples. The first one cited in the Appendix occurs in lines 3222-26. In the lines that follow almost immediately (3250-51), Arthur tells his dream. After setting the scene entirely in the preterit, he switches to the present for one verb before switching back to the preterit.

Most of the presents in *Piers Plowman* occur in statements of gene-

ral -- usually moral -- truth; the infrequency of narrative tense
switching in this work is proportional to the infrequency of narrative
passages, but it does occur, as in lines 113-127 and 241-43.

Visser's disclaimer, "Since in visions the actions are seen as
really happening at the present moment the present tense is normally
used in relating them", can hardly account for passages containing
both preterits and presents.

Failure to account satisfactorily for the occurrences of tense
switching in alliterative verse is a very damaging weakness of the
rhyme/meter hypothesis. Middle English poets, moreover, had available
to them a number of easy, almost automatic alternative devices for the
manipulation of rhyme and meter. It seems both unnecessary and arro-
gant to assume that even the poorest of versifiers had to rely on tense
switching for this purpose to an extent that would account for its wide-
spread use. Poets availed themselves freely, for example, of the semantically empty tense-carrier *gan*, as in line 301 of the General Prologue
of the *Canterbury Tales*. Line 301 is Chaucer's alternative to a line
in which the preterit *preyde* would not have rhymed with *scoleye* in the
next line.

Variable realization of the reduced vowel during the Middle English period, while the transition from schwa to zero was still in progress, is too well known and too well established to require documentation. That this variability provided Middle English poets with great
metrical flexibility is beyond question. And though there is a strong
predominance of "feminine endings" in both alliterative and nonallitera-
tive lines, this "frequency...does not amount to universality" (Davis
1968:149; see also Baugh 1963:xl and Robinson 1957:xxxvi). Passages
from *Gawain*, *The Destruction of Troy*, and the *Canterbury Tales* are appended as evidence.

The rhyme/meter hypothesis throws no light on the status of tense
switching in the grammar of Middle English because it relegates occurrences in literature, our primary source of data, to mere conventionalized poetic license. It consigns the usage to the poet's emergency

kit, a bag of tricks to which a poet has recourse when the mechanics
of versification and the rules of his natural language are in conflict.
Probably the most familiar example of items in the poet's emergency kit
is the use of near-rhyme and eye-rhyme, along with and somewhat over-
lapping the conventional rhyming of words that, as a result of sound
change, have ceased to rhyme in the natural language. Such devices
illustrate what usually happens in a tug-of-war between the conventions
of a verse form and the rules of the language -- the verse form yields
to the language by relaxing its requirements. But tense is a grammatical category, not a poetic convention.

Poets do of course invoke poetic license to use language that de-
viates from the norm in a number of ways. The simplest of these is the
figurative use of language; a more complex manifestation of abnormal
-- or paranormal -- syntax. When such deviance is not purposeful, when
it is not controlled -- when, in other words, poetic license is invoked
as a desperation measure -- it hits the reader right down in his Sprachgefühl. The following lines from a song (Gershwin 1930) that was popular a generation ago illustrate the point: "I'm bidin' my time, 'Cause
that's the kind of guy I'm". One of the authors of this paper recalls
her uncomfortable response, even as a child, to what she now knows to
be a violation of English contraction rules, unmotivated here except
as an ad hoc deviation to meet the requirements of rhyme.

Quite a different effect can be produced when the syntactic deviation is purposeful and controlled. This is the poet's use of paranormal syntax that James Peter Thorne (1964) discusses in "Stylistics
and Generative Grammars". Such deviance may be extreme, as in E. E.
Cummings's "Anyone Lived in a Pretty How Town". Thorne observes that
the total effect of reading a sentence like *he danced his did* "is controlled by the fact that the kind of irregularity it exhibits is *regular in the context of the poem*" (1964:58; our emphasis). The deviance
may be more subtle, as in Donne's "A Nocturnall Upon S. Lucie's Day",
for which Thorne postulates "a gender system much more complicated than,
and quite contrary to, that of Standard English....It does not seem en-

tirely fanciful to suggest that these gender rules explain the effects
of chaos and strangeness which so many literary critics have associated
with the poem" (1964:59). Such syntactic deviance is unique to and constitutes an integral element of a given poem.

Apparently it is also possible for a particular type of syntactic
deviation to be incorporated as one of the conventions of a verse form,
such as the contrapuntal arrangement of two different sentences in Skaldic verse. But this convention differs in several ways from the interpretation of tense switching forced by the rhyme/meter hypothesis.
First, its use was not a desperation measure but a carefully cultivated
embellishment. Second, its use was limited to a highly specialized gen-
re that existed side-by-side with other, simpler verse forms, whereas
tense switching is attested in every type of Middle English narrative
poetry. And third, syntactic counterpoint can be employed without disturbing the syntactic relationships internal to any syntactic unit, as
tense switching, if it existed for the exclusive use of poets in a metrical bind, could not.

We have shown that tense switching is attested in Middle English
literature where neither rhyme nor syllable-count would have required
the substitution of a present form for a preterit; moreover, the flexibility provided by variable forms available to a Middle English poet
would have reduced the necessity for recourse to such poetic license so
greatly that such a necessity could hardly account for the frequency
of tense switching even in rhymed isosyllabic verse. The rhyme/meter
hypothesis automatically brands tense switching in Middle English poetry as syntactically deviant -- not as unfashionable or rural or sub-
standard, but as nonexistent in the grammar of normal (i.e., nonpoetic)
Middle English. Yet we have shown that tense switching differs in a
number of ways from other kinds of linguistic deviation classified as
poetic license -- most radically from those invoked, as the rhyme/meter
hypothesis claims tense switching to have been, as a way out of a metrical dilemma. If tense switching can be shown to have been purposeful and systematic in Middle English literature, then it differs from

the controlled, deliberately artificial devices of poetic license only in that it was neither a poem-specific irregularity, regular within the context of a single poem, nor one that had been conventionalized as a highly valued embellishment of a specific verse form. But this difference -- extreme specialization -- is precisely what sets deviations like the gender system in Donne's poem and the syntactic counterpoint of Skaldic verse apart from the linguistic norm and defines them as deviations. Tense switching in Middle English literature, therefore, may not have been a poetically licensed deviation at all, but a reflection of the linguistic norm.

It is in the *Canterbury Tales*, by virtue of its structure and the genius of its author for exploiting to the utmost the total linguistic competence of his audience, that unambiguous confirmation is to be found.

IV.

A structural analysis of the poem reveals that Chaucer has integrated seven distinct categories of discourse and narration in the *Canterbury Tales*, each of which displays syntactic properties stylistically appropriate to it. These categories, arranged one within the other in a multiply embedded speech set are as follows:

1.   External Direct Discourse (ED): Chaucer the poet directly addressing his audience outside the narrative of the journey to Canterbury;

2.   External Narration (EN): Chaucer the poet narrating the episode of the journey;

3.   Primary Internal Discourse (PID): the dialogue of the pilgrims within the narrative of the journey;

4.   Primary Internal Narration (PIN): the pilgrims' narration of their tales during the journey;

5.   Secondary Internal Discourse (SID): the dialogue of characters within one of the pilgrims' tales;

6. Secondary Internal Narration (SIN): the narration of a
    story by a character within one of the pilgrims' tales;

7. Tertiary Internal Discourse (TID): the dialogue of char-
    acters within a story in Secondary Internal Narration.

To provide a graphic representation of the manner in which the speech
sets form progressively embedded constituents of the enclosing narrative, we have borrowed the familiar notational device of labeled bracketing. The subscripts indicate the seven categories as abbreviated
above:

$$[\quad [\quad [\quad [\quad [\quad [\quad [\quad] \quad] \quad] \quad] \quad] \quad] \quad]$$
$$ED \quad EN \quad PID \quad PIN \quad SID \quad SIN \quad TID \quad \quad TID \quad SIN \quad SID \quad PIN \quad PID \quad EN \quad ED$$

The speech of Chaucer directly addressing his audience (ED) is
outside of and contains the entire narrative. Notice that there are
two general classifications, Discourse and Narration, into which the
individual speech sets are grouped. It is important to understand
the function of tense in each of these two general classifications.

In natural speech, which direct discourse represents, morphological tense is systematically related to the time of the events spoken about with respect to the moment of speaking. A character whose
speech is set within a particular tale is understood to be speaking
at a time present with respect to that tale. Thus we expect to find
natural tense usage in each category of discourse.

In narration, past events are described, for the most part, in
the preterit. The "historical present", as it occurs and as it is
constrained in Modern English narration, is probably a Modern English
development (it may indeed have developed as a specialization of Middle English Narrative tense); nevertheless, we would have excluded
passages in which the use of the present is sustained throughout the
narration of an episode, had we found any, on the grounds that these
could be incipient historical presents. Even in such passages as the
tournament scene in "The Knight's Tale", however, where the present

predominates, the longest series of presents unbroken by a preterit is
fifteen verbs (KT 2600-2611), and the episode contains several such
series.

It is possible that some Middle English present perfects (especially, perhaps, those of intransitive verbs, which were still formed
with *be* in Middle English) should be considered present tense forms.
But since the present perfect does sometimes appear to be equivalent
to the simple preterit (see Visser 1966:749; Mossé 1952:105) -- at
least in narrative use -- we do not count any Middle English present
perfects as presents.

Style switching is inherent in the very structure of the *Canterbury Tales*, and -- fortunately for our purposes -- Chaucer displays an
extraordinary genius for it. The literary style is appropriate to
Chaucer the poet, both in discourse and in the enclosing narrative.
The pilgrims, on the other hand, including Chaucer the pilgrim, are
people enjoying themselves, talking informally among themselves and
telling stories for their mutual entertainment. Their discourse and
their narration, unlike those of Chaucer the poet, call for appropriately more casual styles of informal speech. The erroneous notion
that Chaucer blurred and ignored the element of time is due in part
to his conscious juxtaposition of styles, in part to the occurrence
of tense switching as a syntactic feature of the oral narrative style
of the characters in the *Canterbury Tales*.

The categories of discourse and narration are so thoroughly integrated that contiguous categories must be considered together in the
following close examination.

Tertiary Internal Discourse, the mostly deeply embedded speech
set, is a minor category represented only by the speech of the characters in the three ancedotes told by Chauntecleer in "The Nun's Priest's
Tale". Natural tense occurs in this category. Secondary Internal Narration, which is narration by a character in a pilgrim's tale, is also
a minor category, limited to the three anecdotes told by the rooster
to justify his feelings of apprehension after a foreboding dream. He

begins his first exemplum with line B 4174 (see Appendix). Tertiary
Internal Discourse is represented by lines 4194-97 of this passage.
These lines serve only to illustrate this category and are not intended
to be exhaustive; the narratives of Chauntecleer contain additional passages of direct discourse. Note that *dye* in line 4196 could be either
the present subjunctive or the simple present with future sense. This
construction is still found in such expressions as *either he stops in-
sulting me or I leave.*

Secondary Internal Narration begins on line 4175 with "that whilom two felawes wente". Although most of the narrative is in the preterit, there is an occasional present form; the only one in this passage is *gooth* in line 4184. The degree to which tense switching is
present in this category is not particularly significant, for it is
used here with very little force. The relevant fact is that the category in which it occurs falls into the same general classification as
Primary Internal Narration, in which it assumes considerable importance.
It must be remembered that Secondary Internal Narration exists within
another set of narration and that this results in multiple time refer-
ents in relation to the narrator, who is the Nun's Priest, not Chaucer.

In accordance with medieval practice, Chauntecleer attributes his
story to a great (in this case, unnamed) author (4174-75) in order to
lend authority and validity to the point he is about to make. These
lines occur in the direct speech of Chauntecleer, which is classified
as Secondary Internal Discourse. Statements of the form *X says Y* occur
also in External Direct Discourse and in Primary Internal Discourse and
are consistently in the present. It is still conventional to cite
authorities in the present tense. Line 4190, spoken to Pertelote to
emphasize the ever-present rôle of fate in the lives of all, is also
Secondary Internal Discourse.

The words of the fox to Chauntecleer provide another example (B
4473-82). The speech of the fox, which continues for twenty-nine more
lines, employs natural tense. Note that *were* in line 4477 and *wolde* in
line 4478 are subjunctive forms. This discourse is introduced by Pri-

mary Internal Narration, for the Nun's Priest is narrating the events
and the fox's speech: the preterit is used.

Tense switching is found in Primary Internal Narration in the passage from the same tale beginning with line B 4362; the verbs *looketh*,
rometh, *chukketh*, and *rennen* are present tense forms which occur in the
midst of preterits.   This is narrative tense.   Lines 4374-76 exemplify
Primary Internal Discourse in which the Nun's Priest explains to the
other pilgrims that his narrative is about to change scenes.

Most of the *Canterbury Tales* consists of the pilgrims relating
their tales.   This is Primary Internal Narration, which displays a
considerable amount of tense switching.   The narration begins in the
preterit, which is used for the introductory lines and often continues
for fifty to a hundred (or more) lines.   As the narrator becomes involved in his tale or when important details are presented, tense
switching begins.   Sometimes, as in the example from "The Pardoner's
Tale" (C 463-71), tense switching is introduced almost as soon as the
tale begins.   It is not surprising that the Pardoner gives his tale
the impact of tense switching right from the beginning, for he wants
the moral to strike the conscience of each of his listeners.   He has
explained in his prologue that he extracts large offerings from the
members of his congregation by directing his parables at their vices.
Despite the fact that he has just revealed his modus operandi to his
fellow pilgrims, he has the audacity to point his tale at the Host and
to demand payment for the latter's sins.   The Pardoner's narrative
style is in keeping with his motive.

"The Parson's Tale", a sermon in prose without even the thin narrative thread of the "Melibee", exhibits no narrative tense; since the
tale is not a narrative at all, it should be classified as Primary Internal Discourse.   The usage conforms to natural tense, and authorities
(in this case, usually saints) are cited in the normal present tense
forms.   A sample of the style of the sermon is appended (Robinson 1961:
229).

Lines D 1286-1300, D 1665-74, and D 1761-64 illustrate Primary In-

ternal Discourse, which includes the pilgrims' conversation among themselves, their individual prologues, and their asides and proverbial
comments throughout their tales, in juxtaposition with External Narration: Chaucer's account of the entire episode of the journey. The
presents in the dialogue are entirely natural and appropriate. The
journey, however, is a past event. It is narrated by Chaucer the poet,
not Chaucer the pilgrim; therefore, consistent use of the preterit is
appropriate to this category, except for statements of general validity,
descriptions of regularly recurring events, and proverbial phrases --
all of which can be characterized (e.g., Mustanoja 1960:482) as statements of unlimited time.

The majority of lines in the General Prologue are also External
Narration. Lines A 285-308 are appended as an example.

The first eighteen lines of the General Prologue describe regularly recurring events. These lines are in the present tense. In lines
nineteen through the first half of thirty-four, the poet begins the
description of the events of one particular spring in the past. These
lines are in the preterit. Similes, metaphors, and proverbs are in the
present. Notice the simile in line A 287 and the proverbial comments
of lines A 179-80 and A 500-02.

External Direct Discourse is Chaucer the poet speaking to his audience. As in the other discourse categories, natural tense is appropriate to External Direct Discourse, as exemplified in lines 35-42 of the
General Prologue.

The following lines, also from the General Prologue, represent a
change of category -- from External Narration to External Direct Discourse -- and do not constitute tense switching:

Of twenty yeer of age he was, I gesse   (A 82)

For aught I woot, he was of Dertemouthe   (A 389)

But wel I woot he lyed right in dede   (A 659)

The General Prologue contains the only sure example of tense switching attributable to rhyme (line A 588) in the *Canterbury Tales*:

> The Reve was a sclendre colerik man.
> His berd was shave as ny as ever he kan.

Another apparent exception is *wol* in line A 816. However, since *wold* is found is some editions, including Skeat's, this occurrence of *wol* is at least questionable as an exception. In any case, we think we can concede, without damage to our argument, two exceptions in more than 18,000 lines.

If tense switching had not been part of Chaucer's design, we should expect to find it scattered sporadically throughout the poem. This is not the case; out of seven categories of discourse and narration, only two display tense switching, and these two have something in common: they are both internal character narration, where stylistic features appropriate to storytelling in natural, unselfconscious speech are to be expected. Moreover, if tense switching had been an undesirable feature, we should expect a higher concentration of it in the incomplete and less carefully revised tales and less of it in the more polished tales. This is not the case. "The Franklin's Tale" makes extensive use of tense switching, whereas the fragment of "The Cook's Tale" exhibits none at all. In fact, "The Cook's Tale" breaks off just about where tense switching might have begun if the tale were complete.

Chaucer's exploitation of the Sprachgefühl of his audience includes a number of well-known uses of linguistic detail for realism, for comic effect, for characterization. For Chaucer's audience, the northern dialect of the two Cambridge students in "The Reeve's Tale" was a source of comedy in a broad sense (Hussey and others 1968:91; see also Tolkien 1934) and possibly a more specific joke on a famous Northumbrian family (Robinson 1961:688). The way the Prioress speaks French, "after the scole of Stratford atte Bowe", is germane to the "delicately poised ambiguity" (Hoffman 1954:36) which creates a "tension between the person and her office, between the given human nature and the assumed sacred obligation" (1954:37). The significance of the Summoner's habit, when drunk, of speaking nothing but Latin, in which his competence is limited to the parrot-like repetition of two or three phrases culled from decrees, is as obvious to modern readers as it was to the original audience. Chaucer's use of tense switching is one more example of his exploitation, however intuitive, of the Sprachgefühl of his audience, and such exploitation in literature constitutes evidence that rules governing tense switching were part of the grammar of Middle English.

APPENDIX

From *The White House Transcripts* (Gold 1974):

(81) D-- ....When they considered the resolution on the Floor of the Senate I got the record out to read it. Who asked special permission to have their Staff man on the floor? Kennedy brings this man Flug out on the floor when they are debating a resolution. He is the only one who did this. It has been Kennedy's push quietly [*sic*], his constant investigation. His committee did the (unintelligible) subpoenas....

(111) D-- Funny thing is this fellow goes down to the Court House here before Sirica, testifies as honestly as he can testify, and Sirica looks around and called him a liar.

(241) H-- ....He [Dean] said he [Ervin] probably wouldn't do it, but it'd still give him an awkward stand on a stickly [*sic*] position. The only other idea he comes up with is he said....

(313) P-- ....I thought our relations with MacGregor were not strained. I thought he felt pretty good.

H-- He does.

P-- Why does he go out and say....

From *The Trial of Dr. Adams* (Bedford 1958:172; quoted in Joos 1964:126):

Mr. Lawrence [wholly second violin] "Looking at the nursing notes
to the spring of 1950, what do you say is a fair summary of the
position?" -- Dr. Harman [trenchant and urbane] "I should say
she had recovered from her stroke as far as she is ever going to;
that she has reached a stage at which one might describe her as
being partially crippled, but there are no signs of anything further about to happen". -- Mr. Lawrence: "What do you say about
the continued medication at that period...?" -- [Lively] "The
clearest thing about that is that by that time it has been going
on for a year and some months... It would certainly have to be
continued even if it was producing no good. I can see no evidence
it was producing any harm".

From *The Daughter of Time* (Tey 1951):

(90)   "After practically promising me that she would write it!
            After all our get-togethers and my plans for when this
            endless thing finally comes to an end. I had even talked
            to Jaques about clothes! And now she decides that she
            must write one of her awful little detective stories.
            She says she must write it while it is fresh -- whatever
            that is".

(92-93)   "Sure. Edward died on April the 9th 1483. In London.
            I mean, in Westminster....The young prince was doing les-
            sons at Ludlow Castle in charge of the Queen's brother,
            Lord Rivers. The Queen's relatives are very much to the
            fore, did you know? The place is just lousy with Wood-
            villes".

            "Yes, I know. Go on. Where was Richard?"

            "On the Scottish border".

            "What!"

            "Yes, I said: On the Scottish border. Caught away off
            base. But does he yell for a horse and go posting off
            to London? He does not".

            "What did he do?"

            "He arranged for a requiem mass at York, to which all
            the nobility of the North were summoned, and in his pre-
            sence they took an oath of loyalty to the young prince".

(121)   "That was *after the Princes had been 'murdered'*. (Auth-
            or's emphasis) Yes, and I'll tell you something else.

With her two boys done to death by their wicked uncle, she writes to her other son, in France -- Dorset -- and asks him to come home and make his peace with Richard, who will treat him well".

(141)   "Tyrrel confesses that way back in 1483, nearly twenty years ago, he pelted up to London from Warwich, got the keys of the Tower from the Constable -- I forget his name --"

"Brackenbury. Sir Robert Brackenbury".

"Yes. Got the keys of the Tower from Sir Robert Brackenbury for one night, murdered the boys, handed back the keys, and reported back to Richard. He confesses this, and so puts an end to what must have been a much canvassed mystery, and yet nothing public is done with him".

        ....

"Didn't they even bring Brackenbury in to affirm or deny the story of the keys being handed over?"

(166)   "...It wasn't until Stillington confessed to the council that he [Richard] sends for troops of his own. And he has to send all the way to the North of England at a critical moment. Yes, you're right, of course. He was taken aback".

From Chaucer's *Boece* (in Robinson 1957):

I prosa 3:   ...I sette myne eien on hir and fastned my lookynge. I byholde my noryce, Philosophie, in whoos hous I hadde conversed and hauntyd fro my youthe.

III metr. 12 (This is the one cited by Visser):

        "And Tantalas, that was destroied by the woodnesse of long thirst, despyseth the floodes to drynken".

I prosa 6:   "I nas nat desseyved", quod sche, "that ther ne faileth somewhat, by which the maladye of perturbation is crept into thi thought".

III metr. 12: "The foul that highte voltor, that etith the stomak or the gyser of Tycius, is so fulfild of his [Orpheus's] song that it nil eten ne tiren no more".

IV metr. 7:   [Agamenon] "unclothide him of pite of fadir; and the
              sory preest yeveth in sacrifyenge the wrecchide kut-
              tynge of throte of the doughtor".

From the "Melibee" (Speght 1602:fol. ixvii; this line is cited with
slight orthographic differences in Visser 1966:706, fn.):

   To this sentence answereth anone dame Prudence, and said....

From *Sir Gawain and the Green Knight* (Davis 1968):

   (134-44)   For vnethe watz þe noyce not a whyle sesed,
              And þe fyrst cource in þe court kyndely served,
              Þer hales in at þe halle dor an aghlich mayster,
              ....
              For of back and of brest al were his bodi sturne,
              Both is wombe and his wast were worthily smale

   (179-84)   Wel gay watz þis gome gered in grene,
              ....
              Fayre fannand fox vmbefoldes his shulderes;
              A much berd as a busk ouer his brest henges,
              Þat wyth his higlich here þat of his hed reches
              Watz euesed al vmbetorne abof his elbowes,
              ....

From *The Alliterative Morte Arthure* (Owen and Owen 1971):

   (3222-26) Bot be ane aftire midnighte all his mode changede:
              He mett in the morne-while full mervailous dremes,
              And when his dredefull drem whas drefen to the ende,
              The kinge dares for doute, die as he sholde,
              Sendes aftire philosophers and his affraie telles.

   (3250-51) Than discendes in the dale down fra the cloudes
              A Duches dereworthily dighte in diaperde wedes

From *Piers Plowman* (Kaiser 1958):

   (113)   Þere preched a pardonere, as he a preest were;
              Broughte forth a bulle with bishopes seles,
              ....
   (125)   Ac it is naugt be þe bischop þat þe boy precheth.
              For the parisch prest and þe pardonere parten þe siluer
              That þe poraille of þe parisch sholde haue gif þei nere.

(241) Falsenesse for fere þanne fleig to þe freres.
    And Gyle doþ hym to go agast for to dye.
    Ac marchantz mette with hym and made hym abide,
    And....

For line 301 of the General Prologue, see below.

Examples of lines without "feminine endings":

Gawain	10 b	Arthóur I hát
	858 b	Of túly and társ
Dest. Troy	473	...bléssid were Í
	846	...dóse hym to góo
CT	A 4	Of which vertú engéndred ís the flóur
	A 180	Is líkned tíl a físsh that is wáterlées

From "Anyone Lived in a Pretty How Town" (quoted in Thorne 1964):

    Anyone lived in a pretty how town
    With up so floating many bells down
    Spring summer autumn winter
    He sang his didn't he danced his did
    ...
    When by now and tree by leaf
    She laughed his joy she cried his grief
    Bird by snow and stir by still
    Anyone's any was all to her.

From *The Canterbury Tales* (line references, unless otherwise noted, are to Baugh 1963):

B 4174-97
    Oon of the gretteste auctour that men rede
    Seith thus: that whilom two felawes wente 4175
    On pilgrimage, in a ful good entente;
    And happed so, they coomen in a toun
    Wher as ther was swich congregacioun
    Of peple, and eek so streit of herbergage,
    That they ne founde as muche as o cotage 4180
    In which they bothe myghte ylogged bee.
    Wherfore they mosten of necessitee,
    As for that nyght, departen compaignye;
    And ech of hem gooth to his hostelrye,
    And took his loggyng as it wolde falle. 4185
    That oon of hem was logged in a stalle,
    Fer in a yeerd, with oxen of the plough;

That oother man was logged wel ynough,
As was his aventure or his fortune,
That us governeth alle as in commune.   4190
          And so bifel that, longe er it were day,
This man mette in his bed, ther as he lay,
How that his felawe gan upon him calle,
And seyde, "Allas! for in an oxes stalle
This nyght I shal be mordred ther I lye.   4195
Now help me, deere brother, or I dye.
In alle haste com to me!" he sayde.

B 4473-82   This Chauntecleer, whan he gan hym espye,
He wolde han fled, but that the fox anon
Seyde, "Gentil sire, allas! wher wol ye gon?   4475
Be ye affrayed of me that am youre freend?
Now, certes, I were worse than a feend,
If I to yow wolde harm or vileynye!
I am nat come youre conseil for t' espye,
But trewely, the cause of my comynge
Was oonly for to herkne how that ye synge.   4480
For trewely, ye have as myrie a stevene
As any aungel hath that is in hevene.

B 4362-76   And with that word he fley doun fro the beem,
For it was day, and eek his hennes alle,
And with a chuk he gan hem for to calle,   4365
Real he was, he was namoor aferd.
He fethered Pertelote twenty tyme,
And trad hire eke as ofte, er it was pryme.
He looketh as it were a grym leoun,
And on his toos he rometh up and doun;   4370
Hym deigned nat to sette his foot to grounde.
He chukketh whan he hath a corn yfounde,
And to hym rennen thanne his wyves alle.
Thus roial, as a prince is in his halle,
Leve I this Chauntecleer in his pasture,   4375
And after wol I telle his aventure.

C 463-71   In Flaundres whilom was a compaignye
Of yonge folk that haunteden folye,
As riot, hasard, stywes, and tavernes,   465
Where as with harpes, lutes, and gyternes,
They daunce and pleyen at dees both day and nyght,
And eten also and drynken over hir myght,
Thurgh which they doon the devel sacrifise
Withinne that develes temple, in cursed wise,   470
By superfluytee abhomynable.

ParsT 92-102 (Robinson 1961:229):

>   And now, sith I have declared yow what thyng
> is Penitence, now shul ye understonde that ther
> been three accions of Penitence./ The firste
> is that if a man be baptized after that he hath
> synned,/ Saint Augustyn seith, "But he be
> penytent for his olde synful lyf, he may nat
> bigynne the newe clene lif."/ For, certes, if
> he be baptized withouten penitence of his olde
> gilt, he receyveth the mark of baptesme, but
> nat the grace ne the remission of his synnes,
> til he have repentance verray./ Another de-
> faute is this, that men doon deedly synne af-
> ter that they han receyved baptesme./ The
> thridde defaute is that men fallen in venial
> synnes after hir baptesme, fro day to day./
> Therof seith Seint Augustyn that penitence of
> goode and humble folk is the penitence of every
> day./

D 1286-
1300

>   Oure Hoost tho spak, "A! sire, ye sholde be
>   hende
> And curteys, as a man of youre estaat;
> In compaigne we wol have no debaat.
> Telleth youre tale, and lat the Somonour be."
>   "Nay," quod the Somonour, "lat hym seye
>   to me   1290
> What so hym list; whan it comth to my lot,
> By God! I shal hym quiten every grot.
> I shall hym tellen which a greet honour
> It is to be a flaterynge lymytour;
> And eek of many another manere cryme   1295
> Which nedeth nat rehercen at this tyme;
> And his office I shal hym tell, ywis."
>   Oure Hoost answered, "Pees, namoore of this!"
> And after this he seyde unto the Frere,
> "Tel forth youre tale, my leeve maister deere.

D 1665-74

>   This Somonour in his styropes hye stood;   1665
> Upon this Frere his herte was so wood
> That lyk an aspen leef he quook for ire.
>   "Lordinges," quod he, "but o thyng I desire;
> I yow biseke that, of youre curteisye,
> Syn ye han herd this false Frere lye,   1670
> As suffreth me I may my tale telle.
> This Frere bosteth that he knoweth helle,
> And God woot, that it is litel wonder;
> Freres and feendes been but lyte asonder.

D 1761-64

"Nay, ther thou lixt, thou Somonour!" quod
the Frere.   1761
"Pees," quod oure Hoost, "for Christes
mooder deere!
Tel forth thy tale, and spare it nat al."
"So thryve I," quod this Somonour, "so I
shal!"

A 285-308

A clerk ther was of Oxenford also,   285
That unto logyk hadde longe ygo.
As leene was his hors as is a rake,
And he nas nat right fat, I undertake,
But looked holwe, and therto sobrely.
Ful thredbare was his overeste courtepy; 290
For he hadde geten hym yet no benefice,
Ne was so worldly for to have office.
For hym was levere have at his beddes heed
Twenty bookes, clad in blak or reed,
Of Aristotle and his philosophie,   295
Than robes riche, or fithele, or gay sautrie.
But al be that he was a philosophre,
Yet hadde he but litel gold in cofre;
But al that he myghte of his freendes hente,
On bookes and on lernynge he it spente, 300
And bisily gan for the soules preye
Of hem that yaf hym wherwith to scoleye.
Of study took he moost cure and moost heede.
Noght o word spak he moore than was neede,
And that was seyd in forme and reverence, 305
And short and quyk and ful of hy sentence.
Sownynge in moral vertu was his speche,
And gladly wolde he lerne and gladly teche.

A 1-25

Whan that Aprill with his shoures soote
The droghte of March hath perced to the roote,
And bathed every veyne in swich licour
Of which vertu engendred is the flour;
Whan Zephirus eek with his sweete breeth 5
Inspired hath in every holt and heeth
The tendre croppes, and the yonge sonne
Hath in the Ram his halve cours yronne,
And smale foweles maken melodye,
That slepen al the nyght with open yë   10
(So priketh hem nature in hir corages), --
Thanne longen folk to goon on pilgrimages,
And palmeres for to seken straunge strondes,
To ferne halwes, kowthe in sondry londes;
And specially from every shires ende   15
Of Engelond to Caunterbury they wende,

       The hooly blisful martir for to seke,
       That hem hath holpen whan that they were
         seeke.
         Bifil that in that seson on a day,
       In Southwerk at the Tabard as I lay   20
       Redy to wenden on my pilgrimage
       To Caunterbury with ful devout corage,
       At nyght was come into that hostelrye
       Wel nyne and twenty in a compaignye,
       Of sondry folk, ...   25

A 179-80   Ne that a monk, whan he is recchelees,
       Is likned til a fissh that is waterlees,   180

A 500-02   That if golde ruste, what shal iren do?   500
       For if a preest be foul, on whom we truste,
       No wonder is a lewed man to ruste

A 35-42   But nathelees, whil I have tyme and space,   35
       Er that I ferther in this tale pace,
       Me thynketh it acordaunt to resoun
       To telle yow al the condicioun
       Of ech of hem, so as it semed me,
       And which they weren, and of what degree,   40
       And eek in what array that they were inne;
       And at a knyght than wol I first begynne.

REFERENCES:

Anttila, Raimo. 1976. "The Reconstruction of Sprachgefühl". Paper presented at the Second International Conference on Historical Linguistics, Tucson, Arizona.

Baugh, Albert C., ed. 1965. *Chaucer's Major Poetry*. New York: Appleton-Century-Crofts.

Bedford, Sybille. 1958. *The Trial of Dr. Adams*. New York: Simon and Schuster.

Benson, L. D. 1961. "Chaucer's Historical Present, Its Meaning and Uses", *English Studies* 42.65-77.

Davis, Norman, ed. 1968. *Sir Gawain and the Green Knight*. 2nd ed. and revis. of J. R. R. Tolkien and E. V. Gordon, eds., 1925.

Economou, George D. 1975. "Introduction: Chaucer the Innovator", in George D. Economou, ed., *Geoffrey Chaucer*. New York: McGraw-Hill.

French, Robert D. 1955. *A Chaucer Handbook*. 2nd ed. New York: Appleton-Century-Crofts.

Gershwin, Ira. 1930. *Bidin' My Time*. From George and Ira Gershwin, *Girl Crazy*. New York: Chapell.

Gold, Gerald, gen. ed. 1974. *The White House Transcripts*. New York: Bantam.

Graef, A. 1889. "Die präsentischen Tempora bei Chaucer", *Anglia* 12. 532–77.

Hoffman, Arthur W. 1959. "Chaucer's Prologue to Pilgrimage: The Two Voices", in Edward Wagenknecht, ed., *Chaucer: Modern Essays in Criticism*. Oxford: Oxford University Press.

Hussey, Maurice, Spearing, A. C., and Winny, James. 1968. *An Introduction to Chaucer*. Cambridge: Cambridge University Press.

Joos, Martin. 1964. *The English Verb*. Madison: University of Wisconsin Press.

Kaiser, Rolf, ed. 1958. *Medieval English*. West Berlin: Rolf Kaiser.

Ker, W. P., ed. 1961. *Essays of John Dryden*. New York: Russell and Russell.

Lounsbury, Thomas R. 1892 (page references are to the 1962 printing). *Studies in Chaucer: His Life and his Writings, III*. New York: Russell and Russell.

Mossé, Fernand. 1952. *A Handbook of Middle English*. Translated by James Walker. Baltimore: Johns Hopkins.

Mustanoja, Tauno F. 1960. *A Middle English Grammar: Part I, Parts of Speech*. Helsinki: Société Néophilologique.

Owen, Lewis J. and Owen, Nancy H., eds. 1971. *Middle English Poetry: An Anthology*. New York: Bobbs-Merrill.

Robinson, F. N., ed. 1961. *The Works of Geoffrey Chaucer*. 2nd ed. New York: Houghton Mifflin.

Roloff, H. 1921. *Das Präsens historicum im Mittelenglischen*. Diss. Giessen.

Skeat, Walter W., ed. 1894–97. *The Complete Works of Geoffrey Chaucer*. Vols. IV–VI. London: Oxford University Press.

Speght, Thomas, ed. 1602. *The Works of our Ancient and Learned English Poet, Geoffrey Chaucer*. London: Adam Islip.

Tey, Josephine. 1951. *The Daughter of Time*. New York: Berkley Medallion.

Thorne, James Peter. 1964 (= 1965). "Stylistics and Generative Grammar", *Journal of Linguistics* 1/1.49–59.

Tolkien, J. R. R. 1934. "Chaucer as Philologist", *Transactions of the Philological Society* 1934.1ff.

Visser, F. Th. 1966. *An Historical Syntax of the English Language, Part II, Syntactical Units with one Verb*. Leiden: E. J. Brill.

Warton, Thomas. 1781. *The History of English Poetry from the Eleventh to the Seventeenth Century*. Reprint. London: Vincent Brooks, Day and Son.

EVIDENCE OF AUSLAUTSVERHÄRTUNG IN OLD SAXON

KARL ODWARKA
University of Northern Iowa

INTRODUCTION

This study is based on Ms. M (Monacensis or Bamberg-Munich) of the *Heliand* which is the largest and most reliable of the early Old Saxon manuscripts.[1]

As part of a larger study of the early Old Saxon consonant system approximately 5500 forms (words of different graphemic shape) suspected of containing obstruents were examined by computer.[2] The significant positions for this study were NC#, lC#, rC#, and VC#, where N = nasal, C = consonant, V = any vowel, # = pause, l and r = liquids.

The analysis of the stops and spirants in Ms. M in final position differs from all previous investigations into the *Heliand* in several respects.[3] For example, all findings are based on the entire corpus of M; the number of occurrences is given for every form presented; comparative evidence for all forms utilized in determining phonemic and allophonic distributions is cited; and where extant, Middle Low German reflexes are included.

Based on the observable graphemic evidence as became available through easily readible computer print-outs, a tentative analysis of allographs revealed the probable graphemic structure of Ms. M.[4] The detailed phonological analysis which follows interprets the graphemic data.

THE OLD SAXON CONSONANTS

Based on a study of all consonants in Ms. M[5] the following phonemic and allophonic structures may be presented:

labials[6] /p/ = [p], /b/ = [b], /f/ = [f] and [v], /m/ = [m];

dentals /t/ = [t], /d/ = [d], /þ/ = [þ] and [ð], /s/ = [s] and
    possibly [z], although no overt evidence was found in M
    (see also Moulton 1954:32), /n/ = [n] and probably [ŋ];

velars /k/ = [k] and possibly [k'], /g/ = [g] and [ɣ], /x/ = /x/
    and /h/;

palatal /j/, and labiovelar /w/;

also liquids /r/ and /l/, whose phonemic assignment is based pri-
    marily on graphemic evidence.

Although we may posit four labial and five dental phonemes with
confidence, the identification of the allophones of these phonemes entails some difficulties.

The few observable distinctions in the corpus indicate a three-
way phonemic contrast in the velar order. The velars may actually en-
compass palatal, velar, and glottal allophones, although it is difficult to assign precise phonetic value to the Old Saxon symbols that
represent this order. One may posit allophones [k'], [k], [g], [ɣ],
[x], [h], [ŋ], and [j].

No overt minimal contrasts can be found for [k'] and [ŋ], which
can be assigned to /k/ and /n/, respectively. · [j] is established as
a phoneme /j/ outside of the velar order. [g] and [ɣ] are in complementary distribution with each other and with [x]. All three could be
classified as allophones of a phoneme /g/.

The limited evidence of M suggests assignment of [x] and [h] as
allophones of /x/. Sometimes they are in free variation with each
other, or with zero.

The above presentation of the consonant system of Ms. M, especially the phonemic and allophonic structure of stops and spirants, is the result of a close examination of consonants in the following twelve positions:

1.   Initial consonant (C-): consonant under investigation at the beginning of a word;

2.   Double consonant (CC): two identical consonants in gemination, occurring in any position within a word;

3.   Consonant preceded by a nasal consonant, and followed by a vowel (NCV): in any position within a word, preceded by *m* or *n*, and followed by any vowel, i.e., *i e a o* and *u*;

4.   Consonant preceded by a nasal and followed by a pause (NC#): preceded by *m* or *n* at the end of a word;

5.   Consonant preceded by *l* and followed by a vowel (lCV): in any position within a word, preceded by *l*, and followed by any vowel;

6.   Consonant preceded by *l* and followed by a pause (lC#): preceded by *l* at the end of a word;

7.   Consonant preceded by *r* and followed by a vowel (rCV): in any position within a word, preceded by an *r*, and followed by any vowel;

8.   Consonant preceded by *r* and followed by a pause (rC#): preceded by *r* at the end of a word;

9.   Consonant preceded and followed by a vowel (VCV): in any position within a word, preceded by any vowel and followed by any vowel;

10.   Consonant preceded by a vowel and followed by a pause (VC#): preceded by any vowel at the end of a word;

11.   Consonant preceded by a vowel and followed by *s* (VCs): in any position within a word, preceded by any vowel, and followed by *s*;

12.   Consonant preceded by a vowel and followed by *t* (VCt): in any position within a word, preceded by any vowel, and followed by *t*.[7]

A preliminary assessment of evidence of Auslautverhärtung in M

would be as follows: Some data point to unvoicing of all final consonants by the end of the Old Saxon period. No contrasts exist in the
labial, dental, or velar order in the context NC#. A voiceless velar
stop may, however, contrast with a voiced velar stop or with a velar
nasal which developed from a nasal plus a voiced velar stop. In all
other environments in final position (lC#, rC#, and VC#) a voiceless
stop contrasts with a voiceless spirant or a glottal aspirate in both
the labial and the velar order. A voiceless and a voiced dental stop
may still contrast with each other in these contexts. A contrast between dental stops and voiceless dental spirants cannot be convincingly
established.

A detailed description of stops and spirants in final position
will include earlier findings as well as cite comparative evidence
from the other Germanic languages and, where extant, list the Middle
Low German reflexes.

THE LABIALS IN FINAL POSITION

The Context NC#: *b* is the only labial that occurs in the context
NC#.

N*b*# occurs twice in one form only. *lamb* (2)[8] "lamb, lambs" occurs
in the same shape in Gothic, Old Norse, Old High German, and Old English. The MLG reflex is *lam* with *b* assimilated to *m*, gen. sg. *lammes*.

Only Holthausen interpreted the spelling *b* in the context NC# as
representing voiceless *p*. He assumed that all stops became voiceless
finally, and cited an example from the smaller monuments of OS for a
spelling with final -*p*.[9]

The Context lC#: *p*, *b*, and *f* occur in the context lC#.

p in the context lC# occurs five times in three forms representing
two stems: *gelp* (3) "scorn", ON *gjalp*, OHG *gelf*, OE *gielp*; and *halp*
(1) "helped" and *help* "help" 2 sg. imp. of *helpan* "to help", Go. *hilpan*,
OHG *helfan*, OE *helpan*, OFris. *helpa*.

MLG reflexes are *gelp* "insolence", and *helpan* "to help".

b in the context 1C# occurs twice in one form: *selb* (2) "self"; it will be treated together with 1f#.

f in the context 1C# occurs nineteen times in two forms representing two stems: *half* (4) "side" acc. sg. of *halƀa* "side", Go. *halba*, ON *halfa*, OHG *halba*, OE *healf*, OFris. *halve*, and *self* (15) "self", also occurring as *selb* (2) (see 1b# above), Go. *silba*, ON *sjalfr*, OHG *selb*, OE, OFris. *self*.

MLG reflexes are *halve*, *half* "side", and *sulf*, *sulve*, *self* "self".

Because of comparative evidence and the MLG reflexes, the *p* in the context 1C# is assigned to the phoneme /p/, *b* in *selb* probably represents a spirant. Since both comparative evidence and the MLG reflexes point to a spirant for *b* and *f*, they are assigned to the phoneme /f/.

There is general agreement among scholars that in final position the contrast in the labial order was between a voiceless stop /p/ and a voiceless spirant /f/. The limited evidence of M supports this view.

The Context rC#: only *p* and *f* occur in the context rC#.

p in the context rC# occurs six time in five forms representing two stems: *skarp* (1) "sharp", ON *skarpr*, OHG *scarph*, OE *scearp*, OFris. *skerp*, and *uuarp* (2) "threw", of *uuerpen* "to throw", Go. *wairpan*, ON *verpa*, OHG *werfan*, OE *weorpan*, OFris. *werpa*.

MLG reflexes are *scharp* and *werpen*, *warpen*.

f in the context rC# occurs thirty-two times in five forms representing three stems: *huarf* (4) and *huuarf* (1) "crowd, gathering" and *huarf* (3) "went, surrounded" and their related form *umbihuarf* (1) "surrounded" of *huerƀan* "to go to, go (back and forth)", Go. *hvairban*, ON *hverfa*, OHG *hwerban*, OE *hweorfan*, OFris. *hwerva*; *suarf* (1) "wiped off" of **swerƀan*, Go. (*af-*, *bi-*) *swairban*, ON *sverfa*, OHG *swerban*, OE *sweorfan*, OFris. *swerva*; *tharf* (19) "need" nom. sg., *tharf* (3) "need, needs" pret.-pres. vb. 1 and 3 sg. pres. of **thurƀan*, Go. *þarba*, *þaúrban*, ON *þorf*, *þurfa*, OHG *darba*, *durfan*, OE *þearf*, *þurfan*, OFris. *therve*, *thurva*.

MLG relfexes are *werf*, *warf*, and *werven*, *darven* "to need, to lack" and *derven* "to suffer want, starve"

As in the context lC#, *p* can be assigned to the phoneme /p/; *f* is assigned to the phoneme /f/.

The Context VC#: *p*, *b*, *ƀ*, and *f* occur in the context VC#.

p in the context VC# occurs fifty-five times in thirteen forms representing eleven stems: *biscop* (6) "bishop", Go. *aipiskaupus*, ON *biscup*, OHG *biscof*, OE *bisceop*, *biscop*, OFris. *biskop*, Lat. *episcopus*; *diap* (3) "deep", Go. *diups*, ON *djúpr*, OHG *tiof*, OE *dēop*, OFris. *diap*; *drop* (1) "dripped" 3 sg. pret. of *driopan* "to drip", ON *drjúpa*, OHG *triofan*, OE *drēopan*, OFris. *driapa*; *forsuuep* (1) "driven away" 3 sg. pret. of **farsuuēpan*, ON *sveipa*, OHG *sweifan*, OE *(for-)swāpan*, OFris. *swēpa*; *gescop* (3) and *giscop* (5) "created, ordered" of **giskeppian*, Go. *gaskapjan*, OHG *giscaffan*, *giscepfen*, OE *gescieppan*; *hop* "band, crowd", OHG *houf*, OE *hēap*, OFris. *hāp*; *hriop* (3) "called" 3 sg. pret. of *hrōpjan*, ON *hrópa*, OHG *(h)ruofan*; OE *hrōpa*; *skip* (3) "ship", Go. ON *skip*, OHG *skif*, OE *scip*, OFris. *skip*; *stop* (2) "stepped, went" of **steppian*, OHG *stephen*, OE *stæppan*, OFris. *steppa*; *up* (28) "up", Go. *iup*, ON *upp*, OHG *ûf*, OE *ŭpp*, OFris. *up*; *uueop* (1) "lamented" 3 sg pret. of **uuopian*, and *uuop* (1) "lament", Go. *wōpjan*, ON *ǿpa* and *ópa*, OHG *wuofen* and *wuof*, OE *wāpan* and *wōp*, OFris. *wēpa*.

MLG reflexes are *bischop*, *dêp*, *depe*, *drêpen*, *swepe*, *sweppe* "wip", *geschappen*, *hôp*, *hope*, *hoppe*, *hupe*, *ropen*, *schip*, *schep*, *stappen*, *up*, *wopen*.

b in the context VC# occurs eleven times in five forms representing four stems: *fargab* (4) "gave, lent" of *fargeƀan* "to give, lend", Go. *fragiban*, ON *fyrirgefa*, OHG *fargeban*, OE *forgiefan*, OFris. *urieva*; *geb* (1) "when, if" is considered a scribal error for *ef* (Sehrt 1966:90), Go. *ibai*, ON *ef*, OHG *ibu*, *oƀa*, OE *gif*, OFris. *ief*, *ef*, *iof*, *of*; *lib* (2) "life" and *sinlib* (3) "eternal life", ON *lîf*, OHG *lîb*, OE, OFris. *lîf*; *liob* (1) "dear, friendly", Go. *liufs*, ON *ljúfr*, OHG *liob*, OE *lēof*, OFris. *liaf*.

MLG reflexes are *vorgeven*, *ef*, *of*, *af*, *if*, *lîf*, *lêf*.

Since the above forms also occur in Vf#, the phonemic assignment of *b* in Vb# is being postponed until all labial graphs in the context of VC# have been presented.

ƀ in the context VC# occurs twice in two forms representing two stems: *liƀ* (1) "life" (see Vb# above); *loƀ* (1) "foliage (leaves)", Go. *laufs*, ON *lauf*, OHG *loub*, OE *lēaf*, OFris. *lāf*.

MLG reflexes are *lîf*, *lôf*.

Both *liƀ* (1) "life" and *loƀ* (1) "foliage" also occur with final *f*. They are discussed together with their variant forms with final *f*.

f in the context VC# occurs 194 times in twenty-nine forms representing nineteen stems. All forms that belong to representative stems are listed including all those stems with variant forms spelled with *b* or *ƀ*: *gaf* (9) "gave" of *geƀan* "to give" and eleven related and inflected forms, Go. *giba*, *giban*, ON *gjǫf*, *gefa*, OHG *geba*, *geban*, OE *giefu*, *gifu*, *giefan*, OFris. *ieve*, *ieva*; *ef* (78) and *of* (1) "when, if" (see *geb* under Vb# above); *fif* (1) "five", Go. *fimf*, ON *fimm*, OHG *fimf*, OE, OFris. *fîf*; *lif* (20) "life" and *sinlif* (3) "eternal life", ON *lif*, OHG *lîb*, OE, OFris. *lîf*; *leof* (1) and *liof* (10) "dear, friendly" (see Vb# above); *lof* (9) "praise" (not the same stem as in *loƀ* [1] "foliage [leaves]" under Vƀ# above), ON *lof*, OHG *lob*, OE, OFris. *lof*; *thief* (1) "thief", Go. *þiubs*, ON *þjófr*, OHG *diub*, OE *þēof*, OFris. *thiaf*; *uuif* (23) "wife", ON *vif*, OHG *wîb*, *wîp*, OE, OFris. *wîf*.

MLG reflexes of the forms not listed above are *gave* and *geven*, *vif*, *loven*, *dêf*, *dief*, *deif*, *wîf*.

Comparative evidence, graphemic analysis, and the MLG reflexes all point to a contrast between a phoneme /p/ on one hand and a voiceless spirant on the other. *b*, *ƀ*, or *f* in the context VC# can be assigned to a phoneme /f/ in final position.

THE DENTALS IN FINAL POSITION

The Context NC#: Only *t* and *d* occur in the context NC#.

t in the context NC# occurs sixteen times in two forms represent-

ing two stems: *mornont* (1) "grieve" 2 pl. imp. of **mornian*, **mornon*
"to grieve", Go. *maúrnan*, OHG *mornên*, OE *murnan*. The ending in *mornont* may have been influenced by Old High German. The corresponding
form in manuscript C is *mornot* (see also Holthausen 1921:143); *sint*
(15) "are" 3 pl. pres. of *uuesan* "to be". Forms from the other Germanic languages for *sint* are: Go. *sind*, OHG *sint*, OE *sindon*, *sind*,
sint.

The MLG reflex of *sint* is also *sint*.

d in the context NC# occurs 354 times in forty-four forms. It
is in free variation with *t* in *sind* (40) "are" 3 pl. pres. Among the
forty-four forms one can find some of the most common words easily
recognizable through Modern English and German, such as *aband* (2),
hand (15), *kind* (11), *wind* (4), and, of course, *heleand* (8).

The above evidence does not allow assignment of *t* and *d* in the
context NC# to two contrasting phonemes. Holthausen describes *d* in
final position as being unvoiced (1921:83). This would require *d* =
[t] to be assigned to the phoneme /t/.

The Context lC#: Only *t* and *d* occur in the context lC#.

t in the context lC# occurs twenty-nine times in five graphically
different forms representing six stems: *geuualt* (1) "power, might",
OHG *giwalt*, OE *geweald*, OFris. *wald*; *halt* (1) "lame in the feet", Go.
halts, ON *haltr*, OHG *halz*, OE *healt*, OFris. *halt*; *halt* (1) "more", Go.
haldis, ON *heldr*, OHG *halt*; *salt* (1) "salt", Go., ON *salt*, OHG *salz*,
OE *sealt*, OFris. *salt*; *scalt* (23) "must, ought to" 2 sg. pres. of **skulan*, Go. *skulan*, ON *skulu*, OHG *scolan*, OE *sculan*, OFris. *skela*; *uuilt*
(1) "want to, wish" 2 sg. pres. of *willian*, comparative evidence from
other Germanic languages is Go. *wileis*, ON *vilt*, OHG *wili*, MHG *wil*,
wilt, OE *wilt*.

MLG reflexes are *gewelde*, *gewelt*, *gewalt*, *gewolt*, *helde*, and *heldene* "fetters for the feet", *solt*, *salt*, *schalt*, *schalst*, *scholt*, *wilt*,
wult, *wolt*.

d in the context lC# occurs 129 times in twenty-three forms, such as *ald* (6) "old", Go. *alþeis*, ON *aldinn*, OHG *alt*, OE *eald*, OFris. *ald*, *old*; *geld* (12) "reward, sacrifice" and one composite, Go. *gild*, ON *gjald*, OHG *gelt*, OE *gield*, OFris. *ield*, *geld*; *giuuald* (19) "power, might" and nineteen related forms,[10] OHG *giwalt*, OE *geweald*, OFris. *wald*; *gold* (4) "gold", Go. *gulþ*, ON *gull*, *goll*, OHG, OE, OFris. *gold*; *hald* (1) "more" (see *halt* [1] "more" under 1t# above), and *hald* (1) "hold" 2 sg. imp. (see *haldan* [4] "to hold, take care of"), Go. *haldan*, ON *halda*, OHG *haltan*, OE *healdan*, OFris. *halda*; *hold* (5) "beholden, dear", Go. *hulþs*, ON *hollr*, OHG, OE, OFris. *hold*; *uuerold* (37) "world, mankind, life", ON *verold*, OHG *weralt*, *worolt*, OE *weorold*, OFris. *wrald*, *warld*.

MLG reflexes are *olt*, *ōlt*, *alt*, *gelt*, *gewelde*, *gewelt*, *gewalt*, *gewolt*, *golt*, *helde* and *heldene* "fetters for the feet", *holt* "hold" 2 sg. imp. (see Lasch 1914:239), *werlt*, *werlde*, *werlit*, and *werle*.

A contrast between *t* and *d* in this position could be established on the basis of the final cluster in *salt* (1) "salt" and possibly in *halt* (1) "lame in the feet", as well as the second singular present tense forms *scalt* (23) "must, ought to" and *uuilt* (2) "want to, wish". The *t* and *d* in *halt* (1) and *hald* (1) "more", and in *geuualt* (1) and *geuuald* (16) "power, might" are in free variation.

As in the context NC# the possibility of the unvoicing of all *d*'s in final position must be considered (see also Holthausen 1921:83).

The Context rC#: Only *t*, *d*, and *đ* occur in the context rC#.[11]

t in the context rC# occurs seven times in five forms representing four stems: *gelhert* (1) "wanton, frolicsome", OHG *geilherzî*; *hort* (1) "treasure",[12] a variant spelling of *hord*, Go. *huzd*, ON *hodd*, OHG *hort*, OE *hord*; *suart* (2) and *suuart* (1) "black, dark", also *suart* (1) "darkness", Go. *swarts*, ON *svatr* (*sorti* "darkness"), OHG *swarz*, OE *sweart*, OFris. *swart*; *uurt* (1) "root, plant", Go. *waúrts*, ON *urt*, OHG *wurz*, OE *wyrt*.

MLG reflexes are *geilicheit*, *gêlicheit* (with *-eit* or *-cheit* possibly by analogy from other nouns), *swart*, *wort*, *wurt*.

d in the context rC# occurs 427 times in thirty-eight forms, such as *ford* (60) "forward, forth", OE *forð*, OFris. *forth*, MHG *vort*; *hord* (5) "treasure" and two composite forms (see *hort* under rt# above); *suerd* (2) "sword", ON *sverð*, OHG *swert*, OE *sweord*, OFris. *swerd*; *uuard* (155) "became, happened" 3 sg. pret. of *uuerdan*, Go. *waírþan*, ON *verða*, OHG *werdan*, OE *weorþan*, OFris. *wertha*; *uurd* (4) "fate, death", ON *urðr*, OHG *wurt*, OE *wyrd*.

MLG reflexes are *vort*, *swert*, *ward*.

đ in the context rC# occurs fifteen times in four forms representing three stems: *faruuarđ* (1) "perished" 3 sg. pret. of **faruuerđan*, OHG *farwerdan*, OE *forweordan* (see also *werdan* under rd# above); *forđ* (6) "forward, forth" (see *ford* under rd# above); *uuarđ* (7) "became, happened" of *uuerđan* (see rd# above); *uurđ* (1) "earth, soil", ON *urð*, OE *weorð*, *worð*, *wurð*, *wyrð*.

The MLG reflex not appearing under rt# and rd# above is *wort*, *wurt* "soil, land, estate".

As in the contexts NC# and lC# phonemic assignment of dental graphs is difficult because of the scribe's inconsistency in spelling what seem to be identical forms. For example, although he used *d* 427 times to spell rd#, he nevertheless spelled *forđ* six times with *đ* and sixty times with *d*; he likewise spelled *hord* five times with *d* and once with *t*.

The four forms which are always spelled with *t*, i.e. *gelhert* (1), *suart* (3), *suuart* (1), and *uurt* (1), can be contrasted minimally with forms ending in rd#. This may allow assignment of *t* in the context rC# to the phoneme /t/.

Although a minimal contrast exists between *đ* in *uurđ* (1) "earth, soil" and *d* in *uurd* (4) "fate, death", the other three forms ending in rđ#, i.e. *farwarđ* (1), *forđ* (6), and *uuarđ* (7) are in free variation with forms ending in rd#. A reflex of *uurd* "fate" does not occur in Middle Low German.

A two-way contrast in this position between /t/ and an allophone of /d/ may be assumed.

The Context VC#: *t*, *d*, *đ*, and *th* occur in the context VC#.

t in the context VC# occurs 1,948 times in 195 forms, such as *bet* (5) "better", Go. *batis*, ON *betr*, OHG *baz*, OE, OFris. *bet*; *brengit* (1) "brings" 3 sg. pres. of *brengean* "to bring", OE *brengan*, OFris. *branga* (see also Go. *briggan*, OHG, OE *bringan*, OFris. *bringa*); *cumat* (1) "come" 3 pl. pres., *cumit* (2) and *kumit* (1) "comes" 3 sg. pres. of *kuman* "to come", Go. *qiman*, ON *koma*, OHG *queman*, *kuman*, *koman*, OE *cuman*, OFris. *kuma*, *koma*; *flot* (1) "flowed" 3 sg. pret. of *flioten* "to flow", ON *fljóta*, OHG *fliozan*, OE *flēotan*, OFris. *fliata*; *let* (15) "let, left" 3 sg. pret. of *latan* "to let, leave", Go. *lētan*, ON *láta*, OHG *lâzan*, OE *lætan*, OFris. *leta*; *lut* (1) "little", OE *lȳt*; *magat* (1) "virgin, Virgin Mary", Go. *magaþs*, OHG *magad*, OE *mægð*, OFris. *megith*; *mot* (5) "be able to" 1 and 3 sg. pres. (2) and (3), respectively, of **mōtan* "to be able to", Go. *gamōtan*, OHG *muozan*, OE *mōtan*, OFris. *mōta*; *niut* (3) "desire, zeal", OHG *niot*, *niet*, OE *nēod*, OFris. *niod*; *sat* (14) "sat (down), remained" 3 sg. pret. of *sittean* "to sit (down), remain", Go. *sitan*, ON *sitja*, OHG *sizzen*, OE *sittan*, OFris. *sitta*; *uuit* (7) "we two" nom. dual, Go. *wit*, ON *vit*, OE *wit*; and *uuit* (2) "against, for, with", ON *við*, OE *wiþ*, OFris. *with*.

MLG reflexes are *bet*, *bat*, *bringen*, *brengen*, *komen*, *vlêten*, *laten*, *lutt-el*, *lutt-ik*, *moten*, *nôt*, *sitten*.

d in the context VC# occurs 1,811 times in 436 forms, such as *bed* (1) "bed", Go. *badi*, ON *beþr*, OHG *betti*, OE *bedd*, OFris. *bed*; *blod* (2) "blood", Go. *blōþ*, ON *blóþ*, OHG *bluot*, OE, OFris. *blōd*; *brengid* (1) "brings" (see *brengit*, Vt# above); *cumad* (6) "come(s)" 3 sg. pres. (1) and 3 pl. pres. (5), respectively, *kumad* (6) "come" 2 pl. pres. (2), 3 pl. pres. (3), and 2 pl. imp. (1), respectively, *cumid* (11) and *kumid* (8) "comes" 3 sg. pres. (see *cumat*, above); *flod* (7) "flood, river, water", ON *flóð*, OHG *fluot*, OE, OFris. *flōd*; *led* (3) "hostile, evil", ON *leiðr*, OHG *leid*, OE *lað*, OFris. *lēth*, *lēd*, and *led* (3) "(something) evil, sin", OHG *leid*, OE *lað*, OFris. *lēth*, *lēd*; *lid* (1) "limb", Go. *liþus*, ON *liðr*, OHG *lid*, OE *lið*, OFris. *lith*; *lid* (1) "fruitwine, drink", Go. *leiþu*, ON *lið*, OHG *lîd*, OE *līð*, OFris. *līth*; *lud* (1) "figure", NHG

"Gestalt" (7) (Sehrt 1966:352), see Go. *ludja*, OHG *antlutti*; *magad* (12)
"virgin, Virgin Mary" (see *magat* above); *mod* (3) "mind, courage", Go.
mōþs, ON *mōðr*, OHG *muot*, OE, OFris. *mōd*; *nid* (4) "striving, persecution", Go. *neiþ*, ON *nĭð*, OHG *nĭd*, OE *nĭð*, OFris. *nĭth*; *niud* (3) "desire,
zeal" (see *niut* above); *quad* (137) "spoke, said" 3 sg. pret. of *queden*
"to speak, say", Go. *qiþan*, ON *kveða*, OHG *quedan*, OE *cweðan*, OFris.
quetha; *sad* (1) "seed", Go. *mana-sēþs*, ON *sáð*, OHG *sāt*, OE *sǣd*, OFris.
sēd; *sid* (13) "road, journey, fate", Go. *sinþs*, ON *sinn*, *sinni*, OHG
sind, OE *sĭð*; *sid* (2) "later", Go. *þana-seiþs*, ON *sĭðr*, OHG *sĭd*, OE
sĭð; *uuid* (69) "against, for, with" (see *uuit* [2] above); *uuid* "far,
wide", ON *vĭðr*, OHG *wĭt*, OE, OFris. *wĭd*.

MLG reflexes are *bedde*, *blôt*, *blût*, *vlôt*, *vlût*, *lêde*, *leide*, *lit*
and *let* "limb", *lĭt* "fruitwine", *maget*, *môt*, *moit*, *mout*, *mût*, *nĭt*, *que-
delen* "to gossip", *sât*, *sider* "since, later".

đ in the context VC# occurs eighteen times in six forms representing five stems: *inuuidnĭđ* (1) "enmity", OE *inwitnĭð* (for the last component -*nĭđ* see *nid* under Vd# above); *lĭđ* (2) "fruitwine, drink" (see
lid above); *magađ* (1) "virgin, Virgin Mary" (see both *magat* and *magad*
above); *quađ* (9) "spoke, said" (see *quad* above); *sĭđ* (1) "road, journey, fate" (see *sid* above); *uuiđ* (4) "against, for, with" (see both
uuit and *uuid* above).

MLG reflexes of the forms with *đ* in the context VC# are listed
under Vt# or Vd# where such reflexes can be cited.

th in the context VC# occurs three times in three forms only:
bloth (1) "fearful, disheartened", ON *blauþr*, OHG *blodi*, OE *bleað*, Go.
blauþjan; *geth* (1) "also" *ne...geth* = *neque* (Sehrt 1966:178); *farfioth*
(1) "consume" 3 pl. pres. of *farfion*, *farfehon*, OHG *farfehon*.

MLG reflexes are *blode*, *vorvernen* and *vorverren* "remove".

The forms cited above were chosen to show the complicated phonemic
structure of the dentals in the context VC#.

Minimal contrasts based on the Old Saxon spelling and some etymological evidence reveal a two- or even a three-way phonemic distinction
finally. This three way distinction between /t d þ/ was suggested by

Moulton (1954:28) for the context VC#, as well as for the context rC#.
Holthausen (1921:70) suggests a two-way contrast between /t/ and
/þ/, which, of course, is in agreement with his theory that only voiceless obstruents occurred in final position.

A case could even be made for /t/ as the only dental obstruent
phoneme occurring finally, based primarily on the Middle Low German
evidence and the fact that the spelling in M is inconsistent. Even
Holthausen (1921:70) hinted at this possibility when he wrote:

> Da *th* im Mnd, zu *d* wird, ist mindestens im späteren AS. die
> Spirans überall stimmlos geworden, vgl. Lasch, Mnd, Gr. pgf.
> 319.

Of the three forms with *th*, each occurring once, in the context
VC#, only *farfioth* (1) "consume" 3 pl. pres. can be used as a reliable
example for an etymologically expected /þ/.

Regularized paradigms of Old Saxon present tense verbs show *th* as
the dental in the third singular, and second and third plural endings.
Holthausen (1921:70) writes: "in C ist *th* das häufigste...". This
assumption continues to provide the basis for linguistic studies, e.g.
King (1967:247), and Voyles (1970-71). But there is general agreement
among scholars that in other respects MS. M is the most reliable Old
Saxon manuscript, not C.

Any thorough investigation of the verbal endings has to be based
on statistical evidence from all Old Saxon MSS, especially M. A cursory investigation of M reveals the following evidence for present
tense verbal endings: Some forty present tense forms show free variation between *t* and *d*, such as *cumit* (2) and *cumid* (11), *cumat* (1) and
cumad (6). These forty forms with both *t* and *d* occur approximately
400 times; *th* occurs only once in *farfioth*; and *đ* is never found in
present tense verb forms.

In analogy with the labials a two-way contrast between /t/ and a
spirantal allophone of either /d/ or /þ/ could be assumed. The investigation of the velars and *h* may also influence the proposed phonemic

and allophonic distribution of the dentals. Additional criteria, such as structural symmetry, are used in attempting solutions for an overall structure of the obstruents.

THE VELARS IN FINAL POSITION

The Context NC#: Only *k*, *c*, and *g* occur in the context NC#.

k and *c* occur twenty-one times in ten forms representing seven stems: *dranc* (1) "drank" and one related form of *drinkan*, Go. *drigkan*, ON *drekka*, OHG *trinkan*, OE *drincan*, OFris. *drinka*; *rink* (2) "young warrior, man", OHG *rinch*, OE *rinc*; *sinc* (4) "treasure" and one related form, OE *sinc*; *stank* (1) "stench", OHG *stank*, OE *stenc*; *thanc* (6) and *thank* (1) "favor, thanks", Go. *þagks*, ON *þǫkk*, OHG *danc*, OE *þanc*, OFris. *thanc*, *thonc*; *unc* (3) "the two of us" dat. (2) and acc. (1) dual, respectively, Go. *ugkis*, ON *okr*, OE *unc*; *uulank* (1) "darling, proud", OE *wlanc*, *wlonc*.

MLG reflexes are *drinken*, *drank* "(a) drink", *sinken* "to sink", *stank*, *dank*, *danke*; OS *unc*, dat. and acc. dual, does not appear in MLG writings, though dual forms are still found in some Modern Low German dialects (Lasch 1914:14).

g in the context NC# occurs 198 times in forty-five forms, such as *ahospring* (1) "waterspring, well" and two related forms, OE *ēa*, *ǣ-spring*; *gemang* (2) and *gimang* (9) "crowd, (nom.), between, together (adv.)", MHG *gemanc*, OE *gemang*, OFris. *mong*; *hring* (1) "ring", ON *hringr*, OHG, OE, OFris. *hring*; *iung* (3) "young" and two composite forms, Go. *juggs*, ON *ungr*, OHG, OFris. *jung*, OE *geong*; *strang* (2) "strong, mighty", ON *strangr*, OHG *strengi*, OE *strang*.

MLG reflexes are *sprank*, *gemank*, *rink*, *junk*, *strenga*.

g after nasals in the context NC# may be considered a velar stop [g] of the phoneme /g/ contrasting with /k/.

The Middle Low German evidence points to [g] in Old Saxon rather than [ɣ] in these positions. The latter would have given [-ŋx] not [-ŋk] in final position, where it did not become [ŋ]. All modern studies agree with this analysis.[13]

The Context lC#:   A two-way contrast between /k/ and an allophone
of either /g/ or /x/ is assumed. Unfortunately this contrast is based
on only two forms with l*k#* representing two stems and one form with
l*g#*.

c in the context lC# occurs sixty-five times in seven forms representing two stems: *folc* (57) "people, crowd" and six composite forms,
ON *fólk*, OHG, OFris. *folk*, OE *folc*; *scalc* (2) "servant", Go. *skalks*,
late ON *skalkr*, OHG *scalc*, OE *scealc*, OFris. *skalk*.

MLG reflexes are *volk, schalk*.

g in the context lC# occurs three times in one form: *balg* (3)
"was angry" of *belgan* (1) "to be angry", OHG, OE *belgan*, OFris. part.
pret. *ovir-bulgena*, also ON *belgja*.

Evidence of MLG reflexes is lacking.

Though the *g* in *balg* could be interpreted as either /g/ or /x/,
the *g* in l*g#* most likely had the phonetic value [x]. Holthausen (1921:
79) and Moulton (1954:28) both agree that unvoicing of [g] produced
[x] finally. Only Page (1952:51) assumed voiced obstruents finally
when he assigned [ɣ] to /g/, although he recognized that final *g* represented a spirant.

The Context rC#:   A two-way contrast is assumed for /k/ and /x/
in the context rC#.

k and *c* occur fifty-five times in twenty forms representing two
stems: *stark* (1) and *starc* (1) "strong, evil", ON *sterkr*, OHG *stark*,
starah, OE *stearc*, OFris. *sterk*; *uuerk* (11) and *uuerc* (16) "work, deed"
and twenty-six composite forms, ON *verk*, OHG *wer(a)h*, *werc*, OE *weorc*,
OFris. *werk*.

MLG reflexes are *stark* and *werk, wark*.

g in the context rC# occurs forty times in three forms representing three stems: *berg* (12) "mountain", Go. *baírgahei*, ON *bjarg*, OHG
berc, OE *beorg*, OFris. *berch*, and *gibirgi* (2) "mountains, mountain

chain", OHG *gibirgi*; *burg* (27) "city, castle", Go. *baúrgs*, ON *borg*,
OHG, OE *burg*, OFris. *burch*; *gibarg* (1) "saved, preserved" 3 sg. pret.
of **gibergan* "to save, preserve", Go. *gabaírgan*, OHG *gibergan*, OE *ge-beorgan*, ON *bjarga*.

MLG reflexes are *berch*, *borch*, *bergen*, *bargen*.

h in the context rC# occurs 115 times in two forms representing
two stems: *ferh* (3) "life, soul", Go. *faírhvus*, ON *fjǫr*, OHG *ferah*,
ferh, OE *feorh*; *thurh* (112) "through, because of, with", Go. *þaírh*,
OHG *dur(u)h*, OE *þurh*, OFris. *thruch*.

MLG reflexes are *dorch*, *dor*, *dur*, *dar*.

The MLG reflexes, comparative evidence, and the contrasts between
the limited number of lexical items in the context rCV, together justify assignment of rk# and rc# to /k/ contrasting with rg#, the latter
presumably representing the voiceless spirantal allophone [x] of /x/.
Though there is no spelling evidence for [x] contrasting with [h], morphophonemic writing of *g* for [x] is generally presented as evidence,
e.g. by Holthausen (1921:79) and Moulton (1954:32).

Moulton assigns the *h* in *ferh* to a phoneme different from the [x]
in *burg* because the *h* in *ferh* probably represents glottal [h] (Moulton
1954:32). In the present study, the *h* in both *ferh* and *thurh* is regarded as representing /x/.

The Context VC#: As was assumed in the contexts lC# and rC#, a
two-way contrast existed between /k/ and /x/ in the context VC#.

The inconsistencies in spelling obscure the probable phonemic
structure in final position. In order to illuminate the complex distribution of the velars in final position, all doubtful forms will be
investigated.

k and *c* in the context VC# occur 671 times in eighty-two forms,
such as *ik* (133) and *ic* (87) "I", Go. *ik*, ON *ek*, OHG *ih*, OE *ĭc*, OFris.
ik; *bisuek* (1) and *bisuec* (1) and *bisuuec* (1) "deceived" of *bisuican*
(2) and *bisuuican* (1) "to deceive, hinder", OHG *biswîhhan*, OE *beswîcan*;
ak (1) and *ac* (91) "but", Go. *ak*, OHG *oḥ*, OE *ac*; *bok* (3) and *boc* (1)

"writing tablet(s), book(s)", Go. *bōka*, ON *bók*, OHG *buoh*, OE *bōc*, OFris. *bōk*.

MLG reflexes are *ik*, *ek*, *beswiken*, *ôk*, *bôk*, *bûk*.

In the following forms *k* and *c* are in free variation with *g*: *gehuilic* (17) and *gehuuilic* (3), and *gihuuilig* (1) "each (one)", OHG *gihwelih*, OE *gehwilc*; *ok* (28) and *oc* (40), and *og* (1) "also", Go. *ôuk*, ON *auk*, *ok*, OHG *ouh*, OE *ēac*, OFris. *āk*; *sulik* (3) and *sulic* (28), and *sulig* (1) "such, this", Go. *swaleiks*, ON *slíkr*, OHG *sulîh*, *solîh*, OE *swylc*, OFris. *sullik*, *sel(i)k*, *sek*.

MLG reflexes are *gewelik*, *gewellik*, *ôk*, *solik*, *sollik*, *sollek*, *solk*.

The above two occurrences of final -*ig* may be interpreted as scribal errors possibly explainable by the high frequency of Old Saxon forms ending in the suffix -*ik* and -*ic* (40), which contrast with forms ending in the suffix -*ig* (39); the occurrence of *og* can be explained as a variant spelling.[14]

The forms *gelik* (1) *gelic* (2) and *gilic* (1) "like, some" also occur as *gelich* (2) and *gilih* (2), Go. *galeiks*, ON *glíkr*, *líkr*, OHG *gilîh*, OE *gelîc*, OFris. *gelik*.[15]

The MLG reflex is *gelike*.

Holthausen (1921:81) considers occasional *h* or *ch* for *k* or *c* either due to High German influence or scribal errors.

g in the context VC# occurs 500 times in eighty-nine forms, such as *euuig* (14) "eternal", OHG *êwig*, OFris. *ewig*; *uueg* (17) "road", Go. *wigs*, ON *vegr*, OHG, OE *weg*, OFris. *wei*; *dag* (21) "day", Go. *dags*, ON *dagr*, OHG *tac*, OE *dæg*, OFris. *dach*, *dei*, *dī*; *genog* (4) and *ginog* (1) "enough, much", Go. *ganôhs*, ON *gnôgr*, *nôgr*, OHG *ginuog*, OE *genōg*, OFris. *enōch*, *nōch*.

MLG reflexes are *ewich*, *wech*, *dach*, *genōch*.

h in the context VC# occurs 156 times in twenty-three forms, such as *nah* (2) "near", Go. *nēƕ*, ON *náinn*, OHG *nâh*, OE *nēah*, OFris. *nei*, *nī*; *alah* (3) "temple", Go. *alhs*, OE *ealh*, ON *alh*; *thoh* (71) "yet, however, nevertheless", Go. *þáuh*, ON *þó*, OHG *doh*, OE *þeah*, *þēh*, OFris. *thāh*.

MLG reflexes are *na*, *nage*, *doch*.

g and *h* are in free variation in *noh* (27) and *nog* (1) "still, yet", Go. *nauh*, OHG *noh*, OFris. *noch*.

The MLG reflexes are *noch*, *nocht*.

Minimal graphemic contrasts are found in the following forms with final *-h* and *-g*: *uuih* (9) "sanctuary, temple", ON *vé*, OE *wēoh*, *wīg*; also Go. *weihs*, OHG *wîh(i)* "holy"; and *uuig* (2) "war, battle", ON *vig*, OHG *wic*, *wig*, OE *wīg*, OFris. *wīch*, also Go. *waihjō*; *lah* (1) "find fault with, forbid" 2 imp. sg., ON *lá*, OHG *lahan*, OE *lēan*; also OFris. *lakkia* "to contest"; and *lag* (5) "lay" of *liggen* "to lie, be situated", Go. *ligan*, ON *liggja*, OHG *lig(g)en*, OE *licgan*, OFris. *lidza*; *uuah* (1) "(something) evil", Go. *(un)-wāhs*, OE *wōh*; and *uuag* (4) "wave, flood", Go. *wēgs*, ON *vágr*, OHG *wâg*, OE *wæg*, OFris. *wēg*; *seh* (2) "see" 2 sg. imp. of *sehan*, Go. *saíhvan*, ON *sjá*, OHG *sehan*, OE *sēon*, OFris. *sīa*; and *seg* (2) "sank, moved (forward)" 3 sg. pret. of **sigan* "to sink, move (forward)", ON *síga*, OHG, OE *sīgan*, OFris. *sīga*.

MLG reflexes are *wîen*, *wigen* "to consecrate, sanctify" and *wich*; *laken* and *liggen* (no corresponding inflected forms found); *wâchlik* "dangerous" (?) and *wage*, *wâch*; *sê* imp. of *sên* (Lasch 1914:227) and *sigen* (pret. not extant).

The following forms with final *h* represent preterites of strong verbs: *atoh* (1) "pulled (out)" 3 sg. pret. of **atiohan*, OHG *arziohan*, OE *atēon*; *gitoh* (1) "pulled (out)" 3 sg. pret. of **gitiohan*, OHG *giziohan*, OE *getēon*; *floh* (1) "fled" 3 sg. pret. of **fliohan*, ON *flýja*, OHG *fliohan*, OE *flēon*, OFris. *flīa*; *gisah* (10) and *gesah* (3) "saw, looked at, perceived" 1 sg. (2) and 3 sg. (11) pret. of *gisehan* (8), Go. *gasaíhvan*, OHG *gisehan*, OE *gesēon*; *sah* (4) "saw, considered" 3 sg. pret. of *sehan* (see *seh* above).

MLG reflexes are *tôch* sg. pret., *vlô*, *vlôch*, pret., *sah* sg. pret. (all forms are from Lasch 1914:231 and 235, respectively).

In addition to the above forms, free variation between final *-h* and *-∅* occurs in: *auoh* (1) and *auuh* (1), and *auu* (1) "wrong, evil", ON *ǫfugr*, OHG *abuh*, also Go. *ibuks*; *hoh* (7) and *ho* (3) "high, prominent", Go. *hauhs*, ON *hốr*, *hár*, OHG *hôh*, OE *hēah*, OFris. *hāch*.

MLG reflexes are *ho*, *hôch*, *hoich*, *hoge*.

The evidence presented for *g* and *h* in the context VC# seems to indicate that the scribe was able to use *g* or *h* for [x]. Where *h* and ∅
are in free variation, [x] may have been weakened to [h] or ∅ in the
process of being lost.

CONCLUSION

The analysis offered in this paper does not answer all questions
raised in previous scholarly presentations. Insufficient evidence, e.
g., lack of examples or inconclusive interpretation of rare forms, does
not permit final statements on the distribution of all obstruents. The
study does present, however, an abundance of material for comparison
with evidence found in manuscripts, C, P, and V of the *Heliand*, the Old
Saxon *Genesis*, and in the smaller Old Saxon monuments. It also points
to the difficulty of tracing later developments of the Old Saxon consonants in the various Middle Low German dialects.

Methodologically, the need for using primary sources and observable data is reaffirmed by the approach taken in this investigation.

NOTES:

1) There is almost general consensus that the *Heliand* poem was composed in the early ninth century by a single poet. The poet's use of a
commentary by Hrabanus indicates that the *Heliand* was probably written
after 821 (Behaghel 1965:xxx). Whether the Monacensis (M) manuscript
was copied directly from the original cannot be determined, but it is
clearly placed in the ninth century (Sievers 1878:xxiv).

2) The study was partially supported by a grant for computer time
at the University of Northern Iowa in Cedar Falls. The storage capacity of the IBM 360/40 computer in Cedar Falls does not provide the
necessary memory positions. The computer telephone terminal at Cedar
Falls, however, allows direct access to the storage capacity of the
360/65 computer at the University of Iowa at Iowa City. Though it required less than eight minutes of computer time, small computers do not
possess memory banks capable of storing the amount of information on
which this study is based.

3) Especially the following: Holthausen (1921), Lasch (1914), Moulton (1954), Page (1952), Sievers (1878).

4) In the graphemic analysis I relied primarily on Pulgram (1951), Hall (1962), and Penzl (1967).

5) See Karl Odwarka (1973).

6) Following Moulton, three orders of consonants are recognized (Moulton 1954:29). The term *labial* may include bilabials and labiodentals, while *dental* may include dentals, interdentals, postdentals, and alveolars, etc. The purpose of setting up the three orders of labials, dentals, and velars is to indicate phonemic contrasts.

7) These were used by Moulton (1954) for all early Germanic languages.

8) The number in parenthesis which follows a cited form indicates its frequency in manuscript M. For example, *aband* "evening", is listed as *aband* (2) "evening", but the form *abande* "evening" dat. sg. would be listed as *abande* (1) "evening" dat. sg.; in other words, there is no common listing of forms belonging to the same lexical items.

9) In pgf. 246 Holthausen (1921:83) makes a case for *lamb* which could be interpreted as [l a m p]: "Im Auslaut ist *b* wohl wie *d* und *g* (pgf. 248 und 252) stimmlos geworden, doch herrscht etymologische Schreibung wie in *lamb* 'Lamm'. Einmal nur haben die Wer. Gl. *dump* 'dumm' mit *p* (vgl. Elberfelder *kraump* 'krumm').

10) Sehrt did not record two *giuueld*, lines 3,344 and 5,126, and one *geuueld*, line 2,048 (1966:195).

11) The form *uurht* (1) "fate" in line 2,189 of M is considered a scribal error by Sehrt (1966:725). If the scribe intended to spell it **uurth*, as Sehrt suggests, this would constitute an occurrence of *th* in the context rC#.

12) *hort* in M, line 1,762; Sehrt (1966:539) lists it as *hord*.

13) Holthausen (1921:78) also points to a change of *gn* to [ŋ] which may be represented in alternate spellings *ng* for *gn*: "Vor *n* hatte *g* auch die Neigung zum gutteralen Nasal ŋ zu werden, in dem der folgende Nasal aufgehen konnte, z.B. *gifragn* 'erfuhr', woneben *frang* in CM..." The following forms occur in M: *fragn* (2) "asked" 3 sg. pret. of **fregnan* "to ask", Go. *fraíhnan*, ON *fregna*, OE *frignan*; *gifragn* (9) and *gefragn* (3), and *gifrang* (2) and *gefrang* (1) "learned, came to know" 3 sg. pret. of **gifregnan* "to learn", Go. *gafraíhnan*, OE *gefrignan*.

MLG evidence is lacking.

14) The numbers of forms ending in *-ik* and *-ic*, i.e. (40) and *-ig* (39), refer to the number of graphemically different forms. The total number of forms is 120 and 190, respectively.

15) Sehrt (1966:184) erroneously lists *gilik* for OHG *gilih*. Kluge (1934:209) has *gilih* (*hh*) from Germanic **galīka-*.

SELECTED BIBLIOGRAPHY:

Barnes, Merwin R. 1971. *Phonological and Morphological Rules of Old*

Saxon. Diss., University of California, Los Angeles.

Behaghel, Otto. 1965. *Heliand und Genesis*. Ed. Walter Mitzka, 8th ed. Tübingen.

Hall, Robert A., Jr. 1962. "Graphemics and Linguistics", in *Symposium on Language and Culture*. Cornell University. (Proceedings of the 1962 Annual Spring Meeting of the American Ethnological Society.)

Harms, Robert T. 1968. *Introduction to Phonological Theory*. Englewood Cliffs.

Holthausen, Ferdinand. 1921. *Altsächsisches Elementarbuch*. 2nd ed. Heidelberg.

King, Robert D. 1965. "Weakly Stressed Vowels in Old Saxon", *Word* XXI.19-39.

--------------- 1969. *Historical Linguistics and Generative Grammar*. Englewood Cliffs.

Lasch, Agathe. 1914. *Mittelniederdeutsche Grammatik*. Halle a. S.

Lehmann, Winfred P. 1953. "The Alliteration of Old Saxon Poetry", *Norsk Tidsskrift for Sprogvidenskap*, Suppl. Bind III.

Lübben, August and Walther, Cristoph. 1965. *Mittelniederdeutsches Wörterbuch*. Darmstadt.

Moulton, William G. 1954. "The Stops and Spirants of Early Germanic", *Language* XXX.1-42.

Odwarka, Karl. 1973. *The Consonant System of Manuscript M of the Old Saxon* Heliand. Diss., University of Michigan, Ann Arbor.

Oppermann, Fred. 1959. *The Old Saxon Vowel Phonemes under Medial and Weak Stress in the Manuscript M of the Heliand*. Diss., University of Texas, Austin.

--------------- 1962. "The Old Saxon Vowel Phonemes under Weak Stress", *Journal of English and Germanic Philology* LXI.77-80.

Page, Carl R. 1952. "The Phonological System of the Old Saxon Language", M.A. Thesis, Cornell University, Ithaca.

Penzl, Herbert. 1967. "The Linguistic Interpretation of Scribal Errors in Old High German Texts", *Linguistics* 32.79-82.

Pulgram, Ernst. 1951. "Phoneme and Grapheme: A Parallel", *Word* VII/I. 15-20.

Sehrt, Edward H. 1966. *Vollständiges Wörterbuch zum Heliand und zur altsächsischen Genesis*. 2nd ed. Göttingen.

Sievers, Eduard. 1878. *Heliand*. Halle.

Voyles, Joseph B. 1970-71. "The Phonology of Old Saxon", *Glossa* 4/2. 123-59 (1970) and 5/1.3-30 (1971).

THE APPLICATION OF THE COMPARATIVE METHOD TO PHILIPPINE LANGUAGES

CONSUELO J. PAZ
University of the Philippines

The fact that the numerous languages of the Philippines are closely related should have encouraged a number of studies on the reconstruction of Proto-Philippine. On the contrary, only a few works can be cited which specifically and solely deal with the reconstruction of the
protolanguage or at least part of it. The majority of the studies,
which in some way shed light on the history of Philippine languages,
usually deal with the reconstructed language of a much earlier period,
that is, before the divergence of Proto-Austronesian.

A possible reason for this could be the fact that at the time when
the historical study of languages was the only or prime activity in linguistics, this was up to at least the 1930's, linguistics had gained
the attention of only a few Filipino scholars like Lopez and Viray.
Most, if not all, of the studies done at this time were pursued by foreign scholars like Conant, Brandstetter and Dempwolff, whose interest
was the broader area of Austronesia, touching only on some Philippine
languages. A small number of them took interest in and conducted historical studies on some Philippine languages such as Blake and Conant.
Had there been more Filipino scholars interested in Philippine linguistics at that time, we could have expected more interest in local problems such as the reconstruction of the possible source of the diverse
Philippine languages.

After this era, interest turned to synchronic studies and problems
involving the history of languages were relegated to the background.

It was also during this period that more Filipinos became involved in the study of Philippine languages, especially from the 1950's onward. Their studies were geared to synchronic problems such as descriptive and comparative studies for typological and pedagogical purposes. At present, the historical study of Philippine languages is still dominated by foreign scholars, like Dyen and his students. Cecilio Lopez is to the present the leading Filipino scholar in this field of linguistics, with only two or three other Filipinos doing comparative work.

In my survey of works on the historical comparison of Philippine languages (Paz 1974), I have not come across a published work that establishes the relationship within the geographical boundaries of the Philippines by means of a qualitative approach and by comparing the languages of a single period in time and inductively arriving at the protolanguage. It was for this reason that I decided to conduct a research of this nature.[1] What has been done so far, is showing how Proto-Austronesian as reconstructed primarily by Dempwolff is reflected in Philippine languages.

The subject of this paper concerns explanations for some aberrances or irregularities in the correspondences found in the comparative work which I have been doing on 29 Philippine languages.[2] These languages were chosen out of the approximately 100 languages found in the Philippines and were selected on the basis of phonological, grammatical, and lexical characteristics.[3]

The data of this research was taken solely from present day speakers of the languages and not from available written sources such as dictionaries which, in my opinion, are not reliable enough.[4] Care was taken to gather data from only one location from within the area in which the particular language was spoken to avoid dialect mixing. Informant work was conducted in situ for almost all of the languages and only native speakers were used as informants.

A lot has been said about the reconstructed language which results from the application of the comparative method. One point of discussion is the "uniformity assumption". This assumption implies that the reconstructed language was homogeneous. A few scholars such as Bloomfield (1933) and Hockett (1958) felt this as a necessary assumption for the comparative method to be operational, although they recognized this as "potentially false", since such a state would be contrary to reality, a real language being heterogeneous.

Dyen (1969) presented a proposition to replace the protolanguage uniformity assumption which still allowed the comparative method to operate. He stated that what was necessary to assume was that the protolanguage had an idiolect, the phonemic system of which was reflected in all the daughter languages. This way it makes it easier to accept homogeneity since it characterizes an idiolect. This therefore makes the protolanguage not very different from a real language. I tend to agree with Dyen although I would rather assume homogeneity of a dialect rather than of an idiolect. This for me is more conceivable since even if dialects may not be entirely homogeneous, they certainly are more so than languages. In fact, one might find almost homogeneous dialects in small remote communities, which most probably was the case of a protolanguage such as Proto-Philippine.

Whether this earlier language was a real language which can be assigned to a specific place in time and space is something that this study is not capable of proving, since the recorded history of the Philippines only starts in the middle of the 17th century. Any records prior to this were lost or decayed in the course of the colonial history of these islands.

Viewing the situation from the posited protosound system,[5] it was observed that certain sounds changed or were replaced resulting in the present day languages. But the data belies the fact that the posited protophonemes and their positional variants were regularly reflected in every case. Of course, it might be possible to show regular correspondence in every case by simply taking a few select languages and in turn choosing certain forms that show regular correspondences. But since the intention was to reconstruct Proto-Philippine roots, i.e.,

the protoforms of the roots in all the Philippine languages where these
roots have survived, there was no recourse but to get entagled in the
cognates of some of the languages which did not show the regular sound
correspondence.

Needless to say, sound correspondence is regular, as the Neogrammarians and present-day comparativists advocate, and sporadic or irreg-
ular change should be accounted for by analogy or borrowing. Yet the
comparison of related languages whether confined to a small number such
as three, or a larger number, inevitably confronts the analyst with
sounds which elude explanation in this manner. A careful scrutiny of
environmental factors usually reveal the basis for a plausible interpretation of the aberrant forms. These interpretations involve the
different processes which explain phonological change, some of these
processes being assimilation, dissimilation, metathesis, and the like.
But one would be hard put to show, for example, that metathesis or
sound loss, at least in Philippine languages, is regular or predictable. Assimilation may be explained through environmental evidence
but is not always predictable. There are cognate sets which show obvious similarities which cannot be explained by the regular or automatic sound laws. For example, Yak. *laan* "path, road" is obviously
cognate to Kap., Ilk., Itw., Nag., Buh., Agt., Sub., Buk. *dalan*. The
absence of the medial consonant in the Yak. cognate can be explained
by a loss of a sound, and yet sound loss is not a regular or predictable occurrence in Yak.

In the course of my investigation of the cognates which I compared in attempting to make appropriate statements about the phonetic
correspondences, I found that sound change in these languages could be
characterized as either automatic or nonautomatic. The first type includes the changes which result in regular reflexes and the second type
includes sound change as caused by processes such as assimilation, dissimilation, substitution, reduction, gemination, and metathesis. These
processes do not result in predictable change simply because they are
not automatically operational in the Philippine languages. That is,

identical or very similar situations did not call for the operation of
these processes. Nevertheless, the cognates within sets show a diver-
sity which does not mirror regular or predictable change. And yet,
these forms cannot be taken as anything but cognates and therefore
should permit the reconstruction of their protoroots. In connection
with this, I would like to emphasize the significance of the role of
phonetics or the phonetic features of the sounds in trying to explain
aberrances.

In deliberating the possibilities involved in sound replacement,
I found it necessary to consider as many phonetic features as possible.
This means that in scrutinizing the environment of, let us say, a vowel, not only vowels in preceding and following syllables were considered but also contiguous consonants. Needless to say, that the usual
articulatory features of height, such as high, mid, low, and position,
front, central, and back for vowels; the manner of articulation such
as stop, fricative, lateral, points of articulation such as labial,
alveolar, velar or voicing for consonants, were considered in explaining aberrant sounds. I realized that these aforementioned features
were not adequate explanations for sound replacements in these languages. For example, I found the above mentioned articulatory features
inadequate in explaining the replacement of *ə by a in Ilk. ʔuppát <
*ʔə́mpat "four" or *a by i in Tag., Vir., Kap., Kam. gipú < *gapúk "de-
cayed at the root or trunk". It was on careful scrutiny of the neighboring sounds that I came to conclude that such considerations as the
position of the tongue in consonant production ·had to be taken into
account in explaining sound change. That is, the position of the tongue
in the production of the consonants, whether produced in the front,
central, or back portion of the oral cavity, or whether produced with
the tongue in high or low position was an important factor in the replacement of a neighboring vowel. Furthermore, the activity of the
lips in consonant production was also a point to consider in explaining
such aberrances. Using the Ilk. ʔuppát to illustrate, the u replaced
the ə reflex of *ə and can be explained as the result of the backward

pull by the glottal stop and the influence of the labial p, producing
a labial vowel or a vowel in which the lips are actively involved in
its production. In the case of *gipú* cited above, we find an *i* instead
of the regular *a* reflex. Initially, this can be explained by the influence of the neighboring high *u* resulting in the high *i* replacement,
but then *u* is a back vowel, while *i* is a front vowel. In assessing
the production of p the feature front can definitely be attributed to
it since p is a labial sound. The replacement therefore of a low central vowel by a high front vowel becomes plausible in the light of the
influence or pull of the neighboring high and front sounds. A consonant may also be drawn forward or backward by sounds produced in the
front or back of the mouth. Such is the case of Kap., Png., Sub. *tap-
úŋ* < **galapúŋ* "rice flour" the *g* was pulled forward and replaced by a
t on the pull of the front *p*.

Consequently, in the analysis of the aberrances found in the different languages, I considered the added features front, mid, back,
high, and low, characteristics usually attributed to vowels, as added
features of the consonants, in seeking causes for sound replacements.[6]
Sounds articulated around the labial, dental, and alveolar region were
considered as front sounds, those around the palatal region as central,
and those around the glottal and velar region as back. The sounds produced with the tongue in a raised or arched position were considered
high, those produced with the tongue not arched or raised, in other
words, in a neutral position, were considered low. This way a sound
replacement as that caused by the assimilation of a vowel to a consonant becomes a plausible process. Such replacements are evident throughout the Philippine languages.

I will illustrate only three types of assimilation relevant to this
change, these are backing, fronting, and raising. Png. *gəpə́t* < **gipít*
"lacking in space, time, and means" has *ə* for the **i*, although the regular correspondence is *i* in this language. I propose that the *i* > *ə*
on the pull of the back *g*, then the second *i* was replaced by *ə* on the
influence of the first replacement. This could also be cited as a case

of reciprocal assimilation. Tag. *hánus* < **hanə́s* "gasp, pant" has an
u where *i* (**ə*) would be expected. In this case *i* > *u* due to the velar
nasal which is a back sound. Bon. *kaní* < **kamí* "we" has an alveolar
nasal where all the other languages with cognates for this set exhibit
an *m*. This could be explained by the backing of the front *m* to an *n*
due to the pull of the back sound *k*. Itw. *símid* and Agt. *símə́d* < **sam-*
íg "chin" have a final *d* where other Philippine languages have *g*, *ʔ*,
or *∅*. This aberrance can be explained by the fronting of *g* to *d* on
the pull of the *m*, *s*, and *i* that come before the sound. The replacement by *ʔ* can be accounted for by substitution which will be explained
later.

On the other hand, in Bla. *misáʔ*, Seb. *pisáʔ* < **pəsáʔ* "hatch,
crush", we have cases of raising. The **ə* is regularly reflected as
a in Bla. and as *u* in Seb. but was replaced by *i* in both languages
due to the neighboring high *s* and front *p*. Is. *Etóy* < **kagtə́y* "liver"
is another example. In this case the *a* > *E* due to the following *t*,
a sound articulated in the front of the mouth with the tongue raised.
Consequently, *a* was replaced by a sound which is articulated in a more
fronted position and at the same time in a position which is more
raised.

But then it might be argued that the analysis of sound aberrances
in such a manner as discussed above is unnecessarily forcing the discovery of conditioning factors or influence from the environment. It
could be said furthermore, that it might be simpler to just set up
more correspondence sets, consequently more protophonemes. But the
fact is that aberrances are aberrances or irregularities and therefore cannot be shown as automatic or predictable for a convincing number of occurrences. The result of setting up correspondence sets to
account for every aberrance would result in quite a number of protophonemes (and protoroots) which would be hard to distinguish as separate sounds in the protosound system. This would be even more of a
problem if we support the theory that the reconstructed protosound
system should approximate that of a real language.

For that matter, I have followed the principle of economy in reconstructing Proto-Philippine sounds, again trying to approximate as
much as possible what would be a reasonable inventory of phonemes for
that language. Hoenigswald (1950) calls this the "principle step" in
deciding which possible forms among the various choices that arise out
of a comparative analysis would be the most acceptable.[7] In this study
therefore, I decided to explain aberrances by considering vowels and
consonants as sharing certain phonetic features which could possibly
have been responsible for the irregularities, rather than set up a different correspondence sets each time a set involved different sounds,
which in the case of Philippine languages could get out of hand.

Aside from the nonautomatic change caused by assimilation there
are several other causes or processes which are found to be operational
in the various Philippine languages included in this study. I will
deal with only one other which I found to be significant in the reconstruction of Proto-Philippine roots. This process can account for the
sporadic appearance of certain sounds in otherwise regularly reflected
cognates. I choose to call this process Substitution because I surmise
that speakers had started to drop certain consonant correspondences but
possibly due to uncertainty or inconsistency, did not do so entirely or
completely. Consequently, they substituted either the $ʔ$, h, or y for
the correspondence in question. My initial examination of the cognates
included in this study showed the appearance of these three sounds as
seemingly reflecting a variety of consonants. They appeared in the position of what should have otherwise been occupied by regular reflexes.
For instance, Itw. shows an h occasionally where b, g, l, r would be
expected, or Is. shows h or y where l would be expected, or the $ʔ$ appears where k, b, t, g, s, y would be expected in Tag. Further study
however resulted in this hypothesis of substitution, for it seemed incredulous that $ʔ$, h, or y could be correspondences of at times more
than three different protophonemes in a language, aside from being the
regular reflexes of *$ʔ$, *h, and *y respectively.

The data shows evidence of the sporadic appearances of these three

sounds in all the Philippine languages. In fact, the automatic ʔ before initial vowels in these languages, which is the result of the
structural pressure of CVC, supports this hypothesis of substitution.
Some languages in fact show variants with *h* or ʔ or *h* or *y*, which point
to the instability of these sounds, i.e., Itw. ʔiyúŋ/ʔihúŋ < *ʔaʔrúŋ
"nose", Tag. *hatsíŋ/ʔatsíŋ* < **baksén* "sneeze", Akl. *huyʔáb/kúyʔab* <
*lúŋkab "yawn" (with metathesis in the last variant). To my mind,
this supports the theory of the use of ʔ, *h*, and *y* as substitutes for
complete loss of sounds, which may be due to the speakers uncertainty.
Probably it would be better to attribute this phenomenon to the transition between the use of the correspondence and its loss.[8]

The 29 Philippine languages may be grouped into four, according
to the sounds they use for substitution:

I   ʔ, *h*, *y*   Tag., Iba., Itw., Is., Nag., Vir., Sub., Yak.,
                  Bag., Buk., Bah.

II   ʔ, *h*   War., Bla.

III   ʔ, *y*   Kap., Png., Ilk., Ibg., Kal., Bon., Igt., Kam.,
                  Tbw., Agt.

IV   ʔ   Mar.

The **d* in **dáʔmug* "dew" which is Akl. *hámʔug*, Bah. *dámhug*, Tag.,
Buk. *hamíg*, Tau. *dámug*, Bag. *dámɔw*, Sub. *gámug*, Nag., Seb. *yamíg*, Iba.
yámug, Ilk. ʔámug, Igt. ʔamíg, Bla. ʔámuʔ, Mar. *námog*, Buh. *namíg* is an
excellent illustration for this hypothesis. Buh., Tau., and Bag. show
a regular correspondence to **d*. Assimilation was also responsible for
the replacement of *d* by *n* in Mar. and Buh., due to the influence of the
following *m*. It is in the rest of the languages where we see substitution at work. The *d-* is substituted for by *h* in Akl. by *y* in Nag., Seb.
and Iba., by ʔ in Ilk., Agt., and Bla. In Sub. the ʔ, which resulted
from this process, was lost on affixation of *g-*, part of a noun marker
in this language. Another example is **luŋkáb* "yawn", where most of the
languages show a correspondence to the **l*. But Iba. ʔuŋáb and Tbw.

ʔuʔŋáb, Kap. ʔúyab, Itb. ʔahwáb have a ʔ; Vir. hágab, Seb., Akl. húyʔab,
Nag. hákay have h. It should also be noted that n > y in Kap. ʔúyab
and Seb., Akl. húyʔab.

In summary, I will repeat the two proposals I set forth in this
paper. The first is that the aberrances found in the cognates in the
different Philippine languages can be explained by taking vowels and
consonants as having certain shared phonetic features. This hypothesis
resulted in a Proto-Philippine sound system which consists of a reasonable number of protophonemes. The second proposal is the introduction
of the process of substitution to account for the sporadic and wide-
spread appearance of ʔ, h, and y in a number of correspondence sets.
In my opinion, this process supports the hypothesis that these sounds
were used to substitute for regular correspondences which were in the
process of being dropped or lost.

NOTES:

1) This paper is one of the results of the research project enti-
tled "Proto-Philippine Roots" which was supported by a grant from the
Social Sciences Research Council of the University of the Philippines.
The data gathered for this research consists of over 2,000 cognate sets
from 35 Philippine languages.

2) The languages included in this study are Tagalog (Tag.), Kapang-
pangan (Kap.), Iba Zambal (Iba.), Panggasinan (Png.), Ilukano (Ilk.),
Itbayaten (Itb.), Itawis (Itw.), Ibanag (Ibg.), Isinai (Is.), Kalingga
(Kal.), Bontok (Bon.), Ilongot (Igt.), Naga (Nag.), Virac (Vir.), Kama-
lignon (Kam.), Waray (War.), Sebuano (Seb.), Aklanon (Akl.), Buhi (Buh),
Tagbanwa (Tbw.), Agutaynen (Agt.), Maranaw (Mar.), Tausug (Tau.), Suba-
non (Sub.), Yakan (Yak.), Blaan (Bla.), Bagobo (Bag.), Bukidnon (Buk.),
and Bahi Manobo (Bah.).

3) An earlier research similar to this one, which I conducted on a
smaller scale, "The Sentence Pattern of 26 Philippine Languages" by Constantino (1965), "A Comparative Word-list" by Lopez (1974), along with
the knowledge I acquired of quite a number of Philippine languages which
I worked on during field research in collaboration with Constantino's
extensive research project "Archives of Philippine Languages and Dialects" and "A Structural Comparison of Philippine Languages", helped me
in deciding which languages would show enough differences to establish
their distinction, and what characteristics to look for in selecting
the languages for this comparative work. Efforts were also made to select representative languages from all parts of the Philippines.

4) In my opinion, these are hardly reliable sources for comparative work because the compilers were foreigners who where most likely
influenced or were confined by the orthography and phonological systems of their own languages.

5) As a result of the application of the comparative method to
Philippine languages, the protophonemes emerged as seen in the following chart:

Vowels: i   u

                              ə

                              a

Consonants: p   t   k   ?

                   b   d   ḍ   g̱   g

                               s   h

                   m   n   ŋ

                        l   ḷ

                        r

                   w   y

Diphthongs: ay   uy   əy   aw   əw

Stress: /'/

6) This brings to mind the theory of Chomsky and Halle (1968) on
assigning features to consonants which were previously used exclusively
to characterize vowels. That is, vowels and consonants were taken to
share common features of tongue position and height. In this way the
vowels i, u, and consonants c, k, t^y, t^w were assigned the common feature [high]. On the other hand, u, o, $ɔ$, a, k, q, h, t^w, t were all
considered as sharing the feature [back].

7) He states "If we were not concerned with economy, we could be
content with reconstructing as many phonemes for the protolanguage as
there are sets of corresponding phonemes in the daughter languages --
a frequently criticized flaw in poor comparative work...economy is an
avowed goal of phonemic analysis (however controversial the means of
achieving it may be). It is the same in comparative work...".

8) There is a slight modification to this process in Is., when it
comes to the substitution of a consonant by h. In this language the h,
which comes about as a result of substitution, becomes ɦ, voiced glottal fricative, when occurring in certain positions. These positions

are final, before consonants, and before an a, as in *bígnat "relapse"
> buĥát, *púnsəg "navel" > púsoĥ, *tindég "stand" > ta?dóĥ.

REFERENCES:

Abrams, Norman. 1963. "Historical Development of Bilaan Vowels and
    Some Consonant Reflexes in Bilaan and Related Dialects", Philip-
    pine Sociological Review II (1-2).147-54.
Blake, Frank R. 1906. "Contributions to Comparative Philippine Gram-
    mar", JAOS 27.317-96.
Blake, Frank R. 1907. "Contributions to Comparative Philippine Gram-
    mar II", JAOS 28.199-233.
Bloomfield, Leonard. 1933. Language. New York: Henry Holt.
Capell, Arthur. 1964. "Verbal Systems in Philippine Languages", Phil-
    ippine Journal of Science 93.231-49.
Chretien, Douglas. 1961. "A Classification of Twenty-one Philippine
    Languages", Philippine Journal of Science 91.485-506.
Conant, Carlos E. 1908. "'F' and 'V' in Philippine Languages," Bureau
    of Science, Division of Ethnology Publications, vol. 5, part 2,
    pp. 135-41. Manila: Bureau of Printing.
Conant, Carlos E. 1911. "The RGH Law in Philippine Languages", JAOS
    30.70-85.
Conant, Carlos E. 1912. "The Pepet Law in Philippine Languages", An-
    thropos 7.920-47.
Conant, Carlos E. 1915. "Grammatical Notes on the Isinai Language
    (Philippines)", JAOS 35.289-92.
Conant, Carlos E. 1916. "Indonesian 'i' in Philippine Languages",
    JAOS 36.181-96.
Constantino, Ernesto. 1965. "The Sentence Patterns of Twenty-six
    Philippine Languages", Lingua 15.71-124.
Constantino, Ernesto, Paz, Consuelo, and Posoncuy, Marietta N. 1967.
    "The Personal Pronouns of Tagalog, Ilukano, Isinai and Kapangpan-
    gan", in M. Zamora, ed., Studies in Philippine Anthropology (in
    Honor of H. Otley Beyer), pp. 567-91.
Constantino, Ernesto. 1970. "The Deep Structure of the Philippine Lan-
    guages", The Archive 1 (2) 65-80.
Costenoble, H. 1937. "Monosyllabic Roots in Philippine Languages",
    Philippine Magazine 34 (2) 76, 82, 84, 86.
Costenoble, H. 1937. "Tracing the Original Sounds in the Languages of
    Today", Philippine Magazine 34.24, 38-39.
Dempwolff, Otto. 1926. "Ivatan als 'Test-Sprache' für Uraustronesi-
    schen L", Zeitschrift für Eingeborenen-Sprachen 16.298-302.
Dempwolff, Otto. 1934-38. Vergleichende Lautlehre des austronesischen
    Wortschatzes, Beihefte zur ZES. 15, 17, 19.
Dyen, Isidore. 1947. "The Malayo-Polynesian Word for 'two'", Language
    23.50-55.
Dyen, Isidore. 1947. "The Tagalog Reflexes of Malayo Polynesian D",
    Language 23.227-38.

Dyen, Isidore. 1965. *A Lexicostatistical Classification of the Aus-tronesian Languages (= IJAL, vol. 31, Supplement).*
Dyen, Isidore. 1969. "Reconstruction, the Comparative Method and the Proto-language Uniformity Assumption", *Language* 45.499–518.
Dyen, Isidore. 1973. "Tagalog Reflexes of Proto-Austronesian L", in *Parangal kay Cecilio Lopez (= Philippine Journal of Linguistics, Special Monograph Issue 4)*, pp. 3–7.
Elkins, Richard E. 1957. *Partial Neutralization of PMP Reflexes in Western Bukidnon Manobo.* Fargo, N.D.: University of North Dakota, SIL.
Hockett, Charles F. 1958. *A Course in Modern Linguistics.* New York: The MacMillan Co.
Hoenigswald, Henry M. 1950. "The Principal Step in Comparative Gram-mar", *Language* 26.357–64.
Llamson, Teodoro A. 1966. "The Subgrouping of Philippine Languages", *Philippine Sociological Review* 14.145–50.
Llamson, Teodoro A. 1966. "Tagalog Reflexes of PMP *e", *Anthropolo-gical Linguistics* 8.13–23.
Llamson, Teodoro A. 1969. *A Sub-grouping of Nine Philippine Languages.* The Hague. Martiners Nijhof. xi, 128.
Lopez, Cecilio. 1939. *Studies on Dempwolff's Vergleichende Lautlehre des austronesischen Wortschatzes (= Publications of the Institute of National Language, Bulletin no. 1).* Manila.
Lopez, Cecilio. 1965. "Contributions to a Comparative Philippine Syn-tax", *Lingua* 15.3–16.
Lopez, Cecilio. 1970. "Some New Morphemes in Philippine Languages", *The Archive* 1 (1) 5–32.
Lopez, Cecilio. 1974. *A Comparative Philippine Word-list (= The Ar-chive, Special Monograph Issue No. 1).*
Newell, Leonard E. 1953. "Some Sound Correspondences in Six Philippine Languages", *Asian Folklore Studies* 12.105–07.
Paz, Consuelo J. 1974. *An Appraisal of Historical Studies Made on Phi-lippine Languages.* MS.
Reid, Lawrence. 1974. "Kankanay and the Problem *R and *L Reflexes", in *Parangal kay Cecilio Lopez (= Philippine Journal of Linguistics, Special Monograph issue 4)*, pp. 51–63.
Thomas, David and Healy, Alan. 1962. "Some Philippine Language Sub-groupings: A Lexicostatistical Study", *Anthropological Linguis-tics* 4.21–33.
Viray, Felixberto B. 1941. "Prenasalization in Philippine Languages", *Philippine Social Science Review* 13.119–47.

HISTORICAL ANALOGY AND THE PEIRCEAN CATEGORIES

IRMENGARD RAUCH
University of Illinois

I

"Nothing shows quite so clearly that 'language is a form of life' as does our recourse to analogous expressions." This sort of statement implies that analogy, the topic to be discussed in the present paper, is user-oriented and as such the statement could be found in a current linguistics book concerned with pragmatics or with sociolinguistic factors in language change. This provocative statement, however, comes from the field of philosophy (David Burrell, *Analogy and Philosophical Language*, New Haven, 1971, p. 274), which refreshes our memory to the fact that the burden of understanding linguistic analogy resided originally with other disciplines, preeminently philosophy, and later, also psychology. In linguistics, analogy is one of the concepts which evolved out of the golden era of the comparative method in the early nineteenth century, and which found strong confirmation in its assignment as a corollary to the Neogrammarian Hypothesis later in that century. Thus, we witness, for example, Whitney's early use of Aristotle's four-part geometric proportion in discussing the analogy of the preterite to the preterite participle in the case of English *sung* (*Language and the Study of Language*, New York, 1867), as well as Fick's somewhat visceral attack on what he calls the "Mode- und Kinderkrankheit der Analogisterei" (*Göttinger gelehrte Anzeigen*, 1883, p. 583), notwithstanding the fact that he himself employs analogy in his work.

Interestingly, a century later the analogy controversy is once again in the limelight of linguistic method. Perhaps it is singled out as one of the high priority casualties in the current wave of anti-transformationalism. However, one cannot help but get the impression that the controversy of the preceding century was never even provisionally resolved with regard to analogy, and that, in fact, from 1876 (the Leskien/Brugmann dictum) to the present, analogy simply hobbled along rather aimlessly, by and large under the aegis of sound change.

The question of all or none, that is, outright acceptance or rejection of analogy again appears to characterize the present analogy controversy, but its implications are extremely sophisticated. Thus, we read, for example, in Anttila (*An Introduction to Historical and Comparative Linguistics*, New York, 1972, p. 180), that "The different mechanisms of change share a common analogical core", as though in apparent contrast with King's (*Historical Linguistics and Generative Grammar*, Englewood Cliffs, 1969, p. 128) assertion: "As historical linguistics is treated in generative grammar, grammar is enough:...'analogy' is grammar change". To be sure, the aim of both quotations is radically different, but it is equally true that in both positions analogy is generalized as integral to grammar. And this is the line of thinking which ought to be exploited. It does not imply that we should not pursue those questions, frequently posing binary possibilities and often hearkening back to the first analogy controversy. For example: Is analogy a primary or a secondary process? Does it belong to competence or performance? Is it sporadic or is it regular in every component of the grammar? Nor does this line of thinking imply that we might ignore the valuable results peculiar to competing methodologies. It *does*, however, stress that we might *also* seek to raise novel questions, perhaps even shift the axis of our study with regard to analogy. This is why viewing the Anttila/King citations as a synthesis, rather than as an opposition may be fruitful. For the same reason, it is worthwhile to observe that Henning Andersen, in his presentation to the First International

Conference on Historical Linguistics (Edinburgh, 1973), assimilated
analogical changes into his "Typology of Change" without the use
of the word "analogy" or its congeners. Thus, for example, he types
the case of Middle English *cheri*, a paradigm sample of analogy, as a
"deductive innovation". Can Andersen therefore be accused of rejecting
analogy, or of equating analogical change with sound change? The answer is unequivocally in the negative, and we are reminded that yet
another approach to analogy may be the acceptance of the implicit use
of the concept in research, without insistence upon an explicit definition, a technique familiar to the linguist with regard to the concept
"sentence", or to the physicist with regard to the concept "atom".

II

In the present paper, linguistic analogy is approached by recourse
to, or in this case historically speaking, reversion to another discipline, namely philosophy, and specifically Peircean philosophy. Two
cases of linguistic change serve as the test cases, the first chosen
because it is prehistoric and morphosemantic, the second because it is
historical and phonological. Since these changes, namely the evolution
of the Indo-European perfect tense and the development of the Old High
German diphthong /eo/ in South Rhenish Franconian, are completed changes
in familiar languages with plentiful data, against a background of known
external history, they are ideal for extracting analogical elements.

Recently, Kuryłowicz (*The Inflectional Categories of Indo-European*,
Heidelberg, 1964) and Meid (*Das germanische Präteritum*, Innsbruck, 1971)
have developed intricate hypotheses concerning the evolution of the perfect tense in Indo-European from a verbal adjective in analogy to the
present active system, not only in analogy to the completed system but
also in analogy to the stages of its development. The earliest active
indicative of both present and aorist stems are tenseless, moodless in-
junctives with secondary endings. The minus tense, minus mood injunctive of the present stem builds a present tense by means of an *i*-suffix,

thus producing the opposition *root plus i* (present) versus *root plus zero* (non-present), the latter form signalling the emergence of the imperfect tense. In some Indo-European languages the function of the *root plus zero* form is taken over by an *e-augment plus root* form, thus yielding a three-way opposition in which the bare root is again minus tense but now plus mood. Analogously the perfective stems of the active system take on an *e*-augment yielding a two-way opposition, since a present from by *root plus i-suffix* is impossible according to the rules of natural semantics.

Now, the emergence of the perfect tense emulates the development of the present active system, which has just been described. The proto-perfect form is semantically a medial present or a medial aorist, distinguished purely lexically in its earliest stage. We note immediately that, parallel to the active present and the active aorist, medial here becomes correlated with perfect, so that the category perfect impresses less as an aspect than as a voice. As stated above, the primeval form of the perfect is a verbal adjective; it is in either of the two ablauts, *-e* or *-o*, and combines the meanings of the three aspects imperfective, state, perfective. Parallel to the history of the active, the proto-perfect restructures itself by splitting off a new present stem in *-i* with medial stative meaning, while the original perfect form in *-e* or *-o* ablaut now serves only to signal the secondary meaning of an old perfect, still reflected for example in the history of some preterite-present verbs, namely in tenseless, intensive, iterative features. The earliest form of this intensive, iterative, medial perfect is again injunctive. This injunctive develops further by splitting off a new medial present by means of a dental suffix, thus *t* plus *o* plus *i*, and secondly by retaining its own meaning, either through a parallel form in dental, thus *t* plus *o*, or through the original bare stem in *-e*.

This original bare stem in *-e* is the form leading to the perfect in the historical languages. It is incorporated into the verb conjugation by a set of personal endings and by alternation of the root ablaut (root accent in the singular, suffix accent in the plural and dual) in

analogy to the conjugation of the present active system. These phonological and morphological analogies to the present active system are
claimed to induce semantic analogy, whereby we witness the metamorpho-
sis in which the perfect, originally medial and tenseless, comes to
signal past tense by changing from a medial to an active, that is, by
assuming also the voice of the present active. The intermediate semantic step is considered to be the "resultative perfect", in which the
verb exerts its effect not on the subject as in the case of the medial,
but on the object as is found in transitive relationship. Consequently
the perfect, which had represented a present medial state resulting
from past action, with the change from medial to active concomitantly
favors the feature *completion of the action* over the feature *present*,
thus signalling past tense.

The phonological-morphological analogies posited for the split of
the perfect into the present passive and the perfect active seem fairly
clear and plausible. However, it does not seem reasonable to view the
semantic change from medial to active as an automatic consequence of
these formal paradigm analogies. The semantic change can be reconstructed by a series of independent analogies or correlations somewhat parallel to, for example, the case of "sell" in Contemporary English. The
middle or quasi-passive occurs in such a sentence as "The house sells
well". This correlates with the outright passive in the sentence
"The house is being sold". In the last instance "sold" is a transitive
which accordingly correlates with "sell" in the active sentence "He
sells the house". Thus, an intransitive correlates with the passive
of a transitive, a passive correlates with an active, thereby an intransitive correlates with an active; consider also "appears, is seen,
sees" and many similar sets.

In linguistics we would hold these phonological, morphological,
and semantic analogies all to be of the same type, in this case specifically, the motivation of the verbal adjective (the proto-perfect)
into a verb conjugation according to the rules of the present active
verb conjugation, and the motivation of the medial to an active whether

as a result of those analogies in form and their semantic similarities,
or due to the semantic analogy of the medial with both the passive and
the active. However, the semiotic model of Peirce allows us to distinguish at least two different types of analogy at work here. The first
type is represented by the phonological and morphological analogies,
for example, the factual similarity of the endings, as well as by any
semantic analogies which share like features, for example the factual
similarity of semantic simultaneity (durativity-state) between the present and the perfect paradigm. These are all iconic analogies which
are motivated through the *possible* rules in the grammar. The simple
correlations of the medial with the passive and the active likewise
represent iconic analogy, but only superficially. If we go a step
further to uncover the strategy underlying those correlations, we find
that the crux of the relationships resides in the indexical analogy between the active and passive, which is motivated through a *necessary*
rule in the grammar. This means that the correlation between the active and passive proceeds from the inference that the category passive
has existence only because of the existence of the active, that is,
they are in mutual dependency. In effect then, we arrive at the startling conclusion that it is ultimately not factual similarity of any
sort between the present active and the perfect systems, but it is
rather the factual contiguity between the active and passive, whereby
one is meaningless without the other, that activates the perfect paradigm. Perhaps equally startling here is the realization that the indexical principle deals a severe blow to the reality of the unambiguous
primordial linguistic form.

A similar dynamic can be uncovered in the analogies posited for
the second case of linguistic change chosen for this paper, namely, the
historical development of the Old High German diphthong /eo/ in So. Rhenish Franconian. The data for South Rhenish Franconian come in the main
from the well-known Otfrid who is credited with introducing end-line
rhyme into Germanic verse. Recently, van Coetsem ("Generality in Language Change: The Case of the Old High German Vowel Shift", *Lingua*,

1975) has brought back into prominence the early merger of Old High German /eo/ from *eu and Old High German /ie/ from *ē₂ into South Rhenish Franconian /ia/. The three major dialects of Otfrid's time keep these diphthongs distinct. A raising principle operates in all Old High German dialects, though at differing intervals, whereby the first element of all diphthongs is raised. But for /iu/ and Early Old High German /eo/, the Old High German diphthongs can be assigned to one of two sets: a set of opening diphthongs (*ie*, *uo*) or a set of closing diphthongs (*ei*, *ou*). When Early Old High German /eo/ was influenced by the general raising rule of the first element of the diphthong, it joined the set of opening diphthongs. In two of the major dialects, Old Alemannic and Old Bavarian, a rule lowering the second element of the opening diphthongs is in effect, thus yielding *ea*, *oa*, since it operates prior to the raising rule. However, in neither of these two dialects, nor in the third principal dialect, Old Franconian, is Early Old High German /eo/ changed by this lowering rule. Consequently, when /eo/ becomes /ia/ in Otfrid's South Rhenish Franconian, it is explained as orthographic analogy to Old Alemannic /ia/ from *ē₂, bordering to the South, or as a combination of phonological analogies to the Old Alemannic early lowering of the second element of opening diphthongs (*ea*, *oa*) and to the Old Franconian early general raising of the first element of diphthongs, bordering to the North, or as an indigenous union.

In Peircean terms these analogies are again purely iconic, mirroring the orthographic or phonological processes of neighboring dialects. Otfrid, however, gives evidence of another type of analogy at work. Besides introducing end-line rhyme, Otfrid is credited with other rhythmic conventions such as the insertion of metrical accents and subscript dots to mark vowel elision; he made use of acrostics, and he also rhymed vowels word-initially, that is, he made use of vowel harmony, either at least to some extent or at some time in his history.

This last convention, rhyme within a word as well as rhyme between words, is often adduced as evidence for the merger of Old High German /eo/ with Old High German /ie/ in South Rhenish Franconian. However,

if we view rhyme not just as an iconic analogy, that is factually similar in sound, but as an indexical analogy, the rhyme pairs assume teleological significance, acting more as a cause than as after-the-fact
evidence. This means that, for example, the *ia* of *gibiatan* "to order"
from /eo/ or of *miata* "reward" from $*\bar{e}_2$ is induced by vowel harmony
with the following a in each word, and that, for example, the *ia* of
the rhyme pair *riaf* : *sliaf* "it called : he slept" from /eo/ and $*\bar{e}_2$
respectively, induce each other. The development of the merger of Old
High German /eo/ with /ie/ in South Rhenish Franconian is then motivated, at least in part, by an analogical strategy wherein a necessary
relation or factual contiguity unites two elements.

III

We have seen in the above two cases of linguistic change that the
Peircean distinctions of index and icon which obtain between the sign
and its object allow us to treat linguistic analogies as discrete relational strategies, rather than as unmotivated generalizers. Peirce's
icon, index, and the third member of this semiotic triad, symbol, derive directly from his three pervasive elements or categories inherent
in all phenomena, namely Firstness, Secondness, and Thirdness. Particularly fascinating in the two linguistic changes are the indexical analogical relationships which represent the phenomenological category Secondness. They have been pinpointed as the mechanism of change, because
they represent necessity, existence, what Peirce calls "blind compulsion" or "associational compulsion" (*Collected Works of Charles Sanders
Peirce*, Cambridge, 1932, par. 305-06), which evolves from "otherness"
(1931, par. 296), that is, existence through necessary relationship
with something else.

This lends certainty to historical analogy and to analogy in general. It is precisely this certainty which can contribute to the long
sought *predictability factor* for analogy as a part of linguistics, and

accordingly of science, since in the words of Wells ("De Saussure's System of Linguistics", *Word*, 1947, p. 24), "When it [linguistics] becomes predictive not only of the past but also of the future, linguistics will have attained the inner circle of science". In terms of Kuryłowicz' well-known simile of analogy to the rain which is not inevitable, but whose paths are predictable once it does rain ("La nature des procès dits 'analogiques'", *Acta Linguistica*, 1949), indexical analogies contain predictability. The fact that rainwater will seek its lowest point is indexical, compulsory, just as the fact that grammatical voices as well as rhymes of rhyme pairs necessarily engender one another.

THE PIE WORD ORDER CONTROVERSY
AND WORD ORDER IN LITHUANIAN*

JANINE K. REKLAITIS
University of Illinois at Chicago Circle

Was word order free in PIE? Few would deny that more than one order can be reconstructed for Proto-Indo-European. Independent documentation confirming several positions, most often SOV, VSO, and SVO, can be found in earlier as well as more recent studies. This variation, which occurs in languages such as Sanskrit (Staal 1967 with citations of previous works) and Greek (Friedrich 1975 with citations of previous works), is taken to reflect similar mobility in the sentence structure of PIE. At the same time, it is clearly recognized that the six theoretically possible permutations (SOV, VSO, SVO, OSV, OVS, VOS) do not appear with equal frequency. On the contrary, it is assumed that some of these orders are very infrequent. Evidence for just this kind of skewed distribution has been tabulated, e.g., for Homeric Greek by Friedrich. Nor does anyone claim that "free word order" implies that all elements are free to occupy any position in the sentence. Indeed recognition of restrictions in constituent order and of the tendency for certain kinds of patterns to appear together has become the primary argument, the source of the criteria used, in establishing word order for PIE. Yet despite the fact that recent investigations along these lines start with the same basic set of criteria, Greenberg's (1973) typological principles, different conclusions have been reached.

In 1975 there existed three candidates for PIE word order: SOV (Lehmann 1974), SVO (Friedrich 1975), and VSO (Miller 1975). In 1976

these positions were reviewed, but the impasse persisted. A somewhat
different line of investigation prompted Jeffers (1976:147) to list new
evidence in support of the SVO hypothesis.[1] Acceptance of a new variable, the role of style, led Watkins (1976:316) to propose a variant of
the SOV hypothesis, namely, reconstruction of both verb final and verb
initial orders, in unmarked and marked functions respectively. Up until this time, the controversy on PIE word order had been limited to
two questions: (a) which of the orders is the unmarked or stylistically neutral order, and (b) which of the orders is the original, the
chronologically earliest order? With the introduction of the presence
of a marked order into the pool of candidates the situation has changed.
In view of the commonly recognized free word status of languages such
as Sanskrit, Greek, Latin, and Lithuanian, one might expect to see in
1977 the positing of free word order for PIE as a tempting alternative
to the current deadlock in opinions. In order to forestall such a possibility but, more seriously, because it is my conviction that a solution to the word order controversy will not be found until the development and interrelationship of all the possible orders is investigated,
the results of such an approach are presented in this paper. First,
some of the problems associated with previous positions are briefly
reviewed; then a clarification of the notion "free word order" is presented from a synchronic perspective -- as it exists in Lithuanian today; finally my hypothesis for PIE word order is outlined.

To begin with, one can search for reasons for the inability of
each newly presented argument to negate previous conclusions, and to
be wholly convincing in itself. Definitely a great part of this inadequacy can be attributed both to the nature of the criteria used and to
the method employed for gathering the evidence. The evidence provided
for the determination of unmarked order is usually of two kinds. First,
statistics from frequency studies on the sentence positions of the verb
and on the order of occurrence of the constituents of certain grammatical patterns deemed relevant are given. Secondly, but to a more tentative and lesser degree, evidence of word order is provided by the iden-

tification of elements and constructions whose predominating presence
is said to be strongly indicative of a specific word order type. For
example, prevalence of prepositions indicates the SVO type, while postpositions indicate SOV. All such elements and patterns, many of them
previously identified by Greenberg, are said to correlate with the dominant position of the verb. The flaw rests in this initial assumption
which searches for consistently correlating patterns in constituent order as a means of defining the one dominant order type. The more investigations of this type that are reported, the more apparent is the lack
of consistency in either the expected synchronic correlations or in the
expected diachronic development (Friedrich 1975; Canale 1976, and see
Konneker's comments, p. 66).

Problems in reported inconsistency of expected correlations are
compounded by failure to yield consistent results on data taken from
one and the same text. Perhaps an even greater problem is lack of agreement on what constitutes an acceptable text for sampling. Uniformity
and neutrality of style seem to be the crucial features.

However, results of the earlier studies which report statistics on
the frequency of occurrence for the possible positions of the verb have
not been systematically classified according to the type of text analyzed, whether poetry or proverbs, expository or narrative prose and on
to finer distinctions of marked style. Only lately has there been a
growing awareness that determination of the extent to which the passage
itself is marked is crucial for the proper interpretation of the statistics. It seems that analysis of patterns from even the same text is no
guarantee of reliable figures, since it can present material which supports opposing views. Thus, Friedrich's data from Homeric Greek was
challenged by Watkins who simply referred to a much earlier study based
"further on in the very same book (5) of the Iliad" that furnished statistics and patterns of a different type (1976:317).

Obviously, such variations in statistics, inconsistencies in patterns, and conflicting figures have been of no help in what had promised to be objective solutions to the problem. To give yet another idea

of the inconclusiveness of the data and to illustrate the fact that
portions could well be selected for substantiating either the SVO position or the SOV position, consider the results for Greek assembled by
Dover (as reported in Friedrich 1975:23). His study of the word order
in Lysias (b. 458) revealed a statistical dominance of OV, but the con-
verse VO dominance in his close contemporary Herodotus (b. 485). On
the other hand, in Plato (b. 427) again the OV order is preferred. The
same holds true for other languages. In the Latin data, Friedrich has
isolated inconsistencies in the writings of Caesar, citing a text with
SVO order in contrast to Caesar's normal use of SOV order (1975:54).
Watkins has identified similar inconsistencies in the prose of Cicero
(1976:314).

In addition to such variations of word order in individual representatives of a language, similar problems have been encountered in
attempts to generalize the word order type of entire languages. Friedrich has designated Classical Armenian as SVO alternating with VSO order. Watkins, however, encountered patterns of the SOV type (also with
VSO in marked functions) in the earliest Armenian texts (1976:314).
Much importance is attached by the supporters of the SOV position to
the evidence from Sanskrit. But Friedrich presents an interpretation
which differs significantly from the usual one. He identifies a drift
from the much weaker SOV patterning in Vedic to the stronger SOV patterning in Classical Sanskrit (1975:33). This he claims is an indication that its OV structure was borrowed from the Dravidian languages,
since it would account for its becoming more prominent later. Had the
SOV order been original, the reversed drift should appear. Some of the
arguments and statistics presented by Friedrich might be rebutted on an
individual basis. Nonetheless in its entirety, because of its scope
and its detail, his monograph presents disturbing challenges to the
most widely accepted view, the traditional Delbrückian view of PIE as
SOV. However, even without the testimony of Friedrich's monograph,
the case for SOV as outlined by Lehmann was itself not convincing. Lehmann's cautious conclusion (1974:25), reflecting his inability, despite

a strong emphasis on the positive evidence, to reach a satisfying solution to the problem of PIE word order, underscores this point. A review of the major flaws in his position (Jeffers 1976) has clearly brought out its hypothetical character.[2]

However, it is unnecessary to continue the list of obstacles in the way of resolving the word order debate. It will suffice to recapitulate them. Attempts at finding the original unmarked order for PIE by frequency studies on some one daughter language have been inconclusive. Also these are often criticized for inadequate length of sample and for the marked nature of text sampled. The major deficiency is that very different patterns apparently can be gleaned from writers of the same era, or even from the same writer. Neither have attempts at finding the original, unmarked order for PIE by seeking a common pattern in the daughter languages been successful, since each major word order type is represented. Insular Celtic is VSO; Albanian, Greek, Romance are VO; Persian, Baltic, Slavic, Germanic are both VO and OV; Indic, Tocharian, Anatolian are OV (Lehmann 1974:450).

Because of the failure of the primary criteria to yield an unassailable verdict on word order, each of the investigators of this issue has relied on supplementary arguments to strengthen his theory. Thus, Friedrich brings in the case from areal geography stressing the fact that the trichotomization of PIE with the SVO languages in the central regions, and the non-rigid SVO and VSO language types in the peripheral regions is precisely the situation one should expect if his candidate SVO is reconstructed as the basic order in the homeland area. Miller uses the case from generative syntax marshalling rules that predict the most natural progression in the evolution of typological structures in just the order outlined by his theory. Lehmann depends on several kinds of arguments to correct or balance out the negative elements in his theory, such as, language contact and borrowing, or language in a state of transition, away from or towards the designated order. Again, none of these have been accepted uncritically. Watkins concentrates on providing an impressive array of SOV features from a number of languages.

He rests his case, however, on what might be called the "most common
denominator argument". He, like Lehmann, adheres to the original Delbrückian hypothesis of SOV as the unmarked sentence structure in PIE.
For confirmation of this position, he turns to the essence of the comparative method for reconstructing syntax. By isolating sentences from
Hittite, Vedic, and Greek which are parallel in structure and in cultural content, he offers almost a classic set of cognates in syntactic
form and meaning (1976:314-15). He sums up his proof thus: "That is
how you said that sort of thing in Hittite, Vedic and Archaic Greek.
The syntactic agreements are so striking and so precise, that we have
little choice but to assume the way you said that sort of thing in Indo-
European could not have been very different" (1976:315). Well, interestingly, that is still the way you can say that sort of thing in Lithuanian today. Compare just one example he gives from Sanskrit (1976:
314) with its analogue in the word order of Lithuanian today:

Sanskrit:	*sa*	*yo*	*na*	*ujjeṣyati*	*sa*	
	(ptc.-)he	who	of us	will-win	(ptc.-)he	
	prathamah		*somasya*	*pāsyati*	(AB 2.25.1)	
	first		of the soma	will-drink		

Lithuanian:	*tas*	*kas*	*iš*	*mūsų*	*laimės,*	*tas*
	he	who	of	us	will-win,	he
	pirmas	*somos*	*gers.*			
	first	of the soma	will-drink.			

At first glance the sentences cited by Watkins (not repeated here) and
the counterparts it is possible to provide in regards to word order
from Lithuanian may appear to offer independent evidence from four separate IE branches for the reconstruction of the parent language as the
SOV type. But it must be remembered that this type of sequence is not
the only order in Lithuanian, nor is it the only order that appears in
languages like Greek and Sanskrit.[3] Even if his set is accepted as

proving that this was the most common way, the question remains at
what stage of PIE was this order most prevalent? No one denies the
existence of SOV as an order at some stage of PIE. The debate centers around whether it was the original one. At least, as noted at
the outset, Watkins explicitly incorporates one of the other orders
in his conclusions. Relying on the results of Dressler 1969, he holds
that reconstruction of a single word order is unsupportable and that
both SOV and a marked VSO order must be reconstructed for the parent.
Yet this falls short of being a satisfying solution for a number of
reasons. While granting the marked status of the verb-initial order,
it does not take into account nor seek to explain the presence of various other orders that occur. Its characterization of the marked
function of the verb-initial order as indicating emphasis is incomplete as will be shown later. Finally, in no way does it invalidate
or countermand the many VO features amassed by Friedrich.[4] Though
recognized initially, at the end these are passed over in silence.
While his lengthy exposition did not serve to clinch the case for SOV,
Watkins' forthright remarks on the inadequacy of the typologically
based syntactic framework certainly have paved the way for a more productive approach to this whole issue. In calling for research to establish which variants of word order were stylistically possible for
PIE, he points to but does not capitalize on the means for resolving
the "pseudo-problem". Most of the major investigators actually have
taken the function of word order as a marker of stylistic differences
into consideration. Ordinarily most accounts leave it on the periphery.[5] No systematic analysis of the other possible word order permutations exists. In the final section, my preliminary work in this
direction will be reported.

However, to dispel any remaining doubt on the futility of seeking
a final solution to the PIE word order problem within the confines of
the standard approach, some very general results from its application
in Lithuanian can be summarized. Since verb final position has remained an acceptable order in Lithuanian, and since additionally a

goodly number of other features consistent with this type (such as
preposed adjectives, genitives, adverbs) are standard, Lithuanian is
usually listed in support of the SOV hypothesis. On the other hand,
no one seems to have really looked at the raw data. Friedrich refers
to Berneker's description of Lithuanian as strongly OV. Yet Berneker
also mentions that SVO order is nearly as frequent as SOV, and that
VSO is less common than the others (1900:56). However, Berneker himself does no more than list several examples (borrowed from Schleicher
at that) of each sentence type. My preliminary survey[6] of Old Lithuanian from Sirvydas (b. 1579?) who is generally considered less prone
to foreign influence yielded the following figures. (Passages in Korsakas 1957:69-75.)

Three Term:	SOV	VSO	SVO	OSV	OVS	VOS
	10	1	27	1	8	1

Two Term:	OV	VS	SV	VO
	24	10	14	32

Combined:	OV	VO	VS
	43	73	12

Is the evidence from Lithuanian of any value at all for a new
theory? After all, it is tempting to interpret the documentation of
OV verb order as archaic and VO order as innovating to fit into the
OV hypothesis, especially since VO is most common today. On the other
hand, some VO features (preposed auxiliaries, negative and interrogative markers) are also present in Old Lithuanian. There is no way to
prove that these were introduced later. In fact such an assumption
would be extremely unlikely because identical features are also found
in some of the earliest attested languages. Rather, once again, this
time as a result of research[7] in Lithuanian, we are confronted by the
same fact: the presence of multiple orders and of disharmonious pat-

terns which makes it nearly impossible to determine the one dominant
order on this basis. It is time to expand the basis of the standard
criteria.

Traditionally, there has been no hesitation in designating the
morphological structure of Lithuanian as archaic. In view of the parallel to at least Sanskrit and Greek in the presence of all the possible orders, it is fair to say that free word order also reflects an
inherited feature in Lithuanian. I suggest that the ability to appreciate the function and status of each of these orders in Lithuanian
synchronically presents the opportunity for a better understanding of
this same kind of fluid structure in the classical languages and by inference for the parent PIE. (I leave aside consideration of Hittite.
Its morphology differs by being simpler, its word order typology also
differs by being unusually consistent.)

What can be said of the stylistic function of each of the possible
word orders in Lithuanian? What is their mutual relationship and individual significance? To begin with, SVO very definitely is the most
common, most natural, that is to say, the unmarked order today. On
the other hand, verb initial order is only common, only natural within
the context of a narrative. In that context, this position is used as
one of the devices for highlighting the dramatic tone, the rapid, in-
tense action being described. To achieve that effect, ordinarily two
term patterns in the sequence VS...V(0)...V are used. Once the subject
or hero has been identified, his exploits are recounted in a series of
subjectless sentences. If the subject needs to be referred to again,
the pronominal form ordinarily occurs. Notice that the verb in this
position cannot be called emphatic in the usual sense. On the contrary,
use of the VS pattern at the very beginning of the narrative introduces
the subject in a very neutral manner (compare "There once lived a man").
He will eventually be defined by his deeds and exploits, presented in a
series of verb-initial sentences. It is rather the entire narrative
structure that is marked, while use of a two term followed by the verb
initial sentences is very common for this type of discourse. Use of

three term patterns would slow down the pace, because it is only in
three term patterns that the emphatic status of some one term is vivid-
ly highlighted. Thus in the VSO order, it is the word in the object
slot that is being emphasized, while in VOS -- a very unusual and rare
order -- it is the subject that is emphasized. But the crucial fact
is that the verb initial position of a regular verb is only acceptable
in narrative discourse. To continue the analysis, the markedness of
the three verb final positions again is simple to describe. By the
OSV pattern, the object is topicalized, put in a position of prominence.
By the OVS pattern, the subject is emphasized. The subject-last pattern is less common than the former. This leaves determination of the
stylistic significance of SOV. In Lithuanian it is difficult to generalize and pinpoint its exact status; therefore it is best described
in relation to the others. It is marked in contrast to SVO since it
is less common and more formal. Yet this is a contrast or opposition
which holds true for the entire pattern. From position alone, unlike
for VSO, VOS, OSV and OVS, it cannot be determined whether the subject
or object is being emphasized. In my judgment, neither is intended to
be emphasized (unless phonological emphasis is added). The entire SOV
sentence is marked in relation to the SVO one. The following table
summarizes this discussion of the significance of the various word orders in Lithuanian.

SVO - verb middle

unmarked, stylistically neutral

V_S_ - verb initial	verb final - _O_V
preferred pattern in narrative where S is usually omitted; other- wise underlined term is somewhat marked	once preferred pattern in formal prose; underlined term is some- what marked
VS_O_ VO_S_	_O_SV OV_S_
underlined term very marked; limited to narratives	underlined term very marked

The question arises whether the general outlines of this tripar-
tite division can also be seen in the free word order system of languages such as Sanskrit and Greek. Only an exhaustive analysis of
their occurrence and function in these languages will supply the answer. What has been supplied here is a framework, abstracted from
Lithuanian, which might lead to the discovery of analogous systems
and their stylistic significance in other languages.

Leaving the synchronic matter to await more detailed analysis,
for instance, in regard to implications of the comparative rarity of
subject-last positions, we return to a proposal for the diachronic issue which has been motivated by this investigation of all the orders.

In the course of this paper it has been argued that there is already sufficient evidence (reviewed earlier) that PIE was neither originally SOV nor ever rigidly SOV to relinquish that assumption. The
conclusion that word order was never rigid has one extremely appeal-
ing feature. With this conclusion, one does not expect rigid correlations. Of course, rigid and consistent correlations have never been
possible. It was appreciation of this very fact which led Watkins to
label this issue a pseudo-problem,[8] and to posit two orders for PIE.

One can now propose a plausible theory for how these and other
orders developed in PIE. It will readily become apparent that the
theory for PIE word order which is to be proposed here is not a radical
departure from the others. It relies on Friedrich's data for the ar-
chaicity of SVO features.[9] It combines the evidence offered by others
on the existence of multiple orders in the earliest texts, with the
fact of the continuous existence of free word order in Lithuanian; and
adds other hypotheses on stages of evolution in PIE to present a variant which makes sense out of otherwise seemingly conflicting data. Its
innovating contribution is in the incorporation of questions of stylistic meaning, and of analysis of the entire word order system rather
than of one candidate.

The earliest structural type that can be discerned for PIE is very
likely an analytic, non-inflected type. Although it is not unanimously

accepted that such a stage predates the one that has been traditionally
reconstructed, evidence for this type has been presented.[10] For instance, in nouns it is found in the bare stems that form the first element of compounds. In verbs, evidence is found in the endingless stems
that function as third singulars. A language of this uninflected type
would rely on SVO order for conveying syntactic relations in a sentence.
In addition, Friedrich's evidence for this order and/or VO features as
relics in Greek, pre-Italic, Tocharian, and Classical Armenian supports
this view. So does the even more widely attested presence of the pre-
verbal positioning of negative and interrogative markers characteristic
of SVO structure. The isolating, uninflected morphological structure
was supplemented by various particles in two complementary functions:
for denoting other grammatical relations and the stylistic differences.
At this stage, then, word order had a syntactic function. If one ac-
cepts that imperative forms originally were indicated by the bare stem
of the verb, then one can also see in the change in position to verb
initial the means for signalling commands. As inflections on nouns and
verbs developed, word order could be adapted to signal style. This introduced the VSO and VOS variants. It is unclear whether these were
from the start limited to marking the narrative style. Development of
a more complex morphology, i.e., a case system, could have permitted
the language to change to an SOV type (Miller 1975:48), or, as seems
more likely, permitted it to adopt verb final order from some other language family. The borrowed SOV order became very prevalent, especially
as an indicator of formal style. In turn its two marked variants, OSV
and OVS, came to be used for marking emphasis within that style. Recently proposed evidence from the types of constructions consistent with
SOV order (Jeffers 1976:147) leads to locating the development of non-
finite verbal forms (participles, gerunds, infinitives) and of the absolute constructions (which make use of such non-finite verbals) some-
time after this stage. The variety found in these constructions fits
in with the notion of their late development (Lehmann 1972:989). The
hypothesis of SOV as the later development also fits in with my analysis

of its general or unrestricted marked status, which sets it apart from
the more precisely limited emphatic functions of the other verb final
variants and allows it to form the true marked opposite of the unmarked
SVO. Moreover, interpreting SOV as the borrowed prestigious order can
also explain its uneven distribution through the daughter languages.
Thus, some of the eastern IE dialects such as Hittite came be be influenced by it entirely. Others, as Sanskrit, were affected more gradually. Most likely Tocharian and Armenian were also strongly prone to its
influence. But the central core, Slavic, Germanic, and Baltic, also
Greek and possibly Italic, retained the original and underlying SVO
structure. In the much later stages of PIE, the morphology became even
more synthetic and cumbersome with its ablaut phenomenon, numerous nominal and verbal classes and inflections. This morphological apparatus
began to desynthesize and rely all the more on the SVO order, patterns,
and structural elements such as prepositions, which had been at hand.
Put differently, the disparity between the underlying SVO and superimposed order types with their constructions and case markings reached a
critical peak. The drift towards simplification, the push towards trans
parency has been in progress ever since.

    Such a scenario of coexisting orders is fully supported by the pre-
sence of all these variants in the early texts of some languages. It
explains in a principled way -- as to chronology and division of function -- what had previously seemed completely free, fluid and indeter-
minate. Yet within this general outline of the relationship of the syntactic and stylistic functions of word order, other similar shifts can
be seen on a smaller scale. These need to be investigated. Particularly intriguing are the particles. The role and even meaning of these
particles has been difficult to decipher, because their use has greatly
diminished in the modern languages. For example, they appear with far
greater frequency in Old Lithuanian texts. Leskien (1919:226) labels a
number of them emphatic and considers them equivalent to some of the
Greek particles. Some of these are still listed in the grammars of
modern Lithuanian, but there is a much weaker comprehension of their

meaning and function. They no longer seem relevant. My hypothesis is that at one time, in the early SVO stage of PIE as already mentioned, one of their primary roles was to mark emphasis. At that stage, in the absence of a very developed case system, word order was necessary for separating the subject from object. While word order had the syntactic function, these particles had a stylistic function.[11] As case markers increased, and possibilities for word order became broader and more flexible, their use greatly declined. This change in the primary means for marking stylistic and syntactic functions has gone through a full cycle in languages that are once again analytic in their structure. When their structure was synthetic, it was used for stylistic effect; now, this is only a marginal function of word order. However, it should be remembered that although there ordinarily is a division in the means used for signalling the syntactic relations versus stylistic differences in language, the two are never mutually exclusive.[12] This duality has to be more closely investigated. It is only through this combination of functions that the very special, not at all rigid word order type of PIE will be better understood.

NOTES:

*Due to restrictions imposed on length, this paper deals with only one of the issues discussed in my presentation at Hamburg.

1) Based on his belief that VSO was innovated in Celtic, Jeffers rejects Miller's position with this statement: "SOV and SVO structure are the only viable candidates for consideration in the reconstruction of the parent language" (1976:140).

2) It is to his credit that Lehmann claims no other status for his position than that of best working hypothesis. He energetically campaigns (e.g., 1975) for additional data from all sources in an attempt to stimulate research on an issue which is far from resolved. This paper was in part motivated by this attitude of Lehmann's as well as Friedrich's comment that "more historical and comparative work on Baltic as a whole is needed" (1975:33).

3) As Staal has stressed, recognition of free word order was customary among the Indian theorists. It was the Western Sanskritists who rejecting the idea looked for certain preferential arrangements and treated others as exceptions (1976:60).

4) Although Watkins presents a large body of additional evidence of OV features in individual IE languages, the VO features compiled by Friedrich still stand unquestioned. In fact, in the Greek example given by Watkins, we find a postposed pronominal adjective -- another VO feature (1976:315).

5) But Friedrich in particular takes stylistic differences well into account in his detailed analysis of Homeric Greek. Lehmann too gives examples of marked VSO order in Vedic but is not interested in pursuing the marked patterns.

6) Since Watkins has emphasized the importance of word order in archaic utterances, especially in proverbs, the results of a cursory survey of these might also be mentioned. The majority of proverbs (from Senn 1957:17-18) are in SOV order. Some occur in SVO and even OSV. Only proverbs that are similes (with no subject or object) start with a verb, hence, no VSO order occurred. Thus, apparently some of the same kinds of inconsistent patterns and inconclusive data for constituent order that have been documented for other languages will be found to hold for Lithuanian. A full and detailed investigation on the order of the verb and other relevant grammatical constructions is in progress. Results will be reported at the AATSEEL meeting, Chicago, December, 1977.

7) All the orders occur in the Old Lithuanian texts, and all these orders still are possible in modern Lithuanian. In the following table, results from one passage of current prose are given. (Passage from Sluckis 1973:240-42.)

Three Term:	SOV	VSO	SVO	OSV	OVS	VOS
	2	1	28	1	2	-

Two Term:	OV	VS	SV	VO
	10	9	11	34

Combined:	OV	VO	VS
	15	73	10

8) I disagree with his assessment of the PIE word order controversy as a "pseudo-problem" with the implication that it is not worth pursuing. If a cogent explanation is not provided, investigations will continue along the typological track. This will forestall progress towards the ultimate goal of diachronic syntax -- reconstruction of PIE grammatical categories. Such a goal was outlined by Lehmann over a decade ago (Lehmann and Malkiel 1968). Ironically it is Lehmann who is responsible for the departure from the traditional, genetically oriented approach towards its attainment.

9) Actually very little of that evidence has been mentioned here. To add one more specific conclusion: "The basic conclusion is that Tocharian did definitely exemplify a SOV type, not rigidly, but rather,

as far to the right as Sanskrit, and that *it may contain certain vestiges of an SVO system*" (emphasis mine).
10) Hodge 1970 holds this view but Szemerényi 1970 believes that an even more synthetic structure preceded. Lehmann in 1958 supported it, in 1974 he discusses PIE with the complex morphology.
11) In general, the means of marking emphasis in languages are very limited. These are primarily by word order, repetition, particles, and the special uses made of certain ordinary constructions (Jones 1977: 1,69).

12) For instance, in French word order has a syntactic function, but preposing versus postposing of the adjective occurs to indicate stylistic and semantic differences (see Waugh 1976).

REFERENCES:

Berneker, Erich. 1900. *Die Wortfolge in den slavischen Sprachen.* Berlin: B. Behr Verlag.
Canale, Michael. 1976. "Implicational Hierarchies of Word Oder Relationships", in W. M. Christie, Jr., ed., *Current Progress in Historical Linguistics.* Pp. 39-69. Amsterdam: North Holland.
Friedrich, Paul. 1975. *Proto-Indo-European Syntax (= Journal of IE Studies Monograph No. 1).* Butte: Montana College of Mineral Science and Technology.
Greenberg, Joseph, ed. 1966. *Universals of Language.* Cambridge: MIT.
Hodge, Carleton T. 1970. "The Linguistic Cycle", *Language Sciences* 13.1-7.
Jeffers, Robert. 1976a. "Typological Shift and Change in Complex Sentence Structure", in S. B. Stever et al., edd., *Papers from the Parasession on Diachronic Syntax.* Pp. 136-49. Chicago: CLS.
Jeffers, Robert. 1976b. Review of W. P. Lehmann, *Proto-Indo-European Syntax, Language* 52.982-88.
Jones, Linda Kay. 1977. *Theme in English Expository Discourse (= Edward Sapir Monograph Series in Language, Culture, and Cognition No. 2).* Lake Bluff: Jupiter Press.
Korsakas, K. et al. 1957. *Lietuvių literatūros istorijos chrestomatija. Feodalizmo epocha.* Vilnius: Mokslų akademija.
Lehmann, Winfred P. 1958. "On Earlier Stages of the IE Nominal Inflection", *Language* 34.179-202.
Lehmann, Winfred P. 1972. "Contemporary Linguistics and Indo-European Studies", *PMLA* 87.976-93.
Lehmann, Winfred P. 1973. "A Structural Principle of Language", *Language* 49.47-66.
Lehmann, Winfred P. 1974. *Proto-Indo-European Syntax.* Austin: University of Texas.
Lehmann, W. P. and Malkiel, Y., edd. 1968. *Directions for Historical Linguistics.* University of Texas.

Lehmann, W. P. and Ratanajoti, U. 1975. "Typological Syntactical
    Characteristics of the Śatapathabrāhmana", *JIES* 3.147-59.
Leskien, A. 1919. *Litauisches Lesebuch mit Grammatik und Wörterbuch.*
    Heidelberg: Carl Winter.
Miller, D. Gary. 1975. "Indo-European: VSO, SOV, SVO or All Three?",
    Lingua 37.31-52.
Senn, Alfred. 1957. *Handbuch der litauischen Sprachen. Band II:
    Lesebuch und Glossar.* Heidelberg: Carl Winter.
Sluckis, Mykolas. 1973. *Adomo obuolys.* 2nd ed. Vilnius: Vaga.
Staal, J. F. 1967. *Word Order in Sanskrit and Universal Grammar.*
    Dordrecht: D. Reidel.
Szemerényi, Oswald. 1970. *Einführung in die vergleichende Sprachwis-
    senschaft.* Darmstadt: Wissenschaftliches Buchgesellschaft.
Watkins, Calvert. 1976. "Towards PIE Syntax: Problems and Pseudo
    Problems", in S. B. Stever et al., edd., *Papers from the Parases-
    sion on Diachronic Syntax.* Pp. 305-26. Chicago: CLS.
Waugh, Linda R. 1976. "The Semantics and Paradigmatics of Word Order",
    Language 52.82-107.

ON THE PROBLEM OF MERGER

KRISTIAN RINGGAARD
University of Århus, Denmark

In Old Scandinavian most of the words were either mono- or dissyl-
labic. Longer words did exist, but not in great number. As far as we
are able to discern now, the syllabic system was over-characterized,
as monosyllables were pronounced with a tonal accent, termed toneme 1,
and words of more than one syllable with another, more complex tonal
accent, termed toneme 2. This coupling of syllabicity and tonemicity
was pure redundancy, but as is well known redundancy has its practical
use.

Shortly after the Viking-period developments took place all over
Scandinavia. The insertion of vowels in final clusters and the use of
postponed definite article without altering the toneme created a lot
of dissyllables with toneme 1. Thus the toneme system lost its redundant function of characterizing the syllabic system, and it became
quite superfluous, not to say meaningless. This may possibly be the
reason why it has disappeared in many not-central areas, as Iceland,
the Faroese Islands, around Bergen, in the extreme north of Norway and
Sweden, in most of the Fenno-Swedish dialects, and in most of the Danish dialects -- Denmark is however a special case, which I shall revert
to later.

But the tonemes persisted in the Scandinavian peninsula. And it
might also be argued that they were *not* quite superfluous, that they
by the new development acquired a new function, which was that of distinguishing dissyllables that would otherwise be homonymous. But re-

garded as a reason for retention of tonemicity the case is very weak, as the number of minimal pairs must have been very little at the time. To be sure it is not possible to make a precise estimate. But for modern Swedish, which in this respect is the most conservative of the Scandinavian languages, C.-C. Elert has made a count of some hundred pairs, in slightly archaic Swedish 350 pairs. Far better use of this new possibility was made later on in Norwegian bokmål. Certain developments like vowel lenition and disappearance of final consonant created a lot of minimal pairs -- M. Kloster Jensen has published a list of 2,400 -- and in Norway this discriminating function is consequently often regarded as the raison d'être of the tonemic system.

Probably not earlier than the 16th century certain dialects of the Scandinavian peninsula began apocopating dissyllables, again without altering the toneme. In this way the discriminating power of the tonemic system was greatly reinforced. In these areas monosyllables may have toneme 1 or toneme 2 (in this case in Scandinavian dialectology termed circumflex), and dissyllables may have toneme 1 or toneme 2. Through the developments of centuries we have thus obtained a full-fledged tonal language.

In Denmark tonal accents have completely disappeared, except for a few dialects. But distributionally corresponding to toneme 1 the greater part of Denmark has the Danish stød. (The articulatory change from toneme to stød is still the object of discussion.) Not always, however, as the stød requires a long, voiced sound. As Danish like Norwegian bokmål has had lenition of unstressed vowels the result has been a fair amount of minimal pairs. Nobody has counted them, but it must be somewhere between the Swedish and the Norwegian number (Otto Jespersen once collected nearly 400 pairs), and it is a moot-question in Danish linguistics, if this discrimination could be said to be the function of the stød in Danish.

The Southern Danish islands, however, do not know the stød, so that every trace of original tonemicity has disappeared and only syllabicity exists.

But Danish also knows of apocope.   In fact it is early in history and widespread.   All dialects of the greater part of Denmark, namely, the peninsula of Jutland, are apocopating, and apocopation started in the 13th century and was carried through consistently during the 14th century.   As certain phonotactic structures did not take the stød in Jutlandish, in contradistinction to island-Danish, this resulted in merger of quite a number of mono- and dissyllables, varying in number from dialect to dialect.   The picture is rather complicated, because although tonemicity has disappeared another relic of older dissylla-bicity has persisted for long and still exists in some dialects.   Apo-copated words with a long sonorous sound were pronounced with a dual stress comparable to the dual tone of the tonal dialects, and therefore termed dynamic circumflex.   This circumflex disappeared during the lat-ter half of the 19th century in Eastern Jutland where the amount of mergers consequently is great.

But the greatest interest is due to the dialects of Southern Jut-land.   These dialects do *not* know the stød, and as mentioned they are all apocopating.   Here exist side by side tonal dialects of an almost East-asiatic character with a vast amount of monosyllables distinguished only by tonemes (and a lesser amount of dissyllables distinguished only by tonemes) -- and dialects where not only tonemicity has disappeared, but also the dynamic circumflex is disappearing, so that a vast amount of words has merged completely.   Moreover the former dialects seem to be losing ground, and the latter to be expanding.

*   *   *

Many linguists seem to be of the opinion that linguistic change really ought not to take place, as it is detrimental to communication. This is especially the case of mergers, as distinctions which existed before now disappear.   To my way of thinking the most curious view is held by those who seem to regard language as a living and thinking body which is able to look into the future, detect the danger of an imminent

merger, and take ingenious steps to prevent it. I could give many
quotations.

Nevertheless it is a fact that mergers do occur. Every student
of language history and dialectology will be able to give lots of examples. Most of these are trivial, affect only a little part of the
vocabulary, and the worst consequence seems to be, that they give rise
to word puns, and that they often are the object of derision from neigh-
bors. But the above example shows that it is possible for almost half
of the vocabulary to merge with the other half.

Other linguists advocate a less strong variant of the view, which
is very clearly put by W. Labov: "It is important to note that in the
course of language evolution, change does go to completion... When
this happens, there is inevitably some other structural change to compensate for the loss of information involved" (1972:223).

It is difficult to argue with this opinion, as it is not easy to
know what structural changes you have to look for in each case. But I
would question the "inevitability" of the "structural changes" as I
have been unable to find any such, both in the trivial cases known to
me and in the whole-scale merger mentioned above. Of course the reason may well be that I have not been looking hard enough, you often
find what you are looking for.

On the other hand also I am convinced that it will always be possible to express a former distinction by some new means, if not by a
structural change, then by a string of explaining words. At least if
it is a vital distinction.

So perhaps the phonological system is not vital enough. After all
there is no "meaning" connected with tonemes or syllabemes as such.
They are phonological means of distinction like every phoneme.

Let us therefore end with a brief look at other parts of the grammar.

The Old Scandinavian case system declined early in Danish, somewhat later in Swedish and Norwegian. Iceland still has a full case system, and in central Scandinavian dialects the dative is still fairly

frequent, while the nominative and the accusative have merged and the genitive is rare. It has been postulated that the decline of the case system was a consequence of the lenition of the unstressed final vowels and that prepositions and word order took over. This might seem to support the views of Labov. But the case systems has declined even in dialects without lenition, the decline began before the lenition, and prepositions and fixed word order existed before. It would then be safer to argue the other way around, that it was possible for the case system to decline because other means of expression had already taken over.

Old Scandinavian had a system of three genders. It is not easy to see nowadays what may have been the function, it cannot very well have been the discrimination of the very few homonyms of different genders. Only in Icelandic is the system still in full use, everywhere else it has degenerated. Standard Danish, Standard Swedish and Norwegian bokmål have two genders. Dialects with three genders are widespread in all three countries, but very frequently there is no full agreement between adjective and noun, three genders in nouns and two genders in adjectives is often found. The gender system may be said to have declined very slowly through the centuries because it no longer had any function whatsoever. --Of particular interest is the dialect of Western Jutland. Here gender has completely disappeared, but the pronouns *den* (former masculine/feminine) and *det* (former neuter) are used, quite regardless of former gender, to express a completely novel distinction, between countables and un-countables. This system seems to have emerged during the 14th or 15th century, and it is very unfortunate that we are unable to follow in details how this complete redefinition expressed by old means came about.

I have argued that mergers do take place, also on a large scale. Of course there must be a limit. In order for communication to function language needs a minimum of discriminating entities, phonemes, tonemes, morphemes, syllabemes, syntagmemes or what have you. I also feel sure that these "emes" for some mental reason are structured and in such a way that changes in one part of the overall system may carry with it changes in another part. But the redundancy of language is everywhere so great that even if one opposition disappears there are almost always enough left. Moreover uncompensating splits are just as frequent as uncompensated mergers.

I have also argued that there is not inevitably some other change to compensate for the loss involved. When there are "compensating" changes, and if there is a causal connection, I am of the opinion that the connection is the other way around. If new means of expressing a distinction have cropped up, older ones may disappear.

I do not believe there is any language planning being done by language itself, nor by the great anonymous body of language users.

To my mind the really interesting thing in language evolution is not the merger. More interesting is the study of how entirely new distinctions emerge, and how redundant and even quite superfluous or meaningless phenomena may linger on for centuries and then suddenly by quite unrelated changes acquire a new function or a new interpretation. --Unfortunately emerging, but not yet quite born distinctions are very difficult to observe as normally you will not see them until they are there.

REFERENCES:

Elert, Claes-Christian. 1971. *Tonality in Swedish* (= *Department of Phonetics Publication No. 2*). Umeå.
Hansen, Aage. 1956. "Kasusudviklingen i dansk", in *Festskrift til Peter Skautrup*. Århus.
Jensen, Martin Kloster. 1958. *Bokmålets tonelagspar ("vippere")*. Universitetet i Bergen. Årbok.
Jespersen, Otto. 1897. "Stød og musikalisk aksent", *Dania* IV.
Labov, William. 1972. *Sociolinguistic Patterns*.
Reinhammer, Maj. 1973. *Om dativ i svenska och norske dialekter. 1. Dativ vid verb.* Uppsala.
Ringgaard, K. 1979. "Når tostavelsesord bliver enstavelses", *Sprog og Kultur* XXI.
Ringgaard, K. 1963. "The Apocope of Dissyllables", *Phonetica* 10.
Willkommen, Dirk. 1977. *Ladelunder Dänisch. Phonologie eines Schleswiger Dialekts.* Dissertation, Kiel.

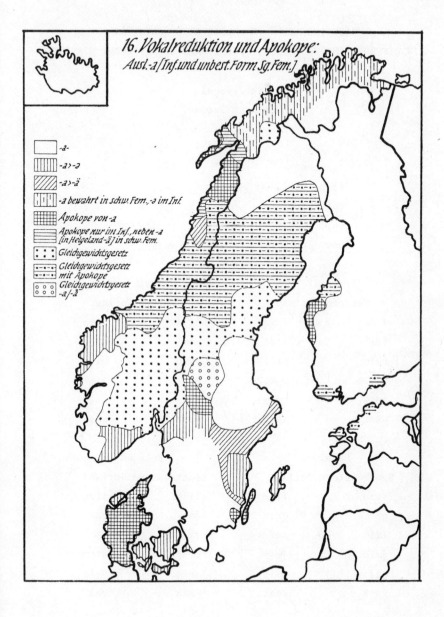

From Oskar Bandle: Die Gliederung des Nordgermanischen. 1973.

DISCRIMINATION OR MERGER BY SYNCOPATION
IN DIFFERENT MORPHOPHONEMIC STRUCTURES IN DIFFERENT DIALECTS

Vendsyssel
Northern Jutland

v:c	ho'r	ho:r
vc:voiced	tåm'	tå:m
vc stop, unv.	sæt	sæ:t
vc voi. c stop unv.	hjælp	hjæ:lp
vc voi., c unv.	hals	ha:ls
vc unv. (c unv.)	wask	wa:sk

Ål — Western Jutland | Houlbjerg — Eastern Jutland

fi'n	^fi:n	fi'n	fi:n
tom'	^tom:	næm'	næm
sæt	sæ?t	mæt	mæt
hjælp	hjæl?p	hjælp	hjælp
hals	hals	hals	hals
wask	wask	wask	wask

Ladelund — Southwestern Jutland | Felsted — Southeastern Jutland

fi:n	fi:n	¹fi:n	²fi:n
gal	gal	¹gal	²gal
læt	læt	¹læt	²læt
jælp	jælp	¹stamp	²stamp
hals	hals	¹hals	²hals
vask	vask	¹vask	²vask

Broad transcription: ' = Danish stød; ? = glottal stop (vestjysak stød). | = merger, ^ = dynamic circumflex, 1, 2 = tonemes 1 and 2.

The table shows the development of different morphophonemic structures in apocopating Jutlandish dialects. The structures are from top to bottom

$$c_o^3 v:c(c), \quad c_o^3 vc:_{voiced}, \quad c_o^3 vc:_{stop,\ unv.}, \quad c_o^3 vc_{voiced}c_{stop,\ unv.},$$

$$c_o^3 vc_{voiced}c_{unv.}, \quad c_o^3 vc_{unv.}(c_{unv.}).$$

In Northern Jutland, original monosyllables and original dissyllables are kept apart by stød and/or by length. In Western Jutland, two structures have merged; the others are kept apart by different means such as stød, dynamic circumflex, glottal stop, length. In Eastern Jutland, four structures have merged, and thus a great part of the vocabulary. In Southeastern Jutland, there is only one means of discrimination, the tonemes. These have disappeared in Southwestern Jutland, resulting in a complete merger of mono- and dissyllables.

THE WORD-AND-PARADIGM MODEL AND LINGUISTIC CHANGE:
THE VERBAL SYSTEM OF OJIBWA

H. CHRISTOPH WOLFART
University of Manitoba

THE LATINATE TRADITION

Hyperbole is hardly a feature one would commonly associate with Bloomfield's scholarly style, yet he seems to have been swayed by the zeitgeist[1] when he wrote, in *Language*, that early travellers and missionaries,

> untrained [as they were] in the recognition of foreign speech
> sounds, could make no accurate record, and, knowing only the
> terminology of Latin grammar, distorted their exposition by
> fitting it into this frame (1933:7).

Linguistic documents of the early modern period undeniably present many difficulties[2] but, as his own successful re-working (1925:130) of Cree and Ojibwa missionary data shows, Bloomfield overstated his case in both respects. Many early records can be salvaged phonologically, and the distortions engendered by the Latin grammatical tradition are no worse, a priori, than those due to other analytical frameworks; indeed, with Algonquian languages at least, classical training appears to have been an advantage rather than a drawback.

Among the more trivial and yet basic precepts of the classical approach to language study is the active use of the language, a condition which traders and missionaries met of necessity. In facing completely novel languages, moreover, the missionaries in particular were far from helpless: the experience of having already learnt and analyzed a second language was an essential feature of their background, with Latin grammar serving as training ground rather than as straitjacket. Some of the results of this laboratory training have fortunately survived,[3] and the Algonquian languages with their complex morphology illustrate quite clearly that the salutary effect of Latin discipline in its breadth far outweighs the isolated cases where its frame has been Procrustean.

It is one of the most prominent aspects of missionary grammars dealing with Algonquian languages that they generally exemplify their inflectional analyses with an abundance of paradigm tables; in one extreme case (Hunter 1875), 14 pages of discourse are followed by 243 pages of paradigms. The inclusion of full, actual paradigms is by no means the least advantage of the Latinate model. It matters little how difficult the transcription or how exotic, occasionally, the theoretical claims, so long as ample actual forms are included which enable the second-hand analyst to verify the claims of the original.

In the verbal system of Ojibwa, for example, there exists a conflict of morphological and syntactic properties which has resulted in several competing analyses and terminologies (cf. Wolfart 1977, especially Table 1). Where full paradigms (ideally including actual stems and explicit glosses) are available, the knot is relatively easy to disentangle; where generalizations of varying succinctness and validity are not, on the other hand, accompanied by the organized data on which they are based and against which they need to be checked, success in this task varies accordingly. In all too many instances it is more difficult to extract adequate and reliable information from the works of modern linguists who fail to include proper documentation than from the paradigm-studded grammars of the missionaries.

OJIBWA TRANSITIVE AND INTRANSITIVE PARADIGMS

The Ojibwa language (known as *Chippewa* in the United States, *Saul-*

teaux in western Canada and by several other regional terms, including *Ottawa* and *Algonquin*) is spoken in an extremely large number of dialects which range from the Montréal area to the western prairies and from the vicinity of Hudson Bay to the shores of Lake Erie (cf. Map 1).

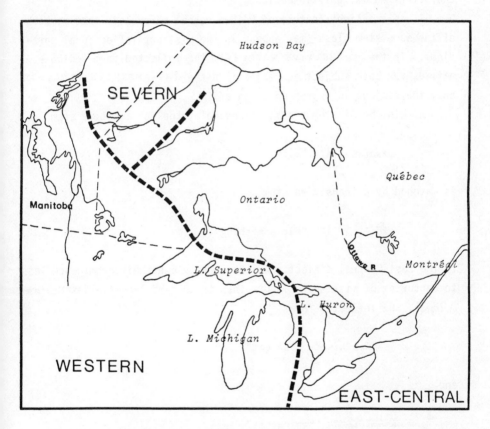

Map 1. Ojibwa dialects: major types and selected local variants.
         Locations in italics are given for orientation only.

The Lower Ottawa Valley, where Jesuits and Recollets wrote the first grammars and dictionaries "de la langue outaouaise et algonquine" (1669) in the mid-17th century, constitutes a temporal and spatial point of

departure for Ojibwa studies. At the opposite extreme, a dialect of
the Severn type was first reported on in 1963 (Rogers 1963), and many
dialects remain completely untouched.

Ojibwa presents a classical case of the highly elaborated morphological structure[4] typical of the Algonquian languages which has been
characterized as "polysynthetic".

It is a salient feature of Ojibwa verbal morphology that members
of the same stem class[5] may appear in two distinct inflectional paradigms. In the TRANSITIVE PARADIGM, the inflected form includes
affixes for both subject and object; in the INTRANSITIVE PARADIGM,
only the subject is expressed by an affix.

Within the AI stem class, for example, the intransitive stem

    wīssini- AI "eat"

is matched by a transitive stem

    mīči-   AI "eat something".

In the East-Central dialects (which probably owe their prominence less
to centuries of missionary labors than to Leonard Bloomfield's *Eastern
Ojibwa*), the inflected forms

    ki-wīssini-min "we eat"

and

    ki-mīči-nān "we eat it"

differ not only semantically and inflectionally but also syntactically:
kimīčinān "we eat it" may be followed by an object complement, e.g.,

    kimīčinān otēhimin "we eat a strawberry";

kiwīssinimin "we eat" never takes an object.

In the transitive form *kimīčinān* the inclusive first person plural is indicated by the prefix *ki-* and the suffix *-nān-*; while there is no overt third person suffix, the plural of the third person category is expressed by the suffix *-in*, e.g.,

> *ki-mīči-nān-in* "we eat them",
> *kimīčinānin otēhiminan* "we eat strawberries".

The intransitive form *kiwīssinimin* expresses only the inclusive first person plural, by *ki-* and *-min*; *-min* is never followed by a third person plural suffix.

The TI class of Ojibwa includes a limited number of cases where the same stem appears in both the transitive and the intransitive paradigm, e.g.,

> *ki-nōnt-ā-nān* "we hear it",
> *ki-nōnt-ā-min* "we hear".

These AMBIVALENT stems are found only in Ojibwa and in Delaware (cf. below).

The morphological distinction between the two paradigms is particularly obvious in those forms where the transitive paradigm shows a third person prefix *o-* (and a suffix *-n-* for the subordinate [or "obviative"] third person), e.g.,

> *o-nōnt-ā-n* "he hears the other";

no prefix appears in the third person forms of the intransitive paradigm, e.g.,

> *nōnt-am* "he hears".

Fuller examples are given in Table 1 which reflects the dialects represented in the earliest documents (notably Anon. 1662) and also Bloomfield's *Eastern Ojibwa*.

STEM CLASS

AI   TI

AI		TI		
[wīssinim]	*["on mange"]*	*nōntām*		indef
niwīssin	*"je mange"*	*ninōntam*		1
kiwīssin	*"tu [manges]"*	*kinōntam*		2
niwīssinimin	*"nous mangeons"*	*ninōntāmin*		1p
kiwīssinimin	*"vous et nous mangeons"*	*kinōntāmin*		21
kiwīssinim	*"vous autres [mangez]"*	*kinōntām*		2p
wīssini	*"il mange"*	*nōntam*		3
wīssiniwak	*"ils [mangent]"*	*nōntamwak*		3p
[wīssiniwan]	*["il mange/ils mangent"]*	*nōntamwan*		3'
nimīčin	*nimīčinan*	*ninōntān*	*ninōntānan*	1-
kimīčin	*kimīčinan*	*kinōntān*	*kinōntānan*	2-
nimīčinān	*nimīčinānin*	*ninōntānān*	*ninōntānānin*	1p-
kimīčinān	*kimīčinānin*	*kinōntānān*	*kinōntānānin*	21-
kimīčināwā	*kimīčināwān*	*kinōntānāwā*	*kinōntānāwān*	2p-
omīčin	*omīčinan*	*onōntān*	*onōntānan*	3-
omīčināwā	*omīčināwān*	*onōntānāwā*	*onōntānāwān*	3p-
omīčini	*omīčini*	*onōntāni*	*onōntāni*	3'-

PARADIGM — intransitive / transitive

subjec

-0   -0p   -0   -0p   object

Table 1.   The transitive and intransitive paradigms of Ojibwa AI and TI stems.

The paradigm of *wīssini-* is from Anon. 1662; forms in square brackets have been supplied.

wīssini-   AI   "eat"
mīči-   AI   "eat something"
nōnt-   TI   "hear / hear something"

THE THREE VERBAL SYSTEMS OF OJIBWA

In the first person plural forms of the transitive paradigm, e.g.,

ninōntānān "we (exclusive) hear it",
kinōntānān "we (inclusive) hear it",

some of the twenty dialects for which we have records[6] show a suffix *-min* while others have *-nān*. While the variation of *-nān* and *-min* has been recognized as a dialect diagnostic at least since 1912 (Michelson 1912:261-69; cf. also Rhodes 1976a:148), its functional rôle within the Ojibwa verbal system appears to have gone unnoticed.

If one compares the left half of Table 1 with the right side, it is evident that the two *transitive* paradigms use the same personal affixes irrespective of stem class:

ni-	*-n*	1	(first person singular)
ki-	*-n*	2	(second person singular)
ni-	*-nān*	1p	(first person plural exclusive)
ki-	*-nān*	21	(first person plural inclusive)
ki-	*-nāwā*	2p	(second person plural)
o-	*-n*	3	(third person singular)
o-	*-nāwā*	3p	(third person plural)
o-	*-ni*	3'	(third person obviative)

The two transitive paradigms are distinguished only by the stems *mīǰi-* AI "eat something" and *nōnt-ā-* TI "hear something" (with the latter including the theme vowel *-ā-*).

The two *intransitive* paradigms, on the other hand, show a number of morphological discrepancies, e.g.,

$$ni\text{-} \quad w\bar{\imath}ssini \quad \text{-}n \quad \text{"I eat",}$$
$$ni\text{-} \quad n\bar{o}nt \quad \text{-}am \quad \text{"I hear".}$$

They do, however, share common ground in the first and second person plural forms:

ni-	*-min*	1p	(first person plural exclusive)
ki-	*-min*	21	(first person plural inclusive)
ki-	*-m*	2p	(second person plural)

These non-third person plural endings, then, most clearly express the unity of the intransitive paradigms across stem classes.

For that reason they are the most obvious point of contrast between the intransitive paradigms on the one hand and the transitive paradigms on the other. The non-third person plural endings thus definitely occupy a pivotal position.[7] Paradigmatic change at this point can be expected to have far-reaching consequences for the entire verbal system of Ojibwa.

The basis for any change must presumably be sought among those members of the TI class where the same stem is found with both transitive and intransitive paradigms. The two forms

$$kin\bar{o}nt\bar{a}min \quad \text{"we hear",}$$
$$kin\bar{o}nt\bar{a}n\bar{a}n \quad \text{"we hear it",}$$

for instance, differ only in the suffix itself. The verb stem, as expanded by the theme sign *-ā-*, is evidently the same in both forms, and it is irrelevant whether the appearance of identity is merely superficial or not: the same sequence *-nōntā-* is heard in both forms.

It would, of course, be fatuous to sketch the kind of situation which might lead an Ojibwa speaker to interpret *kinōntāmin* "we hear" as

"we hear it". But in a large number of dialects, just such a re-inter-
pretation of one of the members of the opposition must have taken place.
While other parts of the transitive paradigm in these dialects still
show the clearest sign of morphologically expressed transitivity, *viz.*,
the suffixal distinction of singular and plural objects, the first person plural (whether exclusive or inclusive) have the *-min* suffix which
is never followed by a plural marker.

The dialects of the *East-Central* type exhibit the maximum differentiation of transitive and intransitive paradigms, with both first and
second person plural suffixes distinct:

	first	second
intransitive	*-min*	*-m*
transitive	*-nān*	*-nāwā*

In the dialects of the *Western* type, the contrast is neutralized in the
first person but maintained in the second:

	first	second
intransitive	*-min*	*-m*
transitive	*-min*	*-nāwā*

It is the dialects of the *Severn* type which have gone furthest in obli-
terating the morphological contrast between the transitive and intransitive paradigms:

	first	second
intransitive	*-min*	*-nāwā*
transitive	*-min*	*-nāwā*

While the intransitive suffix *-min* has crowded out the transitive suffix *-nān* in the first person, in the second person the transitive suffix *-nāwā* has replaced the intransitive suffix *-m*.

Since the Severn dialects show a great deal of interference from Cree, especially in phonology (cf. Wolfart 1973b, Wolfart & Shrofel 1977), it seems almost natural at first to attribute the Severn-specific feature of replacing *-m* by *-nāwā* to the influence of Cree *-nāwāw*. This atomistic interpretation, however, not only fails to account for the expansion of its domain by *-min* (at the expense of its transitive counterpart *-nān*). It also ignores the paradigmatic nature of these changes which, as will be shown in a moment, manifest themselves in different substantive ways yet with identical formal results.

THE INFLECTIONAL NEUTRALIZATION OF THE TRANSITIVITY OPPOSITION

The obligatory replacement of *-nān* by *-min* and of *-m* by *-nāwā* are each found in several dialects; in conjunction with other isoglosses (cf. Wolfart 1977:195-99), they define the three major dialect types of Ojibwa. The further variations of these morphemes which are found in individual dialect records (cf. Table 2) indicate, first, that the development in question is not complete but can be observed in progress; and, second, that it will likely go beyond the domain to which we have restricted our attention.

While the East-Central area generally preserves the *-nān* vs. *-min* distinction, the two suffixes are reported to be in free variation in the dialect of Parry Island. At Island Lake, conversely, the expected *-min* is occasionally replaced by *-nān* even in the intransitive paradigm. That the situation is very much in flux is confirmed by the evidence of the TA paradigm: even in this most overtly transitive paradigm, transitive *-nān* is occasionally replaced by intransitive *-min* in all three major dialect areas.

The most striking case, however, is that of Manitoba Saulteaux (as reported by Voorhis et al. 1976) where *-m* is the only second person plural ending. Whereas the Severn dialects, as shown earlier, syncre-

	INTRANSITIVE (AI–I)		TRANSITIVE Inanimate Object (TI–T)		TRANSITIVE Animate Object (TA)	
	first	*second*	*first*	*second*	*first*	*second*
MAJOR DIALECT TYPES						
East-Central	min	m	nān	nāwā	nān	wā
Western	min	m	*mín*	nāwā	nān	wā
Severn	min	*nāwā*	*mín*	nāwā	nān	wā
LOCAL VARIANTS						
East-Central						
Parry Island			nān/*mín*		nān/*mín*	
Western						
Manitoba Saulteaux				*m*		
Leech Lake				nāwā/(*m*)		
Potawatomi					*mín*, nān*	
Severn						
Round Lake					nān/(*mín*)	
Island Lake		min/(*nān*)			nān/(*mín*)	wā/(*nāwā*)

Table 2. First and second person plural suffixes of the Ojibwa independent indicative.

Suffixes in italics are innovations.
Suffixes in parentheses are significantly less frequent than their counterparts.
* In Potawatomi, *mín* and *nān* occur in distinct parts of the paradigm.

tize intransitive -*min* with transitive -*nāwā* to form their new, neutral sub-paradigm, Manitoba Saulteaux has replaced both transitive suffixes with intransitive ones:

	first	second
intransitive	-*min*	-*m*
transitive	<u>-*min*</u>	<u>-*m*</u>

As summarized in Table 3, Manitoba Saulteaux thus uses the historically and morphologically intransitive forms for both syntactic functions:

> *ninōntāmin* "we hear" / "we hear it",
> *kinōntāmin* "we hear" / "we hear it",
> *kinōntām*   "you hear"/ "you hear it".

In the case of the AI class, the transitivity contrast is expressed both syntactically and by the choice of stem but (just as with the TI stems, above) there is only one suffix, e.g.,

> *kiwīssinimin* "we eat",
> *kimīčimin*   "we eat it".

The evidence of Manitoba Saulteaux (and, in a less apodictic way, of the Leech Lake dialect where -*m* is an optional variant in the transitive paradigm of TI stems) establishes beyond a doubt that the Severn use of -*nāwā* in the intransitive paradigm cannot be attributed to direct Cree interference. Instead, it is now confirmed as part of an intra-Ojibwa development whose target (to risk an eschatological glance) appears to be the complete neutralization of the inflectional expression of the transitivity contrast.

Precise dates are not yet, and may never be, available. Belcourt's treatise of 1839, however, may serve as a terminus ante quem for the appearance of -*min* in the transitive paradigm of Manitoba Saulteaux.

	INTRANSITIVE	TRANSITIVE	
East Central			
1p	ni-nōntā-min	ni-nōntā-nān	ni-nōntā-nān-in
21	ki-nōntā-min	ki-nōntā-nān	ki-nōntā-nān-in
2p	ki-nōntā-m	ki-nōntā-nāwā	ki-nōntā-nāwā-n
Western			
1p	ni-nōntā-min	ni-nōntā-*min*	
21	ki-nōntā-min	ki-nōntā-*min*	
2p	ki-nōntā-m	ki-nōntā-nāwā	ki-nōntā-nāwā-n
Severn			
1p	ni-nōntā-min	ni-nōntā-*min*	
21	ki-nōntā-min	ki-nōntā-*min*	
2p	ki-nōntā-*nāwā*	ki-nōntā-nāwā	ki-nōntā-nāwā-n
Manitoba Saulteaux			
1p	ni-nōntā-min	ni-nōntā-*min*	
21	ki-nōntā-min	ki-nōntā-*min*	
2p	ki-nōntā-m	ki-nōntā-*m*	

Table 3.   Transitive and intransitive paradigms of an ambivalent
TI stem.

The segmentation is intended merely to reflect the surface constituents of these forms: prefix, stem (plus
theme), suffix. Suffixes in italics are innovations.

In the second person plural, *-m* seems to have entered the transitive
paradigm only during the last few decades, i.e., after the 1942 grammar of Dumouchel and Brachet.

THE WORD-AND-PARADIGM MODEL OF LINGUISTIC CHANGE

The progressive neutralization of the transitive : intransitive opposition in Ojibwa verb inflection is not an isolated phenomenon; the intra-systemic variations present an excellent opportunity to observe a far-reaching paradigmatic change as it happens.

Before exploring the further implications of the -nān/-min replacement, one may well ask how such an obvious index of paradigmatic change could have been ignored for so long by students of Algonquian linguistics.[8] The atomistic attitude which apparently persists in spite of structural-systemic protestations provides at least a partial answer which is both simple and realistic.

It seems obvious that neither the Item-and-Process nor the Item-and-Arrangement model which between them have dominated the past fifty years in morphology (cf. Hockett 1954) would have favored the recognition of the pivotal rôle played by the -nān/-min variation. Where the primary concern is with the linear analysis of individual forms, neither synchronic configurations nor their historical evolution receive much attention.

Whatever the respective merits, in synchronic matters, of the IA and IP models and their more traditional competitor, *Word-and-Paradigm* (cf. Robins 1959, Matthews 1965a, 1965b, 1972), may be, they differ in their contribution to historical studies: changes within an inflectional system are more likely to become visible when the Word-and-Paradigm model is employed.[9]

It should be clear from our discussion that we use the term *Word-and-Paradigm* not only in the rather wide sense defined by Robins: as a model which takes "the traditional division between morphology and syntax" as central,

> with morphology covering the formation of words and syntax the structure of sentences stated principally in terms of the relations between words and word groups (1959:119).

In addition we have deliberately appealed to the narrow sense of *paradigm* as the "exemplary paradigm" (Matthews 1972:21 eqs) of Latin traditional grammar. In our interpretation these "παραδείγματα in the

classical sense", the κανόνες or *formulae* of the grammarians, play a
rôle that goes beyond the pedagogical use acknowledged by Matthews
(1972:107) or the heuristic applications exemplified in the present
paper; irrespective of a particular display format, fully documented
paradigms are a powerful way of *characterizing* inflectional patterns.

DRIFT AND TYPOLOGICAL CHANGE

If the evidence of Table 2 were plotted on a map, a fairly clear-
cut geographical orientation would emerge: the inflectional expression
of the transitive : intransitive contrast is complete in the East-Central area; it is reduced in the Western area; and it is suspended entirely in the Severn dialects and in the westernmost representative of
the Western type.

The principle of maximum differentiation alone, or the variations
and paradigmatic mergers which we have discussed, would suffice to let
us interpret the loss of the inflectional expression of the transitivity opposition as a progression from west to east.

Such an interpretation would be compatible with the historical
westward migration of Ojibwa-speaking groups (cf., for instance, Bishop
1975) and the coincidence of the most conservative Ojibwa-speaking area
with the postulated locus of the speakers of Proto-Algonquian (Siebert
1967). Further support for the hypothesis of innovation proceeding
from west to east is found in the fact that an eastern language, Delaware, is the only member of the Algonquian family to share with Ojibwa
the use of essentially the same stem with both transitive and intransitive endings (cf. the TI paradigms of Table 1; for Delaware examples
see Goddard 1974). The same type of double paradigm (or, rather, ambivalent stem [quā VERBUM ANCEPS]) has been reconstructed for Proto-
Algonquian (Goddard 1967), with a choice of transitive or intransitive
endings; in other words, a choice of *-nān* or *-min*.

It is tempting, especially in view of the Delaware evidence, to
go beyond the confines of Ojibwa and search for family-wide develop-

ments which might be identified with geographical directionality. The most obvious instances come from phonology where Voorhis (1976) has observed the loss of intervocalic semivowels in Kickapoo, Fox, Cree, and Ojibwa to take place first in the west and only later in the east. While comparative evidence needs to be examined on a larger scale, the west-to-east pattern is at least suggestive; unfortunately, it is contradicted by another phonological phenomenon, the east-to-west loss of unstressed short vowels in Ojibwa (and, possibly, in Algonquian generally).

Returning to the realm of morphology, we find the eastern conservatism of Ojibwa and Delaware balanced by the innovative pattern of Cree, the western neighbor. Cree has no inflectional indication of transitivity (such as plural markers for the object) in the syntactically transitive TI paradigm; even with TA verbs, the most overtly transitive of all stem classes, there is one entire sub-paradigm where the object itself remains unexpressed (cf. Wolfart 1978:262-66).

Once the pattern of neutralizing the inflectional opposition of transitive and intransitive goes beyond the bounds of one language, any attempt to invoke interference from a neighboring language (in this case, Cree) becomes futile. Instead, we are faced either with a change which antedates the divergence of Proto-Algonquian, with vestigial patterns in Ojibwa and Delaware; or with a case of drift (cf. Sapir 1921: chapter 7 and, most recently, Vennemann 1976). Rather than join Vennemann's "quest for causal explanations" (1976:302), I would be quite content to find a pattern which would be demonstrably common to the observed neutralization in Ojibwa and to the inferred one in Cree and in Proto-Algonquian. How, not why.

The notion of drift, at least in its "almost mystical" version (Hockett 1948: section 8), is closely related to the more recent notion of "favorite targets" (Hoenigswald 1963:40). While we know neither the point of departure, nor the target as such nor, definitely, the cause of the changes we have been discussing, we can identify the *direction* they appear to be taking: since the transitivity contrast is ex-

pressed both inflectionally and syntactically in East-Central Ojibwa
and in Proto-Algonquian, and since it is expressed by syntactic means
exclusively in Cree and in the extreme dialects of Ojibwa, we are wit-
nessing a shift of burden, *a transfer of structural emphasis from morphology to syntax.*

If this generalization, which is inductively based on extensive
first-hand evidence, should sound disturbingly reminiscent of 19th
century evolutionary typology, perhaps it is time to take another look
at that model, too.

NOTES:

1) The rather violent reaction against the "Latinate" model of
traditional grammar which is a commonplace in the linguistic "text-
books" of the first generation, may well be due to the excesses of the
North American school system. Doubtless, it also reflects the cultural
relativism which North American linguists of that period shared with
their anthropological colleagues and, last but not least, the emergent
state of structuralism in linguistics.
2) Some of these are mentioned by Hockett in his review of Bloomfield's Algonquian studies (1948: section 2).
3) Cf. Hanzeli 1969, Wolfart 1967, and several recent editions,
e.g., Fabvre [1695] 1970, Silvy [1678-84] 1974, Mathevet [1748-54]
(Day 1975).
4) Cf. Bloomfield 1946. In spite of many recent studies of selected topics in Ojibwa linguistics, Bloomfield 1958 remains the standard
reference work on Ojibwa.
5) The four stem classes are defined on the basis of formative elements and canonical shapes; stems are frequently paired, either according to the gender of the subject, e.g.,

> *makkatēwisi-*   AI   "be black (animate)",
>
> *makkatēwā-*   II   "be black (inanimate)";

or according to the gender of the object, e.g.,

> *napakahw-*   TA   "flatten someone",
>
> *napakah-*   TI   "flatten something".

Since the traditional labels (AI, II, TA, TI) refer to inflectional-
syntactic properties which are not necessarily shared by all members
of a given stem class, we treat them merely as mnemonic codes; were it

not for the established practice of Algonquianists, arbitrary codes
would be preferable.

6) To the fairly comprehensive list of works cited in Wolfart
1977, add Belcourt 1839, Rhodes 1976b, and Voorhis et al. 1976 (and
cf. the postscript, below). The studies on which the present paper
is based have been supported by the Northern Studies Committee of the
University of Manitoba.

7) Since these forms are the basis for the visible restructuring
of the paradigm, their position is reminiscent (although the details,
of course, are quite different) of the rôle of the third person singular in Indo-European which has been referred to as "Watkins' Law"
(Haiman 1977; cf. Watkins 1962).

8) Even Goddard, whose reconstruction of the double paradigm in
Proto-Algonquian depended on Ojibwa evidence, only notes the extension
of -min without, it appears, pursuing its consequences for the verbal
system as a whole; dismissing intra-Ojibwa variations, he writes that
"The various dialects of the Ojibwa group appear to differ very little
from the Eastern Ojibwa dialect..." (1967:71).

9) This may well be one reason (in addition to its status as the
traditional model) for the prominence of the Word-and-Paradigm model
in studies of highly inflected languages (cf., for example, Kuryłowicz
1964, Watkins 1969).

POSTSCRIPT:

As this volume goes to press, at long last, at the end of 1981,
new material is being collected for several dialects of Ojibwa -- including, for the first time, the Northern Algonquin dialects, whose
internal as well as external relationships are explored in:

> Gilstrap, Roger. 1978. *Algonquin Dialect Relationships in North-
> western Québec*. National Museum of Man, Mercury Series,
> Canadian Ethnology Service Paper 44. Ottawa: National Mu-
> seums of Canada.

> Piggott, G. L. 1978. "Algonquin and Other Ojibwa Dialects: A
> Preliminary Report", in W. Cowan, ed., *Papers of the Ninth
> Algonquian Conference*, pp. 160-87. Ottawa: Carleton Univer-
> sity.

Reports on a number of specific topics appear in:

> Cowan, William, ed. 1978(-80). *Papers of the Ninth (Tenth, Elev-
> enth) Algonquian Conference*. Ottawa: Carleton University.
> 1978 (1979, 1980).

> Drapeau, Lynn, réd. 1981. *Linguistique amérindienne II: études*

algonquiennes. Recherches linguistiques à Montréal 16. Montréal: Université du Québec à Montréal.

(For details and further references, cf. the bibliographical listings in *Algonquian Linguistics* and the forthcoming *Bibliography of Algonquian Linguistics* [by D. H. Pentland & H. C. Wolfart; Winnipeg: University of Manitoba Press].)

Full paradigms and texts, however, remain among the desiderata. While some of the Northern Algonquin evidence, especially as it relates to the Severn dialects, is discussed in my essay on "Marginalia aquilonia" (*Algonquian Linguistics* 5.7-13, 1979), the present study appears in print as written in 1977.

REFERENCES:

Anonymous. 1662. "Principes de la langue algonquine". [From Manuscript No. 12] V. E. Hanzeli, *Missionary Linguistics in New France: A Study of Seventeenth- and Eighteenth-century Descriptions of American Indian Languages*, Appendix A, 103-16. The Hague: Mouton, 1969.

Belcourt, George [sic] A. 1839. *Principes de la langues des sauvages appelés Sauteux.* Québec: Fréchette.

Bishop, Charles A. 1975. "The Origin of the Speakers of the Severn Dialect", in W. Cowan, ed., *Papers of the Sixth Algonquian Conference, 1975*, pp. 196-208. National Museum of Man, Mercury Series, Canadian Ethnology Service Paper 23. Ottawa: National Museums of Canada.

Bloomfield, Leonard. 1925. "On the Sound-system of Central Algonquian". *Language* 1.130-56.

—————————————————— 1933. *Language.* New York: Holt.

—————————————————— 1946. "Algonquian", in H. Hoijer et al., *Linguistic Structures of Native America*, pp. 85-129. Viking Fund Publications in Anthropology 6. New York.

—————————————————— 1958. *Eastern Ojibwa: Grammatical Sketch, Texts, and Word List.* Ed. by C. F. Hockett. Ann Arbor: University of Michigan Press.

Day, Gordon M. 1975. *The* Mots loups *of Father Mathevet [1748-54].* National Museum of Man, Publications in Ethnology 8. Ottawa: National Museums of Canada.

Fabvre, Bonaventure. 1970. *Racines montagnaises [1695].* Transcription par L. Angers et G. E. McNulty. Centre d'Etudes Nordiques, Travaux Divers 29. Québec.

Goddard, Ives. 1967. "The Algonquian Independent Indicative", in A. D. DeBlois, ed., *Contributions to Anthropology: Linguistics I (Algonquian)*, pp. 66-106. National Museum of Canada Bulletin 214. Ottawa: Queen's Printer.

------------ 1974. "Remarks on the Algonquian Independent Indicative", *International Journal of American Linguistics* 40.317-27.

Haiman, John. 1977. "Reinterpretation", *Language* 53.312-28.

Hanzeli, Victor E. 1969. *Missionary Linguistics in New France: A Study of Seventeenth- and Eighteenth-century Descriptions of American Indian Languages*. The Hague: Mouton.

Hockett, Charles F. 1948. "Implications of Bloomfield's Algonquian Studies", *Language* 24.117-31.

------------------ 1954. "Two Models of Grammatical Description", *Word* 10.210-34.

Hoenigswald, Henry M. 1963. "Are There Universals of Linguistic Change?", in J. H. Greenberg, ed., *Universals of Language*, pp. 30-52. Cambridge, Massachusetts: MIT Press.

Hunter, James. 1875. *A Lecture on the Grammatical Construction of the Cree Language*. London: Society for Promoting Christian Knowledge.

Kuryłowicz, Jerzy. 1964. *The Inflectional Categories of Indo-European*. Heidelberg: Carl Winter.

Mathevet, Jean-Claude. 1975. *Mots loups [1748-54]*. See Day 1975.

Matthews, P. H. 1965a. "The Inflectional Component of a Word-and-Paradigm Grammar", *Journal of Linguistics* 1.139-71.

-------------- 1965b. "Some Concepts in Word-and-Paradigm Morphology", *Foundations of Language* 1.268-89.

-------------- 1972. *Inflectional Morphology: A Theoretical Study Based on Aspects of Latin Verb Conjugation*. Cambridge: Cambridge University Press.

Michelson, Truman. 1912. "Preliminary Report on the Linguistic Classification of Algonquian Tribes", *Bureau of American Ethnology, Annual Report 28* [1906-07], pp. 221-90. Washington, D.C.

Rhodes, Richard A. 1976a. "A Preliminary Report on the Dialects of Eastern Ojibwa-Odawa", in W. Cowan, ed., *Papers of the Seventh Algonquian Conference, 1975*, pp. 129-56. Ottawa: Carleton University.

------------------ 1976b. *The Morphosyntax of the Central Ojibwa Verb*. Ph.D. thesis, University of Michigan, Ann Arbor.

Robins, R. H. 1959. "In Defence of WP", *Transactions of the Philological Society* 116-44.

Rogers, Jean H. 1963. "A Survey of Round Lake Ojibwa Phonology and Morphology", *National Museum of Canada Bulletin* 194.92-154. Ottawa: Queen's Printer.

Sapir, Edward. 1921. *Language*. New York: Harcourt, Brace & World.

Shrofel, S. M. 1977. *Cree Admixture in the Verbal Morphology of Island Lake Ojibwa*. M.A. thesis, University of Manitoba, Winnipeg.

Siebert, Frank T., Jr. 1967. "The Original Home of the Proto-Algonquian People", in A. D. DeBlois, ed., *Contributions to Anthropoloy: Linguistics I (Algonquian)*, pp. 13-47. National Museum of Canada Bulletin 214. Ottawa: Queen's Printer.

Silvy, Antoine. 1974. *Dictionnaire montagnais-français [1678-84]*. Transcription par L. Angers, D. E. Cooter, et G. E. McNulty. Montréal: Les Presses de l'Université du Québec.

Vennemann, Theo. 1976. "An Explanation of Drift", in C. N. Li, ed., *Subject and Topic*, pp. 269-305. New York: Academic Press.
Voorhis, Paul H. 1976. Some Observations on the Loss of Semivowels in Central Algonquian Languages. Linguistic Circle of Manitoba and North Dakota, Winnipeg.
Voorhis, Paul H., et al. 1976. *A Saulteaux Phrase Book*. Revised edition. Brandon, Manitoba: Brandon University.
Watkins, Calvert. 1962. *Indo-European Origins of the Celtic Verb. I: The Sigmatic Aorist*. Dublin: Institute of Advanced Studies.
---------------- 1969. *Geschichte der indogermanischen Verbalflexion* (= [J. Kuryłowicz, ed.] *Indogermanische Grammatik III [Formenlehre I]*). Heidelberg: Carl Winter.
Wolfart, H. Christoph. 1967. "Notes on the Early History of American Indian Linguistics", *Folia Linguistica* 1.153-71.
-------------------- 1973a. *Plains Cree: A Grammatical Study*. American Philosophical Society, Transactions n.s. vol. 63, part 5. Philadelphia.
-------------------- 1973b. "Boundary Maintenance in Algonquian: A Linguistic Study of Island Lake, Manitoba", *American Anthropologist* 75.1305-23.
-------------------- 1977. "Les paradigmes verbaux ojibwa et la position du dialecte de Severn", dans W. Cowan, réd., *Actes du Huitième Congrès des Algonquinistes*, pp. 188-207. Ottawa: Carleton University.
-------------------- 1978. "How Many Obviatives: Sense and Reference in a Cree Verb Paradigm", in E.-D. Cook & J. Kaye, eds., *Linguistic Studies of Native Canada*, pp. 255-72. Lisse: Peter de Ridder Press & Vancouver: University of British Columbia Press.
Wolfart, H. C. & Shrofel, S. M. 1977. "Aspects of Cree Interference in Island Lake Ojibwa", in W. Cowan, réd., *Actes du Huitième Congrès des Algonquinistes*, pp. 156-67. Ottawa: Carleton University.

INDEX OF NAMES

•   •   •

SUBJECT MATTER INDEX

U

Überbau 136
Ugaritic 209
Ugaritic cognate 212
unconscious rationality
94, 96
un-countables 391
underlying forms 57
underspecification 184
underspecified 182
unexpressed object 412
unfavorable system 24,
30, 33
uniformitarian prin-
ciple 34
uniformity assumption
347
uninflected 380
universal 25, 75
universalism 63
universals of sound
change 24
unmarked order 377
unnatural changes 24,
26, 28-29
unrelated words 244
unspecific 182
unstressed short vowels
412
unvoicing of final con-
sonants 326
upgliding diphthongs
24
urban centers 13

V

vagueness 184
variable rule 296
variant 255-56, 259,
265
Variationists 59
velar nasal 351
velars in final posi-
tion 336
vendéen 228, 231-32
verb inflection 410
verb primacy 263
verbal base 258
verbal offshoot 247
verbal radicals 249
verbal system 397,
403
vernacular 265
vestiges 245
Vietnamese 81
Virac 349, 353-54
vitality 256
vocabulary 212, 214
vocal cords 80
vocal tract 77
voiced 79-80
voiceless 79-80
voicing 80, 349
vowel 79, 81, 349,
350, 352, 354,
355
vowel lenition 388,
391
vowel quality 197

vowel sequence 41,
47-48
vowel system 30
vowel triangle 25
Vulgar Latin 241, 248

W

wallon 229
Waray 353-54
Watkins' Law 414
WGmc. ai 20-21
WGmc. $\hat{\imath}$ 20-21
Western dialects of
Ojibwa 399, 405,
411
Whig interpretation of
history 131
word-and-paradigm mod-
el 397, 409-10
word families 242
word order 260, 267,
369, 391
word origins 236

Y, Z

Yakan 348, 353-54
Young Grammarians
141, 143-44
Zeitgeist 133, 136,
397
Zend-Avesta 167

• • •